The Arts of Citizenship in African Cities

Africa Connects

Garth Myers (University of Kansas) and Martin J. Murray (University of Michigan), Series Editors

This scholarly series stands at the intersection of globalization and development studies, examining the social, political, and economic effects of these processes on the African continent. For advocates and critics alike, globalization and development are inescapable "facts of life" that define the parameters of social action, not just in Africa, but throughout the world. However, while academic debates and policy discussions careen between praise and criticism, too little attention is given to how these processes actually operate in African settings. Rather than simply reacting to the mainstream scholarly literature, books in this series seek to creatively engage with contemporary debates as a way of developing new perspectives that establish and analyze the linkages between globalization and development.

Published by Palgrave Macmillan:

Encountering the Nigerian State
Edited by Wale Adebanwi and Ebenezer Obadare

Zambia, Mining, and Neoliberalism: Boom and Bust on the Globalized Copperbelt
Edited by Alastair Fraser and Miles Larmer

Fixing the African State: Recognition, Politics, and Community-Based Development in Tanzania
Brian J. Dill

Migrant Women of Johannesburg: Everyday Life in an In-Between City
Caroline Wanjiku Kihato

Urbanization, Urbanism, and Urbanity in an African City: Home Spaces and House Cultures
Paul Jenkins

The Arts of Citizenship in African Cities: Infrastructures and Spaces of Belonging
Edited by Mamadou Diouf and Rosalind Fredericks

The Arts of Citizenship in African Cities

Infrastructures and Spaces of Belonging

Edited by

Mamadou Diouf and

Rosalind Fredericks

palgrave
macmillan

THE ARTS OF CITIZENSHIP IN AFRICAN CITIES

First published in 2014 by
PALGRAVE MACMILLAN®
in the United States—a division of St. Martin's Press LLC,
175 Fifth Avenue, New York, NY 10010.

Where this book is distributed in the UK, Europe and the rest of the world, this is by Palgrave Macmillan, a division of Macmillan Publishers Limited, registered in England, company number 785998, of Houndmills, Basingstoke, Hampshire RG21 6XS.

Palgrave Macmillan is the global academic imprint of the above companies and has companies and representatives throughout the world.

Palgrave® and Macmillan® are registered trademarks in the United States, the United Kingdom, Europe and other countries.

ISBN: 978–1–137–48187–0

Library of Congress Cataloging-in-Publication Data is available from the Library of Congress.

A catalogue record of the book is available from the British Library.

Design by Newgen Knowledge Works (P) Ltd., Chennai, India.

First edition: December 2014

10 9 8 7 6 5 4 3 2 1

Transferred to Digital Printing in 2015

Contents

Figures

Volume Abstracts

The *Arts of Citizenship in African Cities* is a collection of essays that aim to push the frontiers of scholarship that consider African urbanism. Building on a growing literature that resists developmentalist or comparative framings that often end up pathologizing African cities in simplistic terms, the collection offers detailed, nuanced, and ethnographic analyses of life in a diverse range of cities on the continent. Offering a more culturally informed perspective on African politics, the volume includes essays that explore a range of innovative institutions, discourses, and material practices through which claims to citizenship are enacted and contested by a diverse array of actors. The contributions take cities to be sites of experimentation and privilege the below-the-radar, ordinary, and daily negotiations through which emergent reconfigurations of citizenship are being forged. The *arts of citizenship* are used to describe these forms of experimentation, adaptation, and negotiation surrounding claims to the rights and rewards of the city. The *arts* are meant to capture creative innovations that may be out of the range of the familiar, and to conjure the *artifice* that may be entailed in innovative forms of governing. Hegemonic processes of assembling or fixing identities, disciplining space, and materializing power relations are considered side by side with everyday spatial practices and movements that may disrupt plans and associated patterns of inclusion/exclusion.

Specifically, the essays reveal new insight at the intersection of two key themes: infrastructures and spaces of belonging. Through attending to the material and affective contestations surrounding *infrastructures*, the contributions examine how technologies of rule and performances of government are manifested in the built environment and the multiform practices through which these sedimentations are negotiated and transformed in everyday practice. Thus, through examining highways, oil enclaves, mega-churches, and sanitary zones, the material spaces of the city are made to answer for all that they generate, connect, and include/

exclude beyond their technical functions. Problematizing received wisdom about the spatial expressions of claims and imaginings of citizenship, the interventions, instead, privilege relational understandings of the production of *spaces of belonging*. To this end, the contributions examine spaces at the periphery, provisional spaces of mobility, and aesthetic and bodily spaces, all the while fleshing out connections with multiple elsewheres—other cities, "home" villages, the global— that challenge conventional understandings of the locus of citizenship. In this way, the essays contribute to more nuanced understandings of belonging, or the constitution of sociopolitical community throughout these diverse material and discursive realms. Community associations and churches are considered alongside more formal state institutions to interrogate the complex negotiations at play in grappling with custom, imagining new rules of association, and performing civility. Funeral rituals, community courts, elite newspaper columns, and immigrant associations are all exposed for their role in reconfiguring new patterns of community and inclusion. Together, the interventions contribute to a reconceptualization of citizenship and city-ness in Africa that offers insight into recalibrating urban and political theory in general.

Acknowledgments

This book is the product of a conference organized at Columbia University from May 6 to 7, 2011 by Rosalind Fredericks [then post-doctoral scholar with the *Committee on Global Thought* (CGT)] and Mamadou Diouf (Columbia professor and member of the CGT), as part of an annual event series organized by the CGT. The CGT annual series for the 2010–2011 academic year, also organized by Rosalind Fredericks and Mamadou Diouf, was titled *The World and Africa*. The *Arts of Citizenship in African Cities* conference represented the culmination of this year-long series of roundtables, panels, workshops, film screenings, and art exhibitions, and brought together scholars, faculty, students, and others interested in urban and African questions. Over 30 scholars of African urbanism presented papers at the conference, including the 12 authors with chapters in this book. A second book based on the conference assembling research on Senegal was published in French in 2013 under the title, *Les Arts de la Citoyenneté au Sénégal: Espaces Contestés et Civilités Urbaines* (Mamadou Diouf and Rosalind Fredericks, eds).

The success of the *Arts of Citizenship in African Cities* conference was assured by the hard work and dedication of many people, especially from the Institute of African Studies and the Committee on Global Thought. A special thanks is owed to: Robin Stephenson, Lisa Kim, Heather Wylie, Zach Levine, Rebekkah Hogan, Sasha de Vogel, Alioune Badara Dia, Ben Prosky, and Lucia Haladjian. We are grateful for the financing provided for the publication of the volume from the Institute of African Studies and the Committee on Global Thought.

We would, furthermore, like to thank all of those who participated in the conference as paper presenters, moderators, and panel chairs as well as those in attendance who contributed to the lively discussions. All of the chapters represent revisions of papers originally presented at the conference—with the exception of the chapter by Rosalind Fredericks, originally published as an article in *Antipode*.

Rémy Bazenguissa-Ganga's chapter was translated from the French by Catherine Temerson. Hannah Appel's chapter is a revision of an article reprinted with permission from *Ethnography*.

We would like to express our gratitude to the other sponsors who generously contributed to the financing of the conference: The Gallatin School of Individualized Study at New York University, as well as The Graduate School of Architecture, Planning, an Preservation, the Institute for Religion, Culture, and Public Life, the Department of Anthropology, the Middle East, South Asia, and African Studies Department, the School of International and Public Affairs (SIPA), the Global Health Initiative, and the Mailman School of Public Health at Columbia University.

Finally, we are grateful for the support for this project from the series editors, Martin Murray and Garth Myers, throughout the process from its germination at the *Arts of Citizenship* conference. Their editorial comments alongside that of the anonymous reviewer and the editors at Palgrave have assured the fine quality of this work.

Introduction

Rosalind Fredericks and Mamadou Diouf

Decolonizing Urban Theory

Writing about Africa has always been a fraught endeavor, and representing the African metropolis may well be one of the most charged modes of writing about the continent. Essentialist understandings of the continent as rural by nature and of African urbanism as necessarily dysfunctional were foundational to the notions of alterity that have historically haunted ideas of Africa. Despite the fact that a near majority of Africans forge their lives in cities, these assumptions stubbornly persist—at present, yoked to a developmentalist ethos that limits the framing of African cities to invectives of perverse growth, crumbling infrastructure, and flagging economies that demand a series of interventions, often from the outside. This is a central feature of what Jennifer Robinson charted, in her foundational 2002 intervention, as a stark geographical division in urban theory: cities in the Global North are rendered sources of theory, and Global South cities as repositories of poor people and problems that "do not contribute to expanding the definition of city-ness" but are, rather, "drawn on to signify its obverse, what cities are not" (2002: 540). In response, a growing body of scholarship has sought to decolonize urban theory. Jean and John Comaroff contend, "it is the so-called 'Global South' that affords privileged insight into the workings of the world at large" (2012: 114). Precisely because of its presumed "otherness," they argue, the African continent is even more essential as a source of theory for delineating a history of the present.

The last decade has seen an explosion of literature that engages cities in the Global South in a critical reflection on urban practices in relation to theories of globalization. We can cite, among others: the excellent collection edited by Tim Edensor and Mark Jayne on urban trajectories in the non-West (2011); on Africa, the work of Jennifer Robinson (2002), AbdouMaliq Simone (2004a, 2008, 2010), Achille Mbembe and Sarah Nuttall (2004a, 2004b), Edgar Pieterse (2008),

Garth Andrew Myers (2011), and Martin J. Murray (2011); and, on Asia, Ryan Bishop et al. (2003) and Ananya Roy and Aihwa Ong (2011). Drawing upon quite a rich spatiohistorical background, Roy and Ong explore how cities acquire a global dimension in the geography of knowledge—that is, how they become "worlding cities," in their words—and how their epistemological operations are integral to the development of the field of urban studies (2011). They identify two hegemonic theoretical approaches in research situated outside of the West that reduce all urban experiences, that is the urban condition, to two exclusive instantiations: the universal logic of capitalism and postcolonial theory (Ibid.: xv). Ong's introduction rigorously establishes the contrast between the two approaches: the perspective of political economy privileges the "singular script" of the deployment of "global capitalism"; and, the second—postcolonial theory—strongly insists upon "subaltern resistance," of those who were once victims of colonial domination (Ibid.: 6–11). In the script of the expansion of "global capitalism," cities are analyzed as "nodes" in an integrated capitalist network; they serve global interests more than local ones (Ibid.: 6). In this theoretical "*cul-de-sac*," African cities are seen as owing their rapid growth only to large concentrations of poor workers. The logical conclusion of such a premise is, inevitably, urban revolution (Ibid.: 6–7). In contrast, postcolonial theory reasons that, outside of "the West," "the Rest" (to draw upon Stuart Hall's logic (1996)) of the world is invariably postcolonial; it continues to endure shared effects of colonialism. The over-dertermination of urban contexts outside of the West by colonial domination lies at the heart of the theoretical apparatus of postcolonial urban studies.

In this light, the analysis of urbanization in Africa can be seen as dominated by two contradictory representations. The first, and a rather pessimistic one, emphasizes the severity of the crisis gripping organizations, living environments, recreation, and creative activities, as well as the infrastructures that organize them, which facilitate and/or constrain urban practices (Packer 2006, Pieterse 2008, Stren and Halfani 2001, Stren and White 1993). The second representation is more celebratory/optimistic (Diouf 2008, Glaeser 2011, Roberts et al. 2003, Simone 2008, 2011, Tannerfeldt and Ljung 2006, Watson 2014), emphasizing popular African creativity while reinventing Africa's destiny in strict terms of the practices of its so-called indigenous populations—something well illustrated by Dogone tourism in Mali. Thus, a perception of the city as strangely hostile to African populations becomes substituted by a vision in which dynamic urban space is appropriated and by its inhabitants. Further, the pessimists think in terms of policy analysis and of administrative intervention. Their primary preoccupation revolves around the following question: How to render the African city productive, governable, ordered, sanitized, hospitable, and secure, all at once? The optimists, conversely, strive to describe the permanent re-creation of new, specifically African urban spaces, by unearthing the aesthetic and cultural expressions as well as the political, architectural, and economic practices of certain groups. For instance, youth and marginalized people in public and domestic spaces become reinvested in indigenous and cosmopolitan practices, but in ways that diverge from nationalist, administrative reinventions of traditional virtues and values (Diouf 1996).

Roy and Ong propose an ethnographic turn away from the "theoretical dead-end," which presumes singular logics governing urban change. The move is based on the idea of "worlding," which conceives the globalized city as a place of intervention—a source of ambitious visions and speculative experimentations generative of numerous possibilities, positive or negative. We consider, they write, that "such experiments cannot be conceptually reduced to instantiations of universal logics of capitalism and postcolonialism [...]. We therefore focus on the urban as a milieu that is in constant formation, one shaped by the multitudinous ongoing activities that, by wedding dream and technique, form the art of being global" (2011: xv). Joining this commitment, there are, in fact, many studies that stress the fact that "urbanization in developing countries should be studied by privileging a perspective that emphasizes the histories and the distinct postcolonial experiences, the different paths of modernization that are largely influenced by the colonial experience, national liberation, and postcolonial transformation" (Ibid.: 8).

Resonating with the ethnographic turn called for by Roy and Ong, a flurry of debates within Africanist urban theory has endeavored to incorporate African political systems into more cosmopolitan urban and political theories. This emergent literature has driven some of the most innovative and provocative recent scholarly debates considering the urban condition and contributes to refashioning the very basis of how we understand cities and urban citizenship [see, for instance, Myers (2011), Robinson (2006), Pieterse (2008), Murray and Myers (2011), Simone (2010), Mbembe and Nuttall (2004b), and the controversy between Nuttall and Mbembe (2005) and Watts (2005)]. Taking on the "African fable" governing representations of African cities—namely, that they are dysfunctional and subjected to endemic corruption—Garth Myers sets forth an ambitious but simple objective: use the concepts and experiences of urban Africans to interrogate and redesign the allegedly universal models and measuring instruments ordering the epistemological apparatus of conventional urban studies. Further, Edensor and Jayne's work rejects the conventional narrative ("African fable") of the non-Western city (African): spatial disorder; de-beautification; organized violence and crime; inter-ethnic strife; civil disorder; overcrowding flooding; air and noise pollution; unemployment; widespread poverty; traffic chaos; and risk-bearing sexual practices (2011: 4). Following Roy, Ong, and Myers, they make the same invitation to decolonize imaginations of city-ness in order to break free of the categorizing tendencies that dominate urban theory, especially the obsession with archetypical global cities and an associated overemphasis on the structural positions of cities (Ibid.: 3). AbdouMaliq Simone examines the fable of the African city as structurally dysfunctional through an analysis of concepts of informality, invisibility, the spectral ("spectrality"), and the mobility of men and women, resources, ideas, and practices (2004a). In so doing, he highlights the rationality of African urban life despite the appearances of fragmentation and irrationality. Simone operates at the intersection of theory and urban practices to consider colonial urban histories in relation to social and political institutions, always emphasizing stories that enliven the urban scene and the romance of the city and that offer surprising plots and unfinished geographies that sit in contrast with the simplistic imagination of bureaucrats and politicians.

The Arts of Citizenship

Building on this growing literature, the essays in this volume aim to push the frontiers of scholarship considering African urbanism and, in so doing, to recalibrate our understanding of cities, in general. The collection of detailed, nuanced, and geographically diverse[1] ethnographic analyses unpacks the everyday negotiations and practices through which the continent's cities are undergoing processes of "worlding," and through which their residents grapple with everyday life. The essays resist comparative or essentialist framings that simplistically pathologize or celebrate African cities to explore claims to citizenship enacted and contested by a diverse array of actors, across a range of innovative institutions, discourses, and material practices. Thereby, they offer a more culturally informed perspective on African politics than is usually presented in African political studies.

The contributions take cities to be sites of experimentation, and the research privileges the below-the-radar, ordinary, and daily negotiations through which emergent reconfigurations of citizenship are being forged, without neglecting "the impositions of global forces of capitalism, neoliberalism, IMF-styled democratization, and the like" or waxing "romantic about the difficulties of putting new citizenships into practice" (Holston 2010: 9). Following James Holston, the goal is, then "to rub these forces, factors, and difficulties against the grain of local vitalities, to show that they do not preclude them, and that they are, often, reshaped by them" (Ibid.). In this light, recognizing that neoliberal policy has been but one of many forces structuring the lives of urban Africans, the essays elide assumptions of an overarching neoliberalism that have become hegemonic in studies of African cities over the last decade (Parnell and Robinson 2012). Simultaneously, the volume includes representations of urbanites' claims to urban space without presuming a sort of blanket subaltern resistance. Emphasizing "the practices through which power operates, the symbolic and material effects power produces, and its performance" (Moore 1994: 123), the contributions grapple with often ambivalent and contradictory new spaces that are not easily classified within a lens of domination or resistance. A number of the essays portray a sort of "quiet encroachment of the ordinary" (Bayat 1997) through which people dynamically negotiate incremental change while also recognizing the circumscriptions and challenges implied by these new spaces. These innovative daily experiments usher forth new configurations of sociopolitical community entailing new patterns and built spaces of exclusion and inclusion.

Collectively, we use the term *arts of citizenship* to describe these forms of experimentation, adaptation, and negotiation surrounding claims to the rights and rewards of the city. The *arts* are meant to capture creative innovations that may be out of the range of the familiar, and to conjure the *artifice* that may be entailed in innovative forms of governing. The focus on margins and edges—such as symbolic manifestations of the political in the periphery, on the body, in death—of what usually falls under the purview of citizenship practice, therefore, troubles received wisdoms about how we consider what it means to be a citizen. Hegemonic processes of assembling or fixing identities, disciplining space, and materializing power relations are considered next to everyday spatial practices and movements that may disrupt plans and associated patterns of inclusion/exclusion (Secor 2004). In the interaction of people in space and its material sedimentations, the essays, thus, explore the artful processes by which "dominant codings of 'the citizens' and 'the stranger'" are produced, contested, and reconfigured in spatial practices (Ibid.: 352).

Specifically, the essays reveal new insight at the intersection of two key themes: *infrastructures* and *spaces of belonging*. The interventions privilege relational understandings of the production of space in order to problematize received wisdom about the spatial expressions of claims and imaginings of citizenship. To this end, the authors examine provisional spaces of mobility, peripheral sites of connection, and literary and aesthetic representations of the urban, while fleshing out connections with multiple elsewheres—other cities, "home" villages, the global—that challenge conventional understandings of the locus of citizenship. Firstly, material and affective contestations surrounding *infrastructures* demonstrate how technologies of rule and performances of government are manifest in the built environment, and how these sedimentations are negotiated and transformed in everyday, multiform practice. The material spaces of the city—highways, oil enclaves, megachurches, and sanitary zones—in these essays, are made to answer for all that they generate, connect, and include/exclude beyond their technical functions. Secondly, the essays all contribute to the examination of the production of *spaces of belonging*, or the constitution of sociopolitical community throughout these diverse material and discursive realms. Juxtaposing more formal state institutions with community associations and churches, the essays interrogate the complex negotiations through which people grapple with custom, imagine new rules of association, and perform civility. Funeral rituals, community courts, elite newspaper columns, and immigrant associations expose reconfigured cartographies of connection and emplacement in the city. Together, the interventions contribute to a re-conceptualization of citizenship and "city-ness" in Africa that offers insight toward recalibrating urban and political theory in general.

Infrastructures

A central theme taken up by the chapters in this volume considers how delineations of citizenship are codified and contested in the built form of the city. Although urban and African studies have often either relegated infrastructures to the realm of technical or policy discussions or ignored them as irrelevant or uninteresting, there has been a recent deluge of scholarship examining urban infrastructures as key sites for political contestation [see Graham and Marvin 2001, Larkin (2013), the special issue of *Ethnography* on Infrastructural Violence (Rodgers and O'Neill 2012), the symposium in *IJURR* on Political Infrastructure (McFarlane and Rutherford 2008), and the special issue of *Public Culture* on Infrastructures of the Urban (Calhoun et al. 2013]. As Brian Larkin points out in his review of the literature, critical infrastructure scholars demonstrate "how the operation of technologies, ostensibly a neutral practice, becomes the grounds around which forms of citizenship are contested" (2013: 331). Urban studies scholarship from the Global South has been particularly instrumental in re-materializing inquiries around urban citizenship to consider the role of built form—including housing and architecture, public services, and transportation networks—as key sites of performative government practice as well as claims-making by elite and disenfranchised citizens alike (Anand 2012, Fredericks 2014, Kooy and Bakker 2008, McFarlane 2008, von Schnitzler 2008,).

Just as urban space and its infrastructures were produced unevenly in the colonial period in an effort to control populations, often along segregationist lines (Anderson 1995, Betts 1971, Swanson 1977), so do infrastructures in the postcolonial city manifest governmental prerogatives and unequal citizenship across the urban landscape. A key element of the governing work of the built city is in the "staging of infrastructural modernity" or the inscription of state plans and imaginaries in the material space of the city "by which a state proffers [...] representations to its citizens and asks them to take those representations as social facts" (Larkin 2013: 335–336). National development plans and master planning documents are key archives articulating aspirational histories of state performances of modernity through the built environment, and no plans were, perhaps, more ambitious than those proffered by newly minted postcolonial states. The chapters by Giles Omezi and Emily Brownell (this volume) explore the work of master plans in Nigeria and Tanzania, respectively, in the early postcolonial period in conjuring and spatializing nationalist imaginaries through urban form. Omezi's chapter illuminates how large-scale state-planned urban infrastructural interventions—especially road transport systems—in Lagos manifested not only state aspirations for industrialized modernization but also a cohesive national cultural identity. For her part, Brownell explores how discourses of inclusion/exclusion were embedded in infrastructural practices of sanitation and, thus, central to state objectives of planning and control. In this sense, narratives of dirt and discipline undergirded uneven sanitary infrastructures to differentially place and discipline urban residents in development visions for the city.

Central to exerting control over urban development and governing urban subjects is the maintenance of an aesthetic order in the city that keeps people in their proper place. Governmental techniques aimed at defining and enforcing aesthetic norms that render unruly slum spaces unlawful can work to produce specific images of modernity that legitimize the displacement of those deemed "polluting" as unfit to belong in the city. For Asher Ghertner, such techniques undergird the function of what he terms "aesthetic governmentality" in the service of elite "world city" aspirations in Delhi (2010a). As he and other scholars of India have observed, bourgeois environmental discourses are often invoked in such elite projects for urban development (Doshi 2013, Ghertner 2010b, McFarlane 2008). Elite environmentalisms governing uneven practices of infrastructure provision in diverse African cities often represent exclusive aesthetic imaginings of the urban environments much more than they do substantive questions of resource sustainability and access to healthy environments. In these cases, environmental "improvements" in urban areas involve performative display for international donors more than locally derived and legitimate practice. In a similar vein, in her work on modular technologies and intensive enclaving in oil developments in Equatorial Guinea, Hannah Appel's chapter (this volume) demonstrates the profoundly hollow nature of infrastructures that produce the aesthetic facade of public goods that lack all content. In this particular instance, the driving impulse was not bourgeois environmentalism but, rather, discourses of corporate accountability. Her research highlights how the aesthetic power of infrastructure can, thus, be a fetishistic artifice of rule, masking the complicity between state and corporate practice and its associated dispossessions. Walls, buildings, and technical functions can, then, serve "the abdication of responsibility for infrastructure outside the walls" (Appel, this volume).

The provision of urban public services such as water, sanitation, and waste management can be particularly revealing of the intense political contestations surrounding the governance of access to the rewards of the city. Insightful work on water infrastructures, for instance, demonstrates the complex negotiations between state and urban residents surrounding what Nikhil Anand terms "hydraulic citizenship" or "a form of belonging to the city enabled by social and material claims made to the city's water infrastructure" [2011: 545; see also Kooy and Bakker (2008), Ranganathan (2014), von Schnitzler (2008)]. Through pressuring officials, expertly navigating laws and regulations, and intimately engaging with specific water technologies of plumbing, pipes, and pumps, slum-dwellers in Mumbai negotiate access to water resources, thereby exerting their rights to hydraulic citizenship. This shifts the purview of citizenship, from one that assumes that urban membership implies uniform access to the rights of the city to one that emphasizes the positioned expertise involved in exercising citizenship claims through material practices of negotiation.

The power imbued in performances of infrastructural modernity, such as city plans and public service provision, reveals the possibilities for rupture entailed in practices of hijacking, tapping, or disrupting urban infrastructures and the representations they foster. Contestations surrounding sanitation and waste management infrastructure can be especially messy, given the specific materiality of the service and all of its associated dimensions of stigma and abjection. Discourses of waste and sanitation are primary vehicles of modernizing missions through ordering spaces and disciplining bodies and, as such, can be primary sites through which to contest governing projects (Fredericks 2013, Gidwani 2013, McFarlane 2008, Moore 2009). Rosalind Fredericks' research in Dakar, Senegal, emphasizes the possibilities for trash-workers and residents to invert and disrupt such ordering paradigms through blocking the flow of garbage collection via labor strikes and coordinated public dumping (2014). Such trash revolts and the ways that they have reconfigured the benefits of urban citizenship in Dakar are just one particularly provocative expression of the, sometimes, disorderly ways that urban residents contest and confront the governing prerogatives of planners and government officials in their daily negotiations of infrastructure politics. Further, von Schnitzler's research on pre-paid water-meter technologies in South Africa is instructive of how "infrastructure itself becomes a political terrain for the negotiation of central ethical and political questions concerning civic virtue and the shape of citizenship" (2013: 689). Through bypassing, destroying, and, otherwise, tinkering with the technics of this neoliberal layer of infrastructure and, in so doing, gaining illegal access to free water, township residents wage a micropolitics of innovation and subversion that contests ethical regimes of individuation and incentivization.

Although disruption and blockage can be powerful, more often than not, infrastructure politics take place in a constructive mode. Brownell's essay describes the response of residents in Dar es Salaam, faced with being disenfranchised from the rights of sanitary citizenship, through strategically organizing their own systems of waste management and, thereby, insisting on their right to belong in the city. These labors are just one of the myriad expressions of what Simone describes as "people as infrastructure" or the complex "combinations of objects, spaces, persons, and practices" that "become an infrastructure—a platform providing for and reproducing life in the city" (2004b: 408). Simone's essay (this volume) emphasizes how much more than mere survival strategies—for making due or "putting food on the table" under adverse conditions—these coordinated practices represent, and may form the scaffolding through which diverse urban residents forge relations of commonality and reciprocity, map out inventive and synergistic economic relations, and provide laboratories for nation-building. The challenge is in finding ways to coordinate and incorporate such inventions into plans and governing logics, not to ignore or oppose them. Simone and others are, moreover, fully cognizant of the onus placed on city residents by such maneuvering and the limits in flow and function provided by incessant strategizing and provisionality or having "too many things to do." Systematic disinvestment reconfigures the burdens of social reproduction in a profoundly uneven manner (Meehan and Strauss, forthcoming). As is, perhaps, most clearly laid bare in the case of sanitation, furthermore, making one's own infrastructure in the face of state neglect or deliberate abdication of duty can be intensely stigmatizing (Fredericks 2012, Miraftab 2004).

Spaces of Belonging

Alongside a consideration of the politics of infrastructure, the chapters in this volume are keenly concerned with the production of spaces of belonging and their connection to modes of political power and economic accumulation. The tectonic transformations underway in African cities can be understood as dynamic contestations through which different actors stake claims to representing urban space, and negotiate sedimentations of community in everyday practice. Attention to the production of space emphasizes the highly dynamic interrelations between the actors and forces present in the urban landscape, but only in their connection to elsewheres. Instead of boxing cities and their inhabitants and reducing understandings of their growth and form to endogamous factors, these essays understand African cities through the full range of extra-local practices and imaginaries that connect them to the global, the hinterland, other cities, and even other worlds via cosmological imaginings. Drawing on Simone's (2001) articulation of the *worlding* of African cities and Roy and Ong's development of the concept in the context of Asian cities (2011), the collection resists simplistic dualisms between rural and urban and local and global to foreground explorations of urban margins, mobilities, and alternative imaginings of space that emerge in everyday life for their insight into the constitution of sociopolitical communities.

An emphasis on urban margins foregrounds how African cities are produced through their interactions with global movements of capital, people, ideas, and images, and, moreover, how "these movements across territories are not qualitatively equal"—or how the rules by which they are governed may be intensely marginal*izing* (Prakash 2011: 3). Attention to African urbanism, in other words, demands an interrogation of spaces of belonging on a global scale. Although African cities have historically been integrated into global circuits of capital, more often than not, these have been profoundly extractive relationships where the rules of the game are set far from the continent. This demands a more sophisticated understanding of globalization than imaginings of global convergence that leave the African continent conspicuously off the map. Critiquing the naturalized imagery of capitalist globalization as an all-encompassing force that swallows up everything in its path, Ferguson describes international capital as "globe-hopping"; more often than not, it congeals in enclaves of extraction and "development" around geopolitically important resources (2006: 38). Hannah Appel's chapter (this volume) on oil enclaves in Equatorial Guinea provides a particularly powerful demonstration of the violence of such transnational spaces of capitalist accumulation. The empty infrastructures and dramatic insulation of people, money, and laws—away from the local context in Malabo—produce a profoundly uneven urban space defined by exclusion. Such urban spaces raise provocative questions for thinking through "social relations of membership, responsibility, and inequality on a truly planetary scale" (Ferguson 2012: 23).

Central to the marginalizing processes described earlier are specific representations of space and the power to emplace their associated social relations. However, as Appel and the other contributions to this volume recognize, such representations are never complete. Whether deployed by powerful corporate actors (Appel, this volume), states (Brownell, Omezi, this volume), or international development agencies, these "official" representations of space are always subject to competing imaginings of belonging in the city. Jinny Prais' chapter (this volume) details the alternative maps of the city drawn by an urban professional elite in Accra during the colonial interwar years and published in popular newspapers. Through resisting imperial geographies of ethnicity, race, and class, these writers conjured alternative ways of seeing and inhabiting Accra for an Accradian and diasporic international readership. In a very different historical moment in West Africa, Rosalind Fredericks' research on contemporary hip-hop politics (this volume) shows how youth in Dakar deploy and construct alternative imaginings of the city through their artful discourses of transgression and spatial practices of alternative place-making. In this way, rappers and their fans register their disdain for the vision of the nation, as conceived by their "elders," through domesticating a global art form into vernacular practices that forge a new vision of politics and the city. These chapters illuminate that powerful representations of space always sit in fields that are contested, multiple, and, therefore, subject to fracture.

As the Prais and Fredericks chapters make clear, global economic connections via transnational finance and corporate power are, moreover, not the only means through which African cities undergo "worlding." "Worlding from below" (Simone 2001) is brokered by all manner of African institutions and individuals. Key among them are the transnational religious networks through which African Muslims and Christians elaborate "spaces of economic transaction, knowledge production, and cultural influence that are translocal and transnational" in order to envision and materialize their place in the world (Ibid.: 37; see also Diouf 2000, Gifford 2004). Pentecostal churches are centrally involved in city-making processes at the juncture of global and urban worlds. Often situated at the literal margins of cities in peri-urban zones and straddling local, global, and spirit worlds, Pentecostal spaces operate not just as institutions that transform the material architecture of cities—often from the margins—but also sculpt new frontiers in the psychic lives of city-dwellers. Ruth Marshall and Adedamola Osinulu (this volume) both take up the new Pentecostal spaces emerging in Nigeria through examining the Redeemed Christian Church of God (RCCG). A massive place of worship that can accommodate hundreds of thousands of worshippers, Redemption Camp comprises an extensive infrastructure, including its own roads and urban services, on the outskirts of Lagos. As Marshall argues, the mega-church works to deterritorialize urban and peri-urban space through endeavoring to write over and reimagine the ties that bind people along new logics. Central to these alternative imaginings of sociopolitical community are the church's engagement with an "elsewhere"—or global Pentecostal networks and otherworldly arenas. For his part, Osinulu's chapter focuses his attention on the performative spatial politics within the church compound—to explore how the church concretely emplaces new hierarchies and social relations within its ranks through ritual practices.

Due to their "hybrid and ambiguous character" (Trefon 2009: 21), the literal margins of African cities can be particularly generative sites for deriving insight on the production of sociopolitical membership at the nexus of the rural and the urban. Theodore Trefon describes peri-urban spaces as geographies of linkage and "psychological transition, 'hinging' village to a neighbouring city and sometimes beyond" (2009: 17). This builds on a long tradition within African urban studies of resisting simplistic binaries that separate the rural and the urban by showing precisely how the two are interpenetrated in all sorts of complex ways. A key stake of exploring those interpenetrations is the role of custom in historic and contemporary political projects. Stemming from the instrumentalization of customary authority at the core of diverse forms of colonial politics, custom is alive and well in many projects to define the contours of civility today. The tensions and implications of colliding sovereignties implied by citizenship that is defined by custom are, perhaps, most powerfully illuminated where the urban and the rural literally intersect. Juan Obarrio's chapter (this volume) examines the Community Tribunals in peri-urban neighborhoods in provincial Mozambique as a window into the fusion of power systems and authority in the margins and their implications for reconfiguring spaces of political belonging. The innovation here is in highlighting, ethnographically, the very ways that emerging rhetoric and processes of democratization and decentralization that reconstitute custom are codified in the juridical mode.

Although Africanist urban scholarship has consistently explored the persistence of strong links of urbanites with their "home village" since the 1960s, a growing recent literature is exploring the politics of autochthony and the resurgence of claims to belonging "rooted" in land and place. A key voice in that literature, Peter Geschiere has made important interventions revealing the central force that democratization and capitalist globalization play in triggering, reconfiguring, and intensifying the politics of belonging and its rural–urban connections (Geschiere and Gugler 1998, Geschiere and Jackson 2006, Geschiere and Nyamnjoh 2000). These studies affirm the pivotal position of "roots and origins as the basic criteria of citizenship and belonging" (Geschiere and Nyamnjoh 2000: 423), and the function of practices of mobility through which people negotiate spaces of belonging. Geschiere has been especially attentive to the role of the funeral—as a key rite through which belonging is performed—in crystallizing spatial claims to belonging. His chapter (this volume) explodes crude rural–urban binaries through showing how the two spaces are dynamically yoked through mobility in the preparation for, or after, the fact of death. Through reflecting on a diversity of dynamic performances of belonging through funerals, his essay resists facile categorizations of connections to home village and custom.

The challenges posed by mobility for belonging and citizenship are felt particularly acutely by migrants who leave their country of origin in hopes of solidifying their life chances. Christine Ludl (this volume) explores the complexities of community for Senegalese and Malian migrants in South Africa to highlight the often ambivalent spaces of belonging precipitated by movement, transition, and provisionality. Ludl's migrants are defined by their ambivalence to ties and commitments to communities of "strangers," resulting from differing cultural codes of conduct, allegiances to home, and calculations of reciprocity.

In contrast with Simone's characterization of the networking and diversification of affiliations involved in maximizing strategies of reciprocity, many of Ludl's interlocutors can be described as reluctant to invest for all sorts of reasons. Whether involving nearby cities or far away lands, the spatial practice of movement across borders intended to be temporary raises important questions regarding the spatial basis of citizenship and its implied rights and obligations.

Finally, the essays in this volume attend to the embodiment of practices of belonging and their constitution in aesthetic modes and registers. Rémy Bazenguissa-Ganga (this volume) explores aesthetic practices of beautifying urban houses and bodies that citizens in Brazzaville have used to contest state political projects. This joins with a wider body of scholarship looking at range of artistic practices through which urban residents literally write over, embellish, and inhabit the spaces of the city in the likeness of their own desires (Caldeira 2012, Diouf 1996, Diouf and Fredericks 2013). Attention to everyday spatial practices, moreover, highlights the embodied nature of citizenship, or the way that it is constituted in and through bodily practice. Through beautifying their bodies and parading through public space, Bazenguissa-Ganga's *sapeurs* wear their counter-narratives, forging a connection between the urban space and the urban body. Relatedly, hip-hop youth in Dakar claimed space in the city and electoral politics in the last elections through broadcasting their messages through the air with the boom of catchy, sometimes caustic, rap lyrics while also showcasing their politics in hip-hop fashion and brazen t-shirt messages (Fredericks, this volume). This suggests that citizenship is, indeed, worn on the body through practices of adornment and fashion aimed at staking claims and raising voices. Soundscapes, aesthetic, and bodily spaces are, thus, arenas through which the city can be re-made.

Overall, the sections described earlier illustrate how the production of infrastructures and belonging go hand in hand. As each of the chapters will demonstrate, the built material city only comes to life through the lived and imagined practices of city-dwellers. The reconfiguration of discourses of belonging and inclusion, moreover, are inscribed in and through everyday movements and experimentations that inhabit, disrupt, or re-imagine infrastructures. In this way, everyday practice must be understood as "the space of both the routine but also something hidden and evasive" (Prakash 2011: 12). The arts of citizenship are, then, a complex set of competing designs and actions through which sociopolitical communities are formed and enabled through the material space of the city. The following section details the specific contributions of the individual chapters.

Overview of the Chapters

AbdouMaliq Simone's chapter explores the logics of collective action in a diverse set of African cities. Part of a larger effort to demonstrate how postcolonial urban projects go beyond merely failing at development logics, he endeavors to illuminate how urbanization stirs productive relationships. Specifically, Simone maps out the practices of conjunction—or cartographies of connection—produced out of persistent strategizing around how to mobilize resources and "make something out of the city." The picture he paints is one of increasingly intense contestation, where struggles over the fundamental rights and obligations between different social groups—children and parents, men and women, patrons and clients, and, importantly, citizens and government officials—often result in the greater visibility of demands for justice, equality, and accountability. As such, he argues that cities act as laboratories for nation-building, owing to residents' unremitting need to traverse boundaries and find common modes of exchange. Although often seemingly disorderly, these innovative strategies to maximize the capacities of interchange can provide the platforms from which to envision more dynamic, just, and legitimate economies and polities.

Peter Geschiere focuses on the role of the funeral as a key moment that crystallizes urban citizens' definition of belonging and community. Drawing on ethnographic work in Cameroon, he illustrates varying modalities of the funeral in different contexts, and compares these to research on funerals in diverse locations across the continent. As rituals of belonging that emphasize and, in certain respects, politicize the connection of urbanites to their villages of origin, funerals often emerge as elaborate and dynamic performances of "custom" and, in some cases, "invented" traditions. However, the obligation to bury the deceased "at home" in the village is neither static nor ubiquitous. Exploring the dynamic variations in the role of the funeral across space and time, the chapter offers an insightful lens into transformations in rural–urban connections and the spatial imaginings of citizenship.

Juan Obarrio's chapter examines the margins of a provincial city in Northern Mozambique as an ambiguous space of colliding sovereignties and overlapping jurisdictions, to interrogate the ideological and political implications of recent divisions between rural and urban political belonging. Through an ethnographic study of Community Tribunals in peri-urban neighborhoods, he illuminates the paradoxical way in which Mozambique's post-war legal reforms, aimed at democratization and decentralization, have reinstated aspects of colonial governance surrounding the distinction between the rural and the urban through revitalizing "custom" and empowering its authorities. Through interrogating these new reconfigurations of political belonging enacted by the courts—and their perverse political effects in engendering new modes of exclusive citizenship—he offers a provocative analysis of the fate of the "civil" in the contemporary, democratic present.

Ruth Marshall examines the modes of appropriation of urban space by the Nigerian Pentecostal church and their effects on sociopolitical community. Specifically, she focuses on the church's engagement with an "elsewhere," and how it works to simultaneously de-territorialize urban space through transnational networks and imaginaries while re-imagining the local grounds of citizenship and modes of belonging in the city. Part of a broader evangelical project of "global spiritual warfare," evangelical activity has been centered on the reinvestment and re-sacralization of physical and virtual public space. Marshall reveals the project to be, however, highly ambivalent in political terms, because it ends up spectacularizing the sacred and, thereby, rendering it profane. In Lagos, this means not only the massive physical occupation of urban and peri-urban space, as dramatically manifested in material spatialization of the Redeemed Christian Church of God (RCCG), but also through such techniques of redemptive citizenship as "spiritual mapping," in which urban spaces are reclaimed as "prayer sites" in the battle against evil.

Adedamola Osinulu complements Marshall's chapter through an analysis of the worship practices of supplicants who gather at Redemption Camp, an outpost of the RCCG, on the outskirts of Lagos. Osinulu develops the notion of *performative Pentecostal space*, in order to explore the Camp's role as a space through which people re-enact their embodied lived experience in the context of ritual. Paying particular attention to the relationship between the physical layout of the Camp and the social relations performed and enacted during the practice of worship, he examines the way that the spatial dynamics of the city are reconstructed and intensified in the space of the church. Through considering the active production of Pentecostal space, he considers the model of citizenship presented by the Pentecostal church, and raises questions about its role in negotiating and performing the relationship between citizens and the state.

Rosalind Fredericks' chapter seeks to explain why rap emerged as a key medium of protest of a generation of disaffected youth during the 2012 elections in Senegal, and how it was mobilized to create new claims to voice and spaces of citizenship. Through considering the spatial practices and imaginaries of rappers and their followers, she probes the valence of hip hop as a medium of political identity formation and a language of resistance. She argues that hip hop fosters new geographies of citizenship inspiring urban youth to transgress prescribed boundaries in allowed speech and political behavior to make new claims on their city and nation. Specifically, she details the spatial practices of the *Y'en a Marre* youth movement during the elections as both an outcome and an extension of the spaces conditioned by rap and its history. Through tracing their neighborhood-based mobilizations as strategies to critique geographies of exclusion and forge alternative visions of place, she lends insight into the artful spaces of democratic politics in contemporary Senegal.

Rémy Bazenguissa-Ganga offers a historic sociology of the urban aesthetic realm in Congo Brazzaville. He examines the ways that social practices that beautify Brazzaville constitute arts of citizenship through which the Congolese take part in governing and being governed. Through examining beautiful houses and beautiful bodies in the revolutionary and, then, democratic phases of the postcolonial period, he considers the manner in which negotiations in the aesthetic realm "give rise to ways of feeling and result in specific forms of political subjectivity." Overall, he chronicles how, during the revolutionary phase, governed subjects performed beauty on their bodies outside of beautiful houses. For instance, he describes the Society of Ambience-makers and Elegant People (SAPE) movement, through which youth conjoined political claims by making designer clothes. Ostentatious fashion allowed them to inscribe on their bodies forms of resistance to projects and performances of the governing elite. Then, in the later phase of democratization, he argues that the two aesthetic sites were reunited as "the beautiful bodies entered the beautiful houses," paying particular attention to the rise in Masonic architecture. In both phases, he details how these beautification processes are interconnected with the economic landscape and its role in shaping the impulse, resources, and meaning behind beautiful houses and fashionable dressing.

Jinny Prais examines the ways that an urban professional elite in Accra worked to reorder social relations among the African residents of the city and overturn colonial imagery of urban space and people through writing about urban culture in popular newspapers. Through cultural debates in regular columns as well as readers' columns—particularly with regard to imagining spaces of nightlife and dancing—the elite resisted stereotypes related to urban African society and articulated a unified West African culture and new Africa that was primarily stratified according to social class. In so doing, they defied the ethnicity-based mapping of the city and its inhabitants associated with indirect rule, promoted a new understanding of African urban modernity over which they held authority, and laid foundations for contesting colonial rule in the Gold Coast.

Christine Ludl explores the representations of mobility, diversity, and personal and collective ambition of Malian and Senegalese migrants in inner-city Johannesburg. Drawing on ethnographic research with three specific groups of migrants, Soninke and Haalpulaar migrants from the Senegal River region (Senegal and Mali) and members of the two main Senegalese Muslim brotherhoods—the *Muridiyya* and the *Tijaniyya*—it engages with debates on cosmopolitanism, especially as they pertain to the South African context in the wake of xenophobic violence. Ludl resists simplistic portrayals of belonging, networks, feelings, and practices of connection with South African society that would hold African migrants as either transnationals rooted in their country of origin or cosmopolitans participating in the diverse urban fabric. Rather, she fleshes out the ambiguities and complexities of narratives and practices of community for these different groups. Neither cut off from their country of origin nor their South African communities, they forge and negotiate ambivalent spaces of being both inside and outside in Johannesburg.

Hannah Appel examines urban infrastructure connected to the oil industry in Malabo, capital of Equatorial Guinea. Her analysis illuminates how infrastructure becomes a key site through which oil and gas companies as well as Equatoguinean actors negotiate entanglement and responsibility, or more precisely, how material space becomes inscribed in the strive for disentanglement and the abdication of responsibility from the broader social context. Through the performance of intensive enclaving, relations of inequality are materialized and profoundly unequal living conditions normalized. Contrary to the modular fantasy produced by the oil companies, her chapter illuminates the profound work entailed in denying the web of sociopolitical relations required for oil extraction and its range of associated violences.

Emily Brownell explores discourses surrounding waste and sanitation in Dar es Salaam in the late colonial and early postcolonial periods. Through examining the master plans for the city dating from 1940 to 1979, she examines the transformations in narratives about dirt and disorder as well as their associated function in legitimizing forms of urban planning and control. Colonial planners mobilized discourses of dirt and disease to catalyze objectives of segregation and stem the tide of urbanization. Postcolonial administrators under Nyerere shifted the language of planning from an emphasis on race to a narrative connecting urban disorder to laziness and lack of discipline. Ultimately, as the government was faced with the permanence of urban growth and increasingly failed to provide adequate infrastructure, people were forced to find innovative ways of managing their own waste, and Nyerere came to hail such acts as expressions of his philosophy of self-help and discipline. As such, Brownell traces the reconfiguration of discourses of inclusion inscribed in the infrastructural practices of sanitation.

Giles Omezi interrogates how notions of modernity were conjured and spatialized in the city of Lagos during the first 20 years of independence through large-scale, state-planned, urban infrastructure projects. Focusing on a series of National Development Plans spanning three decades from 1960 to 1980, the analysis pays special attention to two major international sporting and cultural events—the Second All Africa Games (1973) and the Second World Black and African Festival of Arts and Culture (FESTAC; 1977). Through the implementation of packages of infrastructural interventions including major sports, civic, residential, and commercial buildings as well as major improvements to the road network of Lagos, these projects were key expressions of state efforts to project nationalist rhetoric locally and internationally, and to sculpt the state's modernization-based development aspirations. At the same time, a conscious effort to reconstitute notions of national identity that departed from Nigeria's recent colonial past can be read off the intent of these development plans and the nature of their implementation. Through burying spatial vestiges of colonial history under new layers of built form, the state deployed architecture and urban infrastructure in its projects of cultural production.

Note

1. With the exception of North Africa, the contributions represent a diversity of cities in West, Central, South, and East Africa from Anglophone, Francophone, Lusophone, and Hispanophone countries.

References

Anand, N. (2011). "PRESSURE: The PoliTechnics of Water Supply in Mumbai." *Cultural Anthropology* 26(4): 542–564.

———. (2012). "Municipal Disconnect: On Abject Water and Its Urban Infrastructures." *Ethnography* 13(4): 487–509.

Anderson, W. (1995). "Excremental Colonialism: Public Health and the Poetics of Pollution." *Critical Inquiry* Spring 21(3): 640–669.
Bayat, A. (1997). "Un-civil Society: The Politics of the 'Informal People'." *Third World Quarterly* 18(1): 53–72.
Betts, R. F. (1971). "The Establishment of the Medina in Dakar, Senegal, 1914." *Africa* 41(2): 143–152.
Bishop, R., Phillips, J., and Yeao, W. W., eds. (2003). *Postcolonial Urbanism: Southeast Asian Cities and Global Processes*. New York: Routledge.
Caldeira, R. P. R. (2012). "Imprinting and Moving Around: New Visibilities and Configurations of Public Space in São Paulo." *Public Culture* 24(2): 385–419.
Calhoun, C., Sennett, R., Shapira, H., eds. (2013). "Introduction to the Special Issue: *Poiesis* Means Making." (Special issue on *Infrastructures of the Urban*). *Public Culture* 25(2): 195–200.
Comaroff, J. and Comaroff, J. (2012). "Theory from the South: Or, How Euro-America Is Evolving Toward Africa." *Anthropological Forum: A Journal of Social Anthropology and Comparative Sociology* 22(2): 113–131.
Diouf, M. (1996). "Urban Youth and Senegalese Politics: Dakar 1988–1994." *Public Culture* 8: 225–249.
———. (2000). "The Senegalese Murid Trade Diaspora and the Making of a Vernacular Cosmopolitanism." *Public Culture* 12(3): 679–702.
———. (2008). "Reimagining an African City; Performing Culture, Arts and Citizenship in Dakar (Senegal), 1980–2000." In Gyan Prakash and Kevin M. Kruse, eds, *The Spaces of the Modern City: Imaginaries, Politics, and Everyday Life*. Princeton, NJ: Princeton University Press.
Diouf, M. and Fredericks, R., eds. (2013). *Les Arts de la Citoyenneté au Sénégal: Espaces contestés et civilités urbaines*. Paris: Karthala.
Doshi, S. (2013). "Resettlement Ecologies: Environmental Subjectivity and Graduated Citizenship in Mumbai." In Rademacher, A. and Sivaramakrishnan, K., eds, *Ecologies of Urbanism in India: Metropolitan Civility and Sustainability*, pp. 225–248. Hong Kong: Hong Kong University Press.
Edensor, T. and Jayne, M., eds. (2011). *Urban Theory Beyond the West: A World of Cities*. London: Routledge.
Ferguson, J. (2006). *Global Shadows: Africa in the Neoliberal World Order*. Durham, NC: Duke University Press.
———. (2012). "Afterward: Structures of responsibility." *Ethnography* 13(4): 558–562.
Fredericks, R. (2012). "Valuing the Dirty Work: Gendered Trashwork in Participatory Dakar." In C. Alexander and J. Reno, eds, *Economies of Recycling*, pp. 119–142. London: Zed Books.
———. (2013). "Disorderly Dakar: The Politics of Garbage in Senegal's Capital City." *Journal of Modern African Studies* 51(3): 435–458.
———. (2014). "Vital Infrastructures of Trash in Dakar." *Comparative Studies of South Asia, Africa, and the Middle East* 34(3): 532–548. Special issue on *Comparative Infrastructures*.
Geschiere, P. and Gugler, J. (1998). "The Urban-Rural Connection: Changing Issues of Belonging and Identification." *Africa: Journal of the International African Institute* 68(3): 309–319.

Geschiere, P. and Jackson, S. (2006). "Autochthony and the Crisis of Citizenship: Democratization, Decentralization, and the Politics of Belonging." *African Studies Review* 49(2): 1–7.

Geschiere, P. and Nyamnjoh, F. (2000). "Capitalism and Autochthony: The Seesaw of Mobility and Belonging." *Public Culture* 12(2): 423–452.

Ghertner, D. A. (2010a). "Calculating Without Numbers: Aesthetic Governmentality in Delhi's Slums." *Economy and Society* 39(2): 185–217.

———. (2010b). "Green Evictions: Clearing Slums, Saving Nature in Delhi." In P. Robbins, R. Peet, and M. Watts, eds, *Global Political Ecology*. London: Routledge.

Gidwani, V. (2013). "Value Struggles: Waste Work and Urban Ecology in Delhi." In A. Rademacher and K. Sivaramakrishnan, eds, *Ecologies of Urbanism in India: Metropolitan Civility and Sustainability*, pp. 169–200. Hong Kong: Hong Kong University Press.

Gifford, P. (2004). *Ghana's New Christianity: Pentecostalism in a Globalizing African Economy*. Bloomington, IN: Indiana University Press.

Glaeser, E. (2011). *Triumph of the City. How Our Greatest Invention Makes Us Richer, Smarter, Healthier, and Happier.* New York: The Penguin Press.

Graham, S. and Marvin, S. 2001. *Splintering Urbanism: Networked Infrastructures, Technological Mobilities and the Urban Condition*. New York: Routledge.

Hall, S. (1996). "The West and the Rest: Discourse and Power." In S. Hall, D. Held, D. Hubert, and K. Thompson, eds, *Modernity: An Introduction to Modern Societies*. Malden, MA: Blackwell.

Holston, J. (2010). "Right to the City, Right to Rights, and Urban Citizenship." Paper read at Mershon Center for International Security Studies. Globalization, Institutions, and Economic Security Workshop.

Kooy, M. and Bakker, K. (2008). "Technologies of Government: Constituting Subjectivities, Spaces, and Infrastructures in Colonial and Contemporary Jakarta." *International Journal of Urban and Regional Research* 32(2): 375–391.

Larkin, B. (2013). "The Politics and Poetics of Infrastructure." *Annual Review of Anthropology* 42: 327–343.

Mbembe, A. and Nuttall, S., eds. (2004a). *Johannesburg: The Elusive Metropolis*. Durham, NC: Duke University Press.

———. (2004b). "Writing the World from an African Metropolis." *Public Culture* 16(3): 347–372.

McFarlane, C. (2008). "Governing the Contaminated City: Infrastructure and Sanitation in Colonial and Post-Colonial Bombay." *International Journal of Urban and Regional Research* 32(2): 415–435.

McFarlane, C. and Rutherford, J. (2008). "Political Infrastructures: Governing and Experiencing the Fabric of the City (Symposium)." *International Journal of Urban and Regional Research* 32(2): 363–374.

Meehan, K. and Strauss, K., eds. (Forthcoming). *Life's Work in Crisis*. Athens, GA: University of Georgia Press.

Miraftab, Faranak. (2004). "Neoliberalism and Casualization of Public Sector Services: The Case of Waste Collection Services in Cape Town, South Africa." *International Journal of Urban and Regional Research* 28(4): 874–892.

Moore, D. (1994). "Optics of Engagement: Power, Positionality, and African Studies." *Transition* 64: 121–127.
Moore, S. A. (2009). "The Excess of Modernity: Garbage Politics in Oaxaca, Mexico." *The Professional Geographer* 61(4): 426–437.
Murray, M. J. (2011). *City of Extremes: The Spatial Politics of Johannesburg.* Durham, NC: Duke University Press.
Murray, M. J. and Myers, G. A., eds. (2011). *Cities in Contemporary Africa.* New York: Palgrave MacMillan.
Myers, G. A. (2011). *African Cities: Alternative Visions of Urban Theory and Practice.* London: Zed Books.
Nuttall, S. and Mbembe, A. (2005). "A Blasé Attitude: A Response to Michael Watts." *Public Culture* 17(1): 193–201.
Rodgers, D. and O'Neill, B. (2012). "Infrastructural Violence: Introduction to the Special Issue." (Special issue on *Infrastructural Violence). Ethnography* 13(4): 401–412.
Packer, G. (2006). "The Megacity: Decoding the Chaos of Lagos." *The New Yorker*, November: 62–75.
Parnell, S. and Robinson, J. (2012). "(Re)Theorizing Cities from the Global South: Looking Beyond Neoliberalism." *Urban Geography* 33(4): 593–617.
Pieterse, E. (2008). *City Futures: Confronting the Crisis of Urban Development.* London: Zed Books.
Prakash, G. (2011). "Introduction." In G. Prakash and K. M. Kruse, eds, *The Spaces of the Modern City: Imaginaries, Politics, and Everyday Life*, pp. 1–18. Princeton, NJ: Princeton University Press.
Ranganathan, M. (2014). "Paying for Pipes, Claiming Citizenship: Political Agency and Water Reforms at the Urban Periphery." *International Journal of Urban and Regional Research* 38(2): 590–608.
Roberts, A. F., Roberts, N., Armenian, G., and Gueye, O. (2003). *A Saint in the City: Sufi Arts of Urban Senegal.* Seattle, WA: University of Washington Press for the UCLA Fowler Museum of Cultural History.
Robinson, J. (2002). "Global and World Cities: A View from off the Map." *International Journal of Urban and Regional Research* 26(3): 531–554.
———. 2006. *Ordinary Cities: Between Modernity and Development.* London: Routledge.
Roy, A. and Ong, A. eds. (2011). *Worlding Cities: Asian Experiments and the Art of Being Global.* Oxford: Wiley Blackwell.
Secor, A. (2004). "'There Is an Istanbul That Belongs to Me': Citizenship, Space, and Identity in the City." *Annals of the Association of American Geographers* 94(2): 352–368.
Simone, A.-M. (2001). "The Worlding of African Cities." *African Studies Review* 44(2): 15–41.
———. (2004a). *For the City Yet to Come: Changing Life in Four African Cities.* Durham, NC: Duke University Press.
———. (2004b). "People as Infrastructure: People as Intersecting Fragments in Johannesburg." *Public Culture* 16(3): 407–429.
———. (2008). "The Last Shall Be the First: African Urbanites and the Larger Urban World." In A. Huyssen, ed., *Other Cities, Other Worlds: Urban Imaginaries in a Globalizing Age.* Durham, NC: Duke University Press.

———. (2010). *City Life from Jakarta to Dakar: Movements at the Crossroads*. New York: Routledge.
———. (2011). "No Longer the Subaltern: Reconfiguring Cities in the Global South." In Edensor, T. and Jayne, M., eds,. *Urban Theory Beyond the West: A World of Cities*, pp. 31–46. London: Routledge.
Stren, R. and White, R. (1993). *Villes africaines en crise: Gérer la croissance urbaine au sud du Sahara*. Paris: L'Harmattan.
Stren R. and Halfani M. (2001). "The Cities of Subsaharan Africa: From Dependency to Marginality." In Ronan Paddison, ed., *Handbook of Urban Studies*. London: Sage Publications.
Swanson, M. W. (1977). "The Sanitation Syndrome: Bubonic Plague and Urban Native Policy in the Cape Colony, 1900–1909." *Journal of African History* 18(3): 387–410.
Tannerfeldt, G., and Ljung, P. (2006). *More Urban Less Poor: An Introduction to Urban Development and Management*. London: Earthscan.
Trefon, T. (2009). "Hinges and Fringes: Conceptualising the Peri-urban in Central Africa." In F. Locatelli and P. Nugent eds., *African Cities: Competing Claims on Urban Spaces*, pp. 15–36. Leiden: Brill.
von Schnitzler, A. (2008). "Citizenship Prepaid: Water, Calculability, and Techno-Politics in South Africa." *Journal of Southern African Studies* 34(4): 899–917.
———. (2013). "Traveling Technologies: Infrastructure, Ethical Regimes, and the Materiality of Politics in South Africa." *Cultural Anthropology* 28(4): 670–693.
Watson, V. (2014). "African Urban Fantasies: Dreams or Nightmares?" *Environment and Urbanization* 26(1): 1–17.
Watts, M. (2005). "Baudelaire over Berea, Simmel over Sandton?" *Public Culture* 17(1): 181–192.

1

Too Many Things to Do: Social Dimensions of City-Making in Africa

AbdouMaliq Simone

The Terms of Urbanization in Africa

Urbanization has much to offer African economic and social wellbeing. This remains the case despite the clear problems inherent in the ways that cities have been put together. These problems include shrinking rural livelihoods, insufficient value-added production, excessive emphasis on rents and administration, and low-cost informal labor. Nevertheless, although much is known about all of the things wrong, biased, distorted, and underdeveloped in African cities, it is also critical to understand urbanization as something capable of stirring productive relationships among people, materials, and places, regardless of specific histories, political conditions, or positions within larger economies.

The relationship between the character of actual existing cities and processes of urbanization is, of course, never straightforward (Brenner 2009). In Africa, this relationship is very heterogeneous. There are primary and secondary cities intensely integrated into global systems of transaction—sites of thriving stock markets, built environments, and popular cultures. There are others that function simply as large military encampments where everyday life centers on struggles to seize goods and territory or ward off incursions by others. There are cities with well-elaborated policy regimes, and others that seem to function through incessantly renegotiated informal accords. There are cities where residents make serious money because nothing official seems to work, and there are cities where people barely survive because everything has to be improvised. These multiplicities follow from how the turbulent relationships among, often, very discrepant agendas and impetus for city-making were stitched together.

The history of urbanization in contemporary Africa has not proceeded in single directions. It embodies the aspirations and procedures aimed toward industrial development, modernization, sectoral specialization, as well as individuated practices of accumulation and subject formation. Moreover, it embodies the constantly mutating collective strategies for creating spaces of operation and livelihood occasioned by the fluid deal-making that has characterized much of city governance throughout late colonial and postcolonial times (Burton 2002, Coquery-Vidrovitch 1991, Fourchard 2006, Salm and Falola 2005). Cities reflect the countervailing exigencies of economic development, citizen formation, and political control (Bayart 2006, Cooper 2008, Gervais-Lambony 2003). What makes "economic sense" according to prevailing norms does not always go together with what makes "social" or "political" sense. Cities are, thus, the bringing together of identities, social positions, and conventions that have been stabilized through different historical eras and social ascriptions that have remained fluid throughout them (Hopkins 2009, Myers 2003).

There have been many explanations for African urban growth and for the massive rural-to-urban migration that took place from the end of World War II to the onset of the global recession in the early 1970s. Obviously, many factors are at work. Rural migrants were forced to the city, in some instances, by land shortages or by the collapse of rural economies. Here, it is important to keep in mind the heterogeneity of rural circumstances. Increasing differentials in wealth and capacity had varied impacts on different rural regions and categories of urban residents. So did the increasing differentiation of land use and production for domestic consumption, as opposed to (or alternating with) domestic production.

Given these circumstances—and without having a lot of resources, political will, and technical capacity to work with—most African cities have frequently demonstrated a substantial ability to link the agendas and practices of individual household livelihood to a broader series of economic, cultural, and religious activities. Here, individuals actively take part in events, places, and networks where many different activities do and could happen. Homes become workshops, workshops become associations, and associations become components of interlinked production systems. Buying, selling, making, cultivating, exchanging, and socializing are tied together in specific, yet changing, patterns of interaction that enable individuals to make effective use of their time, resources, and opportunities (Piermay 2003, Schler 2003).

Because many cities were built with temporary labor markets and curtailed residential rights, they forged highly uneven relationships with territories external to them, and often had fractured linkages with rural areas; moreover, they functioned as places of mediation between locality and mobility, always having to find ways of incorporating new kinds of residents and their articulations to other places (Goerg 2006, Guèye 2007, Guyer and Belinga 1995, Yntiso 2008). As a result, cities were a context for making claims, of figuring particular narratives of legitimacy that enable individual and collective groups of residents to access resources and opportunities such as land, services, participation in institutions, and other entitlements (Abbink 2005, Cueppens and Geschiere 2005, Freund 2009, Hilgers 2009, Lund 2006). Particular modes of address are constituted where residents "put themselves on the map" and seek to have particular identities and needs recognized. These modes of address frequently change, stretching and shrinking to accommodate or exclude particular actors and territories (Boujou 2000, Hilgers 2008, 2009).

As a result, authority is often diffused across sometimes competing, sometimes complementary institutions, and is replete with different meanings and formulas, as well as different forms of consolidation. Some institutions have formal attributes and structures; others are more ephemeral and dispersed, not easily categorized or defined (Bellagamba and Klute 2008, Kelsall 2008, Lund 2006, Miran 2006, Nielsen 2009, Rakodi 2006).

Urbanization Without Cities

Historically, in much of Africa, what was to be gained through an engagement with cities—knowledge, complex social practices, and economic capacity—could never be fully instantiated within the city. Even when substantial rearrangements in cultural life and social economy were precipitated by an urban presence, the potential interconnections among emerging networks of social practice, economic specialization, and cultural reformation were constrained. Clear vehicles of institutionalization were usually foreclosed, largely by the dearth of available public spheres that were not heavily scrutinized or repressed by existing regimes (Coquery-Vidrovitch 1991).

At the same time, for certain migrants, urbanization reflected economic advancement, freedom from the social constraints of rural life, education, and prospects of enhanced social status; therefore, the connections between the attainment of education and urban employment and varying government policies related to cultivating an established urban population became factors in migration (Salau 1979). The complexion of migration varied among regions. The migration of entire families took place more often in West and Central Africa, where the role of women in farming was no larger than that of men, and where there was a strong tradition of trade (O'Connor 1983). The degree to which the elaboration of rural–urban linkages facilitated migration and the extent to which the linkages, in and of themselves, intensified a sense of difference between places were also significant. This sense of difference could be potentially converted into a resource for both rural and urban life. Kinship ties provided a link that enabled people to find a place in the city, and an opportunity to return to ancestral homelands if things did not work out. This is a linkage reinforced by communal land tenure systems and a gendered division of labor, where women were generally responsible for food production.

The sense of linkage went beyond these kinship ties. The concentration of administrative power in cities was so sudden that it had a jarring effect on the rural areas, which were also the objects of this administration. Rural areas were forced to change, particularly as substantial amounts of low-cost imported foodstuffs began saturating urban markets (Hart 1982). Moreover, rural areas resisted the various ways in which they were to be incorporated into more nationally focused production and political systems. Administration was limited in its scope and ability to incorporate rural areas within its ambit (O'Connor 1983). Thus, urban and rural areas existed, in part, as disarticulated spheres. Structuring and plying linkages among them have not only been necessary to reduce "mutual estrangement" and facilitate some sense of overarching coherence. Linkages have, furthermore, become economic instruments in their own right. Linkages are things that can be used and manipulated to facilitate a better life in both domains, compensate for difficulties, and circumvent various social and governmental controls. Increasingly, as people faced conflicts around changes underway in rural areas, the city became a place of refuge, a source for tipping the scales in favor of one party or another, and a place for the short-term accumulation of resources. For urban residents, rural areas became a place to send family members in times of difficulty, to hide assets, to feed urban households, or to garner support or inputs for various urban projects (Englund 2002).

Practices of making something out of the city other than what was expected by a fuller incorporation in capitalist production had to "search" for different organizational forms and auspices under which to operate. Such practices increasingly depended on the identification of loopholes and under-regulated spaces in changing colonial economies. Once identified, these practices acted as compensations and alternatives potentially capable of being appropriated by diverse actors with different agendas (Bertrand 1998, Ferguson 1999, Schler 2003).

Fluidity, thus, remained both a fundamental strength and weakness. These "alternative" economic and cultural practices were unable to remake the city in ways that could serve the objective of expanding agricultural activities for the bulk of rural residents. Nor could they expand the integration of the bulk of the city and its residents into capitalist circuits. Instead, these practices acted as a limiting constraint to both endogenous and capitalist economic expansion. They found ways to urbanize relationships derived from ruralized solidarity and to identify possibilities for urban sustainability in particular ways of engaging under-supervised rural domains. Thus, urban Africa's pursuit of "independent" agendas and aspirations largely took place in this "closed" circuit. These agendas both intersected with and ran parallel to the narrow ways in which the overall urban economy was linked to global capital (Mabogunje 1990).

Contesting the Present

This urban history has produced a situation, today, of intense contestation in many cities of the region. There is contestation in terms of the fundamental rights and obligations embedded in relationships between children and parents, between extended family members, between men and women, patrons and clients, citizens and government officials, among others (Marie 2007). Basic questions as to the place of self-initiative, individual decision-making, and the conditions of belonging to family and other social groups are intensely debated. People are working out many different kinds of accommodation between the needs of autonomous individual action and the security of life that largely remains rooted in long-term forms of social belonging (Marie 1997, Rodrigues 2007, Tonda 2005, 2008).

These dynamics have a direct impact on what governments and civil society can do in terms of managing and changing urban life. Fundamental issues about what people are able to do together and what they can legitimately do on their own are often replete with great tension, controversy, and fluidity. Marked generational divisions remain, and many youth come to rely upon a range of apparent "transgressions" in order to keep open the space by which they can see themselves crafting their own lives (Diouf 2007). There are districts that make a concerted attempt to keep the "larger city" at a distance for fear that progressive integration would mean the loss of the very existence of its residents. However, without incorporation, these districts often experience protracted conflict, which erodes the basis for any consistent authority. For example, in the Kisangani district at the periphery of Kinshasa, I have personally witnessed how adolescent youth are largely in control and run things by virtue of turning all of the familiar conventions upside down—where those practices and behaviors usually most representative of trust and confidence are actively construed as instances of terror. In less extreme ways, some districts are composed of "households" where kinships relations are strikingly absent. Instead, provisional, transitory arrangements of relative strangers prevail whose affiliations are cemented in their ability to ward off obligation and comparison about access to resources and opportunity.

Furthermore, residents have to decide where to locate themselves, how to effectively balance affordability, personal security, economic opportunity, and tenure. For example, some residents have to decide it is more advantageous to spend sizeable amounts of available income to locate themselves in "regular" situations in central parts of the city, or save income by living in more provisional conditions at the periphery (Englund 2002, Ferguson 1999, Guyer et al. 2002, Owusu 2007, SITRASS 2004). There are decisions to make with regard to how much to invest in particular kinds of work or business, how much to invest in maintaining kinship and social relations, and whether residents should affiliate themselves with particular forms of patronage. The intersection of the various ways of working out these decisions theoretically provoke a great deal of discussion and, again, questioning. What are the right things to do; what are the right alliances to make; what are the most effective ways to use limited resources to acquire assets; and, how can these assets be maximized? At the same time, the possibilities that these deliberations can take place in a systematic way in public domains and at scale are often shut down by existing political power. This shutting down of public discussion then disrupts the basic conditions of mediation and problem solving. The trappings of democratic procedures—through municipal elections and decentralization—often become a substitute for wide-ranging public deliberations of policy (Devas 2004).

As such, the greater visibility of demands for justice, democracy, efficiency, and morality that is taking place across African cities is a fruitful place to support a process where political contestation can be waged in terms of those who have been previously kept out of the process. However, what the poor actually win in such a process largely depends on the existence of political parties and institutionalized policies that backup claims for rights. Here, the problem is that more powerful political forces can define the categories and identities through which these claims can be made. For example, the growth of religious movements, both Christian and Muslim, are having an important impact in reasserting practices of economic advancement outside of patronage and communal systems. Moreover, they express commitments to the value of hard work, education, and solidarity across ethnic and regional groupings. The extent to which such religious movements can give rise to a new generation of entrepreneurship is contingent upon the extent to which the elite succeed in capturing these movements for their own economic and political objectives, and how much pastors and imams use these movements to become a new elite (Kaba 2000, Marshall 2009, Miran 2003, van Dijk 2002).

In an important reflection on the long-term political crisis in Côte D'Ivoire, Achille Mbembe and Celestin Monga (2011) talk about the urgent need—a need that has existed for a long time—for the elaboration of institutional relations within language and concepts understandable to diverse constituencies making up the nation or the city, and which are capable of implementing constitutional authority, notions of citizenship, and the governance of resources. The "procedures" of "democracy"—elections, decentralization, and legal transparency—provide little guidance for how to "compose" the instituted threads through which people recognize the willingness to share their futures together.

African Cities as Laboratories for Nation-Building

National institutional frameworks may often do little to cohere the nation or promote a sense of national belonging; however, the day-to-day interactions of residents trying to work out viable distributions of opportunity, or simply trying to live together in adversity, become the important practices of "working out the nation." Even when households may feel that their heart is elsewhere other than the city in which they live, and even if households may primarily stick to their own ethnic or religious grouping, a viable life in the city requires residents to deal with each other in ways that cross the apparent divides. In a divided city such as Abidjan, where political, geographic, ethnic, and religious backgrounds congeal in, often, highly segregated territories—and where boundary crossing can be a high-risk practice—there are many ways in which the divisions get converted into complementarities, sometimes, simply because the value of cross-border transactions is inflated because of the risks entailed. Regardless of the motivation, such transactions take place on a daily basis, as goods have to be moved, and services rendered. Even if some districts can become somewhat self-sufficient, the economic costs of this insularity are high, as social immobility contains its own implicit tax.

Given the long-term economic dependence of many cities on the transnational circuits of trade plied by their residents, the working out of concrete modes of being "Nigerian", "Congolese", or "Cameroonian" come from the practicalities of using common national identity as a means of collaborating in other cities—be it Guangzhou, Paris, Bangkok, or Dallas. Although these residents are operating outside "their" cities, the activities they are engaged with are critical for the economies of these cities and, thus, the ongoing elaboration of national identity remains occasioned by urban conditions. Even when transnational migrants largely originate in rural areas and small towns, as they do for the most part in Senegal, the articulation of cities such as Dakar, Louga, and Touba are inevitably thickened through these migratory circuits—through emerging affiliations and networks among migrants.

Regardless of the particular political histories of distinct nations, cities enable diverse peoples to discover an ability to act in concert and to attain a working sense of responsibility to, and identification with, each other. In fact, reference to the nation becomes an increasingly practical way in which urban residents, in the face of the dissipation of many forms of relied-upon mediation—such as family ties, neighborhood belonging, and cultural practice—are able to concretize a sense of mutual connection (Englebert 2002, Fourchard et al. 2009, Jewsiewicki and Higginson 2008, United Nations Human Settlements Program 2008).

That said, urban residents across the region display little faith in the capacity of national governments to realize these aspirations. The implications of this lack of faith are enormous (Bratton 2007, 2008, Bratton et al. 2004). If a people's commitment to making urban life work is largely based on their belief that the city is the context in which a concrete sense of nationhood can be achieved, and if what can be assumed as the most critical and powerful actor in this process—that is, the state—is seen as an impediment to this project, then, what concrete expectations can be made of urban development in the long run?

At the same time, Africa's capacity for debilitating violence is well known—where many actors, both in and outside of the state, revert to the use of violence as a means of claiming rights and resources. As such, the capacities of large metropolitan areas—full of impoverishment and uncertain futures—to persist without such violence are a critical platform on which to build new institutions and collaborations. Of course, attention has been drawn to the ways in which cities like Kano, Jos, Freetown, Monrovia, Abidjan, Nairobi, Brazzaville, Goma, and

Lomé have been overturned by different waves of internecine violence. What often passes unnoticed in commentaries about urban life is the enormous work residents do, day in and day out, to maintain productive relations with each other. Although criminality and insecurity may be rife in many cities, and violence easily instrumentalized as a means of accumulation and control, everyday economies require reciprocities, negotiation, and cooperation if they are to be effective (Grant 2009).

The ability of cities with millions of inhabitants to maintain these practices over time is a critical resource for any strategy of urban development. Projects that attempt to include participatory planning, decision-making, and management often express frustration over how limited participation often is. However, this frustration often ignores the labor-intensive process, whereby residents are already heavily implicated in each other's lives with the day-to-day work that is necessary in order to maintain functional relationships with neighbors, co-workers, and extended family members. For many urban districts, what is important is their capacity to keep things moving, to facilitate the flow of individuals and materials in and out, and to maximize the capacity of interchange, even if this is, sometimes, at the expense of coherence or an ordered environment (Arnaut 2008; Arnaut and Højbert 2008, Mimche and Fomekong 2008, Nielsen 2007, Pitcher 2006).

Attaining appropriate densities of inhabitation, agglomerated economic activity, and service provision remain priorities; however, it is important to remember that residents live with often vastly different geographies in their minds. In other words, they live with often highly varied maps about where it is safe to go, which spaces belong to whom, and how spaces are connected to each other. These different geographies not only make planning and administration a difficult challenge, but they also constitute a series of checks and balances that insulate against debilitating conflict (Dierwechter 2006, Keith 2005, Marshall-Fratani 2006, Newell 2006, Ndjio 2006). Not content to simply live in well-defined enclaves, the desires of residents to operate across the city as a whole often promotes a sense of sharing and cultivates places where different actors can witness each other and still have access to areas of safety and more circumscribed practices of commonality.

New Links with the Larger World

Just as cities continue to be important contexts for the concretization of everyday aspirations for national belonging and development, so, too, are their roles intensifying as platforms for economic and sociopsychological articulations to a broader regional and global world. Even when particular cities or districts within cities appear marginal in relationship to the "real happenings" of the world, it is important to understand the ways in which even the most seemingly peripheral areas are linked to substantial powers, both near and far.

At the same time, consolidations of new elite territories in the city coincide with the speculative dimensions of urban infrastructure. The rationale for African investment on the part of emerging powers—China, India, Brazil, Taiwan, South Korea, Malaysia, and Russia—is not only to acquire assets in extractive and processing economies. Africa also acts as a locus of intersection among complementary interests, financial modalities, and risk assumption. As an exterior in "need of investment," where both risks and potential profitability are high and where regulatory frameworks are weak, potential synergies among diverse financial streams, competencies, sectors, and networked positions can be explored without long-term commitments or intensive scrutiny. Infrastructure serves as a vehicle of articulation among diverse economic actors. It brings them into close relations that may be specified by certain contractual responsibilities, investment shares, and tasks but need not be restricted to them (Large 2008, Orr and Kennedy 2008, Power and Mohan 2010, Sautman and Yann 2007, Stellenbosch University Centre for Chinese Studies 2006).

At the same time, efforts to consolidate authority and clear development trajectories—to put to an end the diffusion of divergent ways of living in and off the city—are being anchored in terms of building concrete links to the wider world. Facilitating the ease of capital and physical movements across uncertain and "rambunctious" cities becomes the critical conventional strategy to clean up the messiness of African urbanity and set it on a more concentrated, discernible path. African urban economies are, thus, increasingly oriented to scaling up in order to mobilize resources at more universal levels. We have long been familiar with even grassroots organizations scaling upwards to donor organizations and nongovernmental organizations (NGOs) in order to mobilize resources.

Now, even the more informal dimensions of urban economies—far from representing merely deficiencies in those economies—are part of an elaborate latticework of connectivity that will be the basis for future African regional economic development (Söderbaum 2004). The current limited circumference and trajectories of inflows and outflows, of articulations among territories, and of integration among diverse functions, populations, and sectors will be progressively rectified by coordinated infrastructural interventions on many fronts.

This is more than simply building new roads, rails, power lines, and telecommunications. It is more than a matter of constructing synergies between the physical, the institutional, the economic, and the informational (Foster and Bricēno-Garmendia 2010). For this, well-worn circuits of sojourning, trade, and commodity flows, largely outside of formal regulations, have already mapped out a wide range of possibilities, already constitute a large "market-in-waiting."

This is because, despite clear inefficiencies in infrastructure, services, and labor markets, what often does work in the densely populated small- and medium-sized urban production districts is the make-up of labor and the collaborations of entrepreneurs and traders across borders of all kinds. Textiles, shoes, furniture, car parts and repair, household goods, hardware, catering, transport, electronics, and second-hand information technology (IT) products are significant sectors of the urban economy, often constituting specialized districts that absorb tens of thousands of workers in a mix of small- and medium-scale enterprises. Many different kinds of work exist—fabrication, repair, marketing, invention—in the same setting; therefore, there can be a built-in flexibility applied to the specifications of different orders and consumer needs. As the bulk of consumers at this level are locally based, there can be a continuous flow of information between end markets and producers. The key is how to build up from these local-level proficiencies to address a much larger scale of potential markets (Lindell 2010a, 2010b). Here, a full range of activities and services are required to take a service or product from its conception to final sale—including financial, regulatory, supply, and support services, among others.

Past research work shows that the key strength of African urban production is the strong ties that exist at the local level and the ways in which these ties support cross-linkages among different kinds of work and skills (Guyer 2004, Simone 2004). However, accessing larger markets requires the development of a wide range of connections that are often more fluid and short term (Meagher 2010). The question is: how can the different facets of the conception-to-end-use trajectory be efficiently melded so as to reach new markets? Presently, the extent of bottlenecks is legendary. Costly lag times continue to persist between offloading at ports and onward shipment by rail or truck; the absence of storage facilities results in spoilage; sporadic power and other service supplies interrupt production schedules; lack of adequate sanitation and healthcare results in unpredictable labor supplies. A more seamless movement of goods and services is crucial to market expansion, and this will necessitate substantial investment in infrastructure. Even when such infrastructure may be dedicated to the priorities of foreign investors or to synergies among the top sectors of national and urban economies, can this infrastructure also have productive benefits for other lesser scale economies that have been "leading the way" in terms of regional scaling and integration? The needs are so enormous, and the levels of investment remain comparatively paltry, in relationship to what is going on in the rest of the world; therefore, it is difficult to imagine just how sufficient resources will be mobilized.

Practices of Governing

The conventional gospel states that, if only African cities were effectively governed, they would then become "real" cities. Certainly the massive growth of slums and impoverishment has to be grappled with; otherwise, the historical resourcefulness of African urbanities will be choked off—suffocated in the overwhelming absence of anything to work with. Governance entails decisions, mobilization, guidance, and deliberation. These are all practices that are often highly problematic in African cities.

Significant advances have been made in benchmarking, performance-based incentives, use of diagnostic tools and identification systems, as well as the capacity to link strategy formulation to master planning and capital investment planning. The Global Cities Indicators Program (2008) summarizes a suite of indicators available to the urban sector from index-driven approaches to standardize and evaluate various forms of development progress, policy-driven indicators to be used in broad-based consultation and participative planning exercises, and performance measure indicators for governance operations. Some progress has been made to end unfunded national mandates, ensure equitable and transparent intragovernmental transfers, and establish frameworks that will enable municipalities to access credit markets and development bank funds, as well as pool municipal development funds.

Nevertheless, these tools cannot adequately grasp how the "real" administration of cities actually takes place. In this "real" administration, there exists both the intersection and disjunction of different exigencies and aspirations (Muniesa and Linhardt 2009, Randles et al. 2006). On the one hand, municipal governments are faced with the need to generate income to provide essential services and pay for the operations of municipal bureaucracies. Staffing levels, budgets, and technical capacities are usually insufficient to do the job—of collecting fees, managing traffic, monitoring markets, and regulating trade flows, which are only a few examples. Consequently, municipal management relies upon an intermediary sector of brokers and fixers who are not officially part of the municipal system but perform official duties. Because these are not formal sub-contractual arrangements, such intermediaries require certain autonomy of operation as a means of ensuring remuneration for the jobs that they do. They have to have flexibility to collect fees that otherwise would not be necessary if citizens were to deal with the bureaucracies themselves—if they actually could (Blundo 2006).

At the same time, the operations of these intermediaries remain subsumed to the overall agenda of the relevant municipal bureaucracy. Autonomy is displayed in the very manner in which these intermediaries demonstrate their access to the bureaucracy—that is, they have access, although there is no formal reason why they should. As a result, the management of trading, driving, marketing, parking, licensing, or adjudicating also entails the possibility of "citizens" managing the operations of the bureaucracy through such intermediaries who are not necessarily beholden to the official rules and procedures. In many ways, then, the governance of the city cannot be subsumed under conventional normative structures, as they simply do not work. At the same time, the techniques of management that interweave official and unofficial practices in order to effectively accomplish the management of particular activities and bodies also pose a wide range of seemingly unworkable dilemmas (Blundo 2006, Dill 2009, Laurent et al 2004, Prag 2010). Although clearer delineation of institutional competencies and the availability of more money and technical capacity might bring about more conventional dispositions, these, often, are blind to dealing with the accumulated histories of this interweaving of official and unofficial practices and the particular subject positions and spaces of operation they institutionalize over time.

On the other hand, residents have to rely upon the techniques that available municipal administrations use in order to make lines of authority and responsibility visible. Although segments of life can seem very well ordered and defined, it is largely because of the messy assemblages of official institutions and vast networks of unofficial intermediaries that the appearance of clarity can be sustained. Residents must, thus, create and retain concrete possibilities for mixing up distinctions between residence and commerce, licit and illicit work, religion and secularity, and the familiar and entrepreneurial in order to maintain their own semblance of clear identifications, agendas, and life strategies. Of course, these actions make it even more difficult for conventional municipal logics to operate. If things need to be messy in order to be made clear, then making things clear may only create more of a mess.

Governing everywhere, of course, has largely been a function of deal-making. These deals bring together divergent agendas and actors into provisional agreements about dividing up territory or money or, alternately, how these differences will cooperate under specific conditions. Deals are never commitments to the long haul; they do not reflect a progressive sense of reconciliation or the desire for affiliation and cooperation. They largely dispense with ideological commitments; they not only open space to make things happen, but also slow things down when they enforce modest, incremental gains. Importantly, many urban residents believe that this is what governing means. To them, policy pronouncements issued from city hall or press conferences have almost no relevance compared with widespread rumors about which politicians or pastors or tycoons had been seen visiting someone's house after midnight.

As such, more than simply instituting new administrative procedures, there is a need to completely re-visualize just exactly what the municipality might look like. Here, for example, the very physical presence of various amalgamations of youth filling public spaces in cities through political demonstration, cultural festivity, and organized intimidation not only becomes a concrete vehicle of such revising, but also a reactivation of the nation as platform for reaching a larger world (Arnaut 2008, Hansen 2005, Jua 2003, Moyo 2007). Although African governments have often been understandably afraid of the "street" and of youth, this coupling of youth out on the streets is sometimes the only way in which a city is able to see the possibilities of a "new future."

Government ministries across the region are now largely staffed by highly trained, competent, and committed personnel—sometimes even more so than in other countries across the world. These cadres are, increasingly, the visible face of government. Nevertheless, the predominant practices of state politics in numerous African countries—and, thus, fundamental decisions as to the disposition of power and resources—take place in a political world that runs parallel to the state. Although sometimes a world of opaque decision-making, nebulous deals, and arduous balances of competing forces, this parallel domain of decision-making, often, is more effective in bringing together the different range of actors, localities, and tendencies, making up the nation than is the official functioning of the state itself. The problem is that, because it is a parallel, informal world, it is not held to account by its citizens.

Indicators and normative procedures of governance are important; however, what is lost is the array of performative tools that governments potentially have at their disposal as part of their capacity to "make things happen." How municipal government accounts for what it does is a process that can limit the various ways in which government can become a more *visible* actor in the day-to-day lives of urban residents. For government must always consider where it can be *seen* to be actively at work. Of course, municipalities have often been preoccupied with visible displays that supposedly point to its effectiveness, as well as many kinds of "show projects" and public relations exercises. However, here, visibility refers to the ways in which various places and people within the city can actually visualize a government at work in the daily operations of the city.

At the outset, this may mean identifying new ways to use existing municipal assets and, thus, build new categories for urban transactions that work. Municipalities conventionally attempt to recuperate potentially lost value due to various inefficiencies through either subcontracting the management of assets to private firms or selling off those assets outright. In other words, municipal assets are re-categorized as commodities priced according to prevailing market value, and then supplemented by other considerations as public interest. However, this process is often a limited way to think about resources that municipalities control or have access to.

The question is how existing resources can attain wider and more diverse use and in ways that also diversify potential revenue streams and costs. Such a process would build on existing ways by which African urban residents flexibly use different networks of connections—from family members, affiliates, patrons, clients, co-workers, and so forth—to access resources. These resources are, in turn, distributed in quantities that acquire particular value by, again, flexibly using categories that point to different kinds of social relationships and responsibilities. In this way, limited resources find ways to be judiciously distributed by pluralizing the kinds of actors and obligations involved.

Contrary to conventional economic logic that sees markets as places where those making transactions dissociate the goods to be exchanged from any other meaning or network of use other than that of commodity, most African markets have functioned by multiplying the implications of transaction. The buying and selling of goods become occasions to construct and reaffirm the complicated ways in which people are involved in each other's life and the different overlapping networks in which people are involved. Individuals enter these "market relations" for many different reasons and access different opportunities beyond simply a good price or a quick sale, and it is these multiple dimensions that, in large part, drive the dynamism of such markets (Verran 2007).

Municipalities might learn more from the markets they officially manage. For example, as part of their rationale, indicators may be designed and used to curtail the tendency of public institutions to invent their own legitimacy or efficacy. However, in the very process of trying to make explicit that which these institutions do in terms of a system of indicators, a sense of invention is largely maintained. Even when scientific criteria can be stabilized around the statistical robustness of a particular indicator, this does not obviate the need for interpretive flexibility among competing points of view, particularly in terms of what the municipal government actually does and the materials it actually works with. This process of trying to make explicit what is and can be done, then, points to various possibilities where city governments have unanticipated room to maneuver. The process of governance contains within it large degrees of uncertainty that can be mobilized in potentially creative ways (Bolay 2006, Duit and Galaz 2008).

Concluding Note

All of these considerations raise the question of what, then, African cities should be used for. Of course, they house a swelling population of largely slum dwellers, desperate to find a way to stay afloat and lead viable lives. This is not possible without jobs, and a huge number of jobs will need to be created. These jobs will not appear without a substantial expansion of economic activity and, thus, we come back to the question of what cities will be used for. Whether through dense circuits of sojourning, migration, and commodity flows, or simply the concentration of the majority of a nation's population, the major metropolitan areas of Africa have largely reached a point where their anchorage of national and sub-regional economies—similar and divergent—establishes a substantial basis to broaden the articulations among them. Their connections to national territories and global economies make them more than nominal centers of administration (OECD 2007).

Many national economies may be overly tied to extraction and primary production, short-circuiting the conventional industrial underpinnings of urban growth; however, a sufficient history of spin-offs has taken place to partly compensate for this. Most important for the scope of this chapter, the internal pluralities of cities—still far from being viably reconciled within coherent agendas and governmental practices—may be productive in terms of generating more regional, inter-urban collaborations. The question of what an individual African city, then, is to be used for should be increasingly addressed in its plural relationships with other cities, as a means of enacting reciprocities, a complementary use of resources, and a semblance of agglomeration effects. These interchanges will not necessarily solve the problems of slum life, but they do force cities of particular locations, histories, and exteriorities to think more about how to productively shape the spaces that "separate" them.

Urbanization in certain sub-regions certainly is propelling new forms of regionalization and compelling gradual integrations of national populations into regional domains and marking out widening corridors, which expedite new economic synergies. As such, conceptualizing city futures always has to exceed what takes place within given municipal boundaries. This is particularly the case for African cities, as they will not be major production centers in the conceivable future. As such, they must push the ways in which they can be materially and politically implicated in territories far beyond themselves. The basis for this extension will most likely rely upon sharpening inter-city complementarities, plying differential networks, geographic positions, and historical advantages into new scales of investment in infrastructure, social welfare, and economic capacity (World Bank 2009).

The fortunes of the region's cities rise and wane according to dynamics far outside their control as well as how much residents are actually committed to believing in the viability of their futures. Cities facilitate generosity and greed, collaboration and individual parasitism. They are arenas in which individuals can feel like they are living amid a larger world, with all the possibilities of consumption available. When, in that world, they can live as if the hard realities experienced by the majority of urban residents simply do not matter, simply are millions of miles away. Of course, to remain within this imaginary of a well-elaborated urban world when one lives in cities, sometimes not far from the verge of collapse, necessitates all kinds of shortcuts and corruptions. The ways in which these practices have become normalized for so long can lessen the desires of many to do more than toil to make everyday ends meet.

That said, the overwhelming history of African cities is mostly about residents striving hard to "do the right thing." Kids are clothed and fed and made to get to school on time; there are substantial investments in shelter and health; inordinate efforts are made to identify people with talent and skills and make sure they have opportunities to use them. Such pursuits have continued for decades, regardless of the awareness which most residents have that the bulk of these efforts will prove futile. They are futile—not through any fault of their own—but because political interests have been narrowly drawn, resources have been insufficient, and because the attitudes and policies that informed colonization and racism have not changed all that much.

At the same time, urban residents have demonstrated a remarkable inventiveness in making cities something that—despite the prevailing conditions and odds—might be something that could work for them, be somehow supportive of a wide range of aspirations beyond simply putting food on the table. Families and households did internalize an obligation to demonstrate their capacity to do the right thing according to the globalized norms of modernity. No matter how much they did not really believe it, they were always willing to "play at the level of the world" and show how they could be in the world at large. However, they would always have to find a way to valorize the "shadows," that is, those practices and approaches that "got them through" the city, that made the city something vital to them. They know that these shadows will never have the money, status, or support to become a "new norm." Nevertheless, they have to be recognized in some way.

Therefore, oftentimes, the problems of urban development are not so much about the lack of capacity as they are about the persistence of a certain ambivalence. This is an implicit worry that a city re-made too much according to all the modern ways is a city that they will no longer be able to recognize, even if it is, in most respects, welcomed. Unless the real politics of urban life deals with such ambivalence and accords formal recognition to the ways in which cities have actually been experienced and built, there is likely to be an urban development full of stops and starts and messy twists for a long time to come.

References

Abbink, J. (2005). "Being Young in Africa: The Politics of Despair and Renewal." In Abbink, J. and van Kessel, I., eds, (2004). *Vanguard or Vandals: Youth, Politics and Conflict in Africa*, pp. 1–33. Leiden and Boston: Brill.

Arnaut, K. (2008). "Marching the Nation: An Essay on the Mobility of Belonging Among Militant Youngsters in Cote D'Ivoire." *Afrika Focus* 21: 81–105.

Arnaut, K. and Højbjerg, C. (2008). "Gouvernance et ethnographie en temps de crise: De l'étude des ordres émergents dans l'Afrique entre guerre et paix." *Politique Africaine* 111: 5–21.

Bayart J.-F. (2006). *L'Etat en Afrique. La politique du ventre*. L'Espace du politique, 2ème édition augmentée. Paris: Fayard Coll.

Bellagamba, A. and Klute, G. (2008). "Tracing Emergent Powers in Contemporary Africa: An Introduction." In Bellagamba, A. and Klute, G., eds, *Beside the*

State: Emergent Power in Contemporary Africa, pp. 7–22. Köln: Rüdiger Köppe Verlag.

Bertrand, M. (1998). "Villes africaines, modernités en questions." *Revue Tiers Monde* 39: 885–904.

Blundo, G. (2006). "Dealing with the Local State: The Informal Privatization of Street-Level Bureaucracies in Senegal." *Development and Change* 37: 799–818.

Bolay, J-C. (2006). "Slums and Urban Development: Questions on Society and Globalization." *The European Journal of Development Research* 18: 284–298.

Boujou, J. (2000). "Clientélism, corruption et gouvernance locale á Mopti." *Autrepart* 14: 143–163.

Bratton, M. (2007), "Formal versus Informal Institutions in Africa." *Journal of Democracy* 18: 96–110.

———. (2008). "Do Free Elections Foster Capable Governments? The Democracy-Governance Connection in Africa." AfroBarometer Working Paper 104.

Bratton, M., Mattes, R., and Gyimah-Boadi, E. (2004). *Public Opinion, Democracy, and Market Reform in Africa*. Cambridge: Cambridge University Press.

Brenner, N. (2009). "Cities, Territorial Development and the New Urban Politics." In Rumford, C., ed., *Handbook of European Studies*, pp. 442–463. London: Sage.

Burton, A., ed. (2002). *The Urban Experience in Eastern Africa c.1750–2000*. Nairobi: British Institute in Eastern Africa.

Coquery-Vidrovitch, C. (1991). "The Process of Urbanization in Africa (from the Origins to the Beginning of Independence)." *African Studies Review* 34: 1–98.

Cooper, F. (2008). "Possibility and Constraint: African Independence in Historical Perspective." *Journal of African History* 49: 167–196.

Cueppens, B. and Geschiere, P. (2005). "Autochthony: Local or Global? New Modes in the Struggle over Citizenship in Africa and Europe." *Annual Review of Anthropology* 34: 385–407.

Devas, N. (2004). *Urban Governance, Voice and Poverty in the Developing World*. London: Earthscan.

Dierwechter, Y. (2006). "Geographical Limitations of Neo-liberalism: Urban Planning and the Occluded Territoriality of Informal Survival in African Cape Town." *Space and Polity* 10: 243–262.

van Dijk, R. (2002). "The Soul is the Stranger: Ghanaian Pentecostalism and the Diasporic Contestation of 'Flow' and 'Individuality'." *Culture and Religion* 3: 49–65.

Dill, B. (2009). "The Paradoxes of Community Participation in Dar es Salaam." *Development and Change* 40: 717–743.

Diouf, M. (2007). "Social Crisis and Political Restructuring of West African Cities." In Eyoh, D. and Stren, R., eds, *Decentralization and the Politics of Urban Development in West Africa*, pp. 95–116. Washington, DC: Woodrow Wilson Center for International Scholars.

Duit, A. and Galaz, V. (2008). "Governance and Complexity: Emerging Issues for Governance Theory." *Governance: An International Journal of Policy, Administration, and Institutions* 21: 311–335.

Englebert, P. (2002). "Patterns and Theories of Traditional Resurgence in Tropical Africa." *Mondes et Développement* 30: 51–64.
Englund, H. (2002). "The Village in the City, the City in the Village: Migrants in Lilongwe." *Journal of Southern African Studies* 28: 135–152.
Ferguson, J. (1999). *Expectations of Modernity: Myths and Meanings of Urban Life on the Zambian Copperbelt.* Berkeley, CA: University of California Press.
Foster, V. and Bricẽno-Garmendia, C., eds. (2010). *Africa's Infrastructure: A Time for Transformation.* Washington, DC: The International Bank for Reconstruction and Development/The World Bank.
Fourchard, L. (2006). "Résiliences et ruptures en Afrique." *Transcontinentale, sociétés, idéologies, système mondiale* 2: 11–20.
Fourchard, L., Goerg, O., and Gomez-Perez, M., eds. (2009). *Lieux de sociabilité urbaine en Afrique.* Paris: L'Harmattan.
Freund, B. (2009). "The Congolese Elite and the Fragmented City: The Struggle for the Emergence of a Dominant Class in Kinshasa." Crisis States Working Paper No. 2, Crisis States Research Centre, Development Studies Institute, London School of Economics.
Gervais-Lambony, P. (2003). *Territoires Citadins: 4 Villes Africaines.* Paris: Karthala.
Global Cities Indicators Program 2008. *Final Report of the Global Cities Indicators Program.* Washington, DC: The World Bank.
Goerg, O. (2006). "Domination coloniale, construction de 'la ville' en Afrique et denomination." *Afrique and Histoire* 5: 15–45.
Grant, R. (2009). *Globalizing City: The Urban and Economic Transformation of Accra.* Syracuse, NY: Syracuse University Press.
Guèye, C. (2007). "Entre frontières économiques et frontières religieuses: le café Touba recompose le territoire mouride." In Piermay, J.-L. et Sarr, C., eds, *La ville sénégalaise. Une invention aux frontières du monde*, pp. 137–151. Paris: Karthala.
Guyer, J. (2004). *Marginal Gains: Monetary Transactions in Atlantic Africa.* Chicago: University of Chicago Press.
Guyer, J. and Belinga, E. (1995). "Wealth in People as Wealth in Knowledge: Accumulation and Composition in Equatorial Africa." *Journal of African History* 36: 91–126.
Guyer, J., Denzer, L., and Agbaje, A., eds. (2002). *Money Struggles and City Life.* Portsmouth: Heinemann.
Hansen, K. T. (2005). "Getting Stuck in the Compound: Some Odds Against Social Adulthood in Lusaka, Zambia." *Africa Today* 51: 3–18.
Hart, K. (1982). *The Political Economy of West African Agriculture.* Cambridge: Cambridge University Press.
Hilgers, M. (2008). "Politiques urbaines, contestation et décentralisation. Lotissement et représentations sociales au Burkina Faso." *Autrepart* 47: 209–226.
———. (2009). *Une ethnographie á l'èchelle de la ville.* Paris: Karthala.
Hopkins, A. (2009). "The New Economic History of Africa." *Journal of African History* 50: 155–177.

Jewsiewicki, B. and Higginson, P. (2008). "Residing in Kinshasa: Between Colonial Modernization and Globalization." *Research in African Literatures* 39: 105–116.

Jua, N. (2003). "Differential Responses to Disappearing Transitional Pathways: Redefining Possibility Among Cameroonian Youths." *African Studies Review* 46: 13–36.

Kaba, L. (2000). "Islam in West Africa: Radicalism and the New Ethic of Disagreement, 1960–1990." In Levtzion, N. and Pouwels, R. L., eds, *The History of Islam in Africa*, pp. 189–208. Athens, OH: Ohio University Press.

Keith, M. (2005). *After the Cosmopolitan? Multicultural Cities and the Future of Racism*. London: Routledge.

Kelsall T. (2008). "Growing with the Grain in African Development." Discussion Paper No. 1, Power and Politics in Africa, UK Department for International Development and the Overseas Development Institute.

Large, D. (2008). "Beyond 'Dragon in the Bush': The Study of China-Africa Relations." *African Affairs* 107: 45–61.

Laurent, P.-J., Nyamba, A., Dassetto, F., Ouedraogo, B., and Sebahara, P., eds. (2004). *Décentralisation et citoyenneté au Burkina Faso. Le cas de Ziniaré*. Paris-Louvain-la-Neuve: L'Harmattan-Académia Bruylant.

Lindell, I., ed. (2010a). *The Changing Policies of Informality: Collective Organizing, Alliances and Scales of Engagement*. London: Zed Press.

—. (2010b). "Informality and Collective Organising: Identities, Alliances and Transnational Activism in Africa." *Third World Quarterly* 31: 207–222.

Lund, C. (2006). "Twilight Institutions: Public Authority and Local Politics in Africa." *Development and Change* 37: 685–705.

Mabogunje, A. (1990). "Urban Planning and the Post-Colonial State in Africa: A Research Overview." *African Studies Review* 33: 121–203.

Marie, A. (2007). "Communauté, individualisme, communautarisme: hypothèses anthropologiques sur quelques paradoxes africains." *Sociologie et societies* 39: 173–198.

Marie, A., ed. (1997). *L'Afrique des Individus: Itineraires Citadins Dans L'Afrique Contemporaine (Abidjan, Bamako, Dakar, Niamey)*. Paris: Karthala.

Marshall-Fratani, R. (2006). "The War of 'Who Is Who': Autochthony, Nationalism and Citizenship in the Ivorian Crisis." *African Studies Review* 49: 9–43.

Marshall, R. (2009). *Political Spiritualities: The Pentecostal Revolution in Nigeria*. Chicago: University of Chicago Press.

Mbembe, A. and Monga, C. (2011). "Côte D'Ivoire: la démocratie au bazooka?" *Mediapart* January 26, 2011.

Meagher, K. (2010). *Identity Economics: Social Networks and the Informal Economy in Nigeria*. London: James Currey.

Mimche, H. and Fomekong, F. (2008). "Dynamiques urbaines et enjeux socio-démographiques en Afrique noire: comprendre la présent pour prévoir l'avenir." *Revue Internationale des Sciences Humaines et Sociales* 02, L'Afrique subsaharienne à l'épreuve des mutations, pp. 241–264. Paris: L'Harmattan,

Miran, M. (2003). "Vers un nouveau prosélytisme islamique en Côte d'Ivoire: une révolution discrete." In Piga, A., ed., *Islam et villes en Afrique au sud du Sahara: entre soufisme et fondamentalisme*, pp. 271–291. Paris: Karthala.

Miran, M. (2006). "The Political Economy of Civil Islam in Côte D'Ivoire." In Weiss, H. and Bröening, M., eds, *Islamic Democracy? Political Islam in Western Africa*. Berlin: Lit Verlag (for the Friedrich Ebert Foundation).

Moyo, O. 2007. *Trampled No More: Voices from Bulawayo's Townships about Families, Life, Survival, and Social Change in Zimbabwe*. Latham, MD: University Press of America.

Muniesa, F. and Linhardt, D. (2009). "At Stake with Implementation: Trials of Explicitness in the Description of the State." Centre de Sociologie de L'Innovation Working Paper No. 15, MinesParisTech/CNRS.

Myers, G. (2003). *Verandahs of Power: Colonialism and Space in Urban Africa*. Syracuse, NY: Syracuse University Press.

Ndjio, B. (2006). "Douala: Inventing Life in an African Necropolis." In Murray, M. and Myers, G., eds, *Cities in Contemporary Africa*, pp. 103–124. London: Palgrave.

Newell, S. (2006). "Estranged Belongings: A Moral Economy of Theft in Abidjan." *Anthropological Theory* 6: 179–203.

Nielsen, M. (2007). "Filling in the Blanks: The Potency of Fragmented Imageries of the State." *Review of African Political Economy* 34: 695–708.

———. (2009). *Regulating Reciprocal Distances: House Construction Projects as Inverse Governmentality in Maputo, Mozambique*. Danish Institute for International Studies Working Paper No. 33, Copenhagen.

O'Connor, A. (1983). *The African City*. New York: Africana Publishing Company.

OECD. (2007). *Competitive Regional Clusters: National Policy Approaches*. Paris: OECD Policy Brief May 2007.

Orr, R. and Kennedy, J. (2008). "Highlights of Recent Trends in Global Infrastructure: New Players and Revised Rules of the Game." *Transnational Corporations* 17: 95–130.

Owusu, F. (2007). "Conceptualizing Livelihood Strategies in African Cities: Planning and Development Implications of Multiple Livelihood Strategies." *Journal of Planning Education and Research* 26: 450–465.

Piermay, J.-L. (2003). "L'apprentissage de la ville en Afrique sud-saharienne." *Le Mouvement Sociale* 3: 35–46.

Pitcher, A. (2006). "Forgetting from Above and Memory from Below: Strategies of Legitimation and Struggle in Postsocialist Mozambique." *Africa: The Journal of the International African Institute* 76: 88–112.

Power, M. and Mohan, G. (2010). "Towards of Critical Geopolitics of China's Engagement with African Development." *Geopolitics* 15: 462–495.

Prag, E. (2010). "Entrepôt Politics: Political Struggles over the Dantokpa Marketplace in Cotonou, Benin." Danish Institute of International Studies Working Paper 2010:03.

Rakodi, C. (2006). "Social Agency and State Authority in Land Delivery Processes in African cities: Compliance, Conflict and Coordination." *International Development Planning Review* 28: 263–285.

Randles, S., Uyyara, E., Paraskevpoulou, E., Eaton, B., Miles, I., and Howells, J. (2006). *The Use and Limitations of Indicators in the Context of a City-Region Development Strategy*. Institute of Innovation Research, Manchester Business School, University of Manchester.

Rodrigues, C. U. (2007). "From Family Solidarity to Social Classes: Urban Stratification in Angola (Luanda and Ondjiva)." *Journal of Southern African Studies* 33: 235–250.

Salau, A. (1979). "The Urban Process in Africa: Observations on the Points of Divergence from the Western Experience." *African Urban Studies* 4: 27–34.

Salm, S. and Falola, T., eds. (2005). *African Urban Spaces in Historical Perspective*. Rochester, NY: University of Rochester Press.

Sautman, B. and Yan, H. (2007). "Friends and Interests: China's Distinctive Links with Africa." *African Studies Review* 50: 75–114.

Schler, L. (2003). "Ambiguous Spaces: The Struggle Over African Identities and Urban Communities in Colonial Douala 1914–1945." *Journal of African History* 44: 51–72.

Simone, A. (2004). *For the City Yet to Come: Urban Life in Four African Studies*. Durham, NC: Duke University Press.

SITRASS International Solidarity on Transport and Research in Sub-Saharan Africa. (2004). *Poverty and Mobility in Conakry*. Washington DC: The World Bank.

Söderbaum, F. (2004). *The Political Economy of Regionalism: The Case of Southern Africa*. New York: Palgrave MacMillan.

Stellenbosch University Centre for Chinese Studies. (2006). *China's Interest and Activity in Africa's Construction and Infrastructure Sectors*. Stellenbosch, South Africa: Stellenbosch University.

Tonda, J. (2005). *Le Souverain moderne: le corps du pouvoir en Afrique centrale (Congo, Gabon)*. Paris: Karthala.

———. (2008). "Les 'les anges de la mort' du Souverain moderne. Déparentélisation de l'enfance et violence de l'imaginaire des enfants soldats, enfants sorciers et enfants de la rue en Afrique central." *La Pensée* 354: 105–122.

United Nations Human Settlements Programme. (2008). *State of African Cities Report 2008/9*. Nairobi: United Nations Human Settlements Program.

Verran, H. (2007). "The Telling Challenges of Africa's Economy." *African Studies Review* 50: 162–183.

World Bank. (2009). *System of Cities: Harnessing Urbanization for Growth and Poverty Alleviation*. The World Bank Urban and Local Government Strategy 2009. Washington DC: World Bank.

Yntiso, G. (2008). "Urban Development and Displacement in Addis Ababa: The Impact of Resettlement Projects on Low-Income Households." *Eastern Africa Social Science Research Review* 24: 53–77.

2

The Funeral in the Village: Urbanites' Shifting Imaginations of Belonging, Mobility, and Community

Peter Geschiere

Throughout Africa, the continuing involvement of urbanites with the village of origin—for some time, seen as a special trait of urbanization in the continent—seems to be under heavy strain. For the Yoruba area, where urbanization has a relatively long history, Dan Aronson spoke in 1971 of "a single-role system" still uniting city and village, with people constantly moving to and fro between the two poles in different phases of their lives. In the same year, Joseph Gugler suggested for the Igbo, with their powerful "Tribal Unions," that urbanites lived in "a dual system" between city and village (1971). From quite a different perspective, Claude Meillassoux (1975) and Samir Amin (1973) characterized wage-laborers in Africa as "semi-proletarians" because most of them retained a footing in the village economy; this would be the explanation why wages in the capitalist sectors could remain relatively low as the costs of the reproduction of labor were borne by the village economy.

As late as 1992, I saw a report on Cameroon TV news, for several nights running, showing the body of a young kid—probably a *bandit*—who had been found in the streets. What was presented as very shocking was that no one had come forward to claim the body. A few days later, the news showed a French priest burying the body in a small cemetery he had arranged especially for such unclaimed bodies. People were equally shocked that, apparently, it was happening more often that no one came forward to bring these bodies back to the village—their rightful place of burial. This insistence on urbanites' continuing links with the village had important consequences. Many authors have highlighted the crucial role of urban elites as some sort of absentee leaders in village affairs (see Geschiere 1982). This also had (and has) direct effects for urbanites' vision of what constitutes their community and of where they belong.

Nevertheless, it is clear in hindsight that, already in the 1970s, this "rural–urban continuum" (see Geschiere and Gugler 1998) was undermined by increasingly rapid processes of urbanization. In many contexts—for instance, Congo—distances became so great and communication so difficult that it became ever more difficult to maintain relations with the area of birth. The partial or complete collapse of the village economy in other areas had similar effects. Moreover, as was only to be expected, a second generation of urbanites, born in the city, showed themselves less committed to their "brothers" in the village. However, even for first-generation urbanites, relations with the village became ever more complicated.

In Cameroon, for instance, people will say that the leading role of urban elites in village affairs is becoming ever more contested—"even for the Bamileke." This is striking because the Bamileke are seen as migrants *par excellence*, spreading throughout the country. Nevertheless, their elites, in particular, are always cited by people as an example of continuing commitment to the village. Lately, however, this *modéle migratoire*—often quoted as the secret behind the economic success of this group, that indeed controls most of the national trade—shows signs of blockage (Tabappsi 1999). The more successful migrants are still building ever more sumptuous houses in the area of origin—now, often palatial buildings on the top of a hill that have to symbolize their continuing commitment to the village below. Yet, precisely all this ostentation and the fact that they prefer to build at some distance from the village seem to express a growing alienation. Even in the Bamileke area, there seem to be ever more tensions now, with local leaders tired of the arrogance of their "brothers" in the city who are hardly ever on the spot (see Geschiere and Socpa forthcoming).

Nevertheless, recent changes are working in the opposite direction as well. The Post-Cold War moment, with its growing emphasis on political liberalization, also brought a comeback of the village and localist belonging—often somewhat artificial, but nonetheless quite real in its effects. The notorious *Opération Nationale d'Identification* launched (but never fully carried out) by former President Laurent Gbagbo in the Ivory Coast may be an extreme example; yet, it marked the return of autochthony and the emphasis on belonging that has quickly become a hallmark of African new-style politics. Ruth Marshall (2006) reports with clear concern on this operation that would oblige all Ivorians to return to the village "of origin" in order to be registered there as citizens. Abidjan was not to be considered as a "village of origin" except for the Ebrié—its "historical autochthons." All persons who could not claim a village of origin within the country were to be considered immigrants and would, therefore, lose their citizenship. How directly such plans might affect all urbanites is clear from the words of Mr. Séry Wayoro, *directeur d'identification* of this operation: "Whoever claims to be Ivorian must have a village. Someone who has done everything to forget the name of his village or who is incapable of showing he belongs to a village is a person without bearings and is so dangerous that we must ask him where he comes from" (quoted in Marshall 2006: 28).

Clearly, different trends are crossing each other. On the one hand, the commitment to the village becomes ever more strained. However, on the other, there are powerful factors pushing toward a re-affirmation of these links. Moreover, political considerations (like the one mentioned above) are not the only factors that play a role. These are often mixed with powerful emotions. In this respect, the insistence on the "funeral at home"—and "home," here, means the village of origin—stands out as a beacon, be it beset with ambiguities. In many parts of Africa, it is still of utmost importance to be buried in the village of origin. Being buried in the city has the stigma of social disgrace: it is as if one has no family. This has drastic implications. In some areas—for instance, in West Cameroon, but also among the Igbo (E. Nigeria)—one can only be buried in the village if one has built a house there during one's lifetime. It implies, moreover, that urbanites have regularly to return "home" in order to attend the funeral of a family member (often, a fellow urbanite). Most people fear these moments for they are the occasion for villagers to get even with their brothers in the city who are always reproached for not sharing enough. However, dodging the obligation to attend can have terrible consequences as well. Elsewhere (Geschiere 2009), I have tried to show how, in the context of present-day politics of autochthony, the funeral "at home" is turning into a true "ritual of belonging." With the increasing need for ambitious politicians and other elites to emphasize their roots, funeral rituals become ever more elaborate, demanding huge expenditure.[1]

Nevertheless, in this respect as well, nothing is fixed. First of all, it is important to emphasize that, despite their traditional trappings, funeral rites are, in many respects, "neo-traditional." Often, groups—especially the ones who till recently were still semi-nomadic—have copied the emphasis on "burying at home" from neighboring groups, in order to legitimize their own belonging. Moreover, there are important variations regionally and between groups (see the next section). Therefore, rather than seeing the "funeral at home" as a fixed corollary of an African mode of urbanization that would constitute a beacon in urbanites' mapping of community and belonging, this "custom" should be studied as circumscribed in time and space, as a product of constantly changing circumstances. In this chapter, I want to present some data on varying modalities of the funeral in different contexts in Cameroon, and then briefly compare with variations elsewhere. The aim is to understand both—how the funeral can play such an emotionally charged role in urbanites' view of their belonging, *and* the shifts and transformations in this respect.

The Funeral at Home in South Cameroon—A Sacred Obligation?

A brief sketch of the main moments of the funerals I attended in a village in the Maka area since 1971 can serve as an illustration of the unsettling power of these rituals and why they can so easily become high moments in the quest for belonging. Indeed, reading again in my notebooks on the first funerals I attended long ago made me realize how confused I was by these wild occasions that, nevertheless, seemed to follow a clear script—each person playing his or her role with abandon, yet sticking to that role. Almost as confusing was the constant innovation: at nearly every funeral, new touches were added, especially having to do with money, which, nevertheless, seemed to seamlessly fit in with older elements.

The central importance of the funeral in village life was brought home to me, right from the start of my fieldwork when, already on the third day, the whole village was in uproar for 2 days and one long, long night (with a lot of deafening drumming) because of the burial of an old man. At such an occasion, there is always a massive attendance. Especially if the dead person was an important person, people will come from all over the *canton* to attend his funeral. Such larger funerals offer a quite staggering mixture of mourning and merry-making, of solidarity and aggression that brings a dramatic condensation of everyday tensions. The night after someone passes away, there is a long wake, enlivened not only by constant drumming and dancing, but also by fierce outbursts of grieving. The next day, a long series of ostentatious exchanges and gifts follows, culminating in a mock fight over the body, which will, finally, be buried in the course of the afternoon. After this, people will gradually go home. Only on rare occasions will a family stage a repetition of this ritual, for instance, 1 year later, to formally end the mourning. In most cases, the descendants talk about organizing such a second event, but keep delaying it—supposedly, because there would not be enough money.

Only gradually could I discover, mostly thanks to the patient explanations of my assistant Meke Blaise, some pattern in all the tumult and outbursts of emotions. Crucial in all the excitement are rituals that affirm—or rather "perform"—the distinction between patrilineal kin and in-laws. The first ones are seen as "people of the house"; the others stand in a more complicated relation. Basic to kinship in Maka terms is the saying *ba djisse dombe*, "marriage is war," which means that marriage is only possible where there is no kinship—that is, with groups with whom one used to live in a state of *dombe* (war). This tension is enacted in all sorts of ways during the funeral. As soon as the drum of mourning announces that someone has died, the daughters-in-law (i.e., any woman married into the patrilineage) will paint the patrilineal descendants white with chalk, which marks them as mourners. The daughters-in-law themselves, in contrast, put on their dancing gear (a small tuft of raffia-fiber attached to the backside so that it moves frantically with the shaking of the hips) and dance all night, ostentatiously mocking the mourners (and even dancing them down into the mud). Sons-in-law and sisters' sons will give in to similar challenging behavior (insulting speeches, stealing chickens). The high moment in all this, after a whole night of drumming, drinking, and dancing is the *kombok*. The daughters- and sons-in-law gather in the bushes outside the village and form some sort of warriors' column. Then, all of a sudden, yelling loudly, the whole group will rush into the village and charge the house of the deceased. The house is shaken to and fro; the bereaved relatives will offer some symbolic resistance but are chased away from the bier; furniture is thrown outside and set on fire, animals are clubbed to death, sometimes, even guns are fired, and the whole village is in uproar. The daughters-in-law grab clothes of the deceased and put them on, dancing frenziedly. Indeed, the *kombok* is generally associated with "mocking" and "scorn": people will do everything in a crazy and deliberately wrong way—you throw a fowl still with its plumage in the frying pan, you burn chairs, you "cook" palm-nuts on an unlit fire, women dress as men, and so on.

The funeral will be ended the next day by an elaborate set of negotiations, again, full of rivalry. For instance, the daughters-in-law can turn their payment into a true carnival. Dissatisfied by the money offered to them by the elder of the deceased's group, they will chase the mourning descendants away with hilarious mirth, grab the bier, and rush off with it on their shoulders—the corpse bouncing up and down—to "hide" in the bushes behind the house. The elder must then follow them in order to "buy back" the corpse by making a higher bid. As a rule, the women will send him away scornfully a few times but, in the end, they will accept the money. The most difficult negotiations are with the deceased's maternal uncles who have to dig the grave and be paid for their labor. However, more importantly, the corpse must again be "bought" from them: the deceased was also their blood-relative, and if they are offered too little money, they might take the corpse along and bury it in their own village. These negotiations often develop into a long palaver in which the elders of both groups confront each other with much rhetorical prowess. When the elders finally reach an agreement (in the 1980s, up to $100 might have been paid), the time has come for the actual burial. This is the moment when the mourning becomes general: the blood-relatives writhe with grief, but even the sons- and daughters-in-law now show themselves deeply moved.

Although the description here is only a condensed summary of the complexities of the funeral rituals,[2] it may suffice to give an idea of the power of this ritual in affirming someone's belonging within the kinship order. However, it is also important to emphasize that the sketch described earlier is strictly circumscribed in time. Funeral ritual is extremely dynamic and, throughout the 1980s and 1990s, I noticed constant innovations and additions. Characteristically, these had especially to do with the payment of money. Already in the description from the 1970s presented earlier, it is quite striking how central a role money payments had come to play throughout the duration of a funeral. As elsewhere in Africa, the Maka were, indeed, constantly complaining about the rising costs.

In the 1990s, these kinds of funeral rituals quite unexpectedly became a central element in the new-style political debate, as an ultimate test for belonging (and, thus, also for exclusion). Cameroon may not have had an equivalent to the *Opération Nationale d'Identification* in Gbagbo's Ivory Coast. However, democratization led to endless debates here as well about belonging—no wonder, because, under renewed multipartyism, questions like "Who can vote where?" and even more "Who can stand candidate where?" became of vital importance. Oppositions between *autochtones* (autochthons) and *allogènes* (immigrants) acquired new urgency, and the funeral at home became crucial for such distinctions (see Geschiere 2009, ch. 6). For the self-styled *autochtones* in the cities, it is precisely the continuing habit of people who are classified as *allogènes* to bury their deceased "at home"—that is, taking their corpses back to the village although they spent most of their lives in Douala or Yaounde—that justified the conclusion that the village is the place where these "strangers" really belong. So then, they should also go home to vote there. The most pregnant formulation of the funeral as the supreme test of belonging came from Samuel Eboua, an *éminence grise* of Cameroonian politics who, in 1995, blandly stated that a Cameroonian was a stranger anywhere in the country except "where his mortal remains will be buried."[3] It seems that nothing is left here of the idea of national citizenship—so strongly emphasized during the preceding decades of nation-building.

This renewed stress on localist belonging went together with certain changes in the celebration of the funeral throughout the country. The rituals came to increasingly emphasize the obligation of the urbanites and especially the new elites, who had emerged so quickly in the decades after Independence, to return "home" for a funeral (not only their own but also to attend those of their relatives).

In 1991, I had the honor of presiding a jury at the University of Yaounde that had to judge a *thèse de troisième cycle* by Luc Mebenga on funeral rituals among the Ewondo.[4] This was a special time. The whole continent was abruptly affected by a wave of democratization, and this led to particularly fierce riots in Cameroon. Indeed, at the very moment of this defense, the university was occupied by the gendarmes in order to quench the ongoing student protests against the stubborn refusal by President Biya to convene a national conference (as other authoritarian African leaders had accepted to do). The presence of gendarmes at the campus was highly shocking to both students and staff; indeed, there was no precedent for this. They swaggered around the buildings, making it clear that they considered the whole campus to be occupied territory.[5]

In this tense atmosphere, there was—somewhat to my surprise—a lot of attention for a topic that was not really central to the thesis. Mebenga's descriptions of Ewondo funeral ritual reminded, in many respects, the patterns sketched for the Maka earlier: here also, the different kin groups confront each other in fierce performances of aggression and humiliation. Mebenga analyzed the funeral, therefore, as a highly collective moment, affirming the individual's belonging to the kinship group. The members of his jury focused, however, on another aspect: the precarious role of the urbanites during these ceremonies. In fact, the central case of the thesis was the funeral of Mebenga's own father for which he had returned to the village, accompanied by other "sons of the village" who had made their careers in the city. Further, indeed, the thesis contained a few passages that highlighted the author's own commitment to the obligation "to come home":

> Every Ewondo knows very well that, though one is allowed to leave one's natal village, coming back to it—be it to live there or to be buried—is a moral obligation that no one can neglect. This idea finds its concrete expression in the burying of the placenta of a newly born child. This is to remind the child that, even if he becomes a vagrant (*vagabond*), he should never forget to return to the place where his placenta is buried. This act ties any Ewondo to his village, like a child is tied to his mother by the umbilical cord. Indeed, this conception demands that every Ewondo be buried in his village of origin so as to re-affirm this union forged by his birth. Even the authorities respect nowadays this custom—which one finds nearly everywhere in Africa—by facilitating the transportation of the corpse of all its civil servants to their village in order to be buried there. This is one of the few customary norms that are still respected today (Mebenga 1991: 234—translation PG; cf. also Mebenga 2009).

Mebenga analyzed this enduring involvement of urbanites with the funeral in the village as a victory of collective interest in the village despite the rise of individualism marking present-day relations. To him, it is a highly positive sign indicating that some of the old emphasis on the collectivity still remains. Although the socioeconomic interests of these urbanites oblige them to orient themselves toward their new surroundings (the city), it would be their "spiritual interests" that make them retain their links to "the sacred place" of the village. This is why, still in Mebenga's words, they want to be buried in native soil "that does not move despite all social change" (Ibid.: 235).

Nevertheless, during the public defense, a quite different view on the funeral "at home" came to the fore, notably from the interventions of the jury members from the same area. Professor Marcien Towa congratulated the candidate on his courage, because everybody knew how difficult it was to return to the village for a funeral. Professor Jean Mfoulou emphasized this aspect even more strongly: "It is like this among us: anybody who emerges has to excuse himself constantly with those who do not emerge." Both professors stressed that the funeral, in particular, was an occasion when the villagers could make urban elites "excuse themselves" in the most graphical ways. Indeed, many of my colleagues from the forest area told me stories about how they dreaded the moment of return, notably for a funeral. Especially the wild behavior of the sister's sons of the deceased at these tumultuous occasions could easily be directed against urban visitors and their supposed stinginess and egoism. The funeral constitutes, indeed, an ideal moment for the villagers to get even with their "brothers" from the city.

The role of these urban elites at the funeral, therefore, expresses a striking paradox. On the one hand, they feel clearly ill at ease. It is a dangerous moment because they are forced to venture themselves again into the intimacy of their "brothers." They know they will be assailed by all sorts of requests, and it is risky to refuse these outright; everybody knows what disastrous consequences the jealousy of relatives can have if it is not appeased by sharing—after all, there is a direct link between jealousy, intimacy, and witchcraft.[6] Nevertheless, they still feel obliged to attend these wild ceremonies in the village. Apparently, their fears still do not erode their commitment to what, in Mebenga's terms, remains "a sacred place" where they know their placenta was buried at birth.

Changes over Time

Despite all this apparent authenticity, however, there is good reason for relativizing this obligation to be buried "at home" that now seems to be so sacred in some parts of the continent. It is clear that the present-day preoccupation with this topic was encouraged by a special political setting: the new "autochthony" strategy of Biya and his people, who used it most cleverly in order to survive democratization and divide the opposition. One consequence of this strategy was a sudden mushrooming of *associations des originaires* bringing together elites from a certain area. Although, up to 1990, any form of association outside the one-party risked attracting severe sanctions by the ubiquitous *gendarmes*, now, suddenly, urban elites were admonished in no uncertain terms to create their association (see Geschiere 2009, ch. 2 and 6). The main aim of this new policy was to ensure that elites—often, at the pay for the government—would campaign for the president and his party during the hard-fought elections of the early 1990s. These rather new elite associations, especially in the francophone part of the country, came also to play an important role in turning notably elite funerals "at home" into festivals of belonging.[7] It is striking that, in this new context, the ever more elaborate funeral rituals assumed a kind of "natural" self-evidence, as illustrated by the example below.

In 1996, I visited Mamfe in the dense forest of southwest Cameroon on the Cross river, near the Nigerian border. No doubt, people had warned me how bad the road would be. After all, the road to Mamfe enjoys general notoriety in Cameroon as one of the worst in the whole country; and, indeed, we spent a whole night on the *piste*, struggling and pushing behind the car in the mud. On arrival in Mamfe, the many stories around the road suddenly acquired a new turn. The talk of the town was the burial of the wife of a general who originated from Mamfe—he was seen as one of the town's main elites. He had arranged for a spectacular funeral at home, without, however, taking into account that the rains had already begun. There was true *Schadenfreude* in people's stories about how all the region's elites, who evidently *had* to attend the funeral, got stuck in the mud. Some had taken days getting their Pajero (the new status symbol of the elites, replacing the Mercedes) through. Apparently, many people felt this served them right—after all, it was their own fault for not having done anything for so long to get this road tarred. Indeed, for the burial of the general's wife, the transport problems became so overwhelming that, for a moment, it seemed the funeral would have to be postponed to the dry season. However, finally, the general took a drastic decision: he "chartered" several helicopters from the army and had his wife's body, together with the main guests, flown in from Yaounde.

Remarkably, people talked about this as if the whole exercise was, more or less, self-evident: "of course," urbanites had to be brought back to be buried in the village; therefore, it was only "normal" that the general went to such great lengths to bring his wife's body back home. However, it was as striking that older informants, particularly, had other stories to tell. To them, this whole emphasis on burying "at home" seemed to be new.[8]

There are many parallels elsewhere in Africa of similar debates on what appears to be an old tradition, but is seen by others as a new issue in the context of the politics of belonging. The most well-known example is, no doubt, the case of SM in Kenya (see Cohen and Atieno Odhiambo 1992). The funeral of SM, a famous lawyer in Nairobi, led to a fierce fight—finally decided in the national Court of Appeal—between his Luo clan and his Kikuyu widow over where the corpse should be buried. The widow wanted to bury SM at their sumptuous farm in Nairobi. She emphasized his identity as a modern Kenyan citizen. Therefore, he should be buried where he had lived and worked, no matter what his birthplace was. However, the representatives of his Luo clan insisted that modern or not, SM was a Luo and that "custom" dictated a Luo should be buried "at home." Yet, surprisingly enough, Oginga Odinga, then still the grand old man of Luo politics, sided with the Kikuyu widow and declared that, to him, this stress on burying at home was new. According to him, the Luo, as an expansionist group, used to bury their dead in the areas where they migrated to, in order to confirm new claims.[9]

In another example from the Southwest, reported by Francis Nyamnjoh (oral communication, see also Geschiere and Nyamnjoh 2000), similar concerns even led to a violent struggle over the body, and an armed intervention by the *gendarmes*. This funeral was a particularly tragic one because it concerned a Banyangi woman from the Mamfe area, who unexpectedly died during a study period in the United States. Her husband, a Bamileke living in Buea (the Province's capital), had gone to great lengths to have the body transported "home"—in his view, Buea—in order to have her buried near their house there. However, the woman's own family decided that her real home was in the family village near Mamfe, and not with her husband. Therefore, they had the gendarmes interrupt the funeral (which had already started), "arrest" the body, and take it to Mamfe. Apparently, the husband's status as a stranger in Buea (because of his Bamiléké origins, he could certainly not lay claim to any "autochthony" there) weakened his claims to have his wife buried near to his house. Thus, the forces of order were ready to intervene in support of Banyangi "custom" that the corpse should be brought "back home" to her village of birth—clearly, a very flexible custom as, nowadays, Banyangi women are mainly buried in the village of their husbands (see Geschiere et al. 2000, see also Socpa 2002).

The idea of the funeral "at home," self-evident as it seems to be to most people, is clearly full of tensions, which come even starker to the fore now that the burials of important persons have become highly politicized. In a recent article, Nantang Jua (2005) gives an overview of a series of recent cases that created quite a stir. The funeral "at home" of the famous novelist Mongo Beti, a staunch opponent of both President Ahidjo and his successor Biya, became a real scandal because the widow refused any involvement by Biya; however, the village, eager to please the authorities, went directly against her wishes. Jua compares this to an even more contested case of a rich Bamileke man who lived in France and was cremated there. When his French wife brought the urn with his ashes to the village, people were bewildered. Of course, she should have brought back the body to be buried in the ground of the forefathers—after all, this is where her husband belonged. Indeed, the Bamileke are often cited as a group for whom the tradition of bringing back the body to be buried goes back far into the past.[10] However, precisely among Bamileke migrants, the custom to bury at home seems now to be softened among some groups. For instance, in Yaounde, rumors are circulating that, especially the Bangangte (a Bamileke chiefdom), increasingly bury their deceased in the city, sending only a stone—symbolizing the skull—home to the village.[11] Clearly, although burying in the village as proof of one's belonging seems to be a "traditional" obligation, or even a "natural" thing to do, it still allows for all sorts of variations and adaptations.

Emotional Force and Changing Dynamics

Earlier, I dwelt longer on the funeral rituals in Maka villages and their wild performativity to give an idea of their power. On several occasions, I saw urbanites arrive with clear reluctance; often, it concerned people who had not been to the village for some time, but apparently felt obliged to attend. Nevertheless, soon they would be almost literally "sucked up" by the ritual: dancing or grieving (depending on their kinship position toward the dead) with abandon, acting as if they had never been away from the village. Indeed, these funeral rites are a good example of what Birgit Meyer calls "aesthetics," in the sense of a condensation of sensorial experiences. It is a "total experience" that deeply engrains one's belonging to the place (see Meyer 2008; also Geschiere 2009).[12] The sheer force of the "funeral at home"—of the idea by itself but maybe even more its fierce practices—seems to confirm the model quoted earlier of urbanization in Africa, as yet a half-way process: the funeral rituals still seem to bind urbanites to the village with powerful obligations and through emotionally charged occasions.

Nevertheless, precisely because of this almost "natural" self-evidence, it is all the more important to position this "custom" in space and time as a precarious construct, subject to constant change, and certainly not "African" as such. As said, for many societies the very idea of burying as a return to the place of origin is a clear example of a "neo-tradition." The Maka, just like most groups in the forest area, constituted a semi-nomadic society, that until less than a century ago had been moving their family-hamlets every few decades when the surrounding fields appeared to be exhausted. Even in the 1970s, people had little idea where their ancestral villages had been located, and it was very difficult to obtain closer information on where the ancestors had been buried. Several elders even claimed that, in those days, the bodies of the dead were not buried, but put up in a high tree to be picked by the birds.[13] The "custom" of burying someone in front of his/her house was apparently a colonial invention, dating back to the times that the *mise en valeur* of the area finally took off through the spread of cacao plantations (roughly since the 1950s). Only then could the richer planters build bigger houses as a symbol of their success that were seen as an appropriate background for a prestigious grave—often adorned with a stone and a picture of the deceased.

More importantly, it might be that this emphasis on burying at home is not common to the whole of Africa. In South Africa, for instance, there are striking differences between its major cities. In Cape Town, immigrants, especially from the Eastern Cape, still set great store on sending the bodies of their dead back home to be buried there. The townships' famous *stokfels*—the local version of rotating credit associations and often the first form of organization among recent migrants in the anomy of the city—were mainly created for insuring people against the mishap of having to arrange for a costly funeral "at home" (see Lee 2011). In contrast, the townships of Johannesburg (foremost Soweto) have huge graveyards. People in Soweto told me that, at least since the 1930s, urbanites began to bury their dead in their new surroundings rather than sending the body back home to the village.[14]

However, the most intriguing exceptions are the main Congolese cities—Kinshasa and Brazzaville—where there is hardly any trace of the idea that funerals should take place in the village. An easy explanation might be that the village is often far away, and communications have become so difficult that a return to the village is physically impossible. Striking in that is that, here, a very different trend emerged of funerals being taken over by aggressive gangs of young people (boys and girls) who turn it into a confrontation between generations. Filip de Boeck's recent film on the *Cemetery State* (2010) shows most graphically how, especially when the deceased died relatively young, rebellious youth—often, not even relatives—aggressively confront older family members of the dead, accusing them of foul play and secret conspiracies. They take over the bier and march in a most violent procession—the coffin constantly shaking and turning to point out possible evildoers—toward the grave. Joseph Tonda describes similar performances by young revelers, who turn taking over funerals into some sort of profession, for Brazzaville.[15] Interestingly, this author sees a clear contrast in this respect with Libreville where people do still set great store on burying their dead in the village (oral communication, Joseph Tonda and see Tonda 2002). One can add many more variations. It is clear, for instance, that the impact of Islam will directly affect burial practices, even if the concomitant religious obligation to bury people quickly does not always stop Muslim urbanites from continuing to bury their dead in the village of origin (see van Santen 1993 on Mokolo in N. Cameroon).

Furthermore, time will affect the custom of the funeral "at home." It is clear that, with the rapid acceleration of urbanization over the last decades throughout Africa and its ever more chaotic character, it will become more and more difficult—even in cities like Douala and

Yaounde—to keep organizing the funerals in the village. In southern Cameroon in general, urbanization has become so massive—younger people are convinced that it is "impossible" for them to stay in the village—that the threat of an increasing depletion of the countryside is becoming all too real. In many villages, the only adult people remaining are of advanced age. Old men and women still have to work the fields (which, in the case of old men, is really new), because all the young people are in the city. Will the village then continue to exist mainly as a burying ground? This is difficult to imagine. The recent fashion of *bush-falling* (a Pidgin term in which *bush* stands for Europe) further complicates things. *Bush-fallers* (young men and women who try their luck by leaving adventurously for Europe or the Gulf) are now the new role models for many people.[16] But, will these young people, once they manage to "get out," return to the country, let alone the village?

Conclusions

Precisely the uncertainty and the variability that surround this "custom" of the funeral at home—to many still a self-evident obligation—make the vicissitudes of this idea a challenging focal point for further exploring African urbanites' changing sentiments of belonging. Changing attitudes and practices around the funeral highlight crucial parameters in the way the "art of citizenship" of urbanites maps the relation between city and village. The challenge is that opposite trends on this issue seem to cross each other—making the outcome for the near future quite uncertain.

As highlighted earlier, all sorts of factors, including growing geographical and social distance to the village and increasing costs, seem to make it ever more difficult to sustain the notion that the funeral has to take place in the village and that the deceased's body has to be brought back there at all costs. In such a perspective, it becomes tempting to see Brazzaville and Kinshasa with their new styles of burying as some sort of forerunners—pioneers of a more general trend for the continent. However, there are also good reasons for not dismissing too quickly the funeral at home as some sort of relict destined to disappear. As discussed earlier, the post-Cold-War movement of the 1990s—especially the unhappy linking of democratization and decentralization—brought a resurgence of localist belonging and a return of the village, somewhat artificially as a result of political maneuvering, but nonetheless, very effective in everyday life. The implosion of authoritarianism brought, in many countries, new incentives for urbanites to take their belonging to the village most seriously. Furthermore, the funeral at home still is a chosen moment to celebrate such belonging, often with a neo-traditional exaggeration of all sorts of rituals.

It remains, therefore, an open question how the variations in burying customs affect urban citizens' mapping of community and belonging. Can new notions of belonging and solidarities develop more easily where there is no pressure to return to the village for burying the dead? Will this allow for a surpassing of the "traditional" emphasis on localist identifications with the area of origin? The solidarity among the young revelers in de Boeck's film seems to suggest this. Of interest is also a section in Joseph Tonda's book on the commitment of *Brazzavillois* to *la parcelle*—the urban plot where people live (Tonda 2005: 118–120). Is this to be seen as some sort of alternative to the village of origin? An important question in this context is also how the Pentecostal churches and sects, mushrooming throughout Africa (as elsewhere), will position themselves *vis-à-vis* existing funeral practices. In Cameroon, belonging to a Pentecostal group seems not to hinder people from joining with great animation in funeral rites in the village. Nevertheless, the distrust of many Pentecostal groups of the village and the family as locations of the devil would, in principle, imply a stance against bringing back the dead to their rural roots. Will this encourage new and more urban rituals of burying to confirm new religious forms of community and belonging?

Focusing on the funeral not only as a key moment in urban citizens' definition of belonging and community, but also as a highly variable "custom" can help to relativize the view on urbanization in Africa as marked by a continuing commitment to the village. It is clear that issues of burying, and notably the funeral's location, will remain uneasy elements in urbanites' notions of community and belonging. Nevertheless, the idea of the funeral "at home" is not a cultural given that seals urban citizens' ongoing commitment to the village. The challenge is, rather, to follow this idea in its practices with all their variations and shifts. Moreover, this can help to highlight the emergence of new trends of identification and belonging.

Notes

1. Economist Célestin Monga (1995) speaks in this context of a *mauvaise gestion de la mort.*
2. For a fuller description of the Maka funeral and its changing rituals over the last decades, see Geschiere (2005).

3. Interview in *Impact Tribu Une* 5 (1995): 14—my translation.
4. The Ewondo live around Yaounde, the country's capital. They are part of the larger ethnic bloc of the Beti who live in central part of the same forest zone as the Maka and whose sociopolitical organization has similar traits (up to the colonial conquest organized in autonomous family villages with hardly any central authority above the village level).
5. Indeed, once there, I realized that I should never have accepted the invitation to come down for this defense. Clearly, the authorities had insisted that it should take place despite all turbulence as a manifestation that the University was functioning.
6. See Geschiere (2013). See also Smith (2004) on the continuing preoccupation among Igbo to be buried "at home." In this article, Smith similarly emphasizes the flip side of the urbanites' involvement with the village: the funeral is becoming more and more the occasion at which growing tensions between villagers and urbanites come to the fore.
7. Cf. Page (2007) on one of the first projects of elites in America for the village of Bali: a mortuary in order to properly store a body of someone who died in America, while preparing a sumptuous funeral.
8. See Ruel (1969); also Niger-Thomas (2000). Cf. also Roger Orock's forthcoming PhD on Banyangi elite association and funeral at home (University of Aarhus).
9. Cf. also Droz (2003) on constant changes in the funeral practices of the Kikuyu.
10. For these groups—the Bamileke must, rather, be seen as a conglomerate of smaller chiefdoms who, only in colonial times, became grouped together as "the" Bamileke—this related to a tradition that the eldest heir receives his father's skull. Therefore, one's privilege is measured by the length of the series of skulls one has to guard, which indicates belonging to the eldest line for several generations.
11. Antoine Socpa, oral communication. Cf. also the very interesting data of Sverker Finnström (a Stockholm/Uppsala anthropologist) on changing funeral rituals among the Acholi in Kampala (Uganda). In the 1990s, it was becoming too expensive to send the body of a deceased person home for the burial; therefore, people began to take the pole with them that was used to close the grave in the city. However, suspicious bus-drivers began to charge for such poles as if a person was being transported home, or refused to take a pole that clearly symbolized a body. So people tried to hide these poles in their luggage. Finnström plans to publish on this as part of an extremely interesting broader complex of changing funeral rituals developed notably since the time Acholi young men began to serve for the British in the "King's African Rifles"; many thanks to him for allowing me to refer to this here.
12. How deeply engrained the very idea of the funeral at home is, in everyday life, in these parts of Cameroon, was driven home to me when, in 2005, I got stuck in a huge congestion on the road between Yaounde and the West Province (the land of the Bamileke). A few Eton villages along the road had blocked it because they had no electricity although they had paid their bills (another example of failed privatization). Apparently, they had done this quite regularly exactly on Thursday because they knew that on Thursday night Bamileke

from Yaounde would leave for the village to attend funerals during the weekend. Further, indeed, in front of the endless line of cars were three big black cars that each transported a body that had to be buried. The danger of decaying bodies made the strike extra effective.
13. Cf. Droz (2003) on similar habits among the Kikuyu.
14. Unfortunately, I have not been able to find confirmation of this in the literature. A detailed history of burial practices in Johannesburg townships would be of great interest. The difference with Cape Town might relate to the fact that mass-urbanization has a longer history in Johannesburg. A special factor in Cape Town is, no doubt, that over and against groups of "Coloureds" who claim the Western Cape as their home area, immigrants from further away stand clearly out as relative outsiders to the city.
15. Cf. also Noret and Petit (2011) on funerals in Lubumbashi.
16. See Alpes (2011) on the rapid emergence after 2000 of this notion of *bushfalling*, especially in southwest Cameroon, and the great enthusiasm and very optimistic expectations raised by this idea.

References

Alpes, M. J. (2011). "Bushfalling—How Young Cameroonians Dare to Migrate." PhD diss., University of Amsterdam.

Amin, S. (1973). *Le Développement inégal: essai sur les formations sociales du capitalisme périphérique*. Paris: Editions de Minuit.

Aronson, D. R. (1971). "Ijebu Yoruba Urban-Rural Relationships and Class Formation." *Canadian Journal of African Studies* 5(1): 263–279.

Cohen, D. W. and Atieno Odhiambo, A. S. (1992). *Burying SM: The Politics of Knowledge and the Sociology of Power in Africa*. London: Currey/Heinemann.

De Boeck, F. (2010). *Cemetery State*. Brussels: Filmnatie.

Droz, Y. (2003). "Des hyènes aux tombes: Moderniser la mort au Kenya central." In Mapeu, H. and Droz, Y., eds, *Les figures de la mort à Nairobi: Une capitale sans cimetières*, pp. 17–54. Paris: Harmattan.

Geschiere, P. (1982). *Village Communities and the State: Changing Relations Among the Maka of Southeastern Cameroon Since the Colonial Conquest*. London: Kegan Paul International.

———. (2005). "Funerals and Belonging: Different Patterns in South Cameroon." *African Studies Review* 48(2): 45–65.

———. (2009). *Perils of Belonging: Autochthony, Citizenship and Exclusion in Africa and Europe*. Chicago: University of Chicago Press.

———. (2013). *Witchcraft, Intimacy and Trust—Africa in Comparison*. Chicago: University of Chicago Press.

Geschiere, P. and Gugler, J., eds. (1998). "Introduction: The Rural-Urban Connection—Changing Issues of Belonging and Identification," *Africa* 68(3): 309–319 (special issue *The Politics of Primary Patriotism*, eds).

Geschiere, P. and Nyamnjoh, F. (2000). " Capitalism and Autochthony: The Seasaw of Mobility and Belonging." *Public Culture* 12(2): 423–453 (special issue *Millennial Capitalism and the Culture of Neoliberalism*, eds.)

Geschiere, P., Nyamnjoh, F., and Socpa, A. (2000). "Autochthony Versus Citizenship: Variable Effects of Political Liberalization in Cameroon." Report for *Ministère des affaires étrangères*, Paris.

Geschiere, P. and Socpa, A. (forthcoming). "Changing Mobilities, Changing Futures." In Goldstone, B. and Obarrio, J., eds, *African Futures*. Chicago: University of Chicago Press.

Gugler, J. (1971). "Life in a Dual System—Eastern Nigerians in Town." *Cahiers d'études africaines* 11: 400–421.

Jua, B. (2005). "The Mortuary Sphere: Privilege and the Politics of Belonging in Contemporary Cameroon." *Africa* 75(3): 325–355.

Lee, R. (2011). "Death 'On the Move': Funerals, Entrepreneurs and the Rural-Urban Nexus in South Africa." *Africa* 81(2): 248–269.

Marshall, R. (2006). "The War of 'Who Is Who?': Autochthony, Nationalism, and Citizenship in the Ivorian crisis." In Geschiere, P. and Jackson, S. eds, *Autochthony and the Crisis of Citizenship*, *African Studies Review* 49(2) (special issue): 9–43.

Mebenga, L. (1991). "Les funérailles chez les Ewondo: Changements Socio-Culturels, Changements économiques et évaluation de l'esprit de solidarité." Thesis (3ème cycle), University of Yaounde I.

———. (2009). *Anthropologie des rites funéraires en milieu urbain camerounais*. Paris: Harmattan.

Meillassoux, C. (1975). *Femmes, greniers et capitaux*. Paris: Maspero.

Meyer, B. (2008). "Religious Sensations: Why Media, Aesthetics and Power Matter in the Study of Contemporary Religion." In de Vries, H. ed., *Religion, Beyond a Concept*, pp. 704–723. New York: Fordham University Press.

Monga, C. (1995). "Cercueils, orgies et sublimation: Le coût d'une mauvaise gestion de la mort." *Afrique 2000* (21): 63–72.

Niger-Thomas, M. (2000). "'Buying Futures': The Upsurge of Female Entrepreneurship Crossing the Formal and Informal Divide in Southwest Cameroon." PhD diss., Leiden University.

Noret, J. and Petit, P. (2011). *Mort et dynamiques sociales au Katanga (République démocratique du Congo)*. Paris: Harmattan.

Page, B. (2007). "Slow Going: The Mortuary, Modernity and Hometown Associations in Bali-Nyonga, Cameroon." *Africa* 77(3): 419–441.

Ruel, M. (1969). *Leopards and Leaders*. London: Tavistock.

Smith, D. J. (2004). "Burials and Belonging in Nigeria: Urban-Rural Relations and Social Inequality in a Contemporary African Ritual." *American Anthropologist* 106(3): 569–579.

Socpa, A. (2002). *Démocratisation et autochtonie au Cameroun: Variations régionales divergentes*. Munster: LIT Verlag.

Tabappsi, T. F. (1999). "Le Modèle migratoire bamiléké (Cameroun) et sa crise actuelle." PhD diss., University of Leiden.

Tonda, J. (2002). *La guérison divine en Afrique centrale (Congo, Gabon)*. Paris: Karthala.

———. (2005). *Le Souverain moderne—Le corps du pouvoir en Afrique centrale (Congo, Gabon)*. Paris: Karthala.

Van Santen, J. (1993). *They Leave their Jars Behind: The Conversion of Mafa Women to Islam (North Cameroun)*. Leiden: VENA.

3

Citizenship and Civility in Peri-Urban Mozambique

Juan Obarrio

Introduction

In Mozambique, as elsewhere in Africa, the rural–urban divide was central to the juridico-political distinction between citizens and subjects during the colonial period. Paradoxically today, Mozambique's extensive post-war legal reforms aimed at democratization and decentralization, largely mandated by the international donor community, have reinstated aspects of the colonial rural–urban distinction through the revitalization of the "customary" and the legal recognition of its authorities. Post-Socialist, neoliberal policies produced by urban elites attempt to redefine and regulate the "local," through the demarcation of new administrative territories, jurisdictional boundaries, and, especially, the fetishized tropes of "community" and "custom," in order to create a space for post-war reconciliation and a basis for the emergence of a "democratic civil society."

These notes examine the margins of a provincial capital city in Northern Mozambique as an ambiguous space of contending sovereignties. The overlapping jurisdictions of this peri-urban space bring back, in a specular way, aspects of colonial governance folded within the postcolonial democratic present, producing a remarkable effect on contemporary dynamics of citizenship and political belonging. The focus on questions of access to justice and various mechanisms of conflict resolution in peri-urban neighborhoods sheds light on the fate of the concept of the "civil" in Africa, following its trajectory through cities and citizenship, as avatars of "civilization," and their opposing developments as civil war and civil society. This chapter, thus, explores the ideological and political limits of recent divisions between rural and urban political belonging, as well as their negative political effects in terms of new modes of exclusion through restricted forms of citizenship.

In present-day Mozambique, in a run-down, desolate, peri-urban neighborhood, the former People's Courts—currently relabeled by the state as Community Tribunals—continue to accomplish their quotidian work, despite having been excluded from the state apparatus of justice after a constitutional reform during the post-Socialist transition to democracy. Enforcing a mix of state law and "custom," these courts enact a sort of ghostly sovereignty that combines the epoch of Socialism with the current age of a neoliberal democratic regime. The presence of this juridical authority represents a leftover from a previous political era, insofar as, today, its legal practice mixes official norms with elements from normativities that, under Socialism, the courts were specifically mandated to eliminate: kinship, custom, magic, ritual, and local language.

At present, this court is located in an almost ethereal, liminal space: between (Socialist) "popular justice" and the (liberal) "rule of law." It operates at an anachronistic, legal–discursive level situated at a predemocratic moment, equating court, state, and political party, referring the potential relationship with the adversary back to the context of the war, and, thus, excluding the opposition as enemy.

The work of the courts, furthermore, sheds light, albeit by default, on the current FRELIMO politics of recognition of the "customary" that, since 2000, reversed decades of official Socialist ban on custom and traditional authority. "Custom" has played a key controversial role since its manipulation by the Portuguese colonial regime, its promotion by RENAMO during the civil war, and the internal debates on recognition held within FRELIMO during the democratic transition.

What is the import of the resilience of these local sovereignties for a discussion of cities and citizenship in contemporary Africa? How is civility, as an art of citizenship located between ethics and aesthetics, shaping the returning figure of the subject in the subcontinent? A crucial angle to approach these issues lies in the question of what kind of subject these peri-urban community tribunals address today. The subject that the tribunals aim at transforming into a citizen needs to be studied in reference to the context of the postcolonial political history that produced the court itself. This history of citizenship and civility is imprinted on the sites of peri-urban areas that were the border marked by the material effects of the violence of civil war in the 1980s and are, at present, the locus of the democratic reform of the local state.[1]

The (Peri) Urban Scene

Khakhossani[2] is a neighborhood of approximately 14,000 people located in a wide strip of land surrounding the center of Nampula city—the provincial capital. It is an area of a small subsistence economy, where dwellers farm their own *machambas* in the back of precarious cement and straw houses, and each extended family has at least one family member employed in the formal labor markets of the city downtown, most often linked to the public sector and local state services. A ride in one of the mini-buses from the city downtown to Khakkossani takes approximately 30 minutes. The vans follow the damaged dirt road, which runs from the city to the *bairros* or peri-urban neighborhoods, with a large street market of many shacks along its side. The bus stops at a busy crossroads, in front of a carpenter's shop. It takes five more minutes to walk the path that, passing a few houses, goes deeper into the neighborhood, toward the house that lodges the People's court, and the office of the neighborhood Secretary.

The house is approximately 50 years old, nearly derelict. Once owned by a Portuguese settler, it was later appropriated by the new independent state after his flight. The walls must have been painted—all in bright white—for the last time around independence in 1975. Today, the structure appears on the verge of collapse, especially the roof, and the walls are in dire need of a coat of paint; large, sickly mildew stains sprawl across them, inside and out. However, this house in ruins is not just any building: it lodges a minor state apparatus, each space within it enclosing a separate institution of local executive or judicial powers: the bureau of the Secretary of the Neighborhood, the Community Court, the Party cell. These structures are immersed in the minor political struggles unfolding in the area, opposing different ideologies and contested senses of recent history.[3] Local residents who support the FRELIMO government and sided with the party-state during the civil war, take recourse to these authorities, bringing cases to the community court, and demands and petitions to the Secretaries of block and neighborhood. Others, who side with RENAMO, or oppose the government in general, take their conflicts to RENAMO party cells, religious leaders, or customary authorities who extend their chieftaincy in the marginal outskirts of town.

Various juridico-political local actors (former state officers, chiefs, and religious leaders) operating in the area aim at imposing a jurisdiction on both time and space. The force of law and its codes are also, here, a mode for narrating the political effect of a recent past. The house lodging the minor state, as well as the effects it produces on the area of the neighborhood and its inhabitants, is over-determined by a recent history of various coalescing legal and economic transformations. For local residents, the ruined building embodies an imagination of a centralized power. This house is situated on a margin of a peripheral urban neighborhood, a borderline between rural and urban areas. Moreover, it stands within a liminal political zone being somehow simultaneously located inside and outside the official law. Therefore, it is both site and metaphor of the minor state and its decayed yet resilient, indeed, exceptional, order.[4]

From the perspective of local state officers, the loose limits of the neighborhood—signaled by random markers, like a building, a road, or a stream—coincided with the limits of the law. The space in which they work articulates a condensed version of the political at large, as a miniature replica of national politics and the imagination surrounding the central state. The latter involves crucial regional and local variations addressing unique juridico-political, religious or "customary" actors and practices. Moreover, it represents a subjective dimension of the political that instills the law onto the matter of the body, its flesh, and its desires. It is a space where the political is linked to the central state and political parties and blends with a minor politics deployed at the level of segmentary kinship, the body, and subjectivity. This is an urban realm encompassing the public command of the state and the quiet voices of privacy and intimacy. It is a political space that condenses the aspirations of citizenship and the stylized manners of civility.

A Minor State[5]

Until the final stages of the war and the transition toward democracy, around the early 1990s, a political unit called the Dynamizing Group (GD) was the cipher of the party-state system at the level of locality. Aimed at replacing "customary" chiefs as nodes of local governance, the GD was an entity that blended the forms of a local state unit and a FRELIMO party cell. It entailed a limited reform of the political space of locality, because, similar to chiefs, it encompassed all forms of power—executive, legislative, and judicial branches, as well as a local police force—in one single merged form. Immediately following independence, FRELIMO officers held several administrative and political positions at once—something which persists, at present, in the case of the current neighborhood authorities. The GD constituted the embryo of today's minor state, whose praxis originated in those minimal Party units, which, in turn, had as precedent the politico-military cells set up by the guerrilla war machine during the liberation struggle launched from Tanzania in the 1960s—both in the open war of the rural battlefields and in the secrecy of urban insurgency.

Following independence in 1975, conducting their administrative and judicial endeavors in popular public gatherings, local socialist authorities nominated by the party and elected by popular assemblies deployed a mode of government that attempted to "simplify" the intricacies of colonial law and governance, claiming to make them accessible to the local population's needs and dynamics. A few years later, the newly formed base-level People's courts would nominally oppose "custom" and all traditional ritual and language, in a move that mirrored the attempt to replace chiefs with party cells.

"Socialist legality" and the practice of popular justice conducted in those units, furthermore, led to a renewal of an age-old "customary" court that, since precolonial times, had served as a space for conflict resolution and the management of spiritual forces. Yet, the dynamics of "reconciliation," reputedly active in these "customary" chiefly courts, had been transformed, as in other regions of the continent, through the codification enforced by colonial governance (see Chanock 1985).

There are plenty of continuities between the party cells and the current community courts. At present, the two main authorities at work in the peripheral neighborhood—the Secretary of the Neighborhood and the Community Court—are but holdovers from the authorities in old GDs. The position of Secretary was transferred from GD to the locality, and everyday conflicts, which had originally been solved within the GD's Secretary of Social Welfare are now dealt with at the community court. Two of the judges at the Khakhossani court had worked earlier at that office. Albeit by default, in current peri-urban areas, the "minor state"—as the heir to the GD—constitutes a remainder from the former party-state system.

History's effect can be seen in the space of the neighborhood, imprinted on surfaces of the surrounding landscape, over the dense woods, the distant hills, or the rocky paths. A history of political transformation and war is engraved on the walls of the house that lodges the minor state, where the courtroom encloses layers of "historicity"[6] of the political violence behind enforcement of a norm and the current struggles over jurisdiction. The community court constitutes a microscopic version of the larger legal system at the local level. It is but a node in a broader state of things: a disjointed fusion of past and contemporary politics.

The minor state's work is condensed within a local political struggle fought by various actors, and organized around different issues, especially the right to the adjudication of justice. It is a territorial political dispute over jurisdiction—that is, a struggle over the codification through the law of a space and the flow of practices that take place within it. Within that struggle for hegemony and legitimacy, the minor state propagates a narrative about the recent history of the nation. The minor state is a vivid, paradoxical, effect of that history.

The Space of the Law

Tuesday, 9 a.m., in Khakhossani neighborhood. An old, ruined house, the white paint peeling off its walls and ceiling, serves as the neighborhood's Community Tribunal. The house which hosts the minor state has no electricity, and not much daylight seeps in through the cracked panes. To the right of the entrance, along a narrow dark corridor, is located what used to be the kitchen of the settler's house, from whose windows one can see the hills surrounding the neighborhood, some small houses, the palm trees, and the sky. Every other day, before the court's sessions begin, a group of tall, strong young men, wearing bright t-shirts and holding batons, sit on the empty, cracked sink for a while, before leaving to accomplish their duty as the newly formed "Community Police" that, throughout the province, is as much praised for its dutiful help with local security as it is berated for its alleged violent excesses in pursuing "criminals."

On the right of the hall, a cracked wooden door leads into the "Room of Audiences and Trials," where the Community Court holds its twice-weekly sessions (see Centro de Formacao Juridica e Judiciaria 2002). Outside the door, there are two small tables and some precariously built wooden benches. In one of the corners, the Attorney sits behind a table, receiving complaints and filing cases. He gives to each plaintiff a note on a white paper with a blue seal that has a written appointment summoning the person to appear in a few days time before the court, along with the other party, accompanied by several relatives of each. The community tribunal in Khakhossani neighborhood hears cases twice a week, opening its doors every Tuesday and Friday around 8 a.m. in the morning, like every community court in the province. The judges explain that the schedule obeys to official regulations set by FRELIMO in the early 1980s.

Throughout Nampula province, each Tuesday at the same time, a plurality of spaces—be they old, small, settlers' houses or some clearing in the woods, under a tree—become places for the adjudication of justice, where people gather and accusations and complaints, hatreds and loves are vented and, somehow, resolved. Early Tuesday and Friday mornings, people linger in groups of six or seven outside the house, whispering, pausing, and waiting for the court to begin its work.

The house that lodges the minor state bears on it the marks of the passage of time: layers of temporality that are crucial to the effect of historical depth supporting the local legitimacy of justice. This "house of the law," as the community judges call it, has undergone three different political regimes, during each of which it held for the population of the area a symbolic charge related to the political system and the regime of law being enforced at the time. During the late times of the Portuguese regime, it was simply the residence of a settler, a mere "landowner," therefore, a minute sign of the system of extraction by foreign hands of which colonial law was, at the same time, the foundation and the outcome. Taken over by the FRELIMO regime, the house became the site of the party cell. At present, more than three decades after independence and emerging out of the post-civil war agreements, the newly installed post-Socialist regime and its neoliberal stance reconstructs the house, almost by default, as a court that shows national ideologic transformations. Moreover, the house entry is a threshold for the political passage from the "People" to the "community."

Inside the humble, decayed house, which bears no official symbol whatsoever, the court occupies a spacious chamber called the "room of audiences." It is almost in ruins, its dirty walls covered with stains from damp. There is a wire hanging from the ceiling, a power installation that does not work. It is a square room with two windows. There is a window on the wall opposite to where the judges sit that overlooks a larger portion of the landscape lying beyond the courthouse's front: the school, but also the beginning of a road, houses and huts, and trees.

Five community judges sit, chatting and consulting each other, in front of a small group of people in silence. There are two wooden tables: a bigger one, for the president and three other judges, and the smaller one, for the other judge, second in hierarchy, and in charge of the written files. Scattered across his table in an organized disorder are notebooks, folders, copies of legal codes, laws, issues of the *National Gazette*, colored pens, and endless sheets of paper. Behind the table where the judges work are benches and small tables with piles of aging yellowed folders containing hundreds of dusty pages; records of cases that have been tried in the last few years. Next to the judges' table, a small piece of furniture—the court's "archive"—holds pieces of evidence, remainders from several cases and trials clothes from a divorce case, or a talisman from an accusation of sorcery. Facing the judges' table, there is a small bench upon which those summoned to appear before court will sit. Against the wall with the window are several small benches for the relatives and neighbors—eyewitnesses in crimes and disputes, *ad hoc* judges as well as warrantors of future agreements.

The label "community court" reflects both a retreat of the state (see Hibou 1999) as well as the compromised recognition of the legitimacy and authority of the realm of the "customary" as a counterpart in the juridico-political endeavor of the state apparatus. Thus, for the share of the local population that appears before the law twice every week, the courthouse emerges as a sign from a historical past that continues to provide the present with a certain political meaning. Furnished with a somewhat resplendent aura amid the impoverished outskirts of the city, the house stands out as a site of history: a small, modest edifice in ruins where the time of justice emerges out of the force of law.

A history of all the subsequent political transformations that Mozambique has undergone in the last decades has been reflected in changes in the justice system. However, despite the alterations materialized in those different juridical regimes, certain continuities persist. These refer to the limitations of political reform embedded in the postcolonial condition itself: limits of the transformation of jurisdiction and locality, of citizenship as much of subjectivity.

The work of the court takes place amid a contested space of multiple sovereignties and a political struggle over jurisdiction. In this periurban area, state law as well as the normativity of the "customary" shape political subjects. The minor state projects a legal discourse and a practice of government aiming at forging subjectivity as inner folds of exterior power. In order to do this, FRELIMO officers harness a politics of "tradition" and the remainders of ritualized custom that were the main elements of RENAMO ideology during the civil war. Today, when the democratic regime is sustained on the lawful opposition of the two former enemy camps during the war, the RENAMO party wages a struggle to impose another kind of governmentality—one that would shape a different type of subjectivity. The force of law takes hold of subjectivity and politics as a continuation of war unfolds over the battleground of intimacy, desire, and the body. Let us examine an instance of this entangled context of law and custom, of citizenship and civility.

A Case of Debt and Sorcery

The woman, slim, her head covered with a yellow scarf, her legs crossed under the bench, is testifying before the community judges, giving her version of the painful facts that prompted a conflict. It is a case of sorcery in which she is accusing other people, sounding furious, deeply hurt and, yet, somehow managing to maintain a calm tone. Her statement, mostly referring to death, lasts for approximately 20 minutes.

The woman wears a bright white shirt and a skirt with slogans that celebrate the anniversary of the National Women's Association (a FRELIMO organism) and a photograph of a national heroine—a Mozambican female athlete who has established records in the Olympic Games. As she presents her recollections, eating sugarcane, she breastfeeds her baby, who is lying, eyes closed, wrapped against her chest. She is eating sugarcane at the same time as she gives her statement. Speaking about death while giving life appears as a delicate dialectics of invisible forces that might nurture or destroy the body. The legitimacy of the court's legal work seems similarly founded on those modes of becoming, of entangled life and death.

The cascade of words falls clear and, yet, no one can discern truth from nonsense in her rushed speech as yet. The way she speaks about the invisible forces that have harmed her body sounds exaggerated, too extreme. The woman she is accusing of invisible misdeeds is sitting not far from her, wearing a t-shirt with the image of a prominent local politician.

When the first woman finishes giving her speech, the judge president and another judge look at each other and smile sarcastically and turn toward the other plaintiff, a man, asking him about his wife's whereabouts. Before he can answer, the wife starts an agitated speech from her place near the rest of her relatives at the end of the room. After a while, the judge president interrupts her: "I already understood one phase of the problem." Then, another judge speaks for nearly 10 minutes. The first woman, with a melancholic expression, listens to the judge's interpretation of the action of invisible forces that have caused the misfortune of a couple and a deep crisis in her extended family.

Sorcery accusations, in which the offended family asks for an ordeal of ingestion of *mwekathe* (corn flour) to be conducted, are common at the court. Oftentimes, they are connected to cases of divorce and accusations of adultery—the kind of cases that are seen as variations on the theme of indebtedness between people who owe each other respect due to kinship relations (see Macaire 1996).

The President Judge gets in and out of the room. When he returns, he pretends to be taking notes as he interrogates another "mother," and tries to obtain the name of a female sorcerer involved in the accusation. He shouts: "You are all criminals, this is pure deception! You cannot remember the name of the woman at this "hospital" that you visited so many times?" There ensues a tense moment of violence, as he continues screaming, demanding their names to "notify" them and send them to the police station.

After the hearing of the accusations on divorce and sorcery, another judge affirms: "This case of adultery and bigamy is finally solved; the couple will continue living together, we achieved *conciliation*. Now we have to pass judgment on the man's attempt to strangle her with a rope." The judges leave the room, returning 10 minutes later, along with the couple involved in the case. "This, in any tribunal would mean a sentence to prison, because you did it on purpose. But here, in the Community Tribunal it will only imply a fine. You will be *amnestied*; we will not send you to the police or the district court. We will not call the ministers of the church to show them how their Christians behave at their homes." Everybody is silent, and we hear the voice of another judge solemnly reading the sentence: "Nampula Province, June 4th...Disrespect towards his wife and to the whole of society...A fine of Meticais 150,000." The President announces: "you have three days, until Friday to pay, otherwise we will submit the case to a superior court."

Within the framework of the law, measures taken against a moral offense or a crime relate a certain loss to the estimated potential means for recuperation. In this juridico-economic calculus of social relations, transgression is analogous to indebtment, and its repayment is conceived according to a logic of punishment.

Whereas the law constitutes an economy of calculation of equivalences and exchange of sanctions for transgressions, the dynamics at the community court show a different logic. The modality of conflict resolution enforced at the tribunal is strongly permeated by widespread regional patterns of sociability that conceive of the social bond, not as exchange, but as debt. The community court enforces a sense of the law mixed with "customary" perspectives that present communal sociability, not as a closed circle of reciprocity, but rather as open ended, based on the deferral of exchange and of repayment of morally sanctioned debts, implying also the postponement of violence and punishment.

At first, the judges calculate the just compensation—objects, money, or actions—for a given offense. Second, the remnants of a Socialist communal ethos and the resilient "customary" conception of the social as mortgage, intervene to interrupt the actual repayment. Even if some monetary value or object is exchanged, the most important aspect of the agreement, or "reconciliation" has to do with another, more abstract question, the "spirit" of that gift, representing the remainder that cannot be forgotten or erased and needs to be pardoned. The object exchanged as gift is not strictly material, but rather, a local conception of justice.

Beyond bequests and loans through which objects circulate, life itself—conceived as biology and as intimate experience—is considered to be on loan. The "customary" law enforced at the tribunal is a compendium of strategies of borrowing and repayment. Obligations acquired by means of kinship bonds, a physical aggression that requires punishment, or the malicious dealing with property or money, its theft or destruction, connect the intrinsic economic value present in the disputed object with the moral value of norms and duties and punishment dictated by the law.

The Limits of the Law

Although local institutions such as the GDs and the People's courts had been established shortly after independence, in 1975, to oppose tradition and erase "customary" forms of ritual and authority, the resilience of customary forms of life remained in the shadows and folds of formal governance. At present, Northern Mozambique represents a space where various forms of "custom" are implicitly tolerated and mingled with official normativity, producing a sort of "customary" law being enforced today in these (former?) state courts.

The tribunals hear "social" cases about divorce, debt, family or neighborhood quarrels, domestic violence, or sorcery accusations. Crime cases of theft or violence are sent to the police station or official district courts, with which the community courts have loose informal ties. At the tribunals, the entanglement of juridical regimes and historical epochs forms a multifaceted amalgam of postcolonial law, precolonial practices—"custom," "kinship," and "ritual"—and even colonial norms, encompassing from the colonial construction of the "customary" to the Socialist ban on it, and then to the current official reappraisal of "custom" as a legitimate juridico-political category.

When asked about the daily work of the Secretaries and the community courts, local state officers signal to a spot in the small area surrounding the house, as marking the "limits of the law." Beyond this restricted peri-urban space unfolds a realm of different authorities, such as chiefs or spiritual leaders, and various normativities that officers define as "custom," "tradition," the "law of the ancestors," or "FRELIMO law." These limits could be understood as strict territorial boundaries or actual limitations of the law's reach. In fact, both meanings blend through the kind of politics unfolding at the local level. As the officers emphasized, the extent to which a form of law associated with an official, state-sanctioned juridical regime is actually enforced is determined by reference to the orbit of urban political institutions and practices.

Whereas the few state district tribunals in the small city downtown enforced civil law serving a small minority of upper echelon urban population, the minor state in the peri-urban neighborhood enforced a blend of law, custom, and kinship norms. Local state officers considered the neighborhood as the exclusive site for the implementation of the law, with the house of the minor state standing as the fold in space, which condensed these juridico-political relations. Beyond the city's periphery, in the rural areas, a plurality of other normativities disseminated, with a loose relationship to the state apparatus.

The minor state of local tribunals and Party secretaries constitutes an interface between state law and "customary" normativity. Pondering over the court's location, the post-Socialist judges signal the spatial and ideological contours of the condition of liminality in which the neighborhood exists. This is, indeed, a buffer area, not only between spaces, but also between the different juridical regimes. It constitutes the elusive borderline linking the urban ambience of the city center—its boulevards and buildings, its official bureaus and small, decimated shops—and the wide, open fields of the countryside, the rural villages, and the scattered markets along the road.

The peri-urban area represents a threshold between the modernizing, stylized cultural forms of the lettered city and the enduring, yet constantly changing, "customs" of the rural areas. It is a spot in a continuum. Its political and spatial dynamics show that the neighborhood constitutes the forefront of the countryside wedged at the heart of the restricted urban center. A scintillating quotidian collage of economies, legalities, corporeal practices, ritual beliefs, and political languages invalidates the distinction between urban and rural.

The urban–rural divide that represented a crucial juridico-political technology of colonial governance, still delimits the scope of the process of granting full citizenship by the state at present. The various rights associated with belonging to a nation-state are exercised in a differentiated manner, depending on which side of the juridical distinction between urban and rural areas a subject stands. Yet, this divide takes place in the letter of the law and does not hold in regards to the actual material urban flows that constantly crisscross, today as in the past, the various spaces codified by a legal system.

As during colonialism, when a few modernized subjects were granted the right to become *assimilated*, the city is, today, linked to the concept of the "civil" and to a related term—"civilization." The urban is the cradle of civil law, which are norms applied within "civil society." "Civil society" in contemporary Africa appears as a political category, or space, trespassed by the codified ambiguity of "custom" and the falsified complexity of "tradition." However, contemporary juridico-political and economic dynamics, which reproduce former divisions between city and countryside in terms of citizenship rights, generate a social context wherein to speak of a "rural civil society" may be a contradiction in terms. The postcolonial reforms seem to have been unable to transform the juridical space of locality as it was inherited from the late colonial regime. For instance, in Nampula city in 2005, a research project studying regional dynamics of "citizenship" at one of the local universities, designed to inform provincial government policy, encountered problems simply defining the scope of the category in terms of rights, and included "customary" chiefs and even folk healers among leaders of a local "civil society."

Citizenship

The peri-urban community court constitutes a political space apt for the exercise of the subject's rights as a citizen. Inasmuch as it is a space for the provision of justice, of argumentation in defense of individual rights, it is also a site to observe the resonance of liberal doctrines that are supposed to reform both the central state apparatus and the local state. However, the situation of the process of democratization at the local level is somewhat different. An informal—minor—state of which the court is a central part, based on remaining institutions and figures of authority that stem from the previous Socialist regime, exists as a sort of buffering political assemblage between the equally elusive fields of the "customary" and the "state."

Within a nation-state that has recently embraced a liberal–democratic regime, local forms of power and semi-governmental units that diverge from that general orientation still flourish. Within legal jurisdiction of chieftaincy or community courts, liberal rights of individual citizenship that are supposed to be enforced are, in fact, implemented with large deficits due to the blending of state law and "customary" law. The subjectivity that appears before the law as a free subject of rights is the product of a sense of justice born out of an anticolonial struggle and a postindependence political reform. Yet, the current social landscape illustrates how this subject is still an effect of a colonial codification (some of the old colonial codes and rules were still enforced in 2004) that prescribed a differential policy of civil and "customary" rights, and discriminated between urban and rural denizens.

These colonial policies seem to return now under the new guise of neoliberal rule of law, articulated with "precolonial" forms of power and normativity. In light of this, the new official recognition of the "customary" illustrates the extent to which the current postcolonial rural and peri-urban subject—the new democratic citizen—has also been constituted by a complex history of the temporality of "custom," ritualized spirituality, and the malleable, yet mandatory, rules of kinship, filiation, and locality.

The juridical performances held at the court present overlapping aspects of colonial and postcolonial legal regimes, the resilience of "traditional" norms of "custom" and kinship. Historical layers unfold in parallel with various systems of legality, both shaping a subject who, while moving throughout space and in the juridical imagination of the state, from the rural to the urban, falls under the mandate to become a citizen before the law.

One single subject, an individual citizen, can be the measure of all of these historical transformations and their contemporary overlapping and sedimentation. A person enters the space of the court as both citizen and subject. She/he advances into the law begging both the question of citizenship as well as the question of subjectivity. The current broad juridical reforms—recognizing chiefs, bringing back "customary" law—seem to acknowledge that the postcolonial citizen has not absolutely effaced the subject that stems from pre-colonial and colonial regimes of subjection. The legal case that follows offers an example of this historical predicament.

A Case of Debt and Freedom

The woman remains silent, through the hearing of the case. It is not about her life, her deeds, or her sorrows that the men are arguing. She apparently listens as though it is all a distant background noise, undistinguishable words, unclear claims, and rebuttals. She is sitting on the bench, alongside the men who argue, but it is not clear at first who she is. The discussions are about debts, petty violence, labors not performed, and disrespected ceremonial procedures.

Then, suddenly, slowly, a new argument emerges. As the heated back and forth exchanges unfold, the life of the woman begins to be referred. Absent from the quarrel until a moment ago, she becomes centrally entangled with narratives of recrimination and damnation, of an economic and spiritual conflict that mars the lives of these families.

In the narratives of the conflict, the place of the woman appears to occupy a central role; yet, her actual presence seems to be strangely displaced. The statements show that she is but a looming shadow, threatening in a way the men do not describe explicitly, but evidently subdued within the structure of the family.

The case revolved around the woman's unstable but permanent role within these family structures. The issues of debt and deferral disputed involved property, money, and a couple of locales. However, its framing and object were not the most relevant issues. Rather, as the narrative of the case unfolded, the place of the woman evolved from being a marginal voice presence to becoming the center of the dispute. Her manners and desires, her movements or lack thereof, or the possibility of her life itself were not thought of as a gift this time but almost as a commodity.

During that first session (the case was discussed at the court during the following 3 weeks) the references to her life, her position, the chores she accomplished, or her liberty to move began to shed light on the peculiar situation of this woman's life. Not the properties of a life, but life itself as property.

Relatedness evokes different questions of ownership. Local languages and memories intersect with the question of appropriation—of the curtailing of freedom. The woman was the wife of the young man involved in the quarrel, as well as the sister (or first cousin) of the other young man—the other party in the conflict. She lived alongside with her husband at the house of his parents. She "labored all day," she "worked for others," she alleged at the second session, "without receiving anything, neither money, nor a dress, nothing." She could not leave the house freely, either.

When pondering on this case, I had some inkling into how the figure of this woman echoed a distant past, from my reflections about the history of the area or the practices I had observed or that elders had recounted in our conversations. Later, my assistant would confirm my intuition.

"She is a slave," she told me, as she briefed me about a court session that I had not attended due to being sick. We were in the penumbra of the living room of the old, ample house where I stayed. The word reverberated, as though bouncing back from the decrepit walls. The nonchalant, yet loaded tone of my collaborator added nuances to the many deep connotations of the term, within the political culture of the region. Local testimonies I collected, admitting semi-secret practices, informed that this was a singular sign of an extended set of practices of kinship understood as property, strategies that connected relatedness with capture, possession, and control.

The presence of the so-called slave at the tribunal, not as citizen but as subject, questioned the modernity of law and the legacies of the independence project, in the contemporary rural North. Since early modern liberal democratic thought, the citizen has been equated with a proprietor; today, at the crossroads of law and custom, a slave re-emerges as the citizen of a postcolonial democracy, much as the subjects of chiefs that regain state recognition. The subject of kinship structures that provide security and allow for reproduction, as well as for surveillance and servitude, is a citizen-subject. The two corporealities entangled in one individual are the sign of a pervasive "customary citizenship," a condition of subjectivity and subjectivation inflecting, at the level of the local and the singular body, the alleged universality of democratic rights.

Civility

The peripheral neighborhood is the space where micropolitics constitutes subjectivities through the matter of the flesh—the sheer texture of a life lived through an everyday effervescence of desire and emotion, of dreams and nightmares. This corporeal matter, this singular immanent life of desire, is the grounds on which the contest over sovereignty and legitimacy to govern is played out, around the capacity to shape and conduct subjects (see Povinelli 2006).

The dialectics between the juridico-political identities of citizens and subjects in contemporary Africa pivot around the double meaning of the concept of subject, understood both as the product of subjectification and subjection. Juridical practices shaping the subject are over-determined by colonial legal and institutional legacies of arbitrariness and exceptionality still impinging on current forms of governmentality.

Current forms of life are subjected/subjectified by those technologies, which draw the contours of the ethereal quality of dreams, emotions, aspirations, as well as the matter of the body. Intimacy itself is on trial at the court—as a device that rules over the folds of subjectivity, through discussions of conflicts over the body, affect, disease, domestic violence, and spiritual evil. The tribunal is an interface between different political worlds; its juridical dynamics connect the quotidian unfolding of the subject's living and laboring, her passions, desires, and aspirations, with a broader predicament related to larger national and regional political processes, a general political economy, the effects of a political history that constantly transform both the "law" that is implemented in the court (and the juridical status of the court itself), and local modes and scope of "custom."

A person enters into the building of the court under a double appearance: citizen and subject. Subject to the law, she acquiesces to the ritualized movements and rhetoric that will rule over her conflicts and decide upon the folds of her everyday life—subject to the law, the scope of whose rights should neither exceed nor be in default of the space of her indivisible body or the presupposed place of her spirit. Such is the restricted sovereignty of a juridical subject, her entitlements, her emancipatory potential: an autonomous self-possessed individual as defined within the realm of the liberal law. In crossing the threshold of the law—metaphorically, this verge can be located at the doorsill of the room of audiences in the courthouse—the subject trespasses a limit between a private space, which is analogous to the field of the "customary", and the public realm of state law.

The person who arrives at the court is both a national citizen and a "customary" subject, ruled by structures of relatedness, traditional norms, and ritual that are prominent within the dynamics of the community court. This situation begs the question of whether the sphere of the private, as that which is supposedly located beyond the public realm of the state, can encompass the practices of "custom" and "kinship" ruling over the intimate life of desire, thought, and bodily practice. Indeed, current political and developmentalist discourses on Northern Mozambique consider the realm of the "customary" as coextensive with the space limited by the normative concept of a "civil society" located beyond the state apparatus. Nevertheless, actual juridico-political practices in the area present a mix of modernized custom and reformed official law. For instance, the community court constitutes an interface between state law and "customary" normativity.

The subjects who are summoned to the tribunal live in a neighborhood that also functions as a liminal border, or a threshold between the modernizing, stylized cultural forms of the city and the enduring, yet changing, "customs" of the rural areas. Current postcolonial policies reinforce the juridico-political distinction between the rural and the urban shaped during colonial governance. They reify an alleged distinction between the realm of the "customary" and another space linked to the "state" and modern forms of sociability that, since colonial times, have been ruled by "civil," European (Roman) law.

It is a question of citizenship as much as of civility. The concept of "civility" and its etymological root linked to the city acquire, here, a particular resonance. The procedures of the peri-urban court show how, within the transition from a civil war to a civil state, the old division between city as the site of civil law and countryside as the site of "customary" law, remains. In the urban elite's discourse of legal reform, the "customary" still contains traces of that allegedly uncivilized state of nature that, in colonial times, was the context of the category of the indigenous.

At the theatrical stage of the court, in the instant when the subject performs the double guise of her subjectivity—as a private subject and a public citizen—her intimacy becomes the intimacy of the state itself. The folds that compose a given subjectivity are intricately connected, both with juridico-political processes as well as with a whole economy of transformations and political discourses that engage the life of the body and its reproduction, or juridical discourses deployed by the state to define the subject as "subject to the law."

They can constitute ritualized techniques of the body; or, rather, "technologies of the self" through which the subject internalizes the work of those broader dynamics. These techniques include modes of conducting one's body at the court, minimal moves and gestures that reflect other practices exerted on oneself in order to comply with the ceremonies and mandates of justice. For the ultimate technique of the self exerted by the subject-citizen is the conduct of oneself to abide by the law. Those other practices encompass an education in the ritualized imagination of the state, or, in the juridical discourses of governance: pedagogic practices instilled onto the subject so as to make of her a self-restrained, self-possessed teller of truths, a respectful, acquiescent subject to ordinances that blend the enforcement of "custom" and the force of law.

Yet, the court that is the theater of citizenship is also the stage of another kind of civility. Within the court's dynamics, the work of judges is crucially mixed with the intervention of extended families. In the procedures of the tribunals, rites and rights become articulated, and state units seem to merely channel the rules and norms of the "customary." The legal mandate of the state on the correct embodiment of citizenship blends with the forms of subjectivation sanctioned by custom, kinship, and its ritual belief and corporeality. The individual in the peri-urban area becomes a citizen only by passing through the detour of kinship and community.

Citizen-Subject

Anastasio Moculiba was born in a rural district in the hinterland of Nampula province. Like most people from that area, he is a Muslim. In 2005, he lived on the outskirts of the provincial capital although every year, as many other dwellers in the peri-urban neighborhoods did, he worked for 3 months in rural areas 400 km north of the city.

His family owned a small *machamba*, or farmland, behind the two large shacks made of mud and the hut where they lived. Only one member of his extended family had a somewhat stable, albeit intermittent, job related to the "formal" employment sector, working sporadically on the premises of a provincial ministry in the downtown area.

After Anastasio's uncle passed away in 2001, he became the main actor in the extended family. Years later, a bitter dispute with a cousin over a small piece of land that the family cultivated had unsettled relations among his closest kin. His cousin had spread nasty rumors about him in the neighborhood, which damaged Anastasio personally and forced him to seek a settlement through mechanisms beyond those of his family.

As his cousin was close to RENAMO, he took the conflict to local party officers, who transferred it to a chief living on the eastern outskirts of the city. Meanwhile, Anastasio consulted with a local sheikh who gave him advice and put him in touch with a FRELIMO Secretary of the Block, also a Muslim and from the same home district as well as the cousin of a powerful figure in a semi-secret group of Muslim authorities in that rural area. Members of this semi-secret local elite spoke with RENAMO authorities working at the office of the district's mayor (formerly a FRELIMO officer). These officers contacted RENAMO personnel in Nampula city, who spoke with the chief in charge of the case in his informal "customary" court and, together with a FRELIMO neighborhood secretary, they all agreed to take the case to the community court, where a deal was brokered to settle the land dispute between Anastasio and his cousin.

The entanglement of juridical regimes and local political struggles present in this case reference a broader political context of fragmentary state agencies and norms and official authorities, mixed with religious and customary structures. Here, the recourse to official tribunals is out of the question. Personal relations and semi-secret networks involving religious authority mediate interactions with state politics. The peri-urban citizen achieves access to "justice" only through the maze of political networks involving party officers and customary authority.

The individual who approaches the court seeking justice is a concrete subject of rights as well as an abstraction: the citizen of a republic. At present, the court addresses her as a member of a "community," whereas, in the recent Socialist era, she would have been considered an individual element of a collective People. Today, in the postcolonial peri-urban areas, the subject is haunted by an uncanny historical figure.

Through current political practices of subjection, the figure of the slave reappears enfolded within the emancipated democratic citizen.

Today, an African citizen is a non-subject, a free individual emancipated from being a forced laborer and an object-commodity alienated from itself. As a product of the entangled histories of citizenship and subjecthood in Africa, today, the citizen is a 2-fold entity that articulates two jurisdictions within a single self.

Conclusion: Customary Citizenship

The overlapping spatial frontiers and juridico-political boundaries of the neighborhood also mark the limits of a history of postcolonial reform. The area and its institutions of law and justice reflect broader processes occurring at the level of the nation-state. This condition is illustrated by the crucial issue of autonomy, in the double sense of both the self-determination of an independent postcolonial state as well as the autonomous status of its citizens. If a fundamental legacy of the modern spirit of the laws was the emancipation of a free subject who exercises freely her rights, the restricted space of this peri-urban area illustrates the predicament of a nation-state that did not achieve the promises of the immediate postindependence moment. At present, the space of locality seems to be a site most resilient to transformation by political reason and a postcolonial subject who lives in a rural area is, at best, a second-class citizen.

State juridical regimes and international laws operating through them, as well as "customary" practices and kinship norms, construct a subjectivity whose body, emotions, thoughts, and drives are suffused with the flow of the political. This subjectivity is a duplicitous figure. Citizen-subjects crowd the space of the neighborhood.[7] These are individuals defined both by a desire of the state—the ideology of an allegedly centralized apparatus, its proliferation of laws, and its disabled system of services—as well as by more localized, minor forms of power.

Today as yesterday, the rural "customary" is opposed to the notions of urban law and political culture. "Citizenship," as the legal status of a subject of rights that belong to the city, is still denied to the vast multitude of the rural countryside; for instance, in regards to differentiations on the right to vote. The discourse of current governance links the space of the city to the concept of "civil society"—a supposed political and economic association of urban free wills somehow separated from the state that is the apex of the legal reforms propelled by

FRELIMO elites and transnational donor agencies. In the decade of the democratic transition, "civil society" meant, in the urban sphere, organizations that emerged from the very structures of the party-state system and, in the rural areas "traditional authorities": chiefs and local religious leaders.

These are the terms currently being reified by urban political elites in the capital and the agencies of development as structural adjustment that promotes the juridical reform of the state. The liberalization of the justice system via the recognition of the "customary" at the level of local governance emerges, moreover, as a kind of redrafting of a recent conflictive national history. Meanwhile, far away in the North of the country, and almost existing in another temporality altogether, the effects produced by the writing of legal reforms and historical narratives at the site of the central state are delayed. The distant provinces and the capital seem to be disconnected by large gaps and simultaneously linked by subtle lines of flight.

"Citizenship," as the full legal status of a subject of rights that belong to the city or polis, is still denied to the vast multitude of the Mozambican rural countryside. One flagrant example is the restriction in the vote for local authorities. Although the original decentralization project at the end of Socialism included the whole national territory, today, only a few cities elect their officers in a direct way, while most mayors are appointed by the central state in Maputo. Examples from the current democratic dispensation such as this illustrate the current entanglement of incorporation and segregation policies.

What is being inscribed in the flow of the history of the present is a new process of simultaneous social inclusion and exclusion, which can be defined as "customary citizenship." It is a field of force where two vectors converge: "state" recognition and enforcement of custom—its authorities, its ritual norms—alongside official law, and "local" action and demand for autochtony, rights based on relatedness and belief, and an artful inflection on national state ideologies. "Customary citizenship" is a realm of hegemonic struggle, both a technology of governance and a space of expansion of demands of custom over law, of culture over power, of the past over the future.

Peri-urban areas in Africa are crucial spaces wherein to observe the ruptures in the new urban–rural continuum, and where the aporias in the relation between "custom" and "citizenship" are highlighted. These liminal zones show the emergence of novel forms of citizenship and belonging that blend the contours of a neoliberal economic rule of law and a precolonial kingdom of custom.

Notes

1. For a thorough, learned analysis on the structure and conditions of the labyrinthine judiciary system in Mozambique, from People's Tribunals to Supreme Court and "informal" justices, see de Sousa Santos (2006) and the essays in Trindade and Meneses (2006). On People's Courts, see Sachs and Honwana (1990) and Isaacman and Isaacman (1981).
2. All names of places and people have been changed.
3. On micropolitical struggles and ethnographic structures, see Micropolitics and Segmentarity, in Deleuze and Guattari (1987).
4. On urban–rural divide in terms of political citizenship and legal rights, see Mamdani (1996). Also, see Ferguson (1999) and Geschiere and Gugler (1998).
5. A minor state unfolds as an institutional modality of a minor politics. Thus, it is different from conceptualizations of governance in terms of scale, such as a "local state." On the concept of the minor, see Deleuze and Guattari (1986).
6. On "planes of historicity," see Koselleck (2005).
7. Citizen-subject refers to a deconstructive reading of the dichotomic field presented by Mamdani, by means of an analysis of subjectivation/subjection. See also Balibar (1994).

References

Balibar, E. (1994). "Subjection and Subjectivation." In Copcec, J. ed., *Supposing the Subject*, pp. 1–15. London: Verso.

Centro de Formacao Juridica e Judiciaria. (2002). Cruzeiro do Sul, O *Papel dos Tribunais Comunitarios na Resolucao de Conflitos*. Maputo.

Chanock, M. (1985). *Law, Custom and Social Order: The Colonial Experience in Malawi and Zambia*. Cambridge: Cambridge University Press.

Deleuze, G. and Guattari, F. (1986). *Kafka: Toward a Minor Literature*. Minneapolis, MN: University of Minnesota Press.

———. (1987). *A Thousand Plateaus: Capitalism and Schizophrenia*. Minneapolis, MN: University of Minnesota Press.

de Sousa Santos, B. (2006). "The Heterogenous State and Legal Pluralism in Mozambique." *Law and Society Review* 40(1): 39–76.

Ferguson, J. (1999). *Expectations of Modernity: Myths and Meanings of Urban Life on the Zambian Copperbelt*. Berkeley, CA: University of California Press.

Geschiere, P. and Gugler, J. (1998). "Introduction: The Urban-Rural Connection: Changing Issues of Belonging and Identification." *Africa* (London), LXVIII(3): 309–319.

Hibou, B., ed. (1999). "L'Etat en voie de privatization." Special issue of *Politique africaine*, 73 (March).

Isaacman, A. and Isaacman, B. (1981). "A Socialist Legal System in the Making: Mozambique Before and After Independence." In Abel, R. L. ed., *The Politics of Informal Justice*. New York: Academic Press.

Koselleck, R. (2005). *Futures Past: On the Semantics of Historical Past*. New York: Columbia University Press.

Macaire, P. (1996). *L' Heritage Makhuwa a Mozambique*. Paris: L'Harmattan.

Mamdani, M. (1996). *Citizen and Subject.* Princeton, NJ: Princeton University Press.

Povinelli, E. (2006). *The Empire of Love.* Durham, NC: Duke University Press.

Sachs, A. and Honwana, G. (1990). *Liberating the Law: Creating Popular Justice in Mozambique.* London: Zed.

Trindade, J. C. and Meneses, P., eds (2006). *Law and Justice in a Multicultural Society: The Case of Mozambique.* Dakar: CODESRIA.

4

"Dealing with the Prince over Lagos": Pentecostal Arts of Citizenship

Ruth Marshall

Lagos: Between Dreamworld and Catastrophe[1]

Lagos is one of the world's largest mega-cities, projected to reach 20 million people by 2015. Routinely ranked as one of the five worst places to live in the world, it lends itself to all manner of apocalyptic characterizations, with its catastrophically inadequate infrastructure and public services, appalling pollution, and chaotic overcrowding; an unspeakable concentration of anarchy, human misery, crime, and violence. As Kaplan argues, Lagos has become "the cliché par excellence of Third World urban dysfunction" (2000: 15).

These lurid descriptions do not exhaust the experience of the city—at once impossible and extraordinary—and have been countered by a more celebratory view that underscores the inadequacy of dominant paradigms of thinking the city. At the vanguard of this new vision is Dutch architect Rem Koolhaas, whose work on Lagos emphasizes the ingenuity of coping strategies and the intensity of the creative energies required for dealing with everyday life (Koolhaas 2004, see also Haynes 2007). Koolhaas has been roundly, and also rightly, criticized for his aestheticization and dehistoricization of the misery, inequality, and predation that accompanies Lagos' insertion into the global political economy, as well as his dismissal of hope for any rational political and economic change (Gandy 2006, Packer 2006).[2] But is the alternative really between "dreamworld" and "catastrophe"? (Buck-Morss 2002).

Mbembe and Nuttal et al. (2004) rightly stress that the analytic frameworks and normative paradigms of urbanism and urban development (and one could extend this to all "development" studies) effectively result in purely pathological assessments of the African megalopolis, a pathology of which Lagos is arguably the archetype. They argue that, in general, the African "city's fabric has been described as a structure in need of radical transformation and only rarely as an expression of an aesthetic vision" (2004: 353). While attempting to avoid Koolhaas' aesthetic trap, they make a case for a new way of "jamming" the dominant, purely negative, imaginings of Africa through a focus on space and discontinuity—looking at the ways in which spaces circulate and exist in function of connections with an *elsewhere*, and by so doing, bring to light new moral, political, and aesthetic topographies.

Pentecostalism in Africa constitutes one of the most striking examples of reimagining both the city and modes of belonging in it through the staging of an "elsewhere." A predominantly urban phenomenon, 25 years into its dramatic Nigerian expansion, Pentecostalism's public presence in Lagos is absolutely striking. It is impossible to move through the city without being bombarded by a multitude of posters, billboards, and banners advertising churches, services, prayer meetings, revivals, miracles, or hear on the ubiquitous loudspeakers a cacophony of sermons, tongues, and singing. What I want to explore in this chapter are the ways in which the Nigerian Pentecostal engagement with an "elsewhere," both spiritual and material, produces new social and ethico-political topographies, and new ways of thinking about community and citizenship in the polis. The idiom of global spiritual warfare works, if you will forgive the expression, as a double-edged sword. On the one hand, the Pentecostal conversion and de-territorialization of urban spaces and identities through spectacularization and new forms of mediation produces new, transnational, spiritual, and material infrastructures and conduits that open "spaces of hope" (Harvey 2000) that belie these negative imaginings. On the other, these same practices are heavy with political menace and danger. Despite Pentecostalism's individualism and universalizing ambitions, its central political effect can be understood in the ways in which it offers new resources for reconceptualizing local grounds of political belonging and participation in, or escape from, the polis.

In this regard, Pentecostalism might be seen as the contemporary archetype of what AbdouMaliq Simone (2001) has called the "worlding" of African cities, whose themes are taken up by Mbembe and Nuttal (2004). Simone recognizes the difficulty in African cities today of maintaining "recognizable and usable forms of collective solidarity and collaboration" (2001: 17) in the face of the circulation of a seemingly "arbitrary unknown" (Ibid.), or what I have called the experience of "radical uncertainty," which is not merely material, but also epistemological and ontological (Marshall 2009). This is related to the ways in which global processes intersect with local urban practices and networks, such that urban dwellers "now find themselves forced to operate with a more totalizing sense of exteriority" (Simone 2001: 17). He refers to the erasure of boundaries between the "insides" of the city and what Mbembe and Nuttal call an "elsewhere," and argues that the "materialization" of this uncertainty takes a variety of forms, and the city becomes overpopulated by a multitude of what I have called "untrammeled powers," both spiritual and material. Simone argues that, in this context, there is little recourse to effective mediation or clear boundaries.

I have argued that Pentecostalism engages with this unknown by a specific mode of staging—one which claims an effective mode of mediation and reinstitution of clear boundaries by embracing a complex form of exteriority—that could be understood both materially and theologically (Marshall 2009). Materially, it entails the mobilization of new material and symbolic connections with transnational networks of capital, people, and imaginaries whose locus and site of operation is in the world, in its very Christian, indeed, Pauline sense (Derrida 2005: 54). A central trope in the Nigerian Pentecostal expansion has been the image of the city as a place of ethical and spiritual danger, a space of anomie that Pentecostal evangelical practices aim to reclaim and redeem. Unlike the "bush" or the village, which also has associations with dangerous spiritual and supernatural forces, the city is projected as a potential space of order and progress, yet one which, through postcolonial practice, has become a "fallen," chaotic, and lawless place that requires redemption. Evangelical activity has been centered on the reinvestment of physical and virtual public space—part of broader evangelical project of global spiritual warfare in which spatial vocabulary and tropes are crucial. An ever-increasing public presence and visibility is absolutely central to a broader project of redemptive citizenship, and is accompanied by the self-conscious creation of modern, functional spaces of worship and forms of electronic mediation and communication—tapes, CDs, television, films, and the Internet (Marshall 2009: 138, Meyer 2006, 2010). Its expansion throughout Lagos has focused on the investment of physical sites and institutions that instill new forms of worship and self-presentation, modes of sociability, and family structures. Furthermore, there has been a concerted investment of public space such as the market and the void left by an incompetent public service, through the development of new, increasingly globalized networks and the provision of effective forms of social security and services, as well as new attitudes to wealth, labor, and debt that find their expression in the creation of new entrepreneurial structures and modes of accumulation. All of these contribute to the overarching sense of de-localization and de-territorialization that has marked the revival's self-understanding, both materially and symbolically.

Techniques of mass mediation are absolutely central to the ways in which the movement has developed and spread so successfully. Rather than through instances of institutionalized authority, Pentecostalism achieves its power through a verisimilitude, or truth effect, achieved through the public staging and circulation—particularly through forms of mass-mediation, such as television—of prayer, prophecy, testimony, and miracles. Pentecostals have been at the vanguard of the exploitation of electronic media in Nigeria, often outstripping the capacities for production and capitalization of the states themselves (Haynes 2007, Larkin 2008, Marshall 2009, Meyer 2006). The centrality to Pentecostalism of the circulation of mass-mediated religious speech and miraculous performance gives it a singular power. Capitalizing on what Derrida calls the fiduciary structure of language, the "I promise" or "I believe" that is at the basis of every social bond (Derrida 2002: 80); televangelism's "utterly singular" relationship to the media creates a relay between "the ordinary miracle of the 'believe me' and the extraordinary miracles revealed by the Holy Scriptures" (Derrida 2001: 76–77, quoted in Naas 2012: 139). This direct connection between the individual believer and the space-time of the inception of Christianity provides the basis for the delocalization of messages, and gives rise to media-created publics with no sense of place.

If we compare these organizations with other older, more established churches, among mainstream or orthodox denominations, the Aladura churches, and even earlier holiness Pentecostals, we find striking differences in how congregations are set up as communities, and how they identify themselves as co-religionists. As André Corten argues with reference to Pentecostalism in Latin America, "through the media, transversal relations [among churches] are formed. The community of the church still exists as a reference, but is transformed from a place of praise and cohesion to a 'show place' [*lieu de spectacle*] where deliverance and divine healing are staged. In this staging of a 'show,' there is a change of imaginary [*imaginaire*]" (Corten 1997: 17). This imaginary is one in which Pentecostal religiosity cannot really be understood as an institution that furnishes a discrete identity or establishes a clearly bounded community. This leads us to question the capacity of Pentecostalism to mediate the experience of radical uncertainty and developing new forms collective solidarity. Rather than providing a means to specific individual social or political ends, Pentecostal practices of faith appear rather wholly bound up in performing a presentation of the divine—a spectacularization of the sacred that reveals Pentecostalism, like late capitalism, to be a formidable apparatus for the production and consumption of pure means (Agamben 2007, Marshall 2009, Wariboko 2011).

Theologically, conversion deploys new modes of subjectivation under the jurisdiction of the Holy Spirit, where an understanding of divine grace as "transimmanence" would mediate between the self and the world of untrammeled powers (Marshall 2009, 2010, Wariboko 2011). Rather than a drawing of new boundaries, however, this form of mediation takes the Pauline form of the "revocation of every vocation," (Agamben 2005: 25) as in 1 Corinthians 7:17–24, in which the "new creation" does not furnish an identity, but the suspension of every juridical or factical property. This messianic suspension does not nullify or overcome existing divisions (gender, class, age, ethnicity, status, etc.) or give rise to new divisions or distinctions, but renders them inoperative, "in force without signification." This break with old ways is figured through the deliberate restaging of natality, reinvesting it with an ontological priority as regards action, understood as the possibility of beginning anew (Marshall 2009: 50). The idiom of rebirth, the instantiation of an existential principle of endless renewal and an ontology of becoming, the possibility of "making a complete break with the past" that conversion promises—all of these inform the emancipatory effects of breaking with unbelievers as well as with the historical forms of subjection that have structured longstanding forms of domination and accumulation in the postcolony. Yet, this occupation and production of redeemed spaces is conceived in terms of war, a life-and-death struggle to wrest people, places, and destinies from the satanic enemy.

Mike Davis (2004, 2006) has argued that the demographics of Pentecostalism—which now counts half a billion adherents of which the vast majority live in cities in the Global South—make it, potentially, a new revolutionary force, or if not, the best we have to work with: "Indeed, for the moment at least, Marx has yielded the historical stage to Mohammed and the Holy Ghost. If God died in the cities of the industrial revolution, he has risen again in the postindustrial cities of the developing world" (Davis 2004: 34). He credits reformist Islam and Pentecostalism with articulating the most significant response to the process of "urban involution" (labor's self over-exploitation) that characterize the Third World megalopolis: "with the Left still largely missing from the slum, the eschatology of Pentecostalism admirably refuses the inhuman destiny of the Third World city that *Slums* [UN-Habitat 2003] warns about. It also sanctifies those who, in every structural and existential sense, truly live in exile" (Davis 2004: 34). I would like to question this claim from the perspective of Pentecostalism's extraordinary expansion in Lagos and beyond over the past three decades. Does Pentecostalism really "sanctify those who live in exile"? Living in exile in Davis' understanding refers to new global topographies of exclusion wherein the teeming masses of Third World slums have effectively become a form of surplus humanity rather than the reserve labor army of previous phases of capitalist expansion. Davis' claim would presume that Pentecostalism in Africa is predominantly a religion of the slums, and that its eschatology involves sanctifying this surplus in some way that involves an active refusal of this destiny. This strikes me as provocative, but problematic on both empirical and theoretical grounds, in ways I will try to address further. I will proceed by outlining two cases that exemplify modes of Pentecostal expansion in Lagos and beyond. The first, which I will call the "showcase" model, in which the Pentecostal presence (both divine and material) involves the physical re-occupation of space through the acquisition of property and the construction of an idealized space of late capitalist urban living, centered around what may well be the world's largest Pentecostal showplace, capable of welcoming over one million believers. The second, which I will call the "spiritual network" model, involves both a mode of identifying the territorial presence of demonic spiritual forces and conduits, reclaiming these sites and replacing them with "Holy Spirit" networks and connections—a virtual topography largely dependent on new forms of electronic communication, or at least on the imaginaries of connectedness they generate. The argument is that, while, on the one hand, new urban spaces of hope are being produced by this engagement, on the other hand, it also generates new topographies of inequality, violence, and exclusion through the obligation to identify and eliminate the "enemy" as well as the spectacularization and phantasmagorical enchantment so central to its success.

The Redeemed Christian Church of God: God's Own Showcase

Following the early interdenominational movement of the 1970s and 1980s, over the 1990s, effects of a new third wave in global charismatic and Pentecostal Christianity resulted in a massive explosion of church planting. Churches now are found literally on every corner, ranging from modest one-story buildings to lavish complexes in the style of villas or banks as well as huge warehouse-like structures. The most ubiquitous of these new churches are the thousands of parishes of the Redeemed Christian Church of God (RCCG). When I first visited the RCCG national headquarters in 1989, in Ebute-Metta—one of the oldest Yoruba neighborhoods in Lagos comprising predominantly lower middle-class streets and one impressive slum—it was a run-down complex at the end of Cemetery Street, reached by a muddy path, bordering the lagoon and the slums built up around the Ebute-Metta log fields. From its poor Yoruba origins in the 1950s, the RCCG has experienced dizzying growth in the past three decades since Pastor Adeboye took over from its illiterate founder, Pa Akindayomi. Throughout the late 1980s and 1990s, under the impulse of Pastor Tunde Bakare and the energies of Pastor Tony Rapu (both of whom have left the church), RCCG developed new, so-called "model" parishes in middle- and upper-class neighborhoods, with an educated, upper middle-class, ethnically mixed membership. These congregations fast outstripped the older, poorer "classical" parishes in influence, and coincided with the advent of the arrival of the "Word of Faith" or prosperity gospel, fundamentally changing the church's doctrinal emphasis, from a strict other-worldly ascetic holiness, to an emphasis on divine miracles and financial blessings in the here-and-now. The church began to deliberately target the middle and upper classes with fellowship breakfasts at the five-star Eko Le Meridien Hotel and the inauguration of fellowship and outreach groups like the Christ the Redeemer's Friends Universal—an organization of the RCCG that requires potential members to have a post-secondary degree or diploma, as well as women's groups, youth and student fellowships, and mission outreaches.

Today, RCCG has over 14,000 parishes in Nigeria, with approximately five million members. Asonzeh Ukah (2008) claims that RCCG is now the single largest private landowner in Lagos. Adeboye has repeatedly announced that RCCG will plant a church within "five minutes walk" from every urban Nigerian, and a 5-minute drive from every North American. Totally rebuilt and expanded, the new national headquarters now reflects the meteoric expansion of the church in the past 20 years. Its address is no longer 1A Cemetery Street, but 4–5 Redemption Way (figure 4.1).

Nevertheless, as these pictures tellingly reveal, the dramatic expansion of parishes and the striking reconstruction of its headquarters has not meant that RCCG has integrated itself within pre-existing neighborhoods, creating a local site from which to engage in "redeeming" its immediate surroundings and their populations, whether spiritually or materially. In fact, RCCG's relations with the immediate communities in which it has planted itself have often been difficult, litigious, and,

Figure 4.1 National Headquarters of the RCGC, 4–5 Redemption Way. Photo courtesy of Sabine Bitter and Helmut Weber.

at times, violent. Indeed, the acquisition of property precedes the construction of a congregation or community, and is based on the promise of a church a 5-minute walk (or in North America, 5-minute drive) from every person. In North America, the explicit strategy has been to avoid planting new churches in predominantly diaspora neighborhoods, which means that members of these communities must drive more than 5 minutes and traverse previously unfamiliar parts of the cities they live in, while every Sunday the pastor prays over the empty seats. Rather than being outgrowths of specific and localized social formations or neighborhoods, we should think of these parishes as nodes in an ever-expanding network, one which physically and symbolically connects people from disparate neighborhoods, regions, and countries, creating conduits for people and resources that should flow into the "global community" RCCG now sees itself as building (Burgess et al. 2010). The hub of these globally dispersed nodes is found in the extraordinary new complex developed between Lagos and Ibadan: Redemption City.

According to his account, in the late 1980s, faced with the physical impossibility of gathering all his flock in one place, Adeboye had a vision to build a prayer camp outside the city. On what was originally 3.5 hectares of bush at Kilometer 46 on the Lagos–Ibadan expressway, since the early 1990s, RCCG has built a veritable city of some 10 square kilometers, which now functions as the church's international headquarters. Monthly Holy Ghost services attract hundreds of thousands, causing monumental traffic jams that used to paralyze the Lagos–Ibadan expressway for days until a new parking system was put in place. The Holy Ghost Arena measures 1 km long and 500 m wide, and can accommodate over one million worshippers. From 1998 onward, the annual Holy Ghost Congress has attracted between three and six million attendees from across Nigeria and the world. This liminal space between city and bush also functions as a material and symbolic hub, connecting the ever-expanding parishes and networks of the church within the cities of Lagos and Ibadan to the open vistas of the world it claims it will conquer for Christ. RCCG currently has parishes in over 52 countries, on four continents, and is building a new Redemption City on land it acquired outside Dallas, Texas. With over 500 parishes in North America. the RCCG North American mission head, James Fadele, claims that the North American church now boasts a capacity of over one million. (How many empty seats are still being prayed over?)

This veritable empire has been constructed through not only the tithes and offerings of its millions of faithful, but also the mobilization of private capital and entrepreneurial networks and connections, which are increasingly global in character. Symbolically too, the connection to global networks has become increasingly central to the identity of the church and its practices. Even the preferred mode of giving to the Lord in order to receive your blessing now takes place in foreign exchange. Indeed, if the Lord is going to bless your offering "a hundredfold," it is better to give $10 for the Lord than 10 Naira. Illogically, people now exchange their Naira for dollars or pounds before giving it at the Holy Ghost Service. Adeboye's status is now one of a cosmopolitan global leader, as at home in the Presidential palace in Aso Rock as in London, New York, and Dallas. Erstwhile advisor to President Obasanjo, Adeboye also has a street named after him in Abuja and is ranked 49th in *Newsweek's* 2009 list of the world's "top 50 most powerful people." Aspiring state governors or presidential candidates of whatever religious persuasion must now publicly seek Adeboye's "blessing" at highly publicized participation in one of the monthly Holy Ghost nights.

Redemption City is showcased on the RCCG website:

> You are welcome to the Redemption city, where Heaven and Earth meet. The redemption city is in all aspects God's own showcase, as every aspect of its involvement has been a testimony of the awesome revelation of the most High God to His beloved people.... What started as 4.25 acres at Loburo with the exact dimensions of the auditorium then as 150 feet

> by 300 feet...has metamorphosed into a CITY with facilities such as; Banks, Halls, A University, Schools, Chalets, Resort Center, Maternity Center, Clinic, Post Office, Supermarkets, Bookshops, Western Union, an Estate, Security Posts, Churches amongst others. During the June 2008, HGS, Daddy GO announced the completion of the covering of the huge auditorium at the Holy Ghost Arena, glory be to God. The Redemption city hosts the monthly Holy Ghost Service, Special Holy Ghost Service, Annual Convention and the annual Holy Ghost Congress in December. The Story of these special events cannot be overemphasized and has as a matter of fact become one of the leading factors that many people now live permanently in the city development which offers residents a unique lifestyle different from what is generally obtain in many metropolitan city. The peace cannot be quantified. Praise God!' (http://city.rccgnet.org/). (figure 4.2).

"Where Heaven and Earth meet"...Redemption City is indeed a space of exile, but hardly in the sense Davis intends. Developed in deliberate contrast to Lagos, it is an artificial showcase, with all the insubstantiality of the model home: a space of hope that functions at a purely spectacular, phantasmagorical level. Here, we can see how space itself functions as a new form of spectacularized testimonial, as an image rather than a dwelling place. Kehinde Osinowo, leader of

Figure 4.2 Holy Ghost Arena: 1 km × 0.5 km. Photo courtesy of Sabine Bitter and Helmut Weber.

the organization Christians for the Regeneration of the Nation, urges Nigerians Pentecostals to undertake national redemption, quoting Isaiah 58:12: "And they that shall be with thee shall build the old waste places; thou shalt raise up the foundations of many generations, and thou shalt be called the repairer of the breach, the restorer of paths to dwell in" (Marshall 2009: 125). This verse encapsulates the Pentecostal promise to repair the separation between truth and the good, between God's laws and the community of believers, through a process of building and restoration of modes of dwelling in the world. It is difficult to ignore the Heideggerian reference here, for whom man is "insofar as he dwells." His romantic/nostalgic lament was that modern man merely "builds," that is, turns the world into a picture and forgets the ways of dwelling (Heidegger 1971). Redemption City, in this sense, is the perfect picture of the normalized, pacified, and ordered petty bourgeois African city.

If Redemption City is one mode of "repairing the breach," restoring "paths to dwell in," then we can say that it is entirely consistent with late capitalist society of the spectacle and may, in fact, be the best expression of its ethic. RCCG's expansion illustrates how Pentecostalism in Nigeria specifically, but Africa more generally (and arguably in many other places), is a religion of the beleaguered middle classes, or what they have become after their "structural adjustment." Even if it is embraced by more subaltern populations and slum dwellers, it, nonetheless, aspires to a resolutely petty bourgeois ethic and form of subjectivity (see O'Neill 2012). "Surplus humanity" with its chaotic energies has no permanent place here; even the great majority of RCCG members do not have access to loans from Haggai bank that would permit them to purchase a semi-detached Redemption duplex, nor pay the fees for a degree in business administration from Redeemer's University. The best they can do is to participate as spectators in the monthly Holy Ghost night and hope for Adeboye to channel the anointing their way. The event of Pentecostal conversion can be seen to carry with it the same kind of ontological virtue that conversion to capitalism does. All good Marxists remember Marx's enthusiasm for capitalism's capacity to destroy the old hierarchies, ushering in the possibility of modern politics and its principle of equality. Indeed, it might not be going too far to call Pentecostalism an ambiguous form of "desacralization" with respect to its capacity for destabilizing the old order and its difficulty in securing its own sovereign foundation. However, it would be a mistake to simply translate Pentecostalism's capacity for de-territorialization, and the "destitution" that accompanies Pentecostalism's "new life"—"making a complete break with the past"[3]—as a form of resistance to the ways in which dominant political and economic forces in the world today regulate, control, and circumscribe the great mass of the world's population and their possibilities.

"Dealing with the Prince over Lagos": Spiritual Warfare in the City

The "new creation"[4] (2 Cor. 5:17), the new era, and the coming of the Kingdom are to be achieved in Pentecostalism through the waging of an epic battle against the forces of darkness. Further, as we shall see, it is precisely the inability within Pentecostalism to appropriate divine grace—whether to shore up pastoral power and legitimacy or to capture divine blessings—that makes this struggle so very ambivalent. The apocalyptic reading of history that preaches the urgency of evangelism in the end-times and preparing oneself spiritually and ethically for the imminent rapture is a central theme in global Pentecostalism,[5] one that most Nigerian churches and missions also, at least formally, subscribe to. It stages both the dangers and promises of the present in an idiom that presents change not only as urgent, but also as immanent in the present moment. It makes for an experience of the present whose qualities have been altered by the presence of the Holy Spirit and divine grace in the form of miracles, in which the present becomes not only the "only time we have" to struggle, to realize the potentialities that may be released by faith. As Pentecostals say of this struggle, "be of good cheer, we are on the winning side" (Marshall 2009: 126). But, this struggle for redemption is a "battle," a "war" against the forces of darkness:

> The warfare we are presently engaged in is the battle of translating the victory of Jesus over the devil into the everyday, natural realities of our personal lives and also of our political, religious, economic and social systems. It is a battle of reclamation: to reclaim from the devil what he illegally holds in his control...It is warfare. But we are on the winning side. This is the time to muster the army—the Lord's army. Here is a clarion call to battle...We are disadvantaged if we lean on carnal weapons. Prayer—militant, strategic and aggressive prayer—must be our weapon of warfare at this time. It is a spiritual warfare and it needs spiritual weapons. This is a call into the ring to wrestle, to sweat it out with an unseen opponent. For we wrestle not against flesh and blood but against spiritual wickedness, against invisible powers in high places (Ephesians 6:12)[6] (Ojewale 1990: 23–24, 37).

Pastor Tony Rapu, the ex-favored son of Adeboye, and a medical doctor, explains how the battle in the spiritual realm is responsible for many of the socioeconomic and political afflictions that affect contemporary Nigeria in his exposé "Dealing with the Prince over Lagos":

> Everyone is familiar with the account of Daniel and his travails in Babylon...Daniel had prayed, God had responded and somehow given the answer to this unnamed angel to deliver...This angelic messenger carrying Daniel's answer was held in combat by the so-called "prince of Persia" for twenty-one days. The battle was so severe that the angel needed reinforcement and Michael the chief archangel had to come to his aid. Though high in ranking, the prince of Persia was no match for Michael. Grand intrigue in the unseen realm!
>
> What a tale! To the undiscerning ear, this account would sound like another good bible fable embellished for children in Sunday school. But locked up in that account is serious and vital information that reveal the spiritual dimension and dynamics of life not just on earth but around us here in Nigeria. Often times, our secular framework of thought prevent [sic] us from receiving truth as clearly revealed in scripture. Many naïve and uninformed Christians may dismiss the phenomena of angels and other spiritual entities as imaginary because they may not fit well into secular and scientific paradigms. The idea of spiritual beings that can neither be seen nor heard floating around the world is difficult to contextualise its truth in our modern day setting. It is presumed that these demonic princes over the nations were angels, who were in the hierarchy of angelic authority, fell from heaven and have now taken up equivalent positions as "princes" or satanic rulers over nations. When traveling from one country to another one may become aware of a change in the "atmosphere." A feeling that cannot be quantified or measured but discerned within you, perhaps what one senses is a different ruling spirit in operation. Even within this country one can move from one region to another, one city to another and be conscious of discernable spiritual changes...It is thus important to understand that the geopolitical and cultural systems of a nation consist of more than the people, the structures and institutions. There is an attempt by these princes or ruling spirits over nations to exert a negative influence over schools, churches, companies and organizations. We are presently caught in a conflict of forces. The failure to recognize this territorial dimension of the spiritual realm is making many Christians ineffective in fulfilling their purpose. Every sub structure of human society has a spiritual dimension seeking to control and influence the individuals, its economic institutions and the political order. Behind the systems of this country, behind NPA, NEPA, the Nigerian Police Force and the institutions of politics is a raging war! (Rapu 2002)

Here, we are in the presence of a different sort of infrastructure...a complex network of unseen supernatural forces, bringing death and destruction and working to frustrate the Christian project, with specific territorial implantations that need to be specially addressed.[7] It should be pointed out that this conception is not at all peculiar to Africa—the paradigm of spiritual warfare and the action of unseen demonic forces was central to the second wave of Pentecostal revival in the United States and around the world, and has become a growing part of what has been called the "third wave," particularly with the New Apostolic Reformation and Kingdom Now movements pioneered by American evangelists in the 1990s (Holvast 2008. See Wagner 1991, 1993, 1996).

The Nigerian pastors who endorse many of the doctrinal emphases of this new movement (even if they do not always agree with the specific forms it can take, especially those that place an emphasis on hierarchy and total submission to "apostolic leaders," or the connection with dominion theology), are among the most powerful, educated, cosmopolitan, and globally connected pastors in Lagos today. The two most notable are Tony Rapu and Tunde Bakare, who ran in the April 2011 election as the vice-presidential candidate with Muhammadu Buhari on the Congress for Progressive Change ticket. Bakare founded his Pentecostal ministry, The Latter Rain Assembly, after a break with Adeboye in 1989, that has expanded to include a global ministry with mission headquarters in Atlanta, GA. He also heads up an impressive global network of churches and businesses, the Global Apostolic Impact Network (GAIN)—"a network of churches, ministries and kingdom businesses committed to advancing the Kingdom of God on earth" (Bakare website) as well as setting up the International Centre for Reconstruction and Development (ICRD) that he calls a "knowledge industry/think-tank devoted to re-engineering the social, economic and political landscape of Nigeria in particular and Africa in general." Most significantly for Nigerian politics, he was Convener of the "Save Nigeria Group (SNG)," a broad-based civil coalition of pro-democracy groups set up to encourage popular political mobilization. Using his extensive Pentecostal and political networks, Bakare's SNG was very successful in raising civic awareness and voter registration in the run-up to the 2011 elections. The Congress for Progressive Change campaign website declared: "After decades of speaking truth to power and standing on the side of the oppressed, Dr. Bakare has thus extended the frontiers of his political activism in a bid to Save Nigeria, to Change Nigeria and to Make Nigeria Great again in our lifetime" (Congress for Progressive Change).

Political propaganda aside, Bakare is well known for his outspoken and critical views (and daring prophecies) on Nigerian politics, particularly the execrable track record of the ruling PDP party, political corruption, and economic malfeasance, as well as the plight of the poor. Bakare's "social gospel" and political ambition make him a central player in Nigerian politics today. His most recent mobilization had him spearheading the Occupy Nigeria Movement in early January 2012 that organized successful demonstrations against the removal of the oil subsidy. Bakare took the tribune with a collection of left-wing labor leaders and leading intellectuals such as Wole Soyinka and Niyi Osundare (see Osundare 2012). During the summer of 2012, he preached a Sunday sermon on the theme of "President Goodluck Jonathan has to go." This use of the pulpit earned him a visit from the State Security Services, who warned him to "tone it down" (*Vanguard* July 23, 2012). He has also been a violent critic of the current Pentecostal "Church," its miracle mania, prosperity focus, empire-building, and pastoral personality cults. He has, nonetheless, done extremely well for himself through the ministry and his public role, and is one of the wealthier and most influential pastors in Lagos today. Bakare, Rapu, and a growing group of like-minded pastors are developing a somewhat different model of evangelical expansion than the RCCGs: the creation of global networks that are not focused on church planting, but rather, on strategically building what they call global apostolic "corporate culture," linking together institutions and individuals in leading positions in both the public and private sectors, locally and across the globe—a new "spiritual infrastructure" that would serve as a bulwark against the "forces of darkness" in these "end times."

Therefore, what sort of weapons of warfare should be used to deal with the specific problem of the Prince over Lagos? One of the solutions is something called "spiritual mapping." Although I had not seen this widely practiced in Lagos, or in the RCCG a decade earlier, it now appears to be a growing practice. As stated in the Lausanne document:

> Spiritual mapping…involves…superimposing our understanding of forces and events in the spiritual domain onto places and circumstances in the material world…Spiritual mapping is a means by which we can see what is beneath the surface of the material world; but it is not magic. It is subjective in that it is a skill born out of a right relationship with God and a love for His world. It is objective in that it can be verified (or discredited) by history, sociological observation and God's Word (Lausanne 2004).

An RCCG parish in Port Elizabeth, South Africa outlines the strategy in these terms:

- Spiritual mapping is the researching of a city or area to discover any obstacles that Satan has established that prevent the spread of the gospel and the evangelization of a city for Jesus, and to identify spiritual principalities and strongholds over different regions in the city.
- Spiritual mapping is a means to see beneath the surface of the material world. It is a subjective skill born out of a right relationship with God and a love for his kingdom.
- Although spiritual mapping is most often used to identify enemy strongholds, we must remember that not all spiritual activities are dark, and that God also operates in the spiritual domain. Spiritual mapping should also be used to highlight the work that God is doing in the community.
- Our Western world view leads us to believe that the spiritual realm does not even exist, and that makes spiritual mapping even more important a tool for us.
- Spiritual mapping is not an end in itself and is only a powerful weapon or spiritual resource—just a tool that allows us to be more specific in praying for our community. Experience says that specific sniper prayer is more powerful than the shotgun approach.
- Although the final outcome of the battle is already decided, we have to be persistent and steadfast. There will be many battles during this war and constant hostility. Satan knows his time on Earth is running out, and this may explain the increasing worldwide accounts of demonic activity and counterattacks on Christian warriors. Demonic entrenchments or strongholds have been in place for long periods and may have been continually serviced since their inception. They are not just going to leave without a sustained and informed prayer effort.

Many spiritual mappers in Africa, the United States, and Europe "walk the city," identifying sites or physical coordinates on the grid that then become "prayer sites" from which to purify and "reclaim" for Jesus the surrounding areas, "unblocking" the work of the Holy Spirit. They, thus, develop "spiritual maps" with which they can "read the city."

Mbembe and Nuttal note the influence of de Certeau's "Walking in the City" (de Certeau 1984) and Walter Benjamins' concept of *flânerie* (Benjamin 1999) for a conception of cities as a space of open and manifold temporalities, rhythms and circulation, "to read the city from its street-level intimations, as a lived complexity that requires alternative narratives and maps based on wandering" (Mbembe and Nuttal 2004: 361). They correct this for an African context by focusing on not merely the manifest appearances that this practice reveals, but also the "dirty, grubby" underneath, and the radical insecurity experienced by the migrant or informal worker (Ibid.: 363). From the Pentecostal perspective, the practice of walking the city and the significance of the "underneath" takes on an entirely different inflection.[8] In this articulation, Pentecostal practices of space engage in a different form of mediation than the spectacular showcasing of idealized spaces and divine miracles. Spiritual warfare in this formulation functions as a mode of potentially violent reterritorialization. Identifying sites, spaces, and communities as being under the grip of demonic forces requires the deployment of an ambivalent politics of conviction (Marshall 2009: 201–238). The Evil One who threatens the convert's salvation and prosperity, the "Prince above Lagos" responsible for the situation of despair and decay in the city and country today, the sinners and other strongholds of Satan, need to be "convicted," "punished," and "destroyed." In this prayer guide, the convert is given prayers to "castigate the conspirators"[9]:

Father I thank you because sinners will not go unpunished.

1. Let all rumour mongers be ruined. Ez. 7:26
2. It is my turn to enjoy, let all opponents keep quiet. Eccl. 3:13
3. Let all the rebels in my dwelling place and office dwell in dry places. Ps. 68:6
4. Hunger killed the forty men that conspired against Paul, let all conspirators die of hunger. Acts 23:13
5. Ahitophel hanged himself, let all conspirators hang themselves. 2 Sam. 17:23
6. Make a slave of anyone that wants to rob me of my vision. Gen. 50:18
7. All the conspirators in my extended family, be scattered in Jesus' name. I Sam.

In the city itself, slums, Muslim neighborhoods, brothels, bars, sites of old shrines, or current traditional medical clinics, African Aladura churches, and the businesses and domiciles of politicians or the super-rich are among the many possible "demonic strongholds" that are in need of spiritual purification and conversion, entailing practices of identification and boundary-setting without any clear criteria or logic beyond that of division itself—the enemy may be anywhere, even within the church itself.

What is at stake in these practices and imaginaries of divine and demonic spiritual pathways, networks, and inhabitations is, once again, the relationship between material appearances and the real, between the object and its representation. Here, Pentecostalism performs its mediation as revelation. The ability to "see" the spiritual reality behind material appearances is understood in terms of the divine gift of the "spirit of discernment," a sort of inner eye or capacity for moral and spiritual perception, or *aisthesis*, in which judgment and revelation are merged, one that relies upon an unmediated access to grace. This mode of verdiction, or truth telling (Foucault 2001: 18), grounds the post-foundational and politically ambivalent nature of Pentecostal political spirituality.

"If My People Who Are Called by My Name…"

For Pentecostals, Christianity should be a total experience that concerns every aspect of what the believer does and says; As Rapu says, "it not a religion, it is a lifestyle…we don't go to Church, we are the Church!" The explicit corollary of this message is that there is no distinction to be made between the sacred and the secular. In Rapu's terms, society has to be changed, "you can't just camp around Pentecost!":

> The Divine blueprint for National redemption and subsequent transformation begins with a familiar clarion call "*If My people who are called by my name…*" If the people of God will act purposefully, God Himself will heal the land. In practical terms this means that we must begin to understand that the redemption of Nations is tied to the purpose of the Church (Rapu in Marshall 2009: 241).

But, how will this call be answered? Is there any reason to really imagine that Pentecostalism will give rise to emancipatory forms of political action or inclusive forms of citizenship that might do more than merely sanctify the great mass of urban Africans (still) living in exile from humanity? Indeed, what does sanctification imply if not the extrication of a person(s) from the regular, profane commerce of human coexistence? Is sacralization not just another word for death? For many subalterns in the postcolony, conversion does offer a possible escape from a metaphysics of existence through which historical forms of domination have prevailed on the continent. Indeed, the evangelical message takes the form of a universal address that would, in theory, abolish subalternity altogether. However, this emancipatory politics grafts itself, on the one hand, to a phantasmagorical projection of a bourgeois space purified of all difference and division, and on the other, a spiritual warfare against the other that figures the possibility of a war without remainder. Both Bakare and Rapu are acutely aware of the dangers of the spiritual warfare paradigm for the future of citizenship in Nigeria. In the face of the recent spate of deadly bombings of Nigerian churches by the radical Islamist group Boko Haram, Bakare has made a show of aligning with leading Muslim clerics and political leaders in his call for calm, claiming religious violence is a tool in the hands of the political elite to distract popular attention from the desperate state of the political economy. Rapu warns against the spirit of retaliation, citing Martin Luther King:

> Without prejudice to the right of a people to self-defence [sic], reciprocal Christian extremism is no remedy for Islamic terrorism. 'The weapons of our warfare are not carnal'; therefore, we must reach into the treasury of our faith for the appropriate weapons with which to engage the enemy. Reverend Martin Luther King, who carried out his ministry in an atmosphere of racist hatred at a time when African-American were routinely lynched and their churches fire-bombed by terrorists, offers insights on how to respond to persecution. He urged Christians to actualize Jesus' invocation that we love our enemies. 'Hate for hate', King wrote, 'only intensifies the existence of hate and evil in the universe'. The idea of loving our enemies ranks among the more understated aspects of our faith and practice today. It is not only virtually ignored in Nigerian Christianity, but there exists a pattern of prayer that advocates the death of such enemies; commanding them to 'roast and be burned up' in some nebulous Holy Ghost fire. But loving our enemies is a concept that we must actualize today. It is a quality that makes our faith redemptive (Rapu 2012).

Rapu's exhortations notwithstanding, it is very difficult to see how the desire to extricate oneself from these forms of domination and address the vicissitudes of postcolonial urban life will imply a progressive engagement against its violence, or the violence of Capital and Empire that produce the ever-increasing army of surplus humanity crowding cities like Lagos. All the evidence points to a more successful conversion to this violence.

Nigerian Pentecostal theologian Nimi Wariboko rails against what he calls the new "trade-and-barter" attitude to miracles that we can say characterizes Adeboye's brand of Pentecostalism. He argues that Pentecostalism's attitude to miraculous, divine grace is that of a child at play, one that allows grace to float between the serious matter of saving the soul and ordinary, ephemeral, bodily, existential matters—relieving it of the weight of the ends of eternal life. Divine grace as pure means—means without ends. You may recognize Agamben here, and indeed, as his careful reader, Wariboko points out that the "bad news" is that the spirit of Pentecostalism today might be nothing more than the spirit of the latest phase of capitalism. He cites Agamben's observation (taken from Debord) that late capitalism is "a gigantic apparatus for [creating and] capturing pure means" (Agamben 2007: 81, Wariboko 2011: 152), where nothing escapes the logic of commodification, where everything is separated from itself and is exhibited in its separation from itself; becoming a spectacle. Spectacle and consumption are, thus, "two sides of a single impossibility of using" (Agamben 2007: 82).

Wariboko, goes on to warn: "needless to say that in the extreme reaches of Pentecostalism with its array of prosperity gospel, faith healing preachers and flamboyant televangelists, consumption and spectacle are in full force and like capitalism there is an ugly indifference to the caesura between the sacred and the profane" (2011: 153). In this regard then, it appears that conversion to Pentecostalism, with its form of transimmanent grace also constitutes, despite everything, a sort of desacralization, or perhaps a better way of putting it would be that, in its attempt to sanctify every aspect of human practice, everything becomes profane. This puts Davis' claim in a new light.

Wariboko, as a Pentecostal theologian and, indeed, a pastor in the North American RCCG, would rather not see Pentecostalism and its "new creation" as a pure cipher for capitalism, even if, as he says, he is not holding his breath about its current revolutionary potential (154). Yet, it is precisely through its mode as spectacle that the deactivation of divine grace is effected, and that its emancipatory possibilities are opened up, connecting believers with an elsewhere and an "otherwise of being" that figures a new future. It is precisely the impossibility of appropriating or re-presenting the divine, of deploying grace as a means to an end that prevents Pentecostalism from enacting the worst forms of violence. Pentecostalism-as-spectacle, as phantasmagorical projection, encourages believers to inhabit their social identities according to the Pauline suspension of the "as not" where the laws that govern modes of social distinction and the predicates of worldly being—Jew, Greek, Yoruba, Hausa, Muslim, Christian, man, woman, rich, poor, slave and free—are suspended or deactivated, and to experience divine grace as a mode of liberation (Agamben 2005, Marshall 2009: 144). And yet, even if these predicates no longer constitute the terms in which the believer relates to herself, even if Pentecostalism supposedly stages a space in which they would be inoperative, such distinctions are still in force in the church, the city, and in the broader global context, and continue to constrain the life possibilities of millions. Living in hope is better than living in despair, but it does not mean that hope will take the form of emancipatory rather than reactionary political projects. Richard Pithouse, analyzing "resistance in the shantytown," argues that the Hindu fascist movement Shiv Sena based in Mumbai "is one of the many instances of deeply reactionary responses to the need for social innovation," reminding us that "there is no guarantee that the need to invent new social forms will result in progressive outcomes" (Pithouse 2006: 5). It is in the dream of salvation, the desire for the pure, the holy, and the sanctified that the danger lies for Pentecostalism. Nevertheless, the desire for sanctification is also a desire for justice, of a new way of being together. Today, Pentecostalism in Nigeria oscillates dangerously between these two possibilities. On the one hand, as Wariboko argues, spiritual warfare means "cutting the chains of captivity" of given social existence, "returning the light of Being" to the poor on the edge of nonexistence, and sustaining an alternate world of freedom (2012: 159). However, prayer as "the weapon of our warfare" also means the vicious imprecations of "prayer warriors" that drip with blood, tongues as swords excising evil territorial spirits, dropping prayer "smart-bombs" and "strategic prayer missiles" on "enemy strongholds." Nigerian Pentecostals' "first response" to the bombing of Christian churches by the Islamist group Boko Haram in the form of 3 days of national prayer against the enemy illustrates how prayer and curse, benediction and malediction function in tandem in Pentecostal political speech, and its potentially incendiary effects.

Notes

1. Reference to Benjamin's *Passagenwerk* as problematized by Susan Buck-Morss (2002).
2. George Packer (2006) cites Koolhaas' "Fragments of a Lecture on Lagos," and relating how Koolhaas explains that he and his team were too intimidated to leave their car on their first visit to the city: "Eventually, the group rented the Nigerian President's helicopter and was granted a more reassuring view." Koolhaas writes: "From the air, the apparently burning garbage heap turned out to be, in fact, a village, an urban phenomenon with a highly organized community living on its crust... What seemed, on ground level, an accumulation of dysfunctional movements, seemed from above an impressive performance."
3. As Badiou says, "Yet, for Marx, and for us, desacralization is not in the least nihilistic, insofar as 'nihilism' must signify that which declares that the access to being and truth is impossible. On the contrary, desacralization is a necessary condition for the disclosing of such an approach to thought. It is obviously the only thing we can and must welcome within Capital: it exposes the pure multiple as the foundation of presentation; it denounces every effect of One as a simple, precarious configuration; it dismisses the symbolic representations in which the bond found a semblance of being. That this destitution operates in the most complete barbarity must not conceal its properly ontological virtue" (1999: 56–57).
4. "Therefore if any man be in Christ, he is a new creation: old things are passed away, behold, all things are become new."

5. See, for example, the website "Rapture Ready," complete with prediction index, which the site calls "the prophetic speedometer of end-time activity": www.raptureready.com.
6. In his booklet *The Works of the Devil*, Emmanuel Eni clarifies Ephesians 6:12 in this way: "The devil is an excellent administrator. He is the champion of the division of labour. He knows how to organise things in an evil way so as to finally achieve his goal…in Satan's governmental hierarchy, the four mentioned in the above Scriptures are: (a) the "principalities," (b) the "powers," (c) "the rulers of the darkness of this world," (d) the 'spiritual wickedness in high places."…The "principalities" are the "Cabinet members" or the "Federal Ministers" of Satan. They are directly responsible to, and take orders from their "Prime Minister" or "President"—the devil.
7. "What the pioneer of the term, Peter Wagner, and others call "strategic-level spiritual warfare" is praying against these territorial spirits, seeking to "map" their strategies over given locations by discerning their names and what they use to keep people in bondage, and then to bind them in turn so that evangelism may go unhindered. The idea of "spiritual mapping" is one in which people research an area and try to identify the spirit(s) who are in charge over it so that "smart-bomb" praying may loosen the hold of territorial spirits over the people in a territory who may then come to Christ more freely" (Lausanne 2004).
8. At the same time, it puts a totally new spin on de Certeau's "Walking in the City." As Mbembe says, "walking the city" as a figure of "striating openness and flow" depends on "a whole series of rules, conventions, and institutions of regulation and control." In order to walk like de Certeau or Benjamin, certain literal and metaphorical "rules of walking" must be in place. People don't *flâne* or stroll, or even walk, in Lagos. They trek, they rush from place to place, dash across expressways and fight for seats in taxis and buses. From the perspective of the state's rational plan, dashing is not "walking properly." The current governor of Lagos has created a police corps called "Kick Against Indiscipline" that forces people to use the overhead bridges and queue for buses. However, purposeless strolling is not proper walking either. The one time I tried to take a leisurely evening stroll near the lagoon in Lagos, I got arrested at gunpoint.
9. Arowobusoye, *Powerful Prayers for Deliverance and Total Breakthrough*, 43–44.

References

Agamben, G. (2005). *The Time That Remains: A Commentary on the Letter to the Romans.* Stanford, CA: Stanford University Press.

———. (2007). *Profanations.* New York: Zone Books.

Arowobusoye, S. (1999). *Powerful Prayers for Deliverance and Total Breakthrough.* Ibadan, Nigeria: Gospel Teachers Fellowship International.

Badiou, A. (1999). *Manifesto for Philosophy.* New York: SUNY Press.

Benjamin, W. (1999). *The Arcades Project.* (trans. R. Tiedemann). Boston: MIT Press.

Buck-Morss, S. (2002). *Dreamworld and Catastrophe: The Passing of Mass Utopia in East and West.* Cambridge MA: MIT Press.

Burgess, R., Knibbe, K., and Quaas, A. (2010). "Nigerian-Initiated Pentecostal Churches as a Social Force in Europe: The Case of the Redeemed Christian Church of God." *PentecoStudies* 9(3): 97–121.

Congress for Progressive Change. (February 7, 2011). http://buhari4change.com/?p=298. Accessed April 21, 2011.

Corten, A. (1997). "Pentecôtisme et politique en Amérique latine." *Problèmes d'Amérique latine* 24: 17–31.

Davis, M. (2004). "Planet of Slums: Urban Involution and the Informal Proletariat." *New Left Review* 26: 5–34.

———. (2006). *Planet of Slums.* London: Verso.

de Certeau, M. (1984). "Walking in the City." *The Practice of Everyday Life.* Berkeley, CA: University of California Press.

Derrida, J. (2001). "Above All, No Journalists!" In de Vries, H. and Weber, S. eds, *Religion and Media*, pp. 56–93. Stanford, CA: Stanford University Press.

———. (2002). "Faith and Knowledge: The Two Sources of 'Religion' at the Limits of Reason Alone." In Anidjar, G., ed, *Acts of Religion*, pp. 40–101. New York: Routledge.

———. (2005). *On Touching—Jean-Luc Nancy.* Stanford, CA: Stanford University Press.

Foucault, M. (2001). *Herméneutique du Sujet. Cours au Collège de France, 1981–1982.* Paris: Gallimard/Seuil.

Gandy, M. (2006). "Learning from Lagos." *New Left Review* 33(4): 37–52.

Harvey, D. (2000). *Spaces of Hope.* Berkeley, CA: University of California Press.

Haynes, J. (2007). "Nollywood in Lagos, Lagos in Nollywood Films." *Africa Today* 54(2): 131–150.

Heidegger, M. (1971). "Building, Dwelling, Thinking." *Poetry, Language, Thought*, (trans. A. Hofstadter). New York: Harper Colophon Books.

Holvast, R. (2008). "Spiritual Mapping: The Turbulent Career of a Contested American Missionary Paradigm, 1989–2005." PhD diss., University of Utrecht.

Kaplan, R. (2000). *The Coming Anarchy: Shattering the Dreams of the Post Cold War.* New York: Vintage Books.

Koolhaas, R. (2004). "Fragments of a Lecture on Lagos." *Documenta* 11 Platform 4: 175–177.

Larkin, B. (2008). *Signal and Noise: Media, Infrastructure and Urban Culture in Nigeria.* Durham, NC: Duke University Press.

Lausanne Committee for World Evangelism. (2004). *Prayer in Evangelism.* Lausanne Occasional Paper No. 42. http://www.lausanne.org/en/documents/lops/857-lop-42.html. Accessed April 21, 2011.

Marshall, R. (2009). *Political Spiritualities: The Pentecostal Revolution in Nigeria.* Chicago, IL: University of Chicago Press.

———. (2010). "The Sovereignty of Miracles: Pentecostal Political Theology in Nigeria." *Constellations* 17(2): 197–223.

Mbembe, A. and Nuttal, S. (2004). "Writing the World from an African Metropolis." *Public Culture* 16(3): 347–372.

Meyer, B. (2006). "Impossible Representations: Pentecostalism, Vision and Video Technology in Ghana." In Meyer, B. and Moors, A., eds, *Religion, Media, and the Public Sphere*, pp. 290–312. Bloomington, IN: Indiana University Press.

———. (2010). "Aesthetics of Persuasion: Global Christianity and Pentecostalism's Sensational Forms." *South Atlantic Quarterly* 109(4): 741–763.

Naas, M. 2012. *Miracle and Machine: Jacques Derrida and the Two Sources of Religion, Science, and the Media*. New York: Fordham University Press.

Ojewale, M. O. (1989). *A Call to Prayer for Nigeria*. Lagos: Peace and Salvation Publishers.

O'Neill, K. (2012). "The Soul of Security: Corporatism, Christianity, and Control in Postwar Guatemala." *Social Text* 32(2): 21–42.

Osundare, N. (2012). "Why We No Longer Blush." Guest Lecture, Save Nigeria Group Event, "Why We No Longer Blush: Corruption as the Grand Commander of the Federal Republic of Nigeria" Lagos, July 9, 2012. Accessed July 11, 2012: http://savenigeriagroup.com/.

Packer, G. (2006). "The Megacity: Decoding the Chaos of Lagos." *New Yorker Magazine* November 13, 2006.

Pithouse, R. (2006). "Thinking Resistance in the Shantytown." *Mute Magazine* 2(3), August. http://www.metamute.org/editorial/articles/thinking-resistance-shanty-town.

Rapu, T. (2002). "Dealing with the Prince Over Lagos." Sermon, This Present House. July 12, 2002. http://www.thispresenthouse.org/home/firstword.cfm?ContentID=241. Accessed February 9, 2008.

———. An Eye for an Eye. House of Virtue, Blog; January 11, 2012. http://house-ofvirtue.blogspot.ca/2012/01/eye-for-eye-by-pastor-tony-rapu.html. Accessed June 9, 2012.

Simone, A. M. (2001). "On the Worlding of African Cities." *African Studies Review* 44: 15–41.

Ukah, A. (2008). *A New Paradigm of Pentecostal Power: A Study of the Redeemed Christian Church of God in Nigeria*. Trenton, NJ: Africa World Press.

UN-Habitat. (2003). *The Challenge of the Slums: Global Report on Human Settlements 2003*. London: UN-Habitat.

Vanguard. (2012). "SSS Questions Pastor Bakare over Sermon." *Vanguard* July 23, 2012.

Wagner, P. C., ed. (1991). *Engaging the Enemy: How to Fight and Defeat Territorial Spirits*. Ventura, CA: Regal Books.

———. (1993). *Breaking Strongholds in Your City: How to Use Spiritual Mapping to Make Your Prayers More Strategic, Effective, and Targeted*. Ventura, CA: Regal Books.

———. (1996). *Confronting the Powers: How the New Testament Church Experienced the Power of Strategic-Level Spiritual Warfare*. Ventura, CA: Regal Books.

Wariboko, N. (2011) *The Pentecostal Principle: Ethical Methodology in the New Spirit*. Grand Rapids, MI: Eerdmans.

———. (2012). *The Spell of the Invisible: Pentecostal Spirituality in Nigeria*. unpublished book manuscript.

5

The Road to Redemption: Performing Pentecostal Citizenship in Lagos*

Adedamola Osinulu

Arrival

Every month, in ever-increasing numbers, several hundred thousand residents of the Nigerian City of Lagos set out in a search for the transcendent on the expressway that stretches northward out of the city. Believers from many other parts of the country and, indeed, the globe join them. These pilgrims are on their way to Redemption Camp, an outpost of the Redeemed Christian Church of God (RCCG) located on Kilometer 46 of the 120-km (75-mile) Lagos–Ibadan Expressway. Along the way, they are likely to cross paths with worshippers traveling to other religious sites. There are several camps along the expressway including the Deeper Life Bible Conference Center constructed by the Deeper Life Bible Church at Kilometer 42 (right next to Redemption Camp) and Prayer City built and operated by Mountain of Fire and Miracles Ministries at Kilometer 12.[1]

These massive camps are only one symptom of the advent and popularity of Pentecostal Christianity in this part of the world. This form of Christianity, although often defined by its commitment to the ontological reality of Christianity's Holy Ghost, can also be properly marked by its commitment to the performance of divine power through believers' bodies. Throughout Lagos, Pentecostalism's Holy Ghost has become manifest, even as that city has witnessed unprecedented population growth and its infrastructure has become overwhelmed. Pentecostalism's influence can be found on the streets in the form of colorful posters, billboards, and banners advertising upcoming events and various venues. Moreover, it can be found in the city's market places where Pentecostal movies, audio recordings, and publications are sold alongside their secular equivalents. Even in the city's most intimate spaces, the influence of Pentecostalism is felt through the fervent prayers that emerge in the impenetrable language of the Holy Ghost. In addition, virtually every street corner seems to be anchored by a Pentecostal venue of one sort or another. However, it is the massive Pentecostal sites like Redemption Camp and their ability to attract innumerable throngs that most powerfully illuminate the unprecedented scale and rapid emergence of this social phenomenon.

These sites, and their immense congregational capacity, raise important questions about the nature of the gatherings held therein and the broader social milieu out of which they emerge. In particular, we can ask what sort of relationship exists between the often challenging urban conditions of Lagos and the efflorescence of these Pentecostal sites. Further, what forms of belonging or models of citizenship can be found within these religious spaces? In the pages ahead, I seek to answer these questions by examining the nature of the spaces that the Pentecostals have produced in and around Lagos. Using Redemption Camp as a case study, I explore the notion of *performative Pentecostal space*—a space that serves as a site for the re-enactment of one's embodied lived experience in the context of ritual. Such a re-enactment opens the possibility for individual transformation by itself, metamorphosing into a rehearsal for future social mobility. Through the deployment of ardent supplications and cathartic corporeal performances, believers creatively re-imagine their lives, turning the Pentecostal site into a staging ground for desired socioeconomic repositioning. Furthermore, we find that the expressions of desire enacted in the context of ritual performance at Redemption Camp can be understood as a performative representation of power relations with the state—a performance in which the church and its officials stand in proxy for the government and its agents. To that end, the Pentecostals, although ostensibly apolitical, present a model of citizenship in which political action is mediated through religious ritual.

The Redeemed Christian Church of God

The Redeemed Christian Church of God (RCCG) is an indigenously founded body started in 1952 by Josiah Olufemi Akindayomi who had abandoned the worship of the Yoruba god Ogun to join the Christian Missionary Society (CMS). He later joined the Eternal Sacred Order of the Cherubim and Seraphim (C&S), one of the African Initiated Churches (AICs) in southwestern Nigeria (Olaleru 2007: 68). Akindayomi left C&S to form a small prayer band, which he called *Egbe Ogo Oluwa* (the Society for the Glory of God). He later renamed it the Redeemed Christian Church of God, and grew it into a regional

Yoruba church with approximately 40 parishes at the time of his death in 1980. His handpicked successor, Enoch Adejare Adeboye, who took over in 1981, was a university professor of Mathematics.

In the three decades since assuming leadership, Adeboye has expanded the 40 parishes he inherited into an estimated 15,000 parishes today (RCCG n.d.: 14).[2] His transformation of RCCG from a regional Yoruba church into a global organization was achieved through a process of internal reform that included the introduction of "model" parishes:

> The Church had been predominantly traditional with Yoruba language as the primary means of expression...But the church had also begun to witness an influx of more educated people and professionals of diverse cultural backgrounds. To take care of this new breed of worshippers, the 'model' parishes were introduced while the traditional or 'classical' parishes as they were referred to continued to cater for their own members...Both models have, however, begun to witness a convergence in recent years. (RCCG 2008: 7–8)

This development, importantly, allowed the church to package itself within an image of modernity. Further, the introduction of the model parishes allowed RCCG's demographic composition to more accurately reflect the socioeconomic profile of Nigerian society.[3] In addition, the church formulated a group—Christ the Redeemer's Friends Universal (CRFU)—specifically targeted at the society's elite with the goal of "mak[ing] a forum available to the people who are high in society to mix together in the love of God [and] to give them an opportunity to share their problems among people who are their equals or almost equals" (RCCG n.d.: 32). As is clear from RCCG's own words, and as will become clearer as we move through Redemption Camp, RCCG is more interested in mirroring Nigeria's social structure than disrupting it.

Redemption Camp

In addition to modernizing the organization, one of Adeboye's innovations was the purchase, in 1983, of a 4.25-acre property along the Lagos–Ibadan Expressway that has now become the 850-acre Redemption Camp (Marshall 2009: 230, Ukah 2008: 259). The camp's primary function is to host three organization-wide events in RCCG's liturgical calendar (separate from, and supplementary to, the smaller gatherings that occur in its parishes across the globe). The events are:

the Holy Ghost Service (HGS; held on the first Friday of every month save December), the Annual Convention (typically held in the second week of August), and the Holy Ghost Congress (HGC; usually held in the third week of December). Of these three, the Holy Ghost Congress and the Annual Convention attract the largest crowds because they are annual events, whereas the Holy Ghost Service is held monthly.

Even before one arrives at Redemption Camp for one of its events, the camp's presence reverberates in one's consciousness, starting with advertisements disseminated through newspapers and on television, as well as billboards, stickers, flyers, and other promotional materials (figure 5.1). Furthermore, RCCG members are encouraged to and actively invite people within their sphere of influence—friends, relatives, co-workers, and so on.[4] If one has accepted one of these invitations or has been persuaded by the ubiquitous advertisements, one is likely to be caught up in the traffic that is heading into the camp from the expressway. It does not help that portions of the Lagos–Ibadan Expressway are periodically in disrepair due to the constant traffic of 18-wheelers transporting goods. To ameliorate some of that congestion, RCCG has constructed a new 5-mile road connecting the camp to the town of Simawa, which Lagosians can approach by going through Ikorodu (a city to the northeast of metropolitan Lagos) and avoid the expressway entirely.

Figure 5.1 RCCG events are aggressively advertised across a variety of media before the events. Photo: Author.

In order to accommodate the immense crowds that gather at Redemption Camp during these events, RCCG has in place several administrative, commercial, and municipal facilities. The camp is home to the church's international headquarters (distinct from its national headquarters which is in the Ebute Metta neighborhood of Lagos) and also has office facilities that temporarily accommodate church officials during events. Municipal services on the site include a post office, water-processing equipment, and power-generating facilities to supplement the often-interrupted supply from the national grid. Commercial services include six banks, two bookstores, several shops, and a variety of restaurants. These commercial services expand considerably during large events through the use of temporary kiosks, tents, and mobile units. To accommodate and entertain visitors to the camp, there is an International Guest House, a Presidential Lodge, Guest Chalets, and a facility called Redemption Resort. In addition to temporary lodging, the camp features a housing estate where properly accredited members can purchase the right to build on a plot of land provided they complete the structure within an allotted timeframe and provide a room to accommodate an RCCG worker. In addition, there is an estate that consists of prebuilt houses constructed by a developer. To be clear, these facilities can neither accommodate the massive crowds that descend on the camp, nor are they intended to. As such, commercial activity spills over into the neighboring towns, and many attendees simply sleep in their vehicles or in the congregational spaces during multi-day gatherings.

Redemption Camp is, moreover, the home of several of RCCG's ancillary institutions. These include Redeemer's University for Nations (RUN), Redeemer's High School (RHS), and the Redeemed Christian Bible College. Redeemer University's student hostels are appropriated as guest accommodation during major events. Based on the extent of these facilities, one could say that Redemption Camp is indeed a city in miniature and it is, in fact, sometimes referred to as "Redemption City" by RCCG.

The Congress Arena

Despite these various facilities, the Camp's main purpose remains religious gatherings and, as such, congregational spaces are the most significant structures on site. One of these is the Congress Arena, an impossibly large industrial building made up of massive steel columns arranged in a seemingly endless grid to hold up dozens of wide gable roofs (figure 5.2). Each of the modules of this structure spans about 118 feet in both directions. Across its width, there are 13 bays, leading to an overall dimension

Figure 5.2 Redemption Camp's main congregational space, the Congress Arena, a vast structure that seats at least 450,000 attendees. Photo: Author.

of 0.3 miles (half a kilometer). Lengthwise, the building extends for 31 bays giving an overall length of 0.7 miles (just over 1 km). Extrapolating from the seating arrangement used in the forward bays, I estimate that the building can seat approximately 450,000 congregants. For that purpose, a sea of white plastic chairs covers the first third of the space and wooden benches take up most of the rest of the space.

Worship in the Congress Arena is nothing if not participatory. There was a carnivalesque atmosphere that pervaded the evening sessions of the 2009 Annual Convention and which resonated with Durkheim's observation about the intoxicating nature of crowds:

> The very act of congregating is an exceptionally powerful stimulant. Once the individuals are gathered together, a sort of electricity is generated from their closeness and quickly launches them to an extraordinary height of exaltation. Every emotion expressed resonates without interference in consciousness that is wide open to external impression, each one echoing the others. (Durkheim 1995: 218)

As music was generated from the front of the arena and transmitted through the surrounding speakers, congregants participated fully, contributing their own music with tambourines, beaded gourd rattles (*shekere*), whistles, and hand claps. On the floor of the arena, congregants were free to dance without restraint or even to run down the aisles in exuberance, as occurred in many instances. As I clapped along to the singing one evening, a young boy of about 8 or 10, who was just a few seats from me, enthusiastically blew his whistle in rhythm to the beat of the music. Throughout the massive crowd, other whistles pierced the evening air. During transitions between sessions, it was not uncommon for an individual somewhere in the crowd to shout out a call and for the crowd to respond back as in the case of one congregant who during a lull shouted out, "Who did it?" to which those within earshot yelled out "Jesus!" In these actions—the participation of the congregation in the liturgy and the degree to which it is permitted by the church, but even further, the search by congregation members for gaps in the ritual where they can insert themselves—we see a dialog between the laity and the clergy. As Bell puts it, "The deployment of ritualization, consciously or unconsciously, is the deployment of a particular construction of power relationships of domination, consent, and resistance" (1992: 206). In addition, this back and forth serves to inform the observer that, although at points the individuals seem to dissolve into a unitary organism, there are many individuals present here, and theirs is a complex set of motivations.

If one has come to Redemption Camp to escape from the overpopulation of the city, one has certainly come to the wrong place, because here, one is always aware of the crowd. Furthermore, where one is positioned on the grounds of the Congress Arena determines the quality of one's experience. Whenever I was distant from the front of the Arena or even one of several video screens placed around the Arena, my experience was considerably degraded. This gave the space a clear sense of center and periphery where proximity to the center—be that a video screen, audio speaker, or altar—was a more privileged experience. Space within the arena, therefore, became a resource to be competed for. Like many in the mass of humanity that surrounded me during events here, I often tried to secure my piece of sacred real estate with a personal item, in my case, a piece of cloth tied to my white plastic chair. One day during the 2009 Annual Convention, I returned to my spot to find that my chair had been commandeered, along with a number of other seats, to accommodate newly ordained church officials. Attendees' hold on their little piece of this grand space is always precarious; if not properly husbanded and without the right amount of good fortune, losing one's place in the space (and one's symbolic proximity to divine providence) is an ever-present possibility.

The ability to secure good seating in the Congress Arena correlates with one's social standing. Those with the proper relationships (invited guests and so on) have access to reserved seats near the front of the arena. Ushers and security officials diligently guard those reserved seats and demand the proper accreditation before granting access. This makes an excerpt from Adeboye's text *When You Need a Miracle* particularly illuminating:

> Reserved seats are kept for outstanding people. If you are average you need to go earlier for any function before you can find a seat. It is better to stay on top than to stay at the bottom. The river flows from top to bottom. Average people generally drink from waters which outstanding people pass on as leftovers. (Adeboye 2008 [2004]: 26)[5]

Although he wrote this passage to make a larger point about social standing, his words are literally played out on the floor of the arena (figure 5.3). In parallel fashion, those with adequate resources and proper connections can secure housing in the limited hostels or guest quarters in contrast to those who sleep underneath the roof of the Arena or elsewhere on the open campground. However, even more strikingly, qualified church members with enough resources can purchase land or houses in one of the church-owned housing estates on the vast campus.

Figure 5.3 Seating in the Congress Arena is a resource to be competed for. Photo: Author.

The competition for seating and unequal access to preferred seating make it clear that the camp is not some sort of vision of utopian comfort for the majority of attendees, nor is it an argument for a new collective socioeconomic order. Rather, it is a reconstruction and even an intensification of the spatial dynamics in the city. In such a model, the huge crowd present at Redemption Camp mirrors the large population of the city and makes an analogous demand on scarce resources and infrastructure. Furthermore, efforts by the relevant authorities to maintain a degree of formality and order is in constant tension against the needs of the individuals in the social body to clear a space for themselves. As such, the church officials who confiscated my seat to meet the official needs of the church are not unlike the officials of the state who demolish structures deemed illegal by state planning agencies—a frequent occurrence in nearby Lagos.

Therefore, we find that the social structure of the city is maintained and even reinforced on the grounds of the camp. Catherine Bell writes that part of the nature of ritual is that it reproduces the power structures of the society from which it emerges,

> [Ritualization] produces and objectifies constructions of power (via the schemes that organize its environment), which the social agent then reembodies. Ritualized agents do not see themselves as projecting schemes; they see themselves only acting in a socially instinctive response to how things are. Thus, the production and objectification of structured and structuring schemes in the environment involve a misrecognition of the source and arbitrariness of these schemes. (1992: 206)

She further explains that such schemes are experienced as having emerged from forces beyond the community such as its god, tradition, or the larger social organization that subsumes the community. Therefore, the schemes are perceived as illuminating the nature of the cosmos (Ibid: 206–207). In other words, the ritual environment and the sacred narratives become intertwined and self-reinforcing. The primary means of disseminating those sacred narratives is the pulpit of the Congress Arena.

The Pulpit

The climactic moment of virtually all events held in the Congress Arena is the arrival of The General Overseer—Pastor E. A. Adeboye—at the pulpit. He is usually preceded by a performance by the 2,500-member choir led by the church's preeminent saxophonist Pastor Kunle Ajayi.

Ajayi's performances are particularly well received by the congregation as they get a chance to sing along when he plays their favorite choruses. As such, by the time Pastor Adeboye comes to the pulpit and his voice rings out over the P. A. system with his trademark rallying cry, "Let Somebody Shout Hallelujah!" the crowd is thoroughly engaged in the proceedings. Although several speakers would have occupied the pulpit before Adeboye's arrival, it is with his presence that the pulpit achieves its true purpose, for Adeboye's charisma is at the center of the perception of power that many believe is present at Redemption Camp. Asked to account for the popularity of the Holy Ghost Congress, the pastor of the RCCG's Lagos 3 Province, Brown Oyitso, put Adeboye firmly at the center of people's attraction to the site:

> One word: emancipation. Where the sugar is, ants gather. *They are pulled towards the Holy Ghost Congress because there is a man of God there with an anointing that breaks yokes.* They are pulled there because they want to be saved. They are tired of the other kind of life. They want to come into the kingdom of God. They want spiritual emancipation. They want to be born again. Those that are born again want to be free from poverty. (Personal interview with Oyitso, *emphasis added*)[6]

For those supplicants, Adeboye's presence is the key to Redemption Camp's efficacy.

Adeboye is a particularly gifted narrator and storyteller. His ability to effectively communicate his message has played no small part in the conversion of new followers into his fold. Unlike many Pentecostal pastors whose performance from the pulpit involves much shouting and gesticulation, Adeboye speaks in a calm, reassuring baritone. His sermons weave his personal experiences with biblical narratives and exegesis. Furthermore, they are sprinkled with promises of divine favor to the congregants and his words are couched in personal terms—"There is someone here tonight who..."—that pierce through the anonymity of the massive crowds. During his sermons, he often pauses as though interrupted and listens before passing on the message he explains he has just received from God. As such, during his sermon on the sixth night of the 2009 Annual Convention, he made declarations like, "There is someone here tonight whose destiny is about to change." His sermons, moreover, are bookended by prayer sessions he leads the congregation through, guiding their loud, simultaneous prayers with periodic and repeated encouragement.

Adeboye is considered by many in his congregation to be both a prophet whose pronouncements are accurate because they are revealed to him by God and a mediator who is especially qualified to intercede to God on their behalf because of his close relationship with God. Furthermore, as Oyitso noted, he is considered by many in the congregation to be full of divine power or "anointing." Asonzeh Ukah reports that in the old auditorium, after Adeboye departed the stage, people would rush to the area where he had previously stood (Ukah 2008: 264). In the Congress Arena, the pulpit is not directly accessible to congregants, but I witnessed this phenomenon at an outreach event—Let's-Go-A-Fishing—that RCCG held in December 2008 at the Nigerian Police Academy. The moment the service was over, a number of attendees rushed over to the temporary stage where Adeboye had stood moments before so that they could pray there and, thereby, access his power. At work here is the Pentecostal understanding of divine power or "anointing" and how that can be transmitted through an "anointed man of God" and physical objects he comes into contact with. In Ukah's words, "anointing that is mediated through objects and items is supposed to bring about healings and deliverances" (Ibid.).

The Altar

The pulpit from which Adeboye preaches sits on a massive concrete cylinder that serves as the focal point of the whole space. The concrete platform is approximately 60 feet in diameter and rises approximately 16 feet above the floor of the Arena. The floor above the cylinder cantilevers by roughly 2 feet all the way around the cylinder, forming a circular platform along which colorful gauze fabrics are typically draped. The wall of the concrete cylinder is covered with turquoise glazed tiles. The area behind the pulpit and atop the concrete platform seats senior church functionaries and important visiting guests. On the same platform, and by the side of the pulpit, there is an ornate chair that Adeboye once revealed was reserved for Jesus. A lower and smaller circular platform is attached to the larger circular one (to the right of it if one were facing it). This smaller platform is the location from which various singers, musicians, and dancers perform. To the right of that platform, there is a set of bleachers that accommodates RCCG's 2,500-member choir. On the opposite side of the Altar is another set of bleachers that accommodates roughly the same number of officiating ministers who are just a fraction of the many RCCG pastors present for its largest gatherings.

The space between the Altar and the congregation is kept clear of any obstructions because it is periodically occupied by a variety of groups. The meaning of this open area becomes significant as the various groups that gather on it negotiate its meaning, marking it as a site of contestation within the larger space of Congress Arena. As Low and Lawrence-Zúñiga remind us, "contested spaces give material expression to and act as loci for creating and promulgating, countering, and negotiating dominant cultural themes that find expression in myriad aspects of social life" (2003: 18). Furthermore, as we observe these various groups articulating their desires in the context of ritual performance, we should keep in mind Catherine Bell's observation that "ritualization is first and foremost a strategy for the construction of certain types of power relationships effective within particular social organizations" (1992: 197).

Individual expression is brought to the fore at the Altar. On the afternoon of August 3, 2009, as I sat waiting for the Annual Convention's first evening service to start, there were approximately 30 people crowded around the massive altar. One of them was a young woman clad in an earth-colored wax print fabric who slammed her palms on the bench to reinforce each of her utterances. She soon got up and started pacing back and forth while bouncing rhythmically on her feet. She intermittently raised her arms upwards and wide, all the while shaking her head from side to side, her lips in motion. Similarly, a young man, perhaps in his twenties, stomped toward the altar and then away from it, his head crashing down in an emphatic nod with each step. Close by, a woman in her fifties was on her knees and her muscles contracted in rapid fashion as she literally vibrated her whole body. From the crowd, a female voice rang out in Yoruba "Jesu! Jesuuu O!…Oluwosan" ("Jesus! Jesuuus! Healer!").

I propose that these are not just expressions of material desire; there are also debates about existential questions embedded in believers' actions. Each of the players who is represented in the space before the Altar bring his or her own understanding of that space. They also hold a perspective on the nature of power and influence in their society. As Bell writes,

> It is in ritual that we can see a fundamental strategy of power. In ritualization, power is not external to its workings; it exists only insofar as it is constituted with and through the lived body, which is both the body of society and the social body. Ritualization is a strategic play of power, of domination and resistance, within the arena of the social body. (1992: 204)

Through their ritualization before the Altar, believers express a desire to negotiate power relations with the society from which they emerge.

This space in front of the Altar can, therefore, be understood as a product of that very society because it is where these believers, who are well aware of their place in the society and who are motivated by their belief that the Altar is a locus of divine power, stake their claim on a better life (figure 5.4).

It is not only these fervent supplicants who regularly contest the meaning of the Altar and its surrounding space. The most clear-cut event I observed of non-sanctioned use of the space was by a crowd of well over a hundred young men and women that rapidly swept through the space during the night of the October 2009 Holy Ghost Service. As the whole congregation sang and danced to the music emanating from the Altar, this cluster of young participants ran dancing through the aisles this way and that before suddenly breaking through the cordon of ushers securing the Altar clearing. They cheered and danced as they ran, literally somersaulting and tumbling, across the front of the

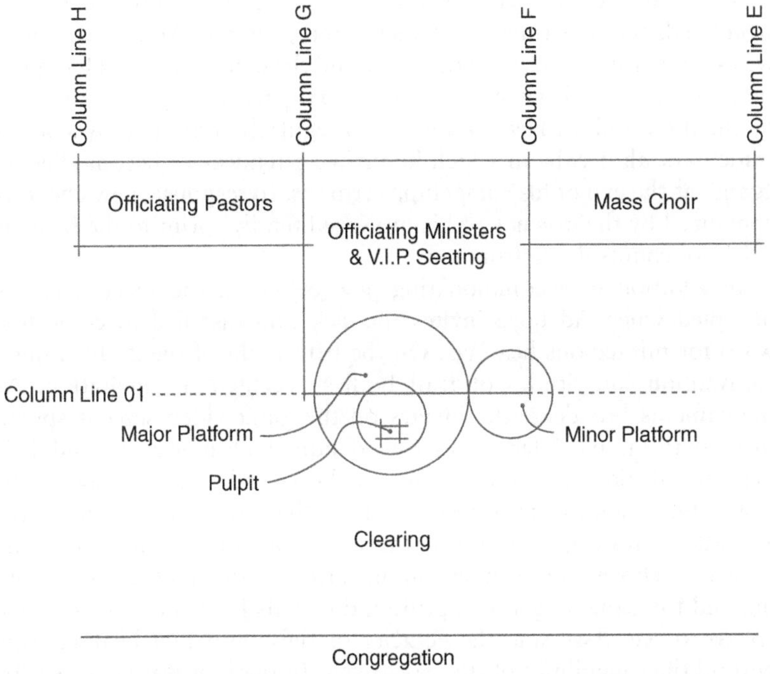

Figure 5.4 The focal point of Congress Arena is a massive concrete cylinder above which the pulpit sits. This altar takes on significance as it and the area around it becomes occupied by a variety of individuals and groups with their own interests. (Author's illustration).

Altar, much to the chagrin of the ushers.[7] Following some acknowledgement from the pulpit, they dissipated as quickly as it had formed. The formation and dissipation of this cluster of boisterous youth at this event points to the degree to which the order maintained during RCCG events comes from the crowds ascription of authority to RCCG and its agents; otherwise, how could control of so many be maintained by so few? There is, in other words, an acceptance of the social hierarchies that have been established by RCCG; yet, the youth demonstrated that such acceptance was not without limits. Bell's perspective that "a participant, as a ritualized agent and social body, naturally brings to such activities a self-constituting history that is a patchwork of compliance, resistance, misunderstanding, and a redemptive personal appropriation of the hegemonic order" proves to be true here (1992: 208). There is, so to speak, a tension between the participant's willing subordination to the power of the institution to generate social structure (in the guise of religious ritual) and her own claim on the purpose of the ritual.

So, what does RCCG itself intend the space to be used for? I had wondered, the first time that I visited the Congress Arena, why there was so much space between the Altar and the congregation. That question was answered when I saw how that space was quickly filled up by the thousands of new converts who regularly respond to Adeboye's trademark altar calls in which he invites attendees to become "born-again" at the end of his compelling sermons. In response, new converts convinced by the urgency of his message literally sprint to the front as Adeboye counts down from ten.

In addition to accommodating new believers, the space becomes occupied when Adeboye invites the sick and disabled to come forward for miraculous healings. On the fifth night of the 2009 Annual Convention, multitudes of frail bodies accepted his invitation. As the cameras broadcast the images on the giant video screens spread through the arena, Adeboye instructed individuals to leave behind their mechanical aids or sick beds. Several brave individuals followed his instructions, appearing to move without their aids. One of these was a toddler, whose appearance on the screen provoked a cheer from the crowd. Adeboye, in return, encouraged those individuals to keep moving and the cameramen to capture individuals he wanted the massive crowd to see. Assessing the veracity of these apparent healings was beyond the capabilities of this researcher. In truth, it was no easier for any of the several hundred thousand attendees that surrounded me. We could not, after all, go up to each person and interrogate him or her on his or her medical histories. Nor could we follow them around after the event to see how long said miracles are sustained. Rather, we had to make a determination of veracity based on the (insufficient) data at hand. However, the willingness to accept the veracity of the claim using the information at hand varies from person to person. One could say, then, that it was left to each individual to be convinced by the staging of the event.[8] To that extent, the degree to which the individual attendee wished to be swayed by the narrative being generated by the altar was up to him or her. Moreover, Adeboye's insistence that the cameras track those cases he felt would be compelling is an acknowledgement of the attendees' freedom to accept or reject the veracity of his claims. For those who wanted alternative narratives to the one being generated from the pulpit, there was a choice to notice, as I did, that not all who went forward appeared to have been healed. For instance, there was a young woman with atrophied legs I observed returning to her seat on the back of her helper, and another groaning woman who returned back down the aisle supported by two helpers on either side of her. What is undisputed is that the meaning of the Congress Arena and Redemption Camp, as a whole, is being intentionally constructed through the images being projected to the attendees and the reports broadcasted afterwards in newspapers and church publications. As one church official put it,

> What draws people, I believe, is the fact that they come and they see God in action. Things do happen, the lame walk, the blind see and they themselves experience miracles. And I believe it is the faith people experience that gives the activity publicity and that's what makes them come month after month, year after year, because the number is increasing.[9]

The efficacy of the site is, in other words, being produced through the practices that attendees observe and the narratives generated about those practices.

Nevertheless, meaning around the Altar is generated, not just by what happens in front of it, but what happens on top of it. During the various occasions I visited the site, the dignitaries sitting on the Altar have included guest ministers from Nigerian and international Christian organizations who have been invited to preach during RCCG events. However, it is not only men and women of the cloth who grace the Altar. Political officials of one kind or another frequently populate it. In December 2003, then president of Nigeria, Olusegun Obasanjo, spoke from the Redemption Camp's pulpit (Marshall 2009: 240). Between 2008 and 2009, I observed four state governors (of Lagos, Ogun, Ondo, and Taraba), as well as a special representative of then Vice President Goodluck Jonathan, seated atop the Altar. In December

2010, Goodluck Jonathan, who had now become the nation's president, attended the Holy Ghost Congress and sat next to Pastor and Mrs. Adeboye on the Altar (Olowu 2010). However, surpassing the actions of his twice-removed predecessor, he knelt in front of Pastor Adeboye to receive his blessings and the prayers of the congregation. It must be noted that the Nigerian elections were scheduled to take place only 4 months later—in April 2011—and Jonathan's presence at the camp is directly correlated to that contest.[10]

By submitting to Adeboye's prayers, Jonathan and political figures like him who attend events at Redemption Camp not only validate the charismatic authority of Adeboye, but also mark the grounds of Redemption Camp as a locus of power. In Ebenezer Obadare's words, "The image of President Goodluck Jonathan kneeling, as if in complete surrender, before the General Overseer of the Redeemed Christian Church of God, marks an epochal moment in the process of the pentecostalisation of our national life" (2010). We can say, then, that Jonathan and his fellow politicians designate this social space as more than just the space of the religious organization in question; rather, they situate it as a national social space. Through their actions, they confirm that the power relations being negotiated at this site include the relationship with the state and its agents, and not just the relationship between the congregation and the institution of the church.

Thus, we find at Congress Arena a variety of groups with various interests represented, each acting to produce meaning at the site. As Hilda Kuper argues, "the same site may be differently manipulated according to specific group interests, but the total spatial arrangements form a general network of communication" (Kuper 1972: 421). In the events I have described, we can clearly identify at least three parties, each of which can be further disaggregated: the supplicants who descend on the site to make requests of God; the agents of the state, such as the president, who come to seek the validation of the congregation and the officers of the church; and, finally, church functionaries who present themselves as mediators to God on behalf of the congregation but who, I argue, are also acting as proxies for the state. To that extent, we can interpret the nature of the exchange happening at Redemption Camp as a dialog between the society and its constituent parts.

It is the desire to move from the margins of society to more durable postures that has brought many supplicants to this site. For those who are participants in the middle class (and Adeboye himself would be a prime example of this), the mechanism by which they were able to arrive there included such things as access to education and proper healthcare. To put it in stark terms, the government is responsible for providing or catalyzing the provision of the sorts of services that enable wealth creation; however, in a society where, as one person put it, each household is its own local government, responsibility has shifted to the individual. One might say, then, that many of the requests that are being expressed at the Altar really should be directed toward the state house or the Presidential Villa, as the case may be. It is fair to assume that, if a crowd of the same magnitude as one finds at Redemption Camp should gather outside the Presidential Villa, making the exact same requests as they make at the camp, and maintaining the same ferocity with which those requests are demonstrated at Redemption Camp, they would be met at the gates by several battalions of riot police. Indeed, this is where ritualization comes in because it performs best in situations where "the relations of power being negotiated are based…on indirect claims of power conferred" and "when the hegemonic order being experienced must be rendered to be personally redemptive" (Bell 1992: 116).

In lieu of appearing at the state house, the vast crowd makes its desires known at the Congress Arena and, at the end of their vigorous demonstrations, Pastor Adeboye emerges with guarantees from God that their desires will be met. He issues palliative promises such as, "Before the end of this month you are going to shout for joy" or "After tonight, you will not suffer another defeat" and "Tonight by the time you're going home, you will have a taste of glory." In that exchange, ostensibly between the people and God, between God and Adeboye, and, finally, between Adeboye and the people, we see a performance of the relationship between the state and the people, wherein Adeboye is a stand-in for the leadership of the state. His perceived moral integrity serves as an alternative to their perceived corruption, and his caring attitude replaces the state's perceived disdain for its citizens. With such an understanding, Jonathan's appearance on the Altar can be seen as an explicit expression of the relationship between the church and the state that had previously only been implied at the site.

However, as we have seen from those congregants gathered around the Altar, "The efficacy of ritualization as a power strategy lies not only in the domination it affords, but in the resistance as well" (Bell 1992: 215). In other words, even as the attendees are conforming to the social structures reproduced at the camp, they are expressing a desire to push beyond them. Clearly, there is a dialectical relationship here between subordination and resistance, and we see the negotiation of that power relationship being played out in the ritualization on the site.

What, then, is the relationship between the space that has been produced and the efficacy of the ritual? One could argue that, in the same way that a stage set must create an illusion of believability, the sacred site must provide an atmosphere conducive to the production of the appropriate "moods and motivations" (Geertz 1973: 90). By replicating the difficult conditions of the city, RCCG promotes an intensification of believers' feelings about their socioeconomic conditions, rendering their ritual performance a genuine refraction of their daily lives.

The efficacy of the site, then, is derived from its believability as a setting for ritual, much in the way a stage set allows the audience to enter the imaginary of the performance. Are the feelings that are provoked genuine enough to engage the imagination of the attendee and make her into a believer? Is Adeboye a credible interlocutor between the people and the abstract conception of power—whether that is God or society? Redemption Camp, I argue, is efficacious because it is able to foster an accurate performance of believers' daily lives and conceal the true nature of their demands in the cocoon of ritual.

Departure

In his book *Last Days*, an exegesis on the New Testament book of Revelation, Pastor Adeboye adopts and extends John the Divine's vision of a post-apocalyptic future in which social solidarity reaches its apotheosis in a transcendent city of God, "We will be worshipping God forever in the New Jerusalem coming down from God, prepared as a bride for her husband…The New Jerusalem is called the city of the living God. This means that God will be there. Jesus will also be there. The angels will be there too" (Adeboye 2002 [1994]: 248). Lagos, because of the difficult physical and social challenges its residents face, has often been described in apocalyptic terms (Koolhaas et al. 2001: 177; Packer 2006: 62). Nevertheless, it is clear from our observations at Redemption Camp that what RCCG has constructed is not a utopian alternative to the rigors of Lagos's urbanism. The disjuncture between Adeboye's "New Jerusalem" and the reality at the camp should make clear that his goal is not to create change through collective action. The immensity of the crowds at Redemption Camp is not the result of a social group working toward a common goal; rather, it is a refraction of the existing social order from the nearby city (and Nigerian society more broadly) into Pentecostal Space.

There is, therefore, a paradox at work at Redemption Camp. The immense crowd does not signify collective action, but points to the possibility of individual transformation. For the individual, the crowd is the background against which she foregrounds her own desires and dreams. It is through the presence of the crowd, that she is able to situate herself in the social order, and by which she knows in which direction she wants to propel herself. Through the deployment of Christianity's sacred narratives, the charismatic leader's encouragement, and all the performative instruments that are rendered available at the Pentecostal site, she is able to imagine her own "New Jerusalem."

RCCG's example at Redemption Camp provides a way forward in the study of African cities by pointing us toward the examination of social spaces in those cities. It is not sufficient to enumerate the ways in which Africans make do amid difficult urban conditions. Rather, it is essential to understand how they carry their experiences with them into the city's social spaces wherein they re-imagine their lives using intellectual and performative mechanisms provided by their social movements. At Redemption Camp, Pentecostalism's openness to performance has allowed us to witness how individuals genuinely express their embodied lived experiences. What spaces like this then offer us is an opportunity to see how Africans themselves understand their societies.

Notes

*The research in this chapter was funded by the Social Science Research Council (SSRC) through its International Dissertation Research Fellowship (IDRF). Funding was also provided by the UCLA International Institute through its Summer Fieldwork Fellowship for International Studies. I would also like to extend my appreciation to Pastor Enoch Adeboye of the Redeemed Christian Church of God for granting me access to the RCCG congregation and to Pastor Tokunbo Olorunnimbe for patiently facilitating my many requests. Thanks also go to Mrs. M. Adediran for her kind hospitality while I was at Redemption Camp. Finally, I am grateful to the many congregants who extended their hand of friendship in my direction.

1. Not only Christian groups have set up shop here. NASFAT, the Nasrul-Lahi-L-Fatih Society, an Islamic group owns a 133-acre property near the Mowe section of expressway.
2. A precise count on the number of parishes is difficult to obtain. Another RCCG publication, for instance, puts the number of parishes in Nigeria at 10,000 (RCCG 2008: 9). Speaking during the 2009 Annual Convention, Pastor Adeboye put the number of parishes in Nigeria as 7,000 and noted that the church had a presence in 151 countries.
3. It must be noted that there are geographic imbalances in RCCG's national composition, partly because of its Yoruba origins but also because of the Islam-North/Christianity-South split in Nigeria. RCCG acknowledges this in its own publications, "The growth pattern has not been uniform across the nation. The encouraging overall growth for Nigeria has been mainly due to the strength of the church in Lagos State, the South-West, and some other states like Delta, Edo, Rivers and the Federal Capital Territory, Abuja" (Oyitso 2009).

4. RCCG's mission statement enumerates among its goals "To have a member of RCCG in every family of all nations" and to accomplish that by "plant[ing] churches within five minutes walking distance in every city and town of developing countries and within five minutes driving distance in ... developed countries" (RCCG n.d.: 10).
5. Adeboye, before his rise as university professor and Pentecostal pastor, had been born into a family that, by his description, was "one of the poorest families in the world" (Adeboye 2008 [2004]: 30). His insistence on an education and his academic brilliance allowed him to transcend that poverty (Ibid: 31).
6. Personal Interview with Brown Oyitso, December 11, 2008, Lagos.
7. Because this particular Holy Ghost Service had been preceded by the Youth Convention, the night was dedicated to "the youth," therefore, their abundant numbers and the exuberance that resulted in the flash mob.
8. I do not mean to imply a falsehood in my use of the term "staging" here; rather, I wish to demonstrate that regardless of their veracity, the sequence of events have to appear not to be falsified in order to be accepted as true by observers.
9. Personal interview with Felix Ohiwerei, March 30, 2010, Lagos.
10. President Goodluck Jonathan also attended the 2012 Holy Ghost Congress.

References

Adeboye, E. A. (2002 [1994]). *The Last Days: A Study of the Book of Revelation*. Lagos: The Book Ministry.

———. (2008 [2004]). *When You Need a Miracle*. Mowe: C.R.M. Bookshop.

Bell, C. M. (1992). *Ritual Theory, Ritual Practice*. New York: Oxford University Press.

Durkheim, E. (1995). *The Elementary Forms of Religious Life*. New York: Free Press.

Geertz, C. (1973). *The Interpretation of Cultures; Selected Essays*. New York: Basic Books.

Koolhaas, R., Boeri, S., Kwinter, S.,Tazi, N., and Obrist, H-U. (2001) *Mutations*. Bordeaux: Arc en rêve centre d'architecture.

Kuper, H. (1972). "The Language of Sites in the Politics of Space." *American Anthropologist* 74(3): 411–425.

Low, S. M. and Lawrence-Zúñiga, D. (2003). *The Anthropology of Space and Place: Locating Culture*. Malden, MA: Blackwell Publishing.

Marshall, R. (2009). *Political Spiritualities: The Pentecostal Revolution in Nigeria*. Chicago: University of Chicago Press.

Obadare, E. (2010). "Pastor Adeboye and the Nigerian state." *Next*, Newspaper. http://234next.com/csp/cms/sites/Next/Opinion/5658678-184/pastor_adeboye_and_the_nigerian_state.csp. Accessed April 11, 2011.

Olaleru, O. (2007). *The Seed in the Ground*. Lagos: Father of Lights Publishers.

Olowu, I. (2010). "Jonathan Visits Redemption Camp." *Next*, Newspaper, http://234next.com/csp/cms/sites/Next/Home/5655441-146/jonathan_visits_redemption_camp__.csp. Accessed April 11, 2011.

Oyitso, B. (2009). "RCCG Missions: The Next Level." *Redemption Light* 13(6): 40, 88.

Packer, G. (2006). "The Megacity: Decoding the Chaos of Lagos." *The New Yorker*, November 13.

RCCG. (2008). *Holy Ghost Congress 2008 Programme*. Lagos: The Redeemed Christian Church of God.

———. (2009). "57th Annual Convention." *Redemption Light* 13(7): 30.

———. (n.d.) *Walking with God: The Testimony of the Redeemed Christian Church of God*. Lagos: The Redeemed Christian Church of God.

Ukah, A. F.-K. (2008). *A New Paradigm of Pentecostal Power: A Study of the Redeemed Christian Church of God in Nigeria*. Trenton, NJ: Africa World Press.

6

"The Old Man Is Dead": Hip Hop and the Arts of Citizenship of Senegalese Youth*

Rosalind Fredericks

Introduction

On the afternoon of Thursday, February 23, 2012, thousands of youth from across Senegal's capital city Dakar gathered in the streets surrounding the city's Independence Square[1] in protest of the elections to be held that Sunday. Waving national flags, wearing political t-shirts, and chanting at the top of their lungs, the crowd's energy was tense and frenetic as everyone braced for the inevitable teargas and rubber bullets that would soon be fired to break up the rally. When the mobile sound system blared the rap songs that had become anthems of the massive opposition movement, the intensity of the protest reached a crescendo. Almost on cue, their caustic chants in Wolof, "*Góor gi doy na, Góor gi dee na, soul na nu ko*" ("Enough of the old man, the old man is dead and buried") and "*Góor gi: Na dem, na dem, na dema dema dem*" ("The old man must go, he must go go go") were interrupted by shots and stinging clouds of teargas.[2] Within minutes, the streets had been cleared. Although on this day the dispersal left no fatalities in its wake, other days had ended on a more somber note.

The chants animating the opposition movement that was spawned during the troubled year leading up to the elections were directed at the elderly[3] incumbent, President Abdoulaye Wade. By 2012, Wade's popularity had declined dramatically owing to economic stagnation, extensive political scandals, and curbs on democratic practice that led observers to characterize his presidency as increasingly patrimonial, autocratic, and even authoritarian (Bingol and Vengroff 2012, Kelly 2012, Mbow 2008). In the direct lead up to the elections, Wade had galvanized the country's opposition movement by insisting on running for a controversial third term, attempting to make significant changes to the constitution, and aggressively cracking down on peaceful protests (Kelly 2012). Violent street clashes between youth and police shocked the nation and sent a message to the international community that Senegal's reputation as a beacon of peaceful democracy in West Africa was critically threatened. On election day, February 26 2012, youth protesters laid low, quietly surveying some neighborhood voting booths in an effort to ensure against any foul play in what was turning out to be one of the country's most dramatic electoral test. After at least ten people had died in the protests leading up the elections, the voting was tense but peaceful and young people jubilantly claimed their share in the victory when Abdoulaye Wade failed to win the first round.

When, on March 25, 2012, Abdoulaye Wade definitely lost the election in the second round of voting[4] to his rival Macky Sall, many international observers hailed the outcome as a solidification of Senegal's reputation as one of Africa's strongest democracies.[5] Offering stark contrast to the previous week's coup in neighboring Mali, the Senegalese elections of 2012 were seen to represent the second major democratic changing of the political guard since Independence in 1960—the other taking place in 2000 when, ironically, Wade was first elected. Echoing the sentiments of many, one young Dakarois told me after the elections: "Botswana has diamonds, Nigeria oil, and Senegal—we have democracy. This is what we do well."[6] But, what had they done and how?

Central to the defeat of President Wade was the audacious movement of youth in Dakar, critically mobilized by rappers and moving to the rhythm of hip hop through Senegal's urban landscape. Through mobilizing their networks in virtual, audio, and urban space, rappers catapulted themselves to the center of the political stage in not only the wave of protest leading up to the elections, but through inspiring a deeper public reflection on citizenship and democratic practice. The youth group, *Y'en a Marre* (YEM) (French for "Enough is Enough" or "We're Fed Up"), in particular, emerged at the forefront of youth contestation and mobilization, crystallizing the grievances of young people in the form an action-oriented, decentralized network rooted in Dakar but operating across the country (see figure 6.1).[7]

Although the role of youth and the ubiquity of rap during these elections can be denied by few, the power of this globalized art form as a force of youth critique and mobilization demands closer attention. The chapter seeks to explain why rap emerged as a key medium of protest of a generation of disaffected youth during the 2012 elections in Senegal and how it was mobilized to create new claims to voice and spaces of citizenship. Specifically, it examines how rap music and hip hop culture

Figure 6.1 A Y'en a Marre activist at a protest rally in July 2012. His sign reads: "Do you have your voter registration card? Hurry up and register. -Y'en a Marre." Author's photo.

act as a locus of political identity formation for youth through offering a language of geographical critique and a spatial practice of alternative place-making.

After briefly historicizing youth and hip hop in Senegal, the chapter makes three interconnected moves. First, I discuss the radicalizing discursive geography of rap as a democratically accessible, unbridled critique that shatters traditions of propriety and rules governing who is allowed to speak for the community. Second, I explore how rappers and their fans engage in resistance that is geopolitically diasporic while rooting their identities deeper into the neighborhood to critique geographies of exclusion and forge alternative visions of place. Finally, the last section details the material spatial practices of the Y'en a Marre youth movement during the elections as both outcome and extension of the spaces conditioned by rap and its history. Bringing together these threads, I aim to illuminate some of the arts of citizenship pioneered by Dakar's youth in a time of great sociopolitical transformation—as well as their limits. The wider implications have to do with how we understand the nexus of space, identity, and music and the spaces of citizenship in an era of urban youth protest.

Theorizing the Spaces of African Youth

Drawing from Deborah Durham, "youth" in Africa is best conceived as a relational, historically constructed social category that is context specific (2000). This understanding emphasizes that youth, as a category of persons, is deeply tied up with power, knowledge, rights, and notions of agency and personhood. Generational struggles have long been a driver of politics on the African continent; therefore, the question of youth and their power is not new to studies of sociopolitical change. However, Alcinda Honwana and Filip de Boeck argue that youth rebellion in the African setting was, until recently, embedded in social dynamics that did not threaten fundamental power structures (2005). Whereas, in the immediate postcolonial period, young African nations made youth the symbol of their future and attempted to channel their involvement in building the nation, African youth have emerged as rebellious "makers and breakers" in the wake of the failure of the nationalist project and the rise of the neoliberal era (Ibid.).

The disproportionate impact of economic crisis and neoliberal reform on African youth has been the subject of a growing literature over the last years. Excluded from education, healthcare, salaried jobs, and even access to adult status, marginalized youth find themselves literally out of place: permanently straddling social categories and lingering in a state of "waithood" (Honwana 2012) when "becoming somebody can no longer be taken for granted" (Cruise O'Brien 1996). Gerontocratic power structures join with the power of millennial capitalism's material fantasies to intensify youth's marginality (Comaroff and Comaroff 2005). Young men, in particular, face the strains of shifting formulas of gender power and the threats to masculinity posed by their impotence in economic and family life (Ralph 2008). Youth are, then, an ambiguous social force: in some contexts, they express themselves through desperate attempts at migration or acts of violence, whereas in others, they have emerged at the heart of democratic movements.

One key mode of expression for African youth to emerge since the 1980s is the explosive influence and popularity of hip hop culture. Paralleling a global explosion of hip hop (Alim et al. 2009, Basu and Lemelle 2006, Mitchell 2001), rap has evolved as a kind of lingua franca for disenfranchised youth across the African continent (Charry 2012, Saucier 2011). In a number of African settings, including Senegal, South Africa, and Tanzania, hip hop artists have fostered political critique of existing or challenging political entities) (Ibid.) However, although there is a burgeoning literature on the rising global influence of rap and a budding interest in its role as the new "mixtape of the revolution"

(Fernandes 2012: 58), limited attention has been paid to the political implication of rap music geographies in fomenting protest, even revolution. Furthermore, precious little focus has been extended to the spatiality of urban music geographies in the tectonic transformations underway in African generational politics and democratic contests.

This analysis is premised on an understanding that youth is a social category particularly associated with circumscriptions in allowed spaces and territories of influence for "the control of spatiality is part of the process of defining the social category of 'youth' itself" (Massey 1998: 127). Generational struggle, as a result, is deeply inscribed in border crossings or the rooting of contestation in the production of transgressive spatialities—imagined and practiced—especially in the context of the new geographies of identity associated with globalization.

There is a growing scholarship examining the way that spaces of youth are being reconfigured in a globalizing Africa (Diouf 2003, Katz 2004), with increasing attention paid to the role of popular media (Barnett 2004a, Dolby 2006, Wasserman 2011) and, particularly, youth music geographies in resculpting citizenship and the public sphere (Barnett 2004b, Hansen 2006). Without presuming that music and its situated practices are necessarily liberatory, youth music geographies can, nevertheless, provide vital arenas for the negotiation of political identities through offering possibilities for rebellion or contestation, a claim to voice, group membership, or a place in the city (Hudson 2006, Kong 1995). Originally the voice of disenfranchised African-American youth, hip hop is particularly associated with its valence as a medium through which to oppose domination and authority. Given the particular power derived from its rooting in geographical critique, hip hop offers a key site for social struggle through alternative spatial imaginings and practices (Forman 2002, Woods 2007). This chapter examines the geographical critique embedded in Senegalese hip hop to explore the role of rap in shaping the spaces of citizenship during the recent Senegalese elections.

Trajectories of Youth Activism in Senegal

Youth in Senegal have a long history of involvement in the political process, but they erupted with particular force during the controversial elections of 1988. In the wake of those troubled elections, Dakar youth endeavored to cleanse the city and, with it, the social and political ills they believed were corroding the nation in the now famous youth clean-up movement, *Set-Setal* (Diouf 1996). Increasingly since 1988, youth—especially Dakarois youth—have been key actors in wider citizenship struggles (Diouf and Fredericks 2013) and key electoral contests. Indeed, youth mobilization was central to Abdoulaye Wade's election to power in 2000 in what was then considered a landmark turning of the political tide after 40 years of Socialist Party rule (*Alternance*). By the elections of 2012, given this history, the rising precociousness of youth culture in the public imagination, and the even more weighty demographic majority represented by youth and their simultaneously declining economic positions, youth were poised to be chief players.

One of the key elements of youth culture and politics during this time has been the central influence of hip hop. Hip hop culture—which includes rapping, breakdancing, graffiti, DJing, and fashion—emerged in Dakar in the mid- to late 1980s as breakdancing emerged into the clubs and rap became more widely available (Herson 2011, Niang 2006). The context of its emergence was the social dislocation caused by the early years of structural adjustment, the profound turmoil surrounding the elections of 1988, and rapidly expanding access to global media. During the political crisis of 1988, major student strikes led the whole school year to be invalidated (*Année Blanche*). With youth out of school, disaffected, and searching for new outlets for expression, Dakar's own hip hop scene took root. Consistent with subaltern rap elsewhere (Alim et al. 2009), at first, Senegalese rappers patterned their music directly after rap emerging from the United States and France. Soon, their art began to take on its own distinct flavor, combining elements of local musical traditions, indigenous languages, and messages that resonated with Senegalese youth. Hip hop has, since, exploded in popularity and, at present, is considered to be the premier music for young people in Senegal, with an estimated 4,000 active groups, mainly in Dakar. Although the founding fathers of Senegalese rap hailed from middle-class central Dakar families who had privileged access to imported records and technology, the central pole of the scene is now concentrated in the city's poor outskirts or *banlieue*. A pioneer in the history of African rap, Senegal is now considered to have one of the largest and most influential hip hop scenes in Africa (Charry 2012).

Born in the context of political crisis, much of Senegalese rap has been highly politicized from the beginning. Senegalese rap founding father, Awadi (originally with Positive Black Soul), has been known for his smart, contestational lyrics going on for 25 years. Other notable foundational groups include WA BMG 44, Rap'adio, and Pee Froiss—all of whom rapped critiquing political corruption, bribery, and the general delinquency of the country's leaders, as well as conditions of economic hardship, legacies of colonialism, and youth struggle. Building on this legacy, in the elections of 2000, rappers emerged as a major force mobilizing the youth and bringing about Alternance (Herson 2007). In 2007 however, in the context of political scandals and a faltering economy, rappers began to criticize Wade. Despite this, the re-election was peaceful, and Wade was re-elected by a surprising landslide in the first round. By the elections of 2012—in which the legality of Wade's candidacy was in question and political scandals had reached their apogee—the rappers were poised to take centerstage in political contest and debate. Some even opted to join the campaigns of individual opposition politicians—notably, Daddy Bibson supporting Ousmane Tanor Dieng and Makhtar le Cagular supporting Ibrahima Fall—however, most rappers endeavored to preserve their reputation as independent critics.[8] The larger spaces they fostered in public critique and the embodied practice of ethical, neighborhood citizenship were, as we shall see further, central to the opposition movement.

The most visible, innovative, and important form of political contestation to emerge from the hip hop scene in the context of the 2012 elections was Y'en a Marre (YEM). Coordinated by the journalist Fadel Barro, the group is led by the rappers Oumar Cyril Touré [aka Thiat ("Junior")) and Landing Mbessane Seck (aka Kilifeu ("Senior")] of the group Keur Gui 2 Kaolack, Simon Kouka (aka Simon), and Malal Almamy Talla (aka Foumalade) in addition to three other friends who help coordinate (namely, Alioune Sané, Sophia Denise Sow, and Mohamed Seck). In January 2011, YEM was formed by Thiat, Kilifeu, and Fadel Barro, who were childhood friends from the city of Kaolack, to protest declining public services and generalized political negligence, as symbolized by the rolling black-outs. Quickly emerging as a major outlet to voice youth discontent, they then played a central role in the massive protests on June 23, 26, and 27, which successfully thwarted President Wade's proposed constitutional reforms. The amendments to the constitution—reducing the percentage of votes required for a first-round victory from 50 percent to 25 percent and creating the position of vice-president—were highly unpopular because of fears that they would allow Wade to ensure his re-election against a split opposition and to make his highly unpopular son the vice president. After huge riots organized around the slogan "Don't Touch My Constitution" took place all over Dakar, with hundreds injured, widespread damage to property incurred, and over 1,000 people arrested, Wade backed down and withdrew his proposed amendments. These events galvanized the opposition coalition of political parties and a wide diversity of citizen groups, including other youth movements, which was thereafter known as M23, for the Movement of the 23 June.

In the months to follow, YEM and its grassroots network of youth chapters across the country conducted widespread voter registration drives, awareness-raising campaigns, and protests. In the direct lead up to the elections, YEM was a central agent of dialog and opposition, fomenting vociferous debates in the press, online through social media, in the airwaves, and in the streets through their various awareness-raising activities, publicity stunts, and demonstrations. Indeed, YEM activists consistently helped drive the protests leading up to the elections, and many of the chants animating the protest rallies drew refrains originating with YEM rappers and singles. YEM became the barometer of youth agitation and the primary expression of youth mobilization. When the former Nigerian President Obasanjo came to Dakar as a delegate of the African Union to observe the elections, in addition to his talks with official candidates, he met with YEM twice.

The YEM basic platform throughout the elections was due process under the constitution and political independence. They refused to endorse candidates and, instead, focused on encouraging voters to resist voting pressure [including *marabouts* (religious leaders[9])] and vote with their conscience. When they disagreed with political developments taking place, they immediately took to the streets. Although YEM always encouraged peaceful protest, faced with repression by Wade's security forces (especially after Wade's bid for a third term was validated on January 27, 2011[10]), some of the protests turned violent.

In many important ways, YEM and youth protest during 2012 can be seen to stem from and to tap the power, philosophy, and ethical practice of hip hop. The following sections will explore the geography of hip hop music and culture in Senegal in order to explain its role in enabling the radical possibility of speaking out of turn and its embodiment in the emergence of YEM.

Rebellious Youth: Rapping Truth to Power

Consistent with the original radicalism of early hip hop in the United States, one of the reasons why hip hop has served as a language of contestation globally is through facilitating new discursive spaces of self-expression for those who may not, otherwise, enjoy such outlets. This is a central element of why hip hop has become a voice of resistance in Senegal. Otherwise disenfranchised from political power and sidelined from traditional avenues of political dialog and critique, underprivileged urban youth in Senegal find a mode of democratic expression in hip hop. Rap's wide accessibility—all one needs is a voice, and an audience can be found and a message conveyed, with no requirements for formal musical training, expensive instruments or equipment, or even literacy—has resulted in its dramatic proliferation across the country.

Through rap, young men, especially, are able to assume the role of spokesmen for not only their generation, but also their communities, city, and even nation.[11] In a country with a strongly hierarchical age-power system, youth's taking the floor in political critique is radical in two important respects. First, it constitutes a transgression of conventional delineations of who is allowed to speak for the community because it usurps gerontocratic traditions of public discourse. Second, this new discursive space constitutes a rupture with inherited conventions of propriety in indirect comment, through involving a direct and uncensored mode of public moral critique. In this way, rap—as a mode of speaking out of turn—embodies a rejection of the status quo that is at the core of a sort of generational revolt. Veteran rapper Keyti[12] (originally with Rap'adio) sums up the impact of rap as direct critique as follows:

> It's about the way Senegalese people can talk about certain things now—naturally. [...]Before hip hop, it was not here. Traditionally the structure of this society is: the elders talk...and the youth they listen and do. But, [...] rappers they broke the rules. [They said] enough of the social structure, enough of the social ladder, we are all citizens. We've got our word to say. And...little by little, people are accepting that a 12 year old can write a rap song and talk about the president. Even though the president is 86 or 90.[13]

Rap gains its power, therefore, from its biting, caustic quality, which supplants traditions of deference. In the refrains from the rap songs quoted at the beginning of this chapter, for instance, the use of *goor gi*, which literally means "adult man" or "elder," instead, takes on an ironic and pejorative connotation of "old man," the object of ridicule. The frequent references to the president by his first name in these and other rap songs convey a clear message of disrespect. These critiques reached their apex on election day in the surprise acerbic booing by young onlookers of President Wade when he cast his vote. The event, perhaps, best manifested the crumbling of traditional rules of propriety in public comment and the systems of power they uphold (see Figure 6.2).

A number of rappers legitimate their claim as the voice of their communities through their role as modern-day *griots* (Appert 2011, Tang 2012). Griots are the endogamous caste (*géwél* in Wolof) of traditional praise-singers, musicians, counselors, and oral historians that

Figure 6.2 A defaced campaign poster of President Abdoulaye Wade. Author's photo.

date back to the precolonial West African kingdoms. Far from disappearing, Senegalese griots have been savvy at adapting their trade to contemporary contexts and pioneering lucrative niches within politics, religious, and cultural spheres. Rapper Baay Bia explicitly connects his music with the training in "deep Wolof" and historic responsibility to be the voice of his people that was bestowed upon him through generations of family griots.[14] He and other griot rappers trace the origins of rap in West African oral traditions in order to justify their authority as its primary spokesmen. One does not have to actually be from a griot family, though, to draw on and perform the function and legitimacy of the griot's role in society. Many other rappers claim the griot's historic responsibility to—in the words of rapper Waterflow's myspace bio—speak "truth to those in power"[15] in functional, rather than genealogical, terms (Appert 2011). This historical and geocultural claim to authenticity works to assert the authority of African knowledge systems and traditions of orality.

Whether as griots or not, central to the imagination of rappers is their self-identification as positioned at the edge of society, looking in. For rapper Foumalade, whose rap name literally means "sick, crazy person," this means rejecting societal rules regarding allowable speech through acting crazy and, thereby, freeing his words. Hailing from the poor district of Guediawaye on the outskirts of Dakar, Foumalade studied at the University of Dakar, but is quick to assert that intellectuals "of the street" are just as important as intellectuals "of the classroom."[16]

The YEM movement has been deeply shaped by—and derives much of its power from—its connection to rap music and culture. Aside from Barro, the key spokespeople of YEM are rappers who have been involved as critics of social institutions and the political process for some time. These artists draw from the long tradition of "hard-core" political rap that has placed rappers as organic intellectuals to whom the youth look for analysis of controversial issues in society. In particular, the construction of the movement as a "sentinel" to the political process is deeply resonant with the role that the rappers have played over the last couple of decades. During the elections, Foumalade and others used this positionality to offer razor-sharp criticism of the president and the democratic process that exceeded the constraints on free speech and democratic debate.

YEM refused to enter the fray of party politics and, instead, focused on fostering substantive dialog about key issues at stake. One of their strategies was to release rap songs and videos geared toward fomenting debate and action among the youth. The scathing lyrics from the *Faux!!! Pas Forcé*[17] single released just a couple of months before the elections are illustrative. Kilifeu raps, "President of scandals; you have dashed the dreams of a whole people" highlighting the series of scandals under Wade. He continues, "You divided the brotherhoods, you no longer have an exit," making an important accusation that Wade had politicized the country's Sufi brotherhoods. For many, this signaled a grave shift in what had been considered a key ingredient of Senegal's recipe for stability. Furthermore, the line "You made the church cry, that will come down on you" accuses Wade's administration of negligence and mismanagement that resulted in the sinking of the *Joola* government ferry in 2002. With almost 2,000 deaths (a large proportion of whom were minority Christians from Senegal's southern region), the tragedy was one of the worst maritime disasters in history and was widely viewed as a symbol of the corruption in Wade's regime. He concludes with "We will be present, you old thug... We'll uproot you before you fleece us,"[18] chanelling youth vitriol with intensity. When asked in a TV interview why they launch their critique through such harsh and violent language, Foumalade explained that a language of contestation must match the power of the injustice being contested.[19]

Through such dialog, rap can be seen to offer youth a way to widen and navigate the public sphere. In light of Wade's limitations on the press (Havard 2004) and the limited access of underprivileged kids' to avenues for political debate, political rap has created an increasingly important and provocative set of discursive spaces—rooted in new media—that generate "innumerable, dispersed dialogues about issues of broad public concern" (Barnett 2004b: 262). It opens up the field of democratic communication to those positioned on the outside of legitimate knowledge and public debate.

Placing Identity on the Edge: Claiming Space Between Ghetto and Globe[20]

If rap as a mode of speech allows the youth of the hip hop generation to occupy more radical, uncensored spaces of critique that are inscribed within generational power struggles, it is also deeply caught up in the production of alternative geographies of the city and the nation, and youth's place therein. Drawing from Lefebvre, Arun Saldanha describes music as the embodied production of space: it "does not just exist 'in' space and refer 'to' space, the space of music is produced and produces identity and politics through its *corporealization*" (2002: 348). In this light, a key element of the way that rap music and its followers reconstitute the democratic public sphere is through producing alternative representations of space through their conjured imaginaries and material practices. It is, thus, through reconfiguring the space of the city and the nation that hip hop youth forge a radical politics.

Although all music can be spatialized, "[i]n hip hop, space is a dominant concern, occupying a central role in the definition of value, meaning, and practice" (Forman 2002: 5). Hip hop has always been known for its intense association with urban places, notably the ghetto and "representing" specific neighborhoods. This has certainly been the case in Dakar, where identification with one's neighborhood—especially for those hailing from the poor "banlieue"—looms large in rap-group identities. In their vision, the city fades into the background and the neighborhood takes center stage as the key locus of identity and collective responsibility.

Especially in the poor periphery of the city, notably in the sprawling unplanned districts of Pikine and Guediawaye, the soundscape of rap music becomes a key ingredient of the "urban ethos" (Krims 2007). At the hands of the artists and their fans, place is conjoined with the sound and aesthetics of hip hop [including fashion, multi-media arts (Rabine 2013), and graffiti] to color the neighborhood with a youthful, urban vibe. Within these neighborhoods, moreover, rappers own the street. Resonating with hip hop narratives in many other locales, most songs make reference to the street as a *way* of living. However, far from denoting a sort of gang lifestyle or delinquency, this signals ownership over the neighborhood—a claim to the rights and rewards of the city through occupying its physical space and the space of public dialog. Whether through the constant buzz of hip hop emanating from radios or the sounds of groups on street corners practicing their art, these youth displace the traditional space and volume of the *penc*—the meeting places where elders discuss neighborly matters—with that of the *banj*, the benches on which young men practice their iconic pastime of tea-making to "kill time" (Ralph 2008) and compose their lyrics. Given the sheer number of rap groups in Dakar, most young people know at least one rapper—if they are not a rapper themselves. Broadcast into the air, the sound and meaning of their craft cannot be contained. It takes possession of the street, grounding youths' claim to voice and authority.

In these neighborhoods, responsibility to remake the "place" in line with hip hop's aesthetics and ethics is taken extremely seriously. Resonating with the wider understanding of hip hop as lived culture, many of Dakar's hip hop generation derive from hip hop an obligation to give back to their neighborhoods and their fellow disadvantaged youth. Central to the neighborhood imaginary is an assertion of the values of "social living" or the ethical obligation to take care of one's own in the face of the state's disregard. Legendary "hard-core" rapper Matador's urban media arts and education center in Pikine, *Africulturban*, has been a pioneer in community building through hip hop since it was founded in 2006. Africulturban has over 1,000 youth members and fosters a range of activities from free concerts to classes offered through its *Hip Hop Akademy* in music production, dance, and web design geared toward empowering underprivileged youth and imparting marketable skills.

Similarly, Foumalade has long been involved in community activism dedicated to reforming literacy education, treatment of the mentally ill, and, especially, improving prisons and the status of prisoners. Reminiscent of African American blues and hip hop musicians, for Foumalade, "the imprisoned are not discarded as outcasts; rather they are often considered witnesses to, and students of" particular geographical conjunctures and their violences (Woods 2007: 72). Through his prison hip hop education programs and rap songs on prison reform, he aims to reconfigure the inside and outside of whose speech is rendered legitimate and authoritative. Building on this and other community-building work, Foumalade recently joined up with some other local rap group collaborators to launch the GHip Hop community center in Guediawaye in April 2013.

Although their spatial imaginaries and practices are deeply rooted in the neighborhood, hip hop youth are also profoundly implicated in literal and symbolic border crossing. Locating themselves at the edge of the city and its poor banlieue, they take ownership over their neighborhood spaces while reimagining the space of the city with the ghetto at its center. Their strategies of mobility and transgression defy the division between city center and periphery, much in the same way that Teresa Caldeira's taggers in Sao Paolo inscribe the center with their *favelano* images (2012). Rap and its messages are profoundly mobile in Dakar, traveling through urban space in graffiti, airwaves, t-shirts, and protest chants.

Some of Wade's most controversial acts had to do with marking, assaulting, or privatizing public space through building elite toll-highways that could only be used by the rich, making street vending illegal, and, probably the most symbolic: building an offensive, and now roundly despised, "African Renaissance Monument."[21] By occupying public space through sound and spectacle, hip hop youth contested this assault on public space; and they often launched their critique in spatial terms. The group Keur Gui (the founders of YEM), directly contest the privatization of public space in their in their song *Coup 2 Gueule* ("Outburst") taking on the failures of the Wade years. In the video, they provocatively juxtapose intensely urban scenes of Dakar (including toll highways) with lyrics describing the city as "our rural world," the poor banlieue of the globe. Thiat and Kilifeu's identities, moreover, as refugees from their city of origin, Kaolack, depressed due to its failing agricultural base, add another dimension to this critique of geographical inequity to highlight the struggles of the non-Dakar, "rural" world. Their art not only directly repudiates the geographies of exclusion they witnessed in Wade's development agenda but also connects this to a wider global critique (common in Senegalese rap) of global uneven development. The ending refrain, "I don't even feel Senegalese any more," suggests that Wade had actually managed to erode the foundations of national identity. In this sense, their imaginary is postnationalist: they draw from global membership to bring into relief the failures of the nationalist project in Senegal and, thereby, register their distain for the vision of the nation as conceived by their "elders."

In addition to reimagining the borders of the city through deploying the ghetto and embodying the street, Senegalese rap is, thus, also centrally preoccupied with working the borders of the nation through geographical imaginings of global citizenship. Rap music has taken root as a key voice of political protest in Senegal because it offers a language that is both anchored in local oral traditions and linked to a global diaspora of youth protest, past and present. The contestation implied in rap, in other words, embodies the desire among young Senegalese for a voice in their own societies as well as their assertion of membership within the global community. Rappers' imaginaries endeavor to reconstruct the space of the nation through domesticating the foreign in order to question a national imaginary from which they feel excluded. Thus, in contrast with *mbalax*, the "national" music of Senegal associated most directly with the international superstar Youssou Ndour,[22] rap gains traction for youth in Senegal precisely because of its diasporic links to multiple elsewheres. Through straddling the border between ghetto and globe, rappers and their listeners use the globalized art form to interrogate and rework the space of the nation. In this vision, moreover, the city stands in for the space of the nation.

Central to this global imaginary is an identification with the black Atlantic and common legacies of struggle within global black history and culture. Senegalese rap is inscribed in the space of the black Atlantic both literally, owing to rappers' explicit identification with a global black diaspora and their geographical practices beyond Senegal, and historically, in legacies of movement, border crossing, and traditions of cultural production within the Atlantic world (Gilroy 1993). Through grounding themselves simultaneously within the local space of the city and transnational diasporic networks, Senegalese rappers, thus, "reaffirm a transatlantic connectivity grounded in commonalities of racialized socio-economic struggle" (Appert 2011: 16). The origin story that rap was born from diasporic connections in the South Bronx including West African oral traditions and then returned to Senegal as a sort of "boomerang"[23] is a foundational instance. However, Senegalese rappers do not take these diasporic connections uncritically. Although they identify with Western rappers and feel part of a global movement of "voiceless" youth, Senegalese rappers are often quick to distance themselves from American rap through asserting that their music is more "authentic" to its original radical roots. They take the high ground when comparing their music to that of gangsta, mainstream, or misogynistic rap. "We can't rap about money, girls, bad behavior in that way! It's not our reality, we are Muslims" Mass of Black Diamonds explained to highlight the important moral underpinnings of Senegalese rap.[24]

The spatial imaginaries of the hip hop generation provided the backdrop for much of the discourse of protest during the 2012 elections. YEM's international connections—including travel abroad to mobilize diasporic groups, strong social media presence, extensive international journal coverage, and an open door for international observers at their headquarters in Parcelles Assainies in Dakar—allowed them convey the global significance of the movement and tap into the legitimizing force of international visibility. This was, moreover, preconditioned and legitimated by their renown in international circuits as rappers. Their global imaginary, in other words, allowed YEM to take on the role of sentinel to the world through straddling international borders as interlocutors with the West. Through inscribing their movement within global youth and democracy movements, they fostered a sense that the whole world was watching, which gave extra force to the protesters and buttressed their pride in the election outcome.

Y'en a Marre's Arts of Citizenship and the Elections of 2012

A central feature of Senegalese hip hop is its deep embedding in urban space—its grounding in intimate geographies of place-"making" (not just representing) in Senegal's urban neighborhoods. YEM built on the tradition within hip hop culture of publically performed ethical action in their campaign during the elections of 2012. Through their innovative education and direct action initiatives—like the *ElectoRap*, *Das Fanaanal*, and the *Foire aux Problemes* campaigns—they channeled transgressive speech and action into a savvy program of social mobilization. For instance, in the Das Fanaanal campaign, which was launched in April 2011 to foster voter registration, YEM urged youth to "protect" themselves, to prepare their weapons for the battle to come. What weapon were they referring to? The vote. The associated slogan, "my voter registration card, my weapon," became a common refrain in protests. Importantly, like the hip hop movement in general, YEM's approach was grounded in a young, information technology-oriented culture. The networks were rooted in new media, much of which was pioneered by online hip hop communities and Facebook pages, which served to get the word out. The mixtape of the movement—or the biting, "hardcore" rap songs released with specific initiatives—became instantly popular online and on the radio.

YEM was, moreover, immediately visible and accessible to young people who saw many of the nation's most celebrated and famous rappers suddenly taking the microphone to talk about politics—live—in their neighborhoods. The rappers of YEM were always front and center at rallies and protests, wearing their characteristic shirts (with Y'EN A MARRE in large block-letters) and, as such, were often caught in the cross-fire when the protests went sour. In the major protests on June 23, 2012, rappers Thiat, Simon, and Foumalade were arrested for protesting peacefully—catalyzing youth outrage and action. A crowd of young people held vigil outside the city prison, demanding the rappers' release and due process under the law. Two months later, when the sentences were due to be released, huge crowds again gathered at the courthouse, in what many feared would become a violent protest. In the end, both rappers' sentences were commuted, but the arrests had bolstered the cult of personality surrounding YEM.

Beyond their tireless press conferences, rap songs, and front and center role at the protests, YEM's most powerful mobilization strategy was its intimate spatial practices in urban neighborhoods throughout Senegal. The following interview with Barro illuminates the way that YEM drew on and extended the power of hip hop:

> When we launched the movement, we built on the 'apparatus' of the hip hop movement. It's a huge scene. In each locality, even the most remote, if there is not a rapper than there is at least a fan of rap. And we built...on this representation of hip hop across the country, to create the network of Y'en a Marre...We produce a lot of music, host a lot of...'pedagogical concerts' where the public comes to take the floor, ask questions and we respond to bring light to questions of citizenship...So, we use the strategies of hip hop to reach a large audience (Haeringer 2011).

In certain ways harkening back to *Set/Setal* in the late 1980s, YEM formed a vast decentralized network of local-associated spin-off groups at the neighborhood level, called *esprits*, or "spirits" of YEM during the summer of 2011. Although there are no formal membership cards, the *esprits* have representatives who interface with the YEM headquarters and *de facto* members who go to meetings and plan specific activities.

Initially, the leaders of YEM hosted "caravans" to spark more than 300 local *esprits* across the country. During the caravan, they worked with the local *esprit* members to hold a community-wide meeting in a public square. YEM leaders would then make presentations on the vision of YEM, answer questions, and lead brainstorming sessions with local community members about local problems. Although hosted by the local youth *esprits*, these meetings often attracted a wide cross-section of the community, including women, children, and older men, including local community leaders and imams (figure 6.3). The debates took on the flavor of the specific context; however, common issues of concern included: garbage and sanitation, electricity cuts, crime, education, unemployment, and, of course, the elections. During voter registration, the *esprits* played a key role in mobilizing their neighbors to vote. After that time, they worked to resolve specific local grievances while fomenting protest on the national stage.

Although the immediate impetus for forming the *esprits* was to mobilize youth voter registration, the broader vision was to catalyze active citizenship practices. Building on the tradition within rap of sustained dialog on broader social and religious issues, YEM also took on a whole set of larger conversations regarding the Senegalese moral universe and quotidian life challenges. The movement proposed no less than a *Nouveau Type de Sénégalais* [New Type of Senegalese person (NTS)] as a credo for improved individual behavior as citizens (*Don't sell your vote!*), urbanites (*Don't throw trash on the street!*), presidents (*Don't abuse your power!*), disciples (*Don't be fooled by corrupt religious leaders!*), and so on. In this light, they aimed to make "politics" relevant by fostering a provocative dialog on issues central to the

Figure 6.3 An *esprit* meeting in the Zone B neighborhood. Author's photo.

lives of everyday Senegalese they saw as elided by politicians and other musical genres.

In the tense weeks leading up to the elections, the NTS was interpreted in many ways by different *esprits* across Dakar. In the protests, sometimes, it meant contesting the assault on public space through forcing entry into a blocked-off Independence Square, or demonstrating at the foot of the African Renaissance Monument. When provoked by Wade's acts of violence, it often meant defending specific symbolic spaces, for instance, in shielding a mosque that had been sacrilegiously tear gassed[25] or even "protecting" residential neighborhoods. The 5-hour, live-broadcast stand-off between police armed with rubber bullets and youth armed with stones in the neighborhood of Cambérène, over the government's inaction in repairing a broken sewer main which flooded the neighborhood, for instance, was one of the most dramatic of the violent clashes. As a potent symbol of state negligence, the insalubrious sewer overflow took on particularly acute meaning in Cambérène, which is considered a saintly locale within the Layenne brotherhood.

The NTS invoked an entrepreneurial morality that was envisioned as a long-term transformative project that would animate the YEM movement well beyond 2012. Leading up to the legislative elections held in July 2012, they continued their caravans around the country. It remains to be seen what role YEM will continue to play now that the electoral crisis is over; however, although less publicly visible on the public radar, they were still able to gather large groups of young people in "brigades" to clean up the city and other neighborhood-based mobilizations since 2012. The leaders stand resolute that they will not give up the fight to unleash no less than a social transformation, or the emergence of the NTS on a grand scale. Our battle has just begun, Fadel Barro told me, "the elections were the easy part."[26]

Conclusions

In 2012, after 12 years of corruption, scandals, economic stagnation, and neoliberal reform, youth in Senegal had had enough of all that was represented by President Abdoulaye Wade. Wade's age had become a metaphor for how far out of touch he was with the realities faced by the nation's youth. I have argued here that the opposition movement should be viewed primarily as an expression of generational revolt where the radical flavor of protest stemmed from the spatial claims-making influence of rap and hip hop culture. Building on the legitimacy of rappers as border-hopping organic intellectuals and tapping the transgressions intrinsic to politically engaged rap, Y'en a Marre youth stoked vitriolic critique and a protest movement which proved crucial to bringing the opposition to power. Paralleling the growing role of hip hop as a language of contestation for subaltern groups across the globe, the specific valence of rap in Senegalese politics derives from particular historically and culturally relevant spaces, imaginations, and practices it inspires on the streets of Dakar.

Although fractured and multivalent, rap music has emerged as the language of Senegalese youth's dispossession, as a powerful mode of direct comment through which young men contest their marginality to assert new logics of debate and action. Hip hop simultaneously fosters a highly developed geographical critique of uneven development while offering an epistemology of place-making for youth in their endeavors to voice and forge alternative imaginings of their city. Through provocative territorial practices, Senegalese rappers and their fans re-imagine their place in Dakar and the world in order to stake claims as global citizens to the rights and rewards of their own city. Sometimes peaceful and, at others, violent, they boisterously occupy and re-appropriate the city, from its edge, thereby upending spatialized control and (re) instilling of notions of duty to neighborhood and country. By deploying alternative representations of space through owning the street and embodying the diaspora, these youth position themselves as whistle-blowers to the political process and witnesses to the world. This emphasizes how material spaces and practices work in concert with discursive and imagined ones, or how spatial representations operate as strategic sites for the contests surrounding communicative power and citizenship.

This analysis highlights, furthermore, the critical pedagogical work of a globalized art form such as hip hop in its vernacular forms as a political language of speaking out of turn. YEM harnessed the important contestational legacy of rap to widen the public sphere and provide new fora for political debate. Rap and the *esprits* it spawned can be seen as fostering a sort of democratic communication through which young people could become aware of, negotiate, and articulate their political identities. This draws attention to the deliberative processes of democracy while emphasizing its performative nature. Moreover, it highlights the importance of new media, music, and popular culture in providing new arenas for political deliberation and change.

Nevertheless, while membership in Dakar's hip hop culture is framed in cosmopolitan terms, we also have to ask what is elided by the movement's projected space of unity. An attention to the multiplicity of publics reveals the elision of women's voices in rap and its so-called democratic spaces. Although young women were very present numerically in the opposition movement overall, behind YEM's proclamations of egalitarianism, their voices are almost nonexistent in rap, and limited in the wider spaces of democracy and protest fostered by the movement. This resonates with observations citing the male "privilege of revolution" in Egypt and elsewhere (Winegar 2012). If the future social critics are going to emerge from this scene in Senegal, women will, most likely, not be among them, highlighting the limitations within YEM's lofty goal of total social transformation.

Finally, it is also important to probe the implications of these new spaces of citizenship in exerting real political economic change and reforming the Senegalese state. The limits of their discourse and practice as independent observers who refuse to enter the fray of party politics will be key questions going forward. The fact that the new president, Macky Sall, was originally part of Wade's party, calls into question the type of substantive political economic transformation to remedy the plight of youth that might come from the top. Only time will tell what the full implications of the artful, rowdy citizenship practices unleashed by the YEM movement will be, going forward; but, it is clear that the time for youth to quietly wait their turn is over.

Notes

*This chapter is a reprint of an article originally published in *Antipode* in January 2014 [Volume 46(1): 130–148] with permission from Wiley. It is based on ethnographic fieldwork (including over 40 personal interviews) conducted between 2010 and 2012 in Dakar and New York with rappers, Y'en a Marristes, and other people implicated in Senegal's hip hop scene in New York and Dakar. The author is grateful to her respondents, Mélanie Sadio Goudiaby for her transcription and translation assistance, and to Sapana Doshi, Tracey Osborne, Malini Ranganathan, Asher Ghertner, Mike Dwyer, three anonymous reviewers, and the Antipode editorial staff for insightful comments. All interviews were conducted by the author in French, Wolof, or English. All mistakes in the text are the author's responsibility.

1. Despite official rights of assembly, opposition protests in downtown Dakar were effectively banned from Independence square through the unlawful denial of permits (Kelly 2012). As a result, protesters congregated behind police barricades in the streets surrounding the square.
2. Both songs "Na dem" and "Goor gi dee na" are by the rapper Red Black.
3. Abdoulaye Wade was officially 85 at the time of the elections, but estimates put his real age near 90.
4. In Senegal, presidential elections consist of two rounds: multiple candidates run in the first round and if no single candidate gains over 50 percent of the vote, a second round is held later between the top two candidates. In 2012, 14 candidates ran in the first round, with Wade winning 35 percent and opposition frunt-runner, Macky Sall, winning 27 percent. In the second round of

voting on March 25, Macky Sall won 66 percent of the vote against Wade's 34 percent.

5. For a sample of international press coverage, see Nossiter (March 25, 2012) and Hirsch and Bojang (March 26, 2012).
6. Personal interview, February 27, 2012, Dakar.
7. For a journalistic history of the movement in French, see Savané and Sarr (2012).
8. Although the vast majority of rappers identify with the opposition movement, some rappers have supported Wade. The rapper Pakoti famously supported Wade in 2007, only to be widely criticized for "selling out." No big-name rappers came out for Wade in 2012.
9. There is a long tradition in Senegal of directives (*ndigël*) by marabouts instructing their disciples to vote for specific candidates. Although there has been no serious *ndigël* since 2000, YEM's direct manner of critiquing marabouts for meddling in politics was fresh and controversial.
10. Wade supported the implementation of a two-term limit on presidential mandates in 2002, but later argued that his first term did not count towards this limit. A controversial constitutional committee reviewed the legality of his bid for a third term, and declared it legal.
11. The overwhelming majority of rappers in Senegal are men. Although it was out of the scope of this chapter to deeply analyze the gendered implications of rap, a few questions are raised in the conclusions.
12. Keyti is one of Senegal's original veteran rappers. Although he is not one of the founders or leaders of YEM, he is considered an "advisor" to the movement.
13. Personal interview, Liberte 6 Extension, Dakar, February 22, 2012.
14. Personal interview, May 28, 2010. Harlem, NY.
15. Waterflow is a member of the hip hop group Wagëblë (http://www.myspace.com/waterflowwageble).
16. Personal interview, 21 June 2010, his home in Guediawaye.
17. Like much rap, the title is a play on words. The immediate meaning is "Don't Force It" but "Faux" is spelled to mean "false" or "fake," lending the statement the meaning "Forced mis-steps."
18. The author provided translation of the French lyrics.
19. Interview on *Le Grand Rendez-Vous* show, broadcast on December 1, 2011.
20. This title is drawn from Simone (2001).
21. The monument was despised because the family it portrays is viewed as culturally inappropriate, the cost of its production was exorbitant and did not rely on local labor, and all visitation proceeds went directly into the President's pocket.
22. Rappers often identified their music explicitly *against mbalax*, which many consider apolitical and old-fashioned, and felt that Ndour's political activism unfairly profited from their work.
23. This is a common metaphor referenced by Senegalese rappers. The internationally known group *Daara J* famously titled one of their albums "Boomerang."
24. Personal interview, June 16, 2010, Dakar.
25. Police fired teargas into the El Hadji Malick Sy mosque on February 17, 2012, in downtown Dakar after protesters took refuge inside. The incident precipitated a violent standoff between protesters and police and was seen

to symbolize Wade's favoring of the Mouride brotherhood (the mosque was Tijani).

26. Personal interview, July 2, 2012, YEM headquarters.

References

Alim, H. S., Ibrahim, A., and Pennycook, A. (2009). *Global Lingustic Flows: Hip Hop Culture, Youth Identities, and the Politics of Language*. New York: Routledge.

Appert, C. (2011). "Rappin Griots: Producing the Local in Senegalese Hip Hop." In Saucier, P. K., ed., *Native Tongues: An African Hip Hop Reader*, pp. 3–22. Trenton, NJ: Africa World Press.

Barnett, C. (2004a). "Media, Democracy, and Representation: Disembodying the Public." In Barnett, C. and Low, M., eds, *Spaces of Democracy: Geographical Perspectives on Citiizenship, Participation, and Representation*, pp. 185–206. London: Sage Publishers.

———. (2004b). "Yizo Yizo: Citizenship, Commodification and Popular Culture in South Africa." *Media Culture Society* 26: 251–271.

Basu, D. and Lemelle, S. J., eds. (2006). *The Vinyl Ain't Final: Hip Hop and the Globalization of Black Popular Culture*. London: Pluto Press.

Bingol, H. B. and Vengroff, R. (2012). "Democratization in Senegal: The Failure of the "Sopi" Revolution." In Adebayo, A. G., ed., *Managing Conflict in Africa's Democratic Transitions*, pp. 105–118. Lanham, MD: Lexington Books.

Caldeira, T. P. R. (2012). "Imprinting and Moving Around: New Visibilities and Configurations of Public Space in São Paulo." *Public Culture* 24: 385–419.

Charry, E., ed. (2012). *Hip Hop Africa: New African Music in a Globalizing World*. Bloomington, IN: Indiana University Press.

Comaroff, J. and Comaroff, J. (2005). "Reflections on Youth: From the Past to the Postcolony." In Honwana, A. and De Boeck, F., eds, *Makers and Breakers: Children & Youth in Postcolonial Africa*, pp. 19–30. Trenton, NJ: Africa World Press.

Cruise O'Brien, D. B. (1996). "A Lost Generation? Youth Identity and State Decay in West Africa." In Werbner, R. and Ranger, T., eds, *Postcolonial Identities in Africa*, pp. 55–74. London: Zed Books.

Diouf, M. (1996). "Urban Youth and Senegalese Politics: Dakar 1988–1994." *Public Culture* 8: 225–249.

———. (2003). "Engaging Postcolonial Cultures: African Youth and Public Space." *African Studies Review* 46: 1–12.

Diouf, M. and Fredericks, R., eds. (2013). *Arts de la Cittoyenneté et Esthétiques du Politiques au Sénégal: Espaces contestés et civilités urbaines*. Paris: Karthala.

Dolby, N. (2006). "Popular Culture and Public Space in Africa: The Possibilities of Cultural Citizenship." *African Studies Review* 49: 31–47.

Durham, D. (2000). "Youth and the Social Imagination in Africa: Introduction to Parts 1 and 2." *Anthropological Quarterly* 73(3): 113–120.

Fernandes, S. (January 29, 2012). "The Mixtape of the Revolution" (Op Ed Contribution). *The New York Times*. New York.

Forman, M. (2002). *The 'Hood Comes First: Race, Space, and Place in Rap and Hip Hop*. Middletown, CT: Wesleyan University Press.
Gilroy, P. (1993). *The Black Atlantic: Modernity and Double Consciousness*. London: Verso.
Haeringer, N. (2011). "Y'en a marre: une lente sédimentation des frustrations," entretien avec Fadel Barro. *Mouvements.info*.
Hansen, T. B. (2006). "Sounds of Freedom: Music, Taxis, and Racial Imagination in Urban South Africa." *Public Culture* 18: 185–208.
Havard, J.-F. (2004). "De La Victoire du 'sopi' à la Tentation du 'nopi'? 'Gouvernement de l'Alternance' et Liberté de L'Expression des Médias au Sénégal." *Politique Africaine* 96: 22–38.
Herson, B. (2007). *Democracy in Dakar* (film). Nomadic Wax Productions.
———. (2011). "A Historical Analysis of Hip Hop's Influence in Dakar from 1984–2000." *American Behavioral Scientist* 55: 24–35.
Hirsch, A. and Bojang, S. (March 26, 2012). "Senegalese President Admits Defeat in Election." *The Guardian*. London
Honwana, A. and De Boeck, F., eds. (2005). *Makers and Breakers: Children & Youth in Postcolonial Africa*. Trenton, NJ: Africa World Press.
Honwana, A. (2012). *The Time of Youth: Work, Social Change, and Politics in Africa*. Sterling, VA: Kumarian Press.
Hudson, R. (2006). "Regions and Place: Music, Identity and Place." *Progress in Human Geography* 30: 626–634.
Katz, C. (2004). *Growing Up Global: Economic Restructuring and Children's Everyday Lives*. Minneapolis, MN: University of Minnesota Press.
Kelly, C. L. (2012). "Senegal: What Will Turnover Bring?" *Journal of Democracy* 23: 121–131.
Kong, L. (1995). "Popular Music in Geographical Analyses." *Progress in Human Geography* 19: 183–198.
Krims, A. (2007). *Music and Urban Geography*. New York: Routledge.
Massey, D. (1998). "The Spatial Construction of Youth Cultures." In Skelton, T. and Valentine, G., eds, *Cool Places: Geographies of Youth Cultures*, pp. 121–129. London: Routledge.
Mbow, P. (2008). "Senegal: The Return of Personalism." *Journal of Democracy* 19: 156–169.
Mitchell, T., ed. (2001). *Global Noise: Rap and Hip Hop Outside the USA*. Middletown, CT: Wesleyan University Press.
Niang, A. (2006). "Bboys: Hip Hop Culture in Dakar, Senegal." In Nilan, P. and Feixa, C., eds, *Global Youth? Hybrid Identities, Plural Worlds*, pp. 167–185. New York: Routledge.
Nossiter, A. (March 25, 2012). "A Turbulence-Free Election in Senegal." *The New York Times*. New York.
Rabine, L. W. (2013). "Pratiques Multimédias et Constructions d'Identité à Dakar." In Diouf, M. and Fredericks, R., eds, *Arts de la Cittoyenneté et Esthétiques du Politiques au Sénégal: Espaces contestés et civilités urbaines*. Paris: Karthala.
Ralph, M. (2008). "Killing Time." *Social Text* 26: 1–29.
Saldanha, A. (2002). "Music, Space, Identity: Geographies of Youth Culture in Bangalore." *Cultural Studies* 16: 337–350.

Saucier, P. K., ed. (2011). *Native Tongues: An African Hip Hop Reader.* Trenton, NJ: Africa World Press.

Savané, V. and Sarr, B. M. (2012). *Y'en a Marre: Radioscopie d'une jeunesse insurgée au Sénégal.* Paris: L'Harmattan.

Simone, A. (2001). "Between Ghetto and Globe: Remaking Urban Life in Africa." In Vaa, M., Tvedten, I., and Tostensen, A., eds, *Associational Life in African Cities: Urban Governance in an Era of Change.* Uppsala: Nordic African Institute.

Tang, P. (2012). "The Rapper as Modern Griot: Reclaiming Ancient Traditions." In Charry, E., ed., *Hip Hop Africa: New African Music in a Globalizing World*, pp. 79–91. Bloomington, IN: Indiana University Press.

Wasserman, H., ed. (2011). *Popular Media, Democracy, and Development in Africa.* London: Routledge.

Winegar, J. (2012). "The Privilege of Revolution: Gender, Class, Space, and Affect in Egypt". *American Ethnologist* 39: 67–70.

Woods, C. (2007). "'Sittin' on Top of the World' the Challenges of Blues and Hip Hop Geography." In McKittrick, K. and Woods, C., eds, *Black Geographies and the Politics of Place*, pp. 46–81. Cambridge, MA: South End Press.

7

Beautifying Brazzaville: Arts of Citizenship in the Congo

Rémy Bazenguissa-Ganga

Translated from the French by Catherine Temerson

The social practices that beautify Brazzaville, the capital of the Congo, partake of the arts of citizenship. They express the way in which the Congolese take part in ruling and being ruled. The reference to the beauty of certain objects initiates them into an aesthetic dimension as it summons a distinctive way of being that belongs to art; they are identified by the fact that they belong to a specific regime of the sensible.[1] What I mean by the arts of citizenship are configurations of experience that give rise to ways of feeling and result in specific forms of political subjectivity. I take inspiration here from Jacques Rancière's analysis based on *le partage du sensible* ("the distribution of the sensible"), namely, a "system of self-evident facts of sense perception that simultaneously discloses the existence of something in common and the delimitations within it that define the respective parts and positions within it" (2006: 12).

In Brazzaville, two objects show this "something in common": beautiful houses and beautiful bodies. They delimit the separation of the political between "container" and "content." Understanding the relative positions of these objects dynamically comes down to showing that the articulation of the arts of citizenship depends on a first form of distribution, which can be understood in reference to history. This articulation can be analyzed through the concepts of phase and sequence. I will call "phase," the form of this first distribution, which makes it possible to understand the plots that configure them.[2] The phase is a historical unit that makes it possible to follow a plot in an exhaustive way, and, the "sequence," a sub-plot that punctuates its moments in articulating the containers, beautiful houses, and the content, beautiful bodies. Two phases, a revolutionary phase and a democratization phase, succeeded one another in the Congo. During the revolutionary phase, the performances of beautiful bodies took place outside the beautiful houses. Democratization reunited the two: the beautiful bodies entered the beautiful houses. I propose to examine the arts of citizenship among the residents of Brazzaville by recalling these two phases, each in turn. I shall reconstruct, in each case, how beautiful houses and beautiful bodies arose out of the interactions between the governing elite and the governed subjects. The chart in figure 7.1 recapitulates this argument.

Phase	*Sequences*	*Dominant political actors*	*Aesthetic paradigm*	*Aesthetic object put forward*
The revolutionary phase: the beautiful bodies come out of the beautiful houses	First sequence: Scientific socialism	*Kalaka*	Writing	–
	Second sequence: Marxist-Leninism	–The military	Writing	Beautiful expropriated house and beautiful built house
		–Fighters and *Sapeurs*	Writing	Ready-to-wear and "collection"
The democratization phase: The beautiful bodies enter the beautiful houses	First sequence: November 1992 to May 1997: confrontations for the legislative and presidential elections	*Kalaka*	Blood	
	Second sequence: October 15 1997 to the present: consolidation of the warrior order of governmentality	*Sapologues* and *Sapelogues*	Blood	Beautiful nomadic bodies captured by beautiful houses.
		Warriors and Freemasons	Blood	Masonic architecture

Figure 7.1 Beautiful bodies and beautiful houses: A genealogy. Author's illustration.

When the Beautiful Bodies Come out of the Beautiful Houses

In the revolutionary phase, the Congolese warded off in vain the aesthetic practices that emphasized the ostentation of government in the capital. The Revolution, the founding event, made this predictable. Indeed, for three decades, the Congolese instituted as revolutionary the political order that was established after a workers' strike turned into a 3-day riot (August 13–15, 1963). The rioters fought against political extravagance. However, the song chanted in the mobilization illustrates the ambiguity of its objectives for it expresses a paradox: "Youlou stole everything, we shall build anew. Congo, all we need is liberty." The first part deplores corruption but this is toned down by the conclusion praising liberty. This shift in meaning clearly conveys the ambiguity of an utterance that simultaneously accuses and excuses.

The revolution occurred after the betrayal of the ideal of citizenship embodied in the singular figure of the *Kalaka,* the local version of the "enlightened." This figure consecrated the distribution of exclusive parts dating back to the colonial order. The *Kalaka* transcended the opposition citizen/native based on the obvious perceptible facts configured by racial separation. Indeed, the word *Kalaka* comes from the local translation of two French nouns: *clerc* and *crack*. It can mean competence, performance and/or elegance. To a large extent, the *Kalaka* constituted a State nobility. Members were all educated in public boarding schools so they could form a subordinate elite and contribute to the consolidation of the colony. Taken away from their families, they inevitably behaved like orphans; they were protected by the administration and, once they were successful, they behaved with arrogance. In a certain sense, this social passion was commensurate with the contribution the *Kalaka* were making in the social distribution of work, and it expressed their way of maintaining their part in the colonial order and exercising their exclusive common part. The colonized non-*Kalaka* saw their arrogance as normal and, in return, they expected the *Kalaka* to use their knowledge to govern the country in an "enlightened" way, to redistribute the benefits obtained through the acquired parts, and to make it possible for everyone to free himself or herself from indigenous status.

The Congolese called them "the writers," which shows they made an operation of transubstantiation insofar as writing takes shape within a social group. It is critical to stress the importance of the writing paradigm in consolidating the experience of citizenship. In this case, writing configures the experience of the fear of the political (see Schmitt 2007) brought on by the death of the body that incarnates it. This paradigm, in its different forms, goes beyond the materiality of the written sheet of paper and links two orders dynamically: the governing elite's impossible attempt to conceal the negative effects of their domination over the bodies of the governed subjects, and the tactics of the governed who reveal the hidden side of this domination by complying with it through protest. This is illustrated in a variety of ways in the political history of the Congo. Initially, the *Kalaka* addressed open letters of complaint to the guarantors of the colonial order contesting the deplorable situation of the indigenous population. The writing paradigm, furthermore, configured the experience of political uncertainty caused by the disappearance of the body of a leader, A. Matswa, and the attempt to clear up the doubts this disappearance raised. Although the colonizers proclaimed Matswa dead, the *Kalaka* launched a messianic movement in his memory (Balandier 1982, Sinda 1972). Several *Kalaka* started epistolary relationships with him and claimed to be corresponding with him. Then, during the elections, over a third of the voters wrote Matswa's name on their ballots, requesting the colonizers return his bones as proof of his death. The messiah's missing body was transmuted into a written body reflecting the body politic. By denying the question of death, the writers brought to light the experience of the two bodies of the person who incarnates the common—namely, the person who never dies and ensures its perpetuity.[3] More broadly, in performances exhibiting their arrogance, the *Kalaka* presented themselves as the most beautiful, because they were the best dressed and displayed the latest fashion trends. Moreover, we may add, the residents of Brazzaville considered the houses of the *Kalaka* as among the most beautiful and prestigious.

The Congolese revolution—the main plot—is the temporal marker that ushers in the first phase. It initiates a one-party political regime that lasts from 1963 to 1991 and configures two sequences or subplots: scientific socialism (1963–1968) and Marxist-Leninism (mid-1968 to 1991). The theme of beautiful houses and beautiful bodies is reconfigured, politically, in the second sequence. In order not to complicate matters, I will concentrate on this latter sequence.[4] It occurs following the rupture of the two orders. On the one hand, after a *coup d'état*, the military came to power for the first time. On the other, in the urban order, the residents of the Bacongo district fought against the emerging political order. This tension configures the arts of citizenship.

From the Beautiful Embezzled House to the Beautiful Built House

Rumors, as they express the mood on the street, serve as a guide to understanding the interaction between the practices of the governing elite and the governed subjects—practices that bring out the social meaning of the beauty of the houses. The beautiful house appears as a linguistic reality, a house in a ditty, evolving with time. At first, it emerges as the container of property empty of bodies, then it becomes the container of the bodies of the governed subjects sacrificed in order to consolidate government power.

In the 1970s, public rumor described the residences of the President's collaborators as the most beautiful. The most persistent rumor concerned the residence of the Chief of Staff and established a specific repertoire for the others. In the rumors, they were essentially viewed as containers. An example: "From the fully equipped living room to the complete range of electrical appliances: everything is automatic. The inside is in marble. There is a television set even in the bathroom." The beautiful house appears as a container of beautiful things, of luxury manufactured goods. However, in evoking these beautiful houses, no reference is made to their occupants or their "beautiful" bodies. On the other hand, in the 1980s, the beautiful house will be seen through the experience of certain bodies that enter them, as the place of the potential death of the governed subjects. Whether the container is empty or full of bodies, the rumors never refer to the house of the highest-ranking personality, the President of the Republic. How are we to understand this omission?

It can be understood by showing that, in spite of the specific references made in the rumors, the designation of beauty refers to a more general situation that makes it possible to grasp other types of practices which, in this case, concern the governing elite. Indeed, let us recall that when the military took power, their moving into official residences befitting their status and social responsibilities became an interesting sociological phenomenon. These houses were located in the center of the city, simply called "the City," the seat of economic and political power. The houses assigned by the State to those in political office were located on the Plateau—the residential and administrative sub-neighborhood of "the City". Not living there stood out, symbolically, as a highly significant political act. The President himself refused to live in the Palace, the Governor General's former colonial residence, where the previous President, considered a *Kalaka,* had lived. Various reasons were given, among them that the military were afraid of powerful "objects" left behind in those houses by the *Kalaka*, just from the fact that they had lived in them. The President's deserting the beautiful houses was understood this way as well as his not wanting to be seen in them. The point was to dissociate the *Kalaka* neighborhood, which had remained vacant, from the military. This was why the President's allies occupied official residences assigned by the Army. The military's desertion of the houses for civil government employees showed that they rejected the conception of legitimacy tied to the presidential Palace. Therefore, the successive presidents lived either at Staff Headquarters, or in the housing for military employees located in the M'Pila neighborhood. During his second term, General D. Sassou Nguesso alone, whose political longevity is exceptional, moved into a new palace built in the Plateau opposite the former palace. These facts show that, in the Marxist–Leninist sequence of the revolutionary phase, the political regime appeared decentered. As the civil seat of power—the locality associated with the *Kalaka*—was left vacant, the real, genuine seat of power became the Staff Headquarters. The government thus let it be known that its legitimacy rested on the Army.

The refusal to live in the official residences brought back the practice of embezzling public property. Corrupt practices arose for occupying the urban space in Brazzaville. This is clear from the statistics on the number of building permits delivered to the military and their allies,[5] and was part of a complex appropriation strategy that did not invalidate the public status of those residences. Indeed, the high-level officials who occupied them did not own the title deeds.[6] The beautiful houses were not built by the principals acting as owners, but were quite simply embezzled and diverted from their original function.

The rise in social wealth changed the conception of the beautiful house. The Congo, whose main resource had been lumber, became an oil-producing country in the 1980s. Many members of the elite used embezzled oil revenue to build houses. Rumor considered these the most beautiful. Most of them were located in M'pila, but there were some also in other neighborhoods. More significantly, the President built a new palace opposite the old one and moved into it. Once again, the Congo found a fixed civil space to represent the centrality of government over the common. During the economic euphoria, the beautiful house was not just the embezzled house but also the newly built house. The Congolese were struck by the speed of construction. In the past, due to lack of financing, houses were usually built very slowly, over many years. Because of the quick pace of construction of these beautiful houses, questions were raised about where the owners' money came from. However, paradoxically, public opinion approved of these "buildings that at least beautify the city." The notion of beautiful houses was a way for the residents of Brazzaville to call attention to the changes in the urban infrastructure made possible by the military elites' investment in construction with their embezzled funds.

After altering the beautiful houses, the political elites began to live in privately built residences. Using the witchcraft schema, rumors denounced them as scenes of human sacrifice where the governing elite took periodic youth baths to "mystically" reinforce their powers. The schema is a variation on the theme of the two bodies of the ruling power: acquiring political longevity through acts of magic that halt the effects of the natural body's degeneration. A residence called the "white house" provides a perfect illustration of this. It belonged to an ally of the President's wife. Located in a neighborhood on the city's outskirts and often empty, *Radio trottoir* (rumor) claimed that people met there every once in a while in order to feast and carry out sacrifices. In the course of my research, I witnessed neighbors mobilizing against the house. After breaking down the doors, they made their way inside, but found nothing. However, the crowd remained convinced that they had not searched thoroughly enough or did not have sufficient power to uncover all its mysteries. Rumors and social mobilizations show how the conception of beauty, in this sequence, becomes more complex, and how strongly it is linked to the powerful fascination with death.

From la lutte *to* la S.A.P.E.

While the mystical body of government was expelled from its container—the palace—the same body brightened the entire urban space and made it possible to politicize the practices of fashionable dressing. These practices are also based on a written perception of the social reality. Fashionable clothes are recognized by their labels and the name of the movement comes from the transformation of a common word, *la sape* (roughly "gear") into an acronym for *Société des Ambianceurs et des Personnes Elégantes* (Society of Ambience-makers and Elegant People). Turning out beautiful bodies is tantamount to the street capturing the mystical body of government through designer clothes.

In this sequence of the revolutionary phase, the propensity to be well dressed and dapper, which until then concerned the residents of all the neighborhoods, now involved the residents of Bacongo particularly. In the new context, where the system of legitimate power was decentered and structured around military decorum, the population in this neighborhood felt trapped in their own bodies because they identified more with the *Kalaka*. In order to continue to take part in the exercise of governing, they established a special link between political power and designer clothes. The link allowed them to resist on several levels: by rejecting the fashion imposed by the elite, which referred explicitly to the revolution or to Marxist–Leninism, or again, by attacking the governing elite's public performances.

Young people living in Bacongo brought back the ostentatious practices of fashionable dressing by creating a first movement in the 1970s called *la Lutte* (the Struggle) (see Gandoulou 1989a, 1989b and Bazenguissa-Ganga 1992a, 1992b). The term referred to the energy spent in obtaining beautiful clothes. They paraded in public spaces (streets, bars, etc.) in processions involving competitions, or *defis* (challenges), to evaluate their respective power. These young people were from modest families. A few were still in school, the majority were dropouts or unemployed; they were only interested in clothes imported from Europe, mainly from France, that they bought in the City shops, where the political elite bought its clothes. They were only interested in ready-to-wear clothes (*prêt-à porter*), for which they used an affectionate diminutive, *prêta*. Actually, they attributed greater value to clothes that were mechanically reproduced than to hand-sewn clothes, the *tounga* (sewn). The celebration of *prêta* brought a technical dimension to the arts of citizenship: fashionable dressing made technical was recognized as partaking of these arts. In a word, this celebration transmuted *prêta* into something other than a product of the technique of reproduction and distribution. Moreover, as several authors have shown, the mechanical arts confer visibility on the masses, or rather on anonymous individuals (see Benjamin 1969: 217–250 and Rancière 2006: 31–34). It is the same principle, therefore, that confers visibility on absolutely anyone and enables *prêta* to participate in the arts of citizenship. Anonymous individuals become the bearers of a specific beauty and *prêta* become mobile containers for beautiful bodies.

The effects of the second revolutionary phase can, therefore, be seen from the wearing of fashionable clothes by any individual, not just the members of the elite. This is how *la Lutte* succeeded in capturing the mystical body of government. To achieve this, *les Lutteurs* (the Strugglers) began by attacking the public performances of the governing elite: for instance, when the President mingled with the crowd and the government ostentatiously exhibited military violence. In the Marxist–Leninist regime, it was common practice to stage scheduled and extraordinary meetings. Knowing how to present oneself before the people is an art. On all such occasions, the governing military always appeared in full uniform. Mingling with the crowd allowed the *Lutteurs* to make the governing body pregnable by introducing a disconnect between the legitimate government's sartorial symbols and the individual incarnating it. For this, the *Lutteurs* favored a particular crowd-mingling situation: the reception for the President of Gabon, O. Bongo. A *Kalaka,* Bongo had worked in Brazzaville during the colonial period. He returned to his country sometime before its independence and eventually took power. The Congolese saw his visits as the pseudo return of a native. The Congolese president, after noticing the prestige earned by his counterpart, became interested in Bongo's "look" and began to diversify his attire, sporting either military dress or civilian clothes depending on the situation.

Another event, among others, conveys the link between ready-to-wear and the rejection of military violence. In the early 1970s, bathing suits were in fashion. Everyone, particularly non-*Lutteurs*, wore them as luxury briefs—articles imported from France and sold at the market. The defeat of a *coup d'état* attempted by P. Kinganga on March 23, 1970, served as a pretext to give this fashion another social meaning. The governing elite exhibited his body riddled with bullets at the stadium of the Revolution. He was naked except for a bathing suit. Several days later, bathing suits lost their prestige with the Congolese; they dubbed them "Kinganga" and began to particularly value briefs with the labels *Hom* or *Eminence,* sold only in the shops in the center of "the City." The ambiguity of *la Lutte*, as revealed by this episode, consisted in competing with the government's sophisticated side and, in fact, in restoring the principle of the two bodies of politics. Thanks to the perpetuation of his name, Kinganga continued to live symbolically. By referring to *prêta*, the public attributed another meaning to the exhibition of his body, which was supposed to have dissuaded the governed from any messianic protest. This emblematic case allows us to hypothesize that the *Lutteurs* incarnated the mystical body. The question of citizenship that then arises is the meaning of the beautiful produced by this act.

It seems obvious that, in this sequence, the ruled see only one way for the body of government to be exhibited: the fashion show. Indeed, outside the palace, another envelope captures the body politic: that of designer clothes. Designer clothing is an envelope analogous to the beautiful house. The *Lutte* escalated in the late 1970s, and grew increasingly popular as President Bongo's success subsided. The prestige of the *Lutteurs* who had immigrated to France weakened his prestige. These *Lutteurs* viewed Paris as the center of the world because it was the center of fashion, and they called their trip the "Adventure." Some Adventurers returned to Brazzaville for vacation, their suitcases filled with clothes, which they wore ostentatiously. Many urbanites admired them. These trips were called "descents."

During this transnational process, the practices of fashionable dressing changed and became *la SAPE*. The members of this society proposed a more global approach to dressing. It involved owning a coherent series of sartorial elements and a specific body type. The series, called *la gamme* (the collection), consisted of designer outfits and shoes. The designer label appeared as the most important element. Its prestige continues to reduce designer clothing to their spoken or read aspect. This fragmentary reading, moreover, points to the ongoing effects of the arts of mechanical reproduction. Labels are not harmed from being copies. *La gamme* also concerns bodily mass—at best, the imitation of the bodies of the governing elite: having curves (cheeks, bellies, and buttocks) and a hairstyle that simulates the beginnings of baldness.

Furthermore, the popularization of *la SAPE* depended on of the economic landscape, and particularly on the prosperity generated by the second oil boom (1979–1984). This boom brought about a lively, joyful atmosphere, the *Nkembo,* which gave a special coloring to the "descents" of *les Sapeurs*. The movement, thereby, had a big influence on social life and on producing the legitimate body incarnating power. In this sequence, the President of the Republic adopted *la SAPE* at the same time as he was building a new palace. In fact, in return, *les Sapeurs* acknowledged that he had the merit of dressing tastefully.

When the Beautiful Bodies Enter the Beautiful Houses

In the democratizing phase, a form of citizenship configured by blood replaced the one configured by written experience. Indeed, the *Kalaka* lose their influence and another socio-body politic emerges that brings together the "warriors" and the Freemasons. The former consecrate the militarization of society; the latter, an escalation of the war in the political–religious sphere. The warriors give a new meaning to the trajectories of the beautiful bodies by directing them to the beautiful houses as their preferred containers; the Freemasons anchor the shape of the beautiful houses and then extend this conception to the public policies for ornamenting the city. A change occurs that confers a more important role on the beautiful houses; being an owner of a beautiful house is seen as an essential sign of social success, including for individuals engaged in the practices of fashionable dressing.

The blood paradigm: warriors and Freemasons should be defined with greater precision. In the arts of citizenship, the blood paradigm makes it possible to stipulate that the seat of government and its mechanisms of reproducibility are divorced from educational achievements. It establishes, at the outset as an obvious fact, that the act of shedding blood permits the acquisition of political power. Moreover, metaphorically, it also configures the practices of patrimony and inheritance. This applies to the experience of individuals who acquire their political entitlement by blood, through a parent who already had this entitlement. The blood paradigm, in all its implementations, is linked, paradoxically, to maintaining life beyond "political" death. In this, the blood paradigm can be contrasted with the writing paradigm, which is transubstantiated by taking shape in a specific social group. As the democratization phase sets in, it engenders competitions for elective mandates; this leads, on the one hand, to the appearance of new players, and, on the other, to the continuation of armed confrontations—both real and metaphoric—beyond the electoral moment. Warriors and Freemasons can be seen as two ideal types whereas true-life cases oscillate between the two. The term "warrior" arose as a way of designating any person—actually or by presumption—involved in the series of armed conflicts that took place between 1990 and 2000.[7] The warriors subsequently exercised the power of life and death. Participating in the armed conflicts became one of the important social occupations that greatly contributed to the new distribution of parts for common. The Freemasons, on the other hand, rallied individuals who, within the framework of the power sharing logic, contributed to the strengthening of presidentialism. Belonging to this allegiance was a sign of a personal relationship with the President of the Republic. The commitment primarily implied the desire to please him. Yet, according to rumor, Freemasons mastered evil rituals calling for bloodthirsty sacrifices in order to reinforce their control over the governed subjects.

As in the first phase, democratization was marked by two sequences. During the first, November 1992 to May 1997, consecrated by the return to power of the civilian *Kalaka* and the reoccupation of the former presidential Palace, a number of confrontations broke out concerning the legislative and presidential elections. In the second phase, from October 17, 1997, to the present, the order produced by these wars became consolidated and formalized. This sequence was also marked by the reestablishment of a decentered government. The former President of the one-party system, General Sassou Nguesso, who had ruled for 9 years, returned to power following his military victory. Like most of his allies, he governed while living in his personal residence. In 2011, he returned to the restored palace opposite the former Governor's palace. Just as in the first phase, the interesting sociological fact appeared in the second sequence: the beautiful bodies entered the beautiful houses.

Sapologie *versus* Sapelogie

For the beautiful bodies to enter the beautiful houses, the old form of *la SAPE* had first to come to an end officially. This event occurred after the war of 1992–1994. Indeed, although they claimed to be nonviolent in the revolutionary phase, the majority of *Sapeurs* became warriors. By carrying out beatings, they signed the death warrant of their former practice. They attacked individuals who continued to celebrate beautiful clothes. The most revealing instance of this change was orchestrated around the figure of Romario and took place in 1994. After the belligerents had signed agreements, Romario tried to revive *la SAPE*. He paraded around the Total market in Bacongo to celebrate the return of peace. Several warriors beat him up publicly and criticized him for not taking into account the complete change of context in the country. The aggressors railed against him in these terms: "the days of *la SAPE* are over, frivolousness is out." Romario made another attempt a few days later, and was treated the same way. By brutalizing beautiful bodies, the warriors drove them off the streets. Through militarization, *les Sapeurs* now made it known that they incarnated a dressed armed body.

La SAPE reacquires its prestige at a later date, in the context of a controversy concerning its heritage. Two tendencies, each bearing a different name, can be distinguished: *Sapelogie* for the Paris version, and *Sapologie* for the Brazzaville version. The name of each of the two practices no longer summons a world governed by fragmentation, words broken up into acronyms, but by concatenation. With the addition of -logie, *la SAPE* becomes a science distinguished by skills, not style. *Sapologie* and *Sapelogie* no longer refer to the writing paradigm but to the blood paradigm insofar as the various armed conflicts contributed in reconfiguring them. *Sapeurs*, being either *Sapologues* or *Sapelogues*, tried to solve the same enigma, namely, how to re-instill desire and *joie de vivre*, at the end of the war, in the residents of Brazzaville's Southern neighborhoods and in the Southern parts of the country. Seen from this point of view, *la SAPE* gave them a pertinent discursive order focused on designer clothes.

Some *Sapelogues* feel they were at the origin of the revival of the movement as a whole. I should immediately emphasize that not all Paris *Sapeurs* see themselves at *Sapelogues*. Nonetheless, I shall adopt this word in order to refer to them globally because, on the one hand, it allows me to stress the generational difference and, on the other, to understand the experience of the individuals who reactivated *la SAPE* from Paris. The influential *Sapelogues* are entrepreneurs (couturiers, shoe designers, restaurateurs, owners of micro-businesses, etc.) who diversified their businesses between France and the Congo. They use the prestige of *la SAPE* as an "eye-catcher" to attract investors and clients. They believe *la SAPE* will bring economic growth to the Congo. The movement's consecration comes from the fact that some *Sapelogues* take part in museum exhibits and performances, or in private or public evenings organized by suburban town halls.[8] These performances contribute in structuring the practice in France and making it visible as an art form. Another vehicle that contributes to the visibility of *Sapelogie* is video. This medium of technical reproduction gives it a new space for the staging of challenges. They become virtual, with videos dematerializing the experience of *la SAPE*. Indeed, DVDs, produced in series, expose the rivalries among *Sapelogues*. All those who are filmed criticize and denigrate one another. "You *Ngaya* (badly dressed person)" is the supreme insult, always used strategically. Whoever is the butt of scorn reacts and retaliates in the next DVD, striking even more forcefully and showing his strength. Several people produced these DVDs. The video-maker makes all the decisions: who to film and how to edit.

As for *Sapologie*, it developed in the Congo, thanks to the influence of a singer—Rapha —and his use of the video medium. Rapha produced a clip called *la Sapologie* in Paris. For the recording, he used the décor of the restaurant "La Sapelogie" whose owner is the *Sapelogue* who claims to have launched the revival of *la SAPE*. The clip had enormous success in the Congo, and Rapha went on to produce other videos in the same vein.[9] This was how the word *Sapologie* became established and spread. Then Rapha gathered former *Sapeurs* around him to give the movement a second wind and they founded an association. During public performances, the *Sapologues* officially march right after the military parades on Independence Day (August 15). This is how *Sapologie* returned to its location of predilection—the street. In addition, it returned to the old form of challenge that took place on the street. *Sapologie* now has the halo of political consecration by delegation, for ministers and other influential members, such as the Prime Minister and the President of the Supreme Court, have the position of Honorary President of the association. The President of the Republic also shares the values of *la SAPE*. In heading the Association, the governing elite convey the importance of fashionable clothes in their political practices.

Unlike the situations described in the first phase, the use of aesthetic objects in the arts of citizenship proves to be more complex. Conditions in the second phase incited some of the people involved in the production of beautiful bodies to build beautiful houses as well. They, therefore, gave concrete expression to one of the ways in which the beautiful bodies gained access to the beautiful houses. Indeed, the *Sapologues* belonging to the elite made their way inside them every day. What of the other *Sapologues* or *Sapelogues*? Their attraction to beautiful houses came after the stigma was lifted. The *leitmotiv* of frivolousness used by the warriors in 1994 to denigrate the movement proved to be very important in this regard. It became an important theme in the criticisms that the *Sapelogues* and *Sapologues* directed against one another. Indeed, many followers publicly recognized the frivolousness of the previous generation, which was satisfied with purchasing beautiful clothes. For the new generation, it became fitting to own other signs of social success in Brazzaville as well: a wife, a beautiful house, a car, and means of production enabling the enjoyment of a substantial income with which to live and support one's family. Blogs and videos relayed these controversial issues. Among these, the theme of owning a beautiful house created a particular problem because during "descents," *Sapelogues* often lived in deplorable conditions. They claimed that this injunction did not apply to them because they owned housing in France. In order to avoid criticism, some went so far as to stay in inns. However, the Brazzaville residents could not bear these infringements and retorted, "you must build here because your life over there doesn't interest us and proves nothing."

To meet these demands, if they could, *Sapelogues* owned residences in both Paris and Brazzaville. From a quick survey, I was able to note that these residences are scattered throughout all the neighborhoods of Brazzaville, but are clustered mainly in the southern districts (Bacongo and Makélékélé) and in the Pool area. The beautiful house here was of a specific type; it does not just reflect the experience of the mystical body's eviction, as in the framework of the revolutionary phase. Indeed, it is a strategic response meant to capture nomadic bodies between the Congo and Europe. These buildings objectivize the experience of a cosmopolitan citizenship. For many *Sapelogues*, building a house in the home country is a sign of patriotism; it shows their wish to take charge of the future of relatives and friends who remained in the Congo, and, possibly, take steps to support the country's economic development.

Masonic Architecture: Shapes of the Houses, Traffic Circles and Mausoleums

Although *Sapelogues* are driven to build a specific type of beautiful house, the spread of these objects in the arts of citizenship does not necessarily depreciate them. As for the governing elite, they allow the former conception based on the witchcraft schema to be reconfigured and generalized. The second sequence of democratization considered here alternates between the decentering and re-centering of political power. The shape of the personal residences (namely their architectural features, façades, ornaments, etc.) now becomes more important than their container aspect.[10] Aside from the residences, the Congolese apply the principles of the beautiful houses to other types of ornaments, such as public spaces, traffic circles, and public buildings.

Just like *la SAPE*, the beautiful houses reappeared after a cycle of violence that had resulted in the destruction of the old houses. These demolitions took place on a larger scale during the lootings that occurred in the course of the armed conflicts in the years 1990 to 2000. However, these acts were not initiated by the governing elite, but by the warriors and some of the governed subjects. As they saw it, lootings permitted the equitable sharing of collectively owned property. They chanted, "To each his share of the national booty." The looting of beautiful houses is a prime example of a boundary line being transgressed, the wall of the household enclosure. In her view of the political realm of the Greek city-state, Arendt establishes a correspondence between the wall and the law.[11] Breaching the walls of a household is invariably the equivalent of breaking the law. Looting does not just call into question the materiality of the wall but its very concept. If walls are no longer physically or conceptually solid, or legally impassable, the spatial order created by them collapses. Looting, consequently, is neither theft, nor predation, but the outward sign of an exceptional state.

After the war, the governing elite, mostly military men and Freemasons, no longer lived in official residences, as in the second sequence of the revolutionary phase, due to their destruction. In time, thanks to the redistribution of oil revenue, they restored their former personal residences and/or built new ones. The building of new residences increased considerably in the 2000s because new international laws made the transfer of funds to Western banks more difficult. Indeed, after the terrorist attacks in New York in 2001, anyone who wanted to transfer funds out of his or her country was required to disclose the provenance of money. Moreover, similar new rules of cooperation in the fight against corruption and tax havens were also implemented. The effects of these laws in the Congo were exacerbated by a specific set of circumstances. After the State was brought to trial for fraudulent business dealings and lost its case, some of the property of the members of the elite was seized or subject to being seized abroad. Lastly, the nongovernmental organizations (NGOs) stepped up their fight against "unlawfully acquired property." To circumvent and counter all of these constraints, the elites invested in the country itself. The prohibition against investing elsewhere, the dread of being seized, drove them to build beautiful houses as well.

These houses stand out, thanks to their architectural shape, and especially because they bear Masonic religious ornaments on their façades, such as a triangle with an eye in the center. This ornament is the owner's way of proclaiming he belongs to the political–religious elite. Aside from the houses, the planning of public space became part of the same trend. It was, first, applied to many official monuments (the Constitutional Court, the Law Courts, etc.), and then spread throughout the Congo in the context of the public policies of "expeditious municipalization." In order to secure their property rights, the elites registered title deeds in the hope of better protecting their property in the future. They became concerned with the question of filiation and inheritance because the exceptional longevity of the Congolese president—in power for 26 years—and the longevity of some of his allies, aroused vague desires for a dynastic form of government. This *de facto* situation consolidated political transfer by inheritance. Belonging to the socio-body politic depends on being "the son of…" However, as the years go by, a growing uncertainty arises concerning succession to the highest political position of government. Who will take power should the President suddenly die? Would the government remain in the hands of his allies or not? Indeed, no one can answer these questions, and this creates a strong feeling of uncertainty among the members of the elite. They cannot anticipate for sure that they will still control state power and if so, for how long. Moreover, every member of the governing elite invokes his responsibility to his children's future. Most of the leaders aspire to insure the continuity of their "government" by inscribing it in both blood and soil. For the elites, the beautiful house has two simultaneous purposes: it is an attempt to settle the uncertainty about the administration of political power, and it is also a way of insuring a future for their descendants.

The governed see these beautiful houses flourish and the public rumor is, "these houses will be handed to the people when the regime collapses." Some people even daydream and say, "these houses will not be torn down; they will be 'nationalized' and become public places." These little comments convey the idea that the public status of these houses does not vanish in spite of their being officially privately owned. These rumors rework the 1980s witchcraft schema of the beautiful houses. However, here, the sacrifices summon the practices of Freemasonry.

The governed share their own broad vision of masonic symbols that allows them to generalize in order to understand the meaning of other structures. This meaning is expressed in controversies that prove to be more impassioned for the building of public monuments than for that of personal residences. The most revealing cases involved the decision of the Brazzaville authorities to grace the most prestigious traffic circles with monuments. These structures are based on two main principles: the historical staging of the city and the representation of Freemasonry's evil powers. They are the target of public controversies that reveal how these city ornaments relate to the beautiful houses.

For the governing elite, the historical staging of the city means erecting statues in memory of the deceased men who held the supreme offices of *Président du Conseil* (Prime Minister) in the colonial period and President of the Republic after the country's independence. It also means displaying the Republic's coat of arms. However, for the governed, these thoroughfare adornments also summon up the quest for the body of a vanished dead political personality. Indeed, the blatant absence among these urban structures of a monument in memory of President Massamba-Débat, the symbol of the *Kalaka*, is striking. He was executed after being sentenced by court-martial; his body was buried anonymously and never returned to his family. The absence of Massamba-Débat illustrates how the blood paradigm excludes the writing paradigm. The second polemic centered around the monument the President and his allies wished to erect in the M'Pila neighborhood in honor of the President's deceased daughter, Edith-Lucie Bongo. The grievances focused on the fact that, for one thing, she was not a significant personality in the political history of the Congo, and, secondly, the President was mixing his private and public life. In order to understand these misgivings, it also seems pertinent to recall the reference made to Bongo, the *Kalaka* president, through whom the capture of the two bodies of government had been consolidated in the 1970s.

The second principle that the Congolese street opposed was the governing elite's use of Egyptian symbols. This was the case of the statue of Ba—half-bird and half-man—placed in the City. The governed subjects felt that this statue belonged to a strategy implemented by the governing elite in order to reinforce their power over society. Another monument of the same nature was the obelisk erected at the traffic circle of a working-class neighborhood. On the day of its inauguration, the Minister of Culture declared, "the Congo is entering the age of modernity because all great cities have their obelisk." Another sort of monument illustrates this disagreement—the traffic circle that the Mayor of Brazzaville decided to build in the center of the city. By taking this initiative, he anticipated future public policies of urbanization. His zeal provoked an angry response from the President and from *Radio-trottoir* (rumor) whose complaint was that the "traffic circle was unattractive."

The principles behind these public constructions aimed at beautifying the city reached a peak with the Savorgnan de Brazza mausoleum—a building bedecked with many masonic emblems. The Congolese currently regard it as the most beautiful and most impressive edifice built since the end of colonization.[12] The fact that the Congolese attribute so much value to this mausoleum is an indication that it is possible to understand the new social meaning of the beautiful houses if we relate their appearance to the reality of the war. Indeed, the decision to build it was made just as the state authorities allowed the exhumation of bodies scattered throughout the country as a result of the armed conflicts of 1990–2000 and their burial in consecrated cemeteries. The governing elite did not connect the two decisions but the "present of history" makes them resonate. The evocation of human remains here means that the beautiful houses entered into a configuration that posits their political treatment in the republican order.

The Arts of Citizenship in the Congo

In tracking the succession of phases and sequences, we have yet to consider the arts of citizenship through the practices of beautifying the city. Seeing the phases as determining the distribution of common parts means postulating the existence of configurations of experience that give rise to specific forms capable of being apprehended by the senses and renewed with time. Indeed, the succession of phases shows that the aesthetic area is where two things take place: firstly, the battle dealing with the promises of national emancipation and, secondly, the illusions and disillusions of history in the form of the non-presentable political dead person. In the first instance, the writing paradigm configures the experience of citizenship and, in the second, the blood paradigm. On the one hand, the writing paradigm that governs the orders of discourse addressed by the governed to the governing elite in order to resolve political doubts underpins the separation between the beautiful bodies and the beautiful house in the revolutionary phase. On the other hand, the blood paradigm that marks the consecration of the warrior order integrates the first within the second, and conveys, in this case, that a strong power that is a power of death accompanies democratization.

Another problem remains to be solved. How is the importance of the second sequence to be understood in the emergence of these aesthetic experiences? This sequence configures a society irrigated by the specific conception of a decentered government anchored in the military institution. In this case, the ambiguous notion of beauty encompasses two things simultaneously. It emerges as the mystical body is evicted from the beautiful houses, its political envelope, namely, the befitting official residences, and the same body is captured by another envelope, the beautiful clothes. Afterwards, it also relates to the reverse movement, namely, the return of the beautiful bodies to the beautiful houses.

These results allow for a deepened understanding of the arts of citizenship by analyzing how beauty—given concrete expression here by two specific objects—participates in the fact of governing and being governed. Further, how does their inclusion in the city makes it possible to interpret the meaning of the practices of citizenship that transcend it? The interactions between two types of subjects, the governing elite and the governed subjects, make it possible to identify these arts of citizenship.

The governing elite, by expropriating and/or building the beautiful houses, testify to a civic model configured by two specific conceptions: revolution, on the one hand, and Freemasonry, on the other. The fact that the financial resources are of state origin indicates that these practices cannot be reduced to some evergetism (see Veyne 1992). The funds do not come from private sources but from the redistribution of state wealth and public property expropriated by the elites. Furthermore, the initiatives are contingent on a person's position in the ruling party, on the quality of the person's relationship with the president of the Republic, more specifically on a desire to please him, and on the economic context marked by the oil booms. Finally, the governing elite create historical plots within the architectural body of the city. Such is the grand operation summoned by the building of beautiful houses, and, in the second sequence of democratization, by the distinction they impart to national heroes.

In contrast, the governed subjects express their aesthetic values mainly through rumors and also, secondarily, by the building of beautiful houses. In their statements, the governed stoke terrifying images of the beautiful houses, emphasizing the fascination exerted by the aesthetics of death. That is how they show their way of being governed, in other words, of both challenging the political power play and subscribing to it. They construct fictions in accordance with a dual regime, ethical and representative. In accordance with the first, the public images that are evoked seek to give the citizens a certain kind of education. Through them, the governed evoke the ethos, the frame of mind of the elites and the group. Rumors stress the existence of houses appropriated for a specific social occupation. As for the representative regime, it links these houses to the order of distributed occupations in the society as a whole. This order takes on an analogy with the global hierarchy of political and social occupations and, therefore, to a fully hierarchical vision of society. Aside from spreading rumors, the governed also start building beautiful houses. In this case, the second generation of *Sapeurs* is embarking on reflexive tactics, questioning certain aspects of their own practices. They convert the financial resources accumulated during their period of transnational mobility into a sign of success in the home country. These buildings objectivize and reinforce an experience of cosmopolitan citizenship. The principle behind the beautiful houses coincides with globalization.

Let us now ask how the beauty of the body, produced by the different practices of fashionable dressing, belongs to the arts of citizenship? We have only to clarify the behavior patterns characteristic of the two subjects distinguished earlier. The governing elite adopt a more passive attitude. The values imposed by the governed fascinate them. In their public appearances, they adopt the fashions of self-presentation configured by the street. Moreover, they become members of *Sapeurs* associations whose prestige they boost by occupying honorary positions in them. By doing this, they are giving *la SAPE* the opportunity to regain the public space as typified by the street. How are we to understand this relative passivity of the governing elite? Is it feigned or simply the effect of the importance of the symbolic order?

For the governed, the practices of fashionable dressing include several acts. The first of these enables them to reconstruct the meaning of colonial history and demilitarize society in the Marxist-Leninist sequence of the revolutionary phase. The Congolese capture military strength in sartorial signs, fragmentary designer clothes—the *prêta* or the label. These practices are seen as a reversal of the order of political domination. The governed impose their sartorial values on the whole of society. In other acts, the *Sapeurs* show their organizational skills. Some of them start businesses using *la SAPE* as an eye-catcher and as a way of joining the system of social occupations. Others create an association linking the two parts of the movement: the inside part and the outside part. In all of these cases, *la SAPE* configures the relationship of beauty to citizenship differently. It brings in a dematerialization of experiences by turning to methods of technical reproduction like video. Museum performances consecrate them as art. Lastly, the system of tastes that informs these practices is clearly expressed in speech. Rumors are gathered that spread news about fashion, and approve or challenge the practices of the governing elite. This discursive order also organizes a body of controversies and encourages a reflexive approach among the members of society. In the arts of citizenship, this reflexivity leads to the establishment of an ethics of responsibility that reinforces their cosmopolitan citizenship. Some *Sapelogues* become organized in order to take part in the country's economic development. This ethics of responsibility, which is based on the accomplishments of *la SAPE*, also represents a way of taking part in the system of the distribution of parts. This system is no longer ruled solely by the State; it is also ruled by the order of globalization.

Whatever the phases and sequences analyzed, the data presented establish the arts of citizenship in the Congo as an element in the mechanism that shows how the political order is torn apart by a tension between an ambivalent criticism of the beautiful houses and a celebration of the beautiful bodies. The beautiful houses rivet the symbolic system of government to a fixed space. Meanwhile, the beautiful body is celebrated in its movement and performance. In this way, the aesthetics of citizenship express the relationship between the effects of government and the positions of the beautiful bodies in the shared space. The beautiful body traces baselines and areas of capture. On the one hand, it positions itself in a transnational space—the space of mobility. On the other, its trajectories prove to be ambiguous to the extent that the beautiful body is initially drawn outside the beautiful house, only to return to it later after having acquired more power.

Notes

1. Sensible here means "perceptible to the senses" as in the expression, "the sensible world."—Translator's note.
2. I constructed this approach to historical sociology in terms of phases and sequences in Bazenguissa-Ganga (2004, 2009: 151). I put forward a conception of time that is not empty, but anchored in specific social dynamics.
3. I am referring here to discussions on the thesis of Kantorowicz (1957).
4. I will not dwell on the characteristics of the sequences, for I have already written about them more extensively in Bazenguissa-Ganga (1997).
5. I discussed these corrupt practices in detail in Bazenguissa-Ganga (1997: 174–178).
6. In the course of my research, I found that, between 1910 and 1972, only 150 plots of land were "correctly" owned in the "City." Whereas, between 1967 and 1972 there were nearly 420 building licenses requested by individuals.

7. Several studies, books, and articles analyze this electoral war. I can suggest, among others: Clark (2008), and Yengo (2006).
8. Such as at the Dapper Museum in Paris or the Musée de Confluences in Lyon.
9. The titles of those DVDs are "Sapologie 2" and "Sapologie 3".
10. In developing this analysis, I take inspiration from the work of Pont (2010).
11. For an analysis of the relation between the wall and the law, see Arendt (1958: 63).
12. I have made a historical sociological analysis of this monument in Bazenguissa-Ganga (2011).

References

Arendt, H. (1958). *The Human Condition*. Chicago: University of Chicago Press.

Balandier, G. (1982). *Sociologie actuelle de l'Afrique noire*. Paris: PUF.

Bazenguissa-Ganga, R. (1992a). "La Sape et la politique au Congo." *Journal des Africanistes* 62(1): 151–159.

———. (1992b). "Belles maisons contre S.A.P.E.: pratiques de valorisation symbolique au Congo." In Haubert, M., ed., *État et Société dans le Tiers-Monde: de la modernization à la democratisation?*, pp. 247–256. Paris: Publications de la Sorbonne.

———. (1997). *Les voies du politique au Congo: Essai de sociologie historique*. Paris: Karthala.

———. (2004). "Approche pluridisciplinaire des pratiques d'exception: sociologie, anthropologie et histoire." Mémoire d'Habilitation à Diriger des Recherches (HDR), University of Lille I.

———. (2009). "Au-delà de l'Atlantique noir: les Afriques des banlieues 'mondialisées'." In Agudelo, C., Boidin, C., and Sansone, L. eds, *Autour de l'Atlantique noir. Une polyphonie de perspectives*. pp. 133–152. Paris: Editions de l'IHEAL.

———. (2011). "The Bones of the Body Politic: Thoughts on the Savorgnan de Brazza Mausoleum." *Journal of Urban and Regional Research* 35(2): 445–452.

Benjamin, W. (1969). "The Work of Art in the Age of Mechanical Reproduction." In *Illuminations*, translated by Harry Zohn, edited and with an introduction by Hannah Arendt, pp. 217–250. New York: Schocken Books.

Clark, J.-F. (2008). *The Failure of Democracy in the Republic of Congo*. Boulder, CO: Lynne Rienner.

Gandoulou, J.-D. (1989a). *Dandies à Bacongo: le culte de l'élégance dans la société congolaise contemporaine*. Paris: L'Harmattan.

———. (1989b). *Au Coeur de la Sape: moeurs et aventures des Congolais à Paris*. Paris: l'Harmattan.

Kantorowicz, E. (1957). *The King's Two Bodies*. Princeton, NJ: Princeton University Press.

Pont, A. V. (2010). *Orner la cité: Enjeux culturels et politiques du paysage urbain dans l'Asie gréco-romaine*. Bordeaux: Ausonius.

Rancière, J. (2006). *The Politics of Aesthetics: The Distribution of the Sensible*. Translated with an Introduction by Gabriel Rockhill, Afterword by Slavoj Žižek, London and New York: Continuum.

Schmitt, C. (2007). *The Concept of the Political*. Translated and introduced by George Schwab, afterword by Tracy B. Strong and Notes by Leo Strauss. Chicago: University of Chicago Press.

Sinda, M. (1972). *Le messianisme congolais et ses incidences politiques*. Paris: Payot.

Veyne, P. (1992). *Bread and Circuses: Historical Sociology and Political Pluralism*, translated by Oswyn Murray and Brian Pearce. New York: Penguin Books.

Yengo, P. (2006). *La guerre civile au Congo-Brazzaville*. Paris: Karthala.

8

Representing an African City and Urban Elite: The Nightclubs, Dance Halls, and Red-Light District of Interwar Accra

Jinny Prais

Introduction

It is well known that cities are not static monoliths. They do not contain an assemblage of tidy spaces packaged into a larger discrete unit. The physical spaces of cities are themselves endowed with social values that are often antagonized and contested. Even more, inhabitants of cities frequently project their own mental maps onto urban topographies, and they do so in ways that shape lived experiences of urban life and physical space. In the 1920s and 1930s, the residents of Accra, the then administrative center of the British Gold Coast, confronted their own complex ordering of space as various segments of society competed to shape its physical and imagined terrain.

This chapter aims to address this complexity, foremost by exploring how Accra's university-educated professional elite imagined the city of Accra in the newspapers that they owned, managed, or edited during the interwar years. Their physical and mental mapping of the city was strongly influenced by their own social and political standing *vis-à-vis* African chiefs, elite Europeans, high-ranking colonial officials, and a growing class of locally educated socially aspirant clerks, clergymen, teachers, and shopkeepers. In the African-owned newspapers, writers—typically of elite orientation with professional degrees—mapped their city according to social status and the mutually informing markers of class and gender of which such status was comprised. Amid this discourse, gendered markers, especially descriptions of women (e.g., their clothing, body shape, livelihood, education), helped stratify the urban environment into high-, middle-, and low-class spaces. This demarcation of space is seen most readily in newspaper articles on dance and nightlife.

During the interwar years, the colonial government strengthened the social, political, and cultural authority of the African chieftaincy, in this case dominated by the Ga ethnic group. These actions were entrenched and reinforced the colonial vision of Accra as divided between a white colonial administration and an ethnically segmented African village. This narrow vision of Accra overlooked its diverse community of English literate and urbane African residents. Among them was a professional elite, comprising lawyers, doctors, headmasters, and business owners, and a growing group of non-elite, clerks, teachers, and shopkeepers. Members of these divergent groups pursued their own political, social, and cultural projects by participating in, or even founding, newspapers and social clubs. Once the exclusive domain of the African and European elite, these dance halls and other entertainment venues became increasingly popular among non-elite Africans. It is primarily within this context that Accra's professional elite shaped its own understanding of the urban space in ways that served its unique political, social, and cultural projects of the interwar years. These professionals were themselves ethnically diverse and in search of a new image of urban Africa—one that celebrated all things "modern" and urban, and transcended ethnic divisions. The professional group's newspaper descriptions of the city (as expressed through dance and leisure activities) reveal its political and social aspirations. They convey an egalitarian relationship between African professionals, elite Europeans, and high-ranking colonial officials, and suggest a superior or unique position *vis-à-vis* the African chieftaincy and a paternalistic relationship with non-elite readers. Representations of women played a key role in the self-positioning of African professionals *vis-à-vis* colonial and African audiences.

Although we have some knowledge of Accra's English literate community, we know less about how different groups within this broader community interacted with one another, particularly around issues of urban space and identity. The African-authored newspaper articles on dancing and nightlife help divulge the nature of their convergences and antagonisms, and illuminate the role women and gender played in the representation of Accra and an urban elite. These articles, endowed with diverse implications, establish a tendency among African professionals to imagine the city through the lens of gender and class and not in ethnically spatial terms. This mental mapping ran contrary to the colonial policy of indirect rule that classified Accra, particularly its African sections, as a Ga city that possessed an ethnically segmented urban landscape. Furthermore, they demonstrate that Accra's African residents physically appropriated, structured, and inhabited space in ways that contravened the colonial perception of a, foremost, ethnically striated urban topography. The newspaper articles in question reflect the self-positioning of the professional elite that, first, sought to convey a new image of urban Africa for broader audiences and to define a sociopolitical ordering of Accra that addressed how aspirant non-elite readers increasingly occupied the city. As less affluent locally educated Africans engaged in leisure activities laden with potential elite connotations and encroached upon physical or mental terrains that the professional elite perceived itself privileged to occupy, newspaper writers used gendered and classed markers to encourage readers to draw proper distinctions between elite and aspirant spaces and parallels between African professionals and European elites, thereby further amplifying the cognitive experience of Accra as an urban topography segmented by class, not ethnicity. In short, these articles enact definitions of properly elite leisure spaces and activities in ways that police distinct boundaries of class and defy the colonial vision of Accra as an indirect rule town.

I, therefore, examine how elite writers endeavored to present a new vision of urban Accra that emphasized the distinction between different social classes and corresponding gender norms among "Accradians." Accradian is a term used by African newspaper writers to describe Accra's urbane African residents. It refers to newspaper writers and readers, and the patrons of Accra's bars, nightclubs, cinemas, and dance halls. Newspaper descriptions of Accra's dances and other leisure activities staged the city by depicting them as microcosms of the social order that various actors sought to organize and, at a certain level, bring into signification. Dance offered an additional physical dimension through which Accradians enacted or imagined their city, its social composition, and its landscape. The dance hall was a seemingly magical space where a cook, dressed in a three-piece suit, could pass as a gentleman and physically mingle with elite Africans, in particular, elite women. As bodies mixed on the dance floor, distinctions of social class blurred. Moreover, as non-exclusive nightclubs, dance halls, and drinking spots sprung up to meet a growing demand for leisure, the social and cultural presence of Accra's less affluent aspirants increased. When combined, these factors provoked anxiety about social mobility and class distinction among Accra's African professional elite, thereby prompting its members to delineate their status as participants in "Society" and to stress the exclusivity of the social spaces they inhabited. In so many ways, the city of Accra created through dance and the articles that addressed it was the "soft city" of "illusion, myth, [and] aspiration..." that was "as real, maybe more real, than the hard city one can locate in maps and statistics, in monographs on urban sociology and demography and architecture" (Raban 1998: 4). For the elite, the "soft city" of Accra was defined by social class, not ethnicity.

Ethnic Segmentation and Indirect Rule

Invigorated by the theory of indirect rule, the colonial regime of the Gold Coast thoroughly invested in African Accra as an ethnic town governed indirectly through the authority of the Ga at the level of the native administration. The Ga were among the earliest ethnic groups to settle along the Accra stretch of the coastline, and represented the majority of people living within the three main townships that formed the core of Accra during the early twentieth century: Nleshi (James Town), Kinka (Ussher Town), and Osu (Parker 2000: 2). During the interwar years, the diversity of Accra's African residents was impressive, and many ethnic groups such as the Akan, Dangme, Ewe, Igbo, and Hausa, as well as a growing community of English literate West Africans inhabited the city (Acquah 1958: 31–32). Other residents included peoples from the British West Indies, India, and Lebanon, in addition to more transient residents that included migrant African workers, European laborers and bureaucrats, and American soldiers briefly stationed in Accra during the 1930s.

John Parker's *Making the Town: Ga State and Society in Early Colonial Ghana*, as the title indicates, examines Accra as being a fundamentally Ga town and explores the complex politics of the Ga over time. His final chapter, which focuses on early twentieth-century Accra, discusses the influx of migrants and the formation of a professional elite, and he links these individuals and their histories to the urbanization and social change of the period (Parker 2000: 194–236). However, his book's foremost preoccupation is with the politics of the Ga and their navigation of Accra's urban transformation. Parker's view of Accra as a Ga town has a solid historical basis. Colonial authorities and Ga ethnics clearly collaborated to define Accra as a Ga city. This categorization had certain implications. It impressed upon newcomers that Accra was, effectively, a Ga town. By the 1920s, a slew of people from various African communities and even from areas beyond the continent had settled in Accra. They do not appear to have been integrated into existing Ga institutions, a practice that Parker and Roger Gocking indicate to have occurred previously (Gocking 1999: 36, Parker 2000: 16–17). Accordingly, although the Ga still densely populated well-established parts of the city, newer districts increasingly housed a variety of people who were not of Ga origin (Acquah 1958: 101).[1] Being, in a sense, foreigners in a Ga city, these various ethnic communities occupied their own residential quarters, created their own urban cultures, and largely regulated themselves; nevertheless, they inhabited a "Ga" urban landscape, wherein Ga held preeminent authority and yielded effective governance through the native administration.

In keeping with the theory of indirect rule, it was "early recognized by the Colonial Government that law and order could be better maintained through the recognition of headmen of migrant tribes who could, through their personal influence and position, keep their followers law-abiding" (Acquah 1958: 101). Accordingly, the diverse ethnicities of Accra resided in specific residential areas and engaged in various forms of self-policing, but their power and authority was limited. Non-Ga headmen, for example, could not set up native courts or "collect levies from their fellow-tribesmen. Only the Ga chiefs (prior to 1953) had these rights" (Acquah 1958: 101). Critically, non-Ga headmen "never had any jurisdiction over Accra" (Ibid). Moreover, although the city's African (Ga and non-Ga) elite could compete for legislative seats, the number of seats open to educated Africans decreased during the interwar period. Thus, through these various policies and actions, the colonial government supported the ultimate authority of the Ga over other local African authorities that included non-Ga headmen and the professional elite. The colonial regime's definition of African Accra as a Ga town, therefore, had two implications. One was the tendency for Accra's urban topography to be reckoned in spatial terms as an array of ethnically segmented spaces. Second, even if diverse ethnicities resided in Accra, they inhabited an urban landscape that was imagined to be monolithically Ga—that is, in principle, possessed and governed by the Ga people.

Despite these circumstances, it is nonetheless reasonable to question to what extent the inhabitants of Accra accepted the definition of a bifurcated town that was both an ethnically segmented Ga town and a European colonial city in the ways that colonial authorities vaunted. What is more, if one had to judge from its newspaper articles, the professional elite, composed of Ga and non-Ga, conceived of itself as a distinct class regardless of its internal ethnic composition. Significantly, it did not view Accra and its social segmentation through the lens of ethnicity. Professional status, education, income, and participation in certain distinctly urban leisure activities and organizations apparently distinguished it from other urban groups, whether Ga or others. In fact, as the professional elite lost its political standing within the town councils and legislative council, it fashioned for itself a new conceptual space that rivaled the colonial and ethnic spaces of the city. A lawyer, newspaper editor, and leading member of the professional elite, J. B. Danquah, used the term African "Society" to denote the professional elite and the spaces it inhabited. African Society occupied parts of the city that were viewed as distinct from that of the native administration and the Christianborg Castle (colonial administration). African Society, which included only the highest elites of the town of all ethnic and country origin, offered the elite a viable third space (outside the native and colonial administrations) for political, cultural, and social action. The newspaper articles of the professional elite aimed to locate this conceptual space within specific areas of the city and the leisure activities that it housed. In this sense, the professional elite engaged in a political project that sought to match (if not surpass) the political authority of Ga chieftains, and to reframe Accra as something other than an indirect rule city that limited and misrepresented African political and social affiliations.

The colonial image of Accra as an indirect rule city divided between a European colonial administration and an ethnically segmented African population overlooked the alternative spaces of cultural, social, and political production in the city. In the eyes of colonial authorities, Accra was "an essentially European domain, unfit for a 'proper' African state" (Parker 1999: 211). They argued that African affairs "were best conducted in the bush, not in the urban showcase of expatriate enterprise and ordered modernity" (Ibid). By implementing indirect rule in urban space, colonials aimed to recreate the "bush" within the city. While doing so, they denied the existence of urban Africans or, when they acknowledged them, pathologized them as disembedded from their natural habitat. In other words, the townspeople they conceived of as "de-tribalized" were reckoned to be mimicking Europeans in ways that did not suit their natural inclinations. The discourse of de-tribalization suggested that Africans were intrinsically incompatible with the urban environment and "modern" forms of governance.

This assumption was as racial as it was political. If Africans were viewed as incapable of functioning within the urban space and of organizing themselves outside of ethnic categories, by implication, they could not practice modern self-government. During the interwar years, the professional elite actively pursued the creation of a new Africa (urban and modern) that transcended ethnic divisions and sought the eventual establishment of a self-governing British West African nation within the empire. In this way, the existence and representation of urbane Accradians and their public sphere was essential to elite political ambitions.

Elite and Non-Elite Accradians

During the early part of the twentieth century, and at least until the 1930s, Accra's public sphere—particularly its literary and political aspects—was dominated by highly educated men and women from the Gold Coast, Sierra Leone, and Nigeria. Many of these elite studied abroad, with London being the most popular destination at this time. Professional degrees in law and medicine were quite common for men. Women tended to complete most of their education in West Africa; however, some attended finishing and secretarial schools in the United Kingdom. The West African Student Union (WASU), formed in London in 1925, became a central meeting point for students. As members of WASU, students published a regular club magazine, hosted dances and public lectures, and socialized with members of Parliament. Their mission was cooperation and unity among Anglophone West Africans in the collective uplift of African peoples. WASU promoted research on the various customs and norms of the many ethnic groups of (British) West Africa, its goal being the eventual development of a homogeneous West African identity and set of legal customs and cultural norms (not tied to any single ethnic group) that would serve as the foundational elements of a united West African nation. Members were strongly encouraged to continue this mission upon their return to West Africa.

Accra was a popular destination for such WASU members. Many, most notably J. B. Danquah, came or returned to the city prepared to use the skills they had gained abroad to promote the WASU's political agenda at home. Amid this trend, the popular styled newspapers that emerged in Accra during the 1930s became a prime venue for the engagement of English-literate Africans in debates on West African unity, self-help, and a diversity of cultural concerns related to the formation of a new Africa that transcended ethnic and geographical divisions. As a result, the local papers carried news from Nigeria, Sierra Leone, and Gambia and included empire-wide news and commentary that promoted a sense of unity among West Africans and an imperial identity. Culture debates, often carried in readers' letters and regular columns—such as the "Ladies' Corner," "Dancing News," and "A Man About Town"—played an important part in elite Africans' effort to articulate a unified West African culture and a new Africa that was itself the product of many influences.

Accra's professional elite had a distinct experience of colonialism that prompted it to define Accra and its social strata in terms of aspirational categories rather than the ethnic divisions that were the foundation of British indirect rule. Although its members were from different ethnic groups, study abroad, affiliation with WASU and its political aspirations, movement among the empire's urban centers, and consumption of Western products in Accra itself facilitated an experience of urban living that was aspirational, socially stratified, and characterized by leisure activities. These elite Accradians, therefore, imagined and experienced their city in terms of class strata illuminated by newspaper articles on dance halls. This experience can be deemed "real" inasmuch as it informed material and ideological class distinctions and dictated social performances predicated upon class stratification and its associated consumption and leisure activities. However, at the same time, it disguised or challenged other realities that made Accra a manageable space for the imperial system. These include the fact that the British Empire governed the Gold Coast through the maintenance and manipulation of ethnic divisions, and that the cultivation of class distinction and its leisure activities by elite Africans disguised the limits that British imperialism placed upon social mobility and compensation for labor.

As stated earlier, Accra's community of writers and readers was diverse, but it mainly comprised elite professionals. During the interwar years, Accra underwent radical transformation in terms of its social composition, and a new social segment of non-elite readers emerged. By the start of the 1930s, the Gold Coast included numerous English literate Africans who had not studied abroad, but completed various levels of education and worked as clerks or teachers. Stephanie Newell discusses this group at length in her book *Literary Culture in Colonial Ghana*. After World War I (WWI), it came to play an increasingly visible role in the public sphere through its club activities, letters-to-the-editor, and freelance articles. According to Newell, this group consisted of "aspirant intellectuals who had not yet entered the elite, but who had achieved the rare distinction of gaining a nominal education and entering the salaried workforce" (Newell 2002: 42). Newell locates this "elusive" and "highly mobile" group just outside the territory of the African professional elite that possessed high social status occupations and greater financial as well as educational resources. She defends this group against the colonial literature of the time that depicted its members as "semi-educated" "imitators of the white man" (Newell 2002: 42). For Newell, this group and their activities suggest a changing landscape of wealth and social status. New markers of social status included: converting to Christianity, wearing European dress, participating in clubs, speaking and writing in English, reading and discussing Western canonical texts, and owning books or a private library (Newell 2002: 43). Their actions within the public sphere as members of literary and religious societies and occasional contributors to the press were largely opportunistic expressions of individual desires for social advancement.

Whereas taking great pains to establish a paternalistic relationship with these literary aspirants, the elite self-consciously used Accra's Anglophone public sphere to pursue its own political, social, and cultural agendas manifested at the local and imperial levels. As the editor to the *West Africa Times*, J. B. Danquah, strategically used the *Times* to bring about radical transformation in the social and cultural lives of Accradians by formulating and promoting a new understanding of Africa that was "modern" (*Wasu* 1926). In his position as Editor to the Accra-based *African Morning Post*, Nigerian writer Nnamdi Azikiwe encouraged a cultural renaissance that he hoped would give way to a "New Africa" (Azikiwe 1969). Azikiwe's "New Africa" was distinct from the "Old Africa" of chiefs and ethnic affiliations. The New Africa, he argued, "must consist of Africans and human beings, not just Fanti or Ga, Temne or Mende, Yoruba or Ibo, Bantu or Tureg, Bubi or Hausa, Jollof or Kru" (Jones-Quartey 1965: 120). As emphasized throughout this chapter, it was primarily in an urban environment such as that of Accra that new forms of civic subjectivity not bounded by religion or ethnicity could emerge and, for this reason, it was where Azikiwe envisioned that his New Africa. Moreover, as Azikiwe, like J. B. Danquah, believed that the project to realize a new Africa required a collective and conscious effort to remodel social life, the press and the public sphere were essential to its realization. However, a new Africa depended on the cooperation and support of readers who were developing their own distinct understandings of the future.

The perspectives of Danquah and Azikiwe regarding the role of the elite in this new vision of Africa influence how we understand their relationship with the aspirant non-elite class. Although Newell, for instance, does not focus on the relationship between the non-elite readers and the professional elite, the sources that she uses, namely the work of Kobina Sekyi, suggests tension between these groups. In her discussion of Sekyi's *The Blinkards*, Newell writes:

> In his satire of literary and debating clubs, then, Sekyi's writing is neither reformist nor transformative. In fact, in this instance it appears to be elitist and superior, poking fun at the newly educated 'scholar' class

> who were busily setting up their own clubs, practising their English language and asserting their own literary tastes and aspirations. (Newell 2002: 169)*

In other words, the professional elite endeavored to stake a paternalistic stance in relation to non-elite Accradians. As such, it was not totally hostile. The professional elite, in fact, offered its support to non-elite club activities. However, this support was not purely altruistic, and reflected the professional class' higher social position and condescension. Newell, again, spells out the nature of this paternalistic relationship quite succinctly:

> Whereas the nineteenth-century fraternities comprised members of the coastal elite, by the 1920s and 1930s, clubs were dominated by the relatively weak and dependent social class of clerks and teachers, who, in an effort to establish their visibility and legitimacy as a social group, appealed for patronage among the local elites, involving African professionals, elders and chiefs in the activities of their clubs, as well as merchants, clergymen and even the occasional colonial administrator. (Newell 2002: 39)

The elite addressed such tensions and staked its paternalistic stance foremost in its treatment of dance. When we look at newspaper articles on social life, dance, and other leisure and nighttime activities, it becomes apparent that some newspaper writers were invested in forging a distinctive elite identity that excluded and, in some cases, diminished the legitimacy of the native administration and aspirant clerks and teachers.

Elite Representations of Accra "Society"

Although references to Ga affairs appeared in the press, professional elite writers such as J. B. Danquah (writing as "Zadig" in the *West Africa Times*) stressed that the native administration did not shape the city and its inhabitants. At best, it had a minor role to play in the making of a new Africa, and Accra Society was, instead, the primary factor in shaping the city and its future. Through open discussion and debate about the social composition of Accra, such newspaper writers defined elite spaces and leisure activities. Writers for the Accra-based *West Africa Times*, for example, often made reference to Accra's "upper-set," "Society" (with a capital S), and the "upper-tenth" (Prais 2008: 209–222). Discussions of social class, likewise, appeared in the *Times*' columns "The Castle and Society," "A Man About Town," and "Ladies' Corner." "The Castle and Society" even announced "select" events, such as dances, literary club meetings, debates, weddings, and private house parties. In this instance, the name "The Castle and Society" intentionally contrasted "Castle," a reference to the colonial power at the Christianborg Castle, and "Society," a reference to Accra's "A-list" African residents (e.g., the professional elite).

A discussion of Accra "Society" by "Zadig," the writer of "A Man About Town" and penname of J. B. Danquah, provides insight into the paper's understanding of the composition and borders of Accra's upper echelon. In an entry on the definition of Society in Accra, "Zadig" clarified that simply belonging to a literary club or receiving an "invitation from the Ga Mantse [the king or paramount chief of the Ga people] to a social function" did not imply "recognition as a member of society" (*West Africa Times* July 13, 1931: 2). "Zadig" wrote, "[i]t is true that when a person belongs to a literary club, he belongs to a society, but that is a totally different sort of society from 'Society' in the sense it is used of the fashionable world" (*West Africa Times* July 13, 1931: 2). Moreover, although there were "many levels of society in Accra," the society he referred to in his column was "exclusive" and did not welcome every "'Tom, Dick, and Harry'" (*West Africa Times* July 13, 1931: 2). Exclusivity was primary to his definition, as "[o]ne would not call a society exclusive in which a cook can exchange ladies with his master in a dance hall" (*West Africa Times* July 13, 1931: 2).

"Zadig" suggested there were only three exclusive societies that made up Accra Society: the African and European high government officials associated with Christiansborg Castle; "the exclusive white society" associated with the European-only Accra Club; and the "exclusive African society" associated with the Rodger Club (*West Africa Times* June 27, 1931: 2). African men who did not receive an invitation to the Rodger Club's annual "At Home," for example, were not among the "upper tenth," and, therefore, had not "yet arrived in society" (*West Africa Times* June 27, 1931: 2). "Bohemians" formed another distinct set that fell outside African Society; however, he noted, they were considered "leaders in fashionable life" (*West Africa Times* June 27, 1931: 2). In response to reader protest, no doubt from Accra's non-elite readers, he conceded that literary society included people outside the exclusive African Society (*West Africa Times* October 27, 1931: 2).

Literary society in Accra—and, in particular, exclusive African Society—had little to do with the African chieftaincy, because, as "Zadig" explained, state and society functions were distinct; a state function had "nothing to do with society as such" (*West Africa Times*

July 13, 1931: 2). Although the "highest in society are [often] the highest in a particular State affair," the situation in Accra, probably owing to indirect rule and the index of social class used by "Zadig" and other writers, was different. According to "Zadig," the James Town Mantse's annual "Odwira" did not count as a "society affair" (*West Africa Times* October 27, 1931: 2). Critically, African Society did not revolve around the native administration. It was separate from the chieftaincy and formed its own place alongside the Christianborg Castle. As the column, "The Castle and Society," implied, the elite imagined an equal and cooperative relationship with European officials. This positioning of the elite allowed it to declare its authority over the urban scene and a new Africa.

Qualification for entrance into African Society, at least for men, was tied to membership at the Rodger Club, which required "good character" and an annual income that approached three figures (*West Africa Times* July 13, 1931: 2). University-educated lawyers, doctors, politicians, headmasters, and their wives as well as single women from wealthy and "respected families" were members of the Rodger Club (*Gold Coast Independent* May 2, 1931: 2). Dances and musicals at the club were reported to be "very select" and by invitation only. When open to the public, tickets were expensive, making it nearly impossible for clerks and low-level bureaucrats to gain access.[2] Thus, although these less affluent men were part of literary society, they would never gain access to African Society and its alleged control over the future of urban Africa (*West Africa Times* October 27, 1931: 2).

Newspaper articles on dance and its regulation constituted focal points of elite definition and participation in Society. Weekly gatherings of "notable" men and women for the purpose of dancing the foxtrot, tango, and waltz to Highlife music, were essential to the production and performance of Society. The most elaborate descriptions of these gatherings are found in the "Ladies' Corner" of the *West Africa Times*. Its columnist, "Marjorie Mensah" (a pseudonym used by Mabel Dove and Kenneth MacNeill Stewart), was introduced as a highly educated elite African woman writer who also edited the paper's "Castle and Society" column.[3] The fictive "Marjorie" was responsible for constituting Society through "Castle and Society." As "she" put it, "[t]he constitution of society is the constitution of my column 'The Castle and Society.' He whom I put there belongs, and she whom I don't doesn't" (*West Africa Times* March 14–15, 1931: 2). Both columns were class conscious. The "Ladies' Corner" provided insights into life in the United Kingdom and reviews of the latest fashions from Paris, English literature, and African American poetry. The column included regular and lengthy descriptions of "select" events around Accra including lectures, debates, literary and musical club meetings, government functions, weddings, sporting events, and dances.

Descriptions of dances, in particular, allowed the elite (through the "Ladies' Corner") to expose readers to the lavish and romantic aspects of Accra's "inner-circle." Society dances were often depicted as "fairy-like," "romantic," and reminiscent of *Arabian Nights* or a private ball at Buckingham Palace (*West Africa Times* August 31, 1931: 2). "Marjorie" took pride in the fact that even "these hard times of depression" did not prevent Accra Society from enjoying the "reverie of ceaseless mirth and moonlit bliss" (*West Africa Times* July 6–7, 1931: 2). Recalling a Dance at the Palladium in 1931, she wrote,

> I arrived at the place beautiful when the dance was in full swing... I had not seen the Palladium look so wonderful for quite an age. How romantic a setting! There were Bands-men with their European conductor—a tall and very imposing figure looking quite 'it' beating the time to one of the most haunting and possessing 'Blues' I have yet heard... To these hypnotic strains, slender feminine figures of beauty bewitchingly robed in the new mode—with long Victorian skirts which fell in graceful folds just tipping the ankles—swayed their luscious bodies rhythmically as the music rose and fell like the dreamy tide of a magic ocean... From the ceiling hung decorative flags of all descriptions and upon the silent moving dream... It was all too dazzling to pause to notice personalities. Stars seemed to out-shine stars... We are, truly, the spoilt darlings of civilization... these pleasantries only suffice to kill tedium and draw from the world a smile in spite of hardship and ever-brewing troubles. (*West Africa Times* April 8, 1931: 2)

In "Marjorie's" description, the elite's sophistication and glamour were denoted by their participation in an event that included "bands-men with their European conductors," innovative "Blues" music, and "slender" elite women clothed in the "new mode." These features in aggregate reflected the event's high social status and modernity. As such, it rivaled "Marjorie's" description of a dance at Buckingham Palace that appeared in her column a few months later (*West Africa Times* August 31, 1931: 2).

In another description of an elite, but less glamorous night filled with "beauty, youth, dance and the thrills of glorious music" hosted by the Accra Youngsters Club," "Marjorie" recalled the "rich flashes of colour, beaming smiles of charming, alluring women—some in our own national dress—and the grace and poise of the well groomed young men as they bore their damsels down to the dance" (*West Africa*

Times July 6–7, 1931: 2). Once again, "Marjorie" emphasized how women marked the space with their "beaming smiles" and "charming" dispositions. Intrigued by elite Indian women's modernity and simultaneous embrace of the sari, "Marjorie" also indicated that the bold mixing of European and indigenous forms of self-expression and identity suggested national maturity and confidence. Although the Youngsters dance was not the most elite event of the year, "Marjorie" preserved her "A-list" status by noting that she watched the excitement of the evening's dance unfold from the privacy of a "handsome Ford Sedan of the latest model" (*West Africa Times* July 6–7, 1931: 2). Considering that a decade later, in 1948, there were a total of 85 Ford cars imported into the Gold Coast, this exclusive commodity further demarcated elite status (Gold Coast Government 1935: 117).

Although elaborate, "Marjorie's" descriptions of society dances were not unusual. Several papers devoted substantial space to "select" dances. Leading the front page of the October 19, 1937, issue of the *African Morning Post*, for example, was a flattering review of a high-society dance at the Trocadero Hotel where "well-dressed couples" and "select ladies and gentlemen" danced to "High-Life" performed by the local Police Band (*African Morning Post* October 19, 1937: 1). Later in the decade, other papers, including *The Echo* and *The Gold Coast Spectator*, carried columns devoted exclusively to dancing news that addressed the concerns of elite and non-elite readers.

African women adorned in fashionable dresses, clubs with European names, and Ford cars of the latest model all served to index the degree of sophistication of the elite. As will be discussed, women prostitutes, cigarettes, and bottles of beer demarcated the lower class leisure spaces. In this way, women and commodities came to signify the high and low spaces of the city. By pairing the elite spaces with glamorous people and prized commodities, these descriptions created the illusion of the elite's control over certain spaces within the city, its authority over other members of the literate community, and its social status *vis-à-vis* elite Europeans.

Accra's Aspirant Readers and Elite Representations

We have already seen how elite newspaper writers associated the grand ballroom and theaters with the leisure pursuits of the elite; however, through this form of categorization, they also endeavored to classify leisure spaces linked to segments of society that did not share their status. They did this by focusing their attention on the middle and lower class dance halls, ballrooms, nightclubs, movie houses, and bars. One such social segment was that of the dance clubs inhabited by a dance-crazed "youth," by which they referred to aspirant clerks, shopkeepers, and teachers. According to a spate of articles written by elite professionals, this so-called youth, inspired by the dance hall and cinema, spent its life in search of fleeting sources of pleasure and prestige—the acquisition of money, fancy suits, and knowledge of the latest dance step. Its craving for the acquisition of the appearance of modernity over the substantial elements of Western civilization—its education, legal structures, literature, and refined leisure time activities—threatened the elite's efforts to establish a new Africa.

In 1937, concerns about an increasingly consumerist and frivolous youth culture surfaced in relation to the opening of what was reported in *The Echo* as Accra's only nightclub. For the *Echo*'s "Tom Blunt," the nightclub inspired lengthy literary descriptions. Situated "just off the Station Road," the "one and only Night Club in town," "The Club" was the place where "'strange bedfellows' met with 'Stranger companions' and glamorous women riot[ed] on a sort of indolent holiday amidst scenes of wild profusion" (*The Echo* October 7, 1937). There, according to the writer, every "Tom, Dick, Harry, and 'Arriette" were "to be found every night smoking a cigarette, sipping an innocent Beer or dancing to a real slap up local tune with a real riotous enthusiasm" (*The Echo* October 7, 1937). "Tom Blunt" also claimed that "'The Club' folks are just like similar folks in any large city: overnoisy; ready to have a scrap for a personal trespass to 'property' or fight themselves into 'possession'" (*The Echo* October 8, 1937). The "girls" there filled the hall as "drink, smoke, dance and song go the rounds" (*The Echo* October 1, 1937). A certain Commissioner of Police was known to patrol the area and, whenever he was there, the "girls" danced their best, and "like the strolling players in one of Dickens' works who all turned eyes on the London Manager, the 'girls' would all turn eyes on the fair, young 'Sup'" (*The Echo* October 1, 1937). He, too, had been seduced by the "magnetic glamour of things in the hall" (*The Echo* October 1, 1937). The chaotic space of the nightclub was, in such ways, both exciting and cautionary to writers, if only because of the licentiousness it supported.

Nevertheless, according to "Tom Blunt," "The Club" was not where police supervision was needed; rather the strip along the Barnes Road was the city's trouble spot. Here, he explained, "molestation, vagrancy and other social and moral wrongs could be found every moment after nine o'clock every night. And the thing goes on until two o'clock in the morning" (*The Echo* October 8, 1937). The men and women who loitered here were described by "Blunt" as "notorious; the scum of a place like an African city; the lowest of low; a very terrible type" (*The Echo* October 8, 1937). Intriguingly, the slum's existence did not tarnish the elite vision of the city, but it even reflected Accra's urbanity and justified the elite's a role in policing non-elite forms of urban leisure. Moreover, it further indicates the stratified character of Accra's urban environment, which newspaper writers had conceptually divided into three spaces: the select spaces within the city, the Rodger Club and the Palladium, and the elite dances and events hosted within them; the spaces inhabited by the "youth," the bars, low-class dance halls, and nightclubs; and the red-light district of city where "the lowest of low" entertained themselves through the night.

"Blunt's" rendering of Accra nightlife had much in common with the nightlife of New York City as represented visually in the Gold Digger films produced in the United States. *The Gold Diggers of Broadway* was released in the United States in 1929, and the subsequent *Gold Diggers* films played in Accra's cinema houses throughout the decade. The film is about a group of young showgirls, "gold diggers," who seek men's affection and money to rescue them from the harsh realities of the depression-era Broadway theater industry. These films were constantly referenced in the Accra press and formed an important visual text in the construction of the city, its inhabitants, and gender norms. Through the appropriation of a vocabulary derived from the cinema, writers argued that non-elite dance halls had become infected by "a certain kind of women"—"gold diggers" who allegedly lured African gentlemen into love relationships of questionable value. With the same literary flare used to describe the "The Club," "Blunt" wrote:

> When night falls in Accra many things happen. The streets then would teem with another sort of population not seen during the day—never. We notice women, all well adorned in the latest fancy prints and adequately slippered, some even in shoes with dangerous heels, stepping to 'The Club' as a sort of entre of the night's sport. It starts here and ends elsewhere. These women are true vamps: they are irresistibly nocturnal. We only see them when night falls, for, indeed, darkness cloaks a multitude of sins. It certainly covers theirs. (*The Echo* October 2, 1937)

As new venues for entertainment emerged, and as new vocabularies and images of modernity arrived in the city, "gold diggers" became the seductive bloodsucking "vamps" of society. The image of the gold-digging "vamp," as used by newspaper writers, symbolized the alleged increasing bawdiness and disorder of urban society. Her physical presence within the elite imagination of the city organized the social body.

In contrast with the "slender feminine figures" robed in "long Victorian skirts" that marked the elite ballroom, the women that frequented the middling and lower class clubs and dance halls dressed in trendy "fancy prints" and wore "shoes with dangerous heels." Existing on the boundaries of the social body (she is only visible at night), she marked the border between the necessary grittiness that denoted Accra's status as an urban space, and the genteel society and identity that "Marjorie Mensah" and other elite writers sought to depict. For the self-definition of the urban elite, the "vamp" was as necessary as the elegant, well-educated, elite woman seen on the dance floors of Accra and in the newspaper pages of the *Times* in the form of the fictive "Marjorie Mensah."

Women were not alone in having their values critiqued by writers of the professional ilk. Men of more middling backgrounds found their leisure to be under scrutiny too. Writers accused men "fresh from school or College" (youth) of focusing on frivolous goals and achievements (*African Morning Post* February 16, 1939). One writer, using the pen-name "Lone Star," argued that youth's only ambition was the perfection of their dance style in order to be "reckoned as one of the 'famous' dancers about town" (*African Morning Post* February 16, 1939). Their alleged unquenchable thirst for glamour left them willing to do almost anything, including squandering meager salaries and borrowing money from friends, family, and moneylenders to be seen at one of Accra's new and fashionable dance clubs. Writer J. K. Appiah also lamented that the "average Gold Coaster" refused to live frugally and indulged a "life too extravagant and vague" (*African Morning Post* February 17, 1939). Indeed, as both writers argued, the desire for luxury goods, such "gorgeous costumes," and a glamorous lifestyle captured these youth so much so that those not in "a position to procure their daily bread" recklessly borrowed money "for the purpose of ordering high class suits to appear gay in the streets—mere vanity!" (*African Morning Post* February 17, 1939). Both authors agreed that their actions threatened "the elevation of themselves and the race" (*African Morning Post* February 16, 1939).

As the articles of the elite indicate, both women and "young" men were not to be trusted with the future of the race and nation. Their experimentation with urban forms of leisure and cultural production were portrayed as wayward and in need of elite guidance. By suggesting that the actions of women and youth threatened the future of the African race (and the elite's vision of a new Africa associated with a self-governing West African nation), the urban elite added another layer of urgency and importance to its presence and regulatory role.

Its articles, therefore, reinforce its authority, particularly over urban leisure and culture.

Conclusion

To conclude, I want to return to Jonathan Raban's notion of the soft city as one of illusion and aspiration. In a letter entitled "stop the dance," a local reader argued that the reports of high-society dances and the act of dancing itself were but a "melancholy delusion" (*Gold Coast Spectator* May 21, 1938: 656). In reality, he boldly asserted, there was no "high-class society in Accra" (*Gold Coast Spectator* May 21, 1938: 656). "Youth" and those who proclaimed to be members of "high society" were equally frivolous, consumerist, and influenced by foreign modernities. Both groups were posing as elite, and neither group had power or authority.

Whirling around the dance floor would not erase the reality of the colonial situation. While it was perfectly acceptable for the European officers in the colony, described as "ballroom lizards," to head to the dance halls of Accra for "pleasure and entertainment," it was quite another for the average Gold Coast African to indulge in the extravagance of the ballroom (*Gold Coast Spectator* May 21, 1938: 656). He pointed out that the average salary of the European officer, at £500 annually, could accommodate many "frivolities." The average salary of the African worker in Accra, a meager £48 to £200 annually, did not afford Gold Coast Africans the same luxury (*Gold Coast Spectator* May 21, 1938: 656). Thus, he argued, a night at the ballroom only served to blind the people of the Gold Coast to the true nature of their circumstances. It was time for the "people of Accra" to turn "their attention to serious things," and to "divert their attention away from dancing halls to literary clubs and education" (*Gold Coast Spectator* May 21, 1938: 656).

The interesting aspect of this reader's comment is the assertion that there was no elite in Accra, at least not one that was economically, politically, and financially secure. Rather, all of the African residents of Accra that made up the literary society—from lawyers to the low-paid office clerk—were essentially "aspirant." Provided this assessment, the city as it was imagined by newspaper writers must also be seen as aspirant—that is, as a city that aspired to exist through the depictions of ballrooms, fancy dresses, and modern dance styles. What these newspaper representations convey then is an understanding of the "soft city," in both its physical enactment and mental mapping, as not only one of illusion and myth, but also of aspiration, desire, and competition that had political and social implications for the people and symbolic figures that came to structure and divide it. Simultaneously being an "unreal" and "real" city, the newspaper articles illuminate how the city was experienced and shaped through and within the site of dance.

In other words, the overall impression conveyed by newspaper editorials is that of a distinctly modern, class-segmented city—and in two distinct but interrelated senses. The editorials, in general, constituted reactions to the material factors and physical movements of the non-elite class that organized and occupied spaces of leisure activity in ways that connoted its social mobility. They responded to an "actual" urban phenomenon that endowed space with social value in ways that encroached upon boundaries between themselves and the non-elite. These articles reflect the efforts of the elite to impose their own mental mapping of the city in response to this phenomenon, one that defined in concrete terms the distinction between truly elite leisure space and activity and that of a less legitimate aspirant group. Furthermore, they illustrate how elites distinguished themselves from colonials and chiefs by discussing dance as a social phenomenon. The ludic positioning of the elites and aspirants in relation to each other and the colonial establishment, in this sense, generated a physical and mental ordering of Accra that formed an alternative vision of the city—one that defied ethnic segmentation and the expectations of colonial indirect rule.

These articles are also significant inasmuch as they reflect an elite experience and conceptualization of class that contravened differences of race or ethnicity. Although colonial perception rendered Accra a city of indirect rule and a specifically Ga space inhabited by diverse displaced ethnic elements, the elite defined itself as inhabiting a "Society" in which British authority figures and educated Africans who shared a distinctly elegant and modern ethos meaningfully participated. Ethnicity and Ga preeminence did not matter in this elite vision of Accra's urban space, which largely excluded the African chieftaincy and discussions of ethnicity. Through this vision, the elite endeavored to present literary Accra as the "new Africa" that defied the governance of ethnic chieftains or colonial bureaucrats. It was to lead Africa and Africans into the future. In this Africa, the elite exercised a cultural authority on par with that of the European elite through patronizing an aspiring middling class.

Notes

1. Adabraka was the most diverse neighborhood in Accra with Ga, Akan, Ewe, Adangme, Nigerian, Sierra Leonean, British, Syrian, Lebanese, American, Indian, and various European residents (Acquah 1958: 101).

2. A dance ticket for men cost as much as 5 shillings. In 1931, teacher and clerk salaries were reported to be 2 shillings and 6 pennies per month, or a penny per day. Editorial, "Why Clubs and Societies in Accra Never Last Long?" *Gold Coast Independent* May 9, 1931. For more information on salaries of the clerk class, see Miescher (2005: 87, 95–97, 108). See also "Dance organized by Chair E. C. Quist, Esq.," *West Africa Times* April 13, 1931: 1.
3. For a lengthy discussion of the writers of the "Marjorie Mensah" column, see Prais (2008: 238–242, especially footnotes 512, 513). I argue that West Indian writer Kenneth MacNeill Stewart was the primary author of the "Ladies Corner" by "Marjorie Mensah," and not Mabel Dove as previously suggested by Audrey Gadzepko, Stephanie Newell, and La Ray Denzer. The fact that a man authored the column using a female pseudonym suggests the importance of a woman's presence in the African press for the professional elite and its political and cultural projects. As discussed in chapter 6, some readers viewed "Marjorie" elite men's fantasy that masked the reality of Gold Coast women. See also Gadzekpo (2001), Denzer (1992), and Newell and Gadzekpo (2004).

References

Acquah, I. (1958). *Accra Survey*. London: University of London Press.

Azikiwe, N. (1969). *Renascent Africa*. New York: Negro Universities Press.

Denzer, L. R. (1992). "Gender and Decolonization: A Study of Three Women in West African Public Life." In Ajayi, J. F. and Peel, J. D. Y., eds, *People and Empires in African History: Essays in Memory of Michael Crowder*, pp. 217–224. London: Longman.

Gadzekpo, A. (2001). "Women's Engagement with Gold Coast Print Culture from 1857 to 1957." PhD diss., University of Birmingham.

Gocking, R. (1999). *Facing Two Ways Ghana's Coastal Communities Under Colonial Rule*. New York: University Press of America.

Gold Coast Government. (1935). *Gold Coast Bluebook*. Accra: Gold Coast Colony Government Printer.

Jones-Quartey, K. A. B. (1965). *A Life of Azikiwe*. Baltimore, MD: Penguin Books.

Miescher, S. (2005). *Making Men in Ghana*. Bloomington, IN and Indianapolis, IN: Indiana University Press.

Newell, S. (2002). *Literary Culture in Colonial Ghana*. Bloomington, IN: Indiana University Press.

Newell, S. and Gadzekpo, A. (2004). *Selected Writings of a Pioneer West African Feminist*. Nottingham: Trent Editions.

Parker, J. (1999). "The Cultural Politics of Death and Burial in Early Colonial Accra." In Anderson, D. and Rathbone, R., eds, *Africa's Urban Past*, pp. 205–221. Portsmouth, NH: Heinemann.

———. (2000). *Making the Town: Ga State and Society in Early Colonial Ghana*. Cape Town, South Africa: David Philip Publishers.

Prais, J. (2008). "Imperial Travelers: The Formation of West African Urban Culture, Identity, and Citizenship in London and Accra, 1925–1935." PhD diss., University of Michigan.

Raban, J. (1998). *Soft City*. London: Harvill Press.

Newspaper Articles

African Morning Post, *Accra, Ghana*

Editorial, October 19, 1937, 1.
Lone Star, "Does the Gold Coast Youth Think?", February 16, 1939.
J. K. Appiah, "Gold Coast Youth Beware!", February 17, 1939.

The Echo, *Accra, Ghana*

Tom Blunt, "What is Happening?", October 1, 1937.
Tom Blunt, "What is Happening?",October 2, 1937.
Tom Blunt, "What is Happening?", October 7, 1937.
Tom Blunt, "Hands off The Club", October 8, 1937.

The Gold Coast Independent, *Accra, Ghana*

Editorial, May 2, 1931, 562.
Editorial, "Why Clubs and Societies in Accra Never Last Long?", May 9, 1931.
"Stop the Dances," *Gold Coast Spectator*, May 21, 1938, 656.

Wasu, *London, England*

J. B. Danquah, March 1926.

West Africa Times (Times of West Africa), *Accra, Ghana*

Zadig, "Diary of a Man About Town," March 14–15, 1931, 2.
"Dance Organized by Chair E. C. Quist, Esq.," April 13, 1931, 1.
Marjorie Mensah, "Ladies' Corner," April 8, 1931, 2.
Zadig, "Diary of a Man About Town," June 27, 1931, 2.
Marjorie Mensah, "Ladies' Corner," July 6–7, 1931, 2.
Zadig, "Diary of a Man About Town," July 13, 1931, 2.
Marjorie Mensah, "Ladies' Corner," August 31, 1931, 2.
Zadig, "Diary of a Man About Town," October 27, 1931, 2.

9

Seeing Dirt in Dar es Salaam: Sanitation, Waste, and Citizenship in the Postcolonial City

Emily Brownell

This chapter examines early postcolonial discussions about infrastructural neglect and environmental change in Dar es Salaam, Tanzania. Scratching below the actual dirt, these changing discourses on waste and cleanliness came to reinforce an exclusionary notion of urbanization without actually leading to a cleaner city. Newspaper articles, letters to the editor, and political speeches sought to instill an ethos of self-discipline aimed at urban citizens. In Dar, as in many urban settings, discussions of dirt and displacement often went hand in hand.[1] Calls to protect public health and urban environments provided a convenient excuse for governmental regulation of specific populations and geographies of the city. After independence, President Julius Nyerere and the state capitalized on colonial narratives of sanitation and urban control to rid the city of its "disorderly" people and rein in the uncontrolled growth of urban spaces. However, in the following decade, as was the case across Africa, urban populations grew dramatically. By the middle of the 1970s, Tanzania's economy was near collapse and its cities were only becoming more crowded. At this time, the rhetoric of waste transformed in two interesting ways. Although it remained a tool for purging urban areas, waste and wasted spaces began to reflect not just personal uncleanliness and laziness but also a larger narrative of the failure of citizens to embrace the national call for self-reliance and self-help. In this moment of rhetorical transformation, some previously reviled urban habits came to be embraced as examples of *Ujamaa*[2] development.

The history of sanitation and disease in colonial African cities is a weighty one, inextricably tied to the racial partitioning of urban neighborhoods. Maynard Swanson in "The Sanitation Syndrome" writes that racist ideas about Africans were reinforced at the turn of the twentieth century by theories about the spread of infectious diseases (1977). At a time of growing African populations in colonial cities, these disease theories laid the groundwork for segregating and isolating non-white populations along color lines. When the bubonic plague appeared in the Cape Colony, arriving on ships in the harbor, the Chinese, African, and Indian dockworkers were the first to contract it, confirming colonial fears that non-white populations in the Cape were particularly volatile disease vectors. In fact, the outbreak of the plague in South Africa fueled the implementation of the Urban Native policy in 1923. Cape Town's Medical Officer Barnard Fuller later wrote that "uncontrolled Kaffir hordes were at the root of the aggravation of Cape Town slumdom" and that it was because of them that "it was absolutely impossible to keep the slums of the city in satisfactory condition" (Swanson 1977: 392). The general municipal reaction to intractable dirt was to isolate communities, and yet, it was this very racism that created a perfect storm of contagion. Europeans rationalized their frequent failure to set up waste management systems in colonial cities by portraying Africans as terminally dirty and incapable of maintaining clean neighborhoods. With poor sanitation, diseases passed around neighborhoods, lending, along the way, "scientific" credence to racist assumptions about African hygiene. The spread of disease was both genuinely feared by colonial administrators and trumped up as an excuse for the segregation of races.

These anxieties came to define the geographies of colonial cities across the continent, particularly at the points of intersection between European and African communities (see LaFontaine 1970, Maude 1938, Reader 1962, Southall and Gutkind 1957). Colonial Dar es Salaam was no exception. Generations of planners used racial segregation as their core-organizing principal for the city, later thinly disguised as low-, medium-, and high-density housing zones (European, Indian, and African, respectively) in their city planning documents. Nevertheless, this segregation also fed a new anxiety that these neighborhoods were potential sites of anarchy and unrest. From the perspective of the colonized, this seemed possible as well. Frantz Fanon, in *The Wretched of the Earth*, suggested that neglected, overcrowded neighborhoods could be incubators for transforming anti-colonial sentiment into outright revolution, where "the insurrection will find its urban spearhead" (1963: 81).

Although not all academic discussions of urban Africa dwelled on the fear of insurrection, much scholarship after independence tended to dwell on dystopian futures, characterizing the periphery of cities as black holes, swallowing up African livelihoods. They were seen as places not only composed of waste, but full of wasted potential.

Daniel Lerner described migrants in 1967 in the urban peripheries as a "suffering mass of humanity, displaced from the rural areas to the filthy peripheries of the great cities" (24–25). Left to languish on the edge of cities, experiencing no transition into an urban industrial labor force, Lerner writes, "these are the 'displaced persons,' the DPs, of the development process as it now typically occurs in most of the world, a human flotsam and jetsam that has been displaced from traditional agricultural life without being incorporated into modern industrial life" (Ibid). Although sympathetic, the depiction is still troublesome for the uniform wretchedness it conveys. Many academics in the 1970s revisited and, in the end, revised this view of shantytowns as repositories of waste with no redeeming features. Lerner's characterization of the periphery reflects an era of scholarship where academics were stumped by the choice of rural Africans to stay "displaced" in these peripheries rather than going back "home."

Postcolonial African fiction, furthermore, has grappled with and employed a political rhetoric of waste and wasted people, often in far more politically potent ways than academic scholarship. Wole Soyinka, for example, used imageries of "shit" to subvert the rhetoric of victimhood and point out the failures of governance and the proliferation of corruption (Soyinka 1972). In his article on "excremental postcolonialism," Daniel Esty notes the prevalence of excrement as a "governing trope" in postcolonial African fiction for a generation stuck between jubilation at the end of colonialism and the disillusionment of nationalist sentiment in the independence era (1999: 23). "Shit has a political vocation," Esty writes, "it draws attention to the failures of development, to the unkept promises not only of colonial modernizing regimes but of post-independence economic policy" (1999: 23). Writers employed it to tell narratives and serve figuratively as "a material sign of underdevelopment; as a symbol of excessive consumption; as an image of wasted political energies" (Ibid.: 14). Thus, just as we see in Dar, urban dirt came ultimately to represent both the failure of citizenry and the state in a broad set of postcolonial African contexts.

Regardless of who was indicted by the dirt, these neglected neighborhoods reflect Mary Douglas' (1966) definition of dirt as matter out of place. Douglas points out that what makes dirt dangerous or taboo is not always its biological composition but its potential to be where it should not be. "Seeing" dirt is often the real issue of dirt itself; having the authority to designate what is dirty and what is clean is more politically salient and rhetorically powerful than actually dealing with it. Considering both the biological and metaphorical role of dirt in a society then becomes an apt way to look at "place" and "displacement." Writ large, Douglas' definition invites us to think about where not just things but also people "ought" to be or not be (Lincoln 2008).[3]

Planning for the City

Examining three generations of Master Plans for Dar es Salaam allows us to trace how colonial fears about contamination and race shaped the physical geography of the city. In the postcolonial era, the rhetoric of what these new "dirty" and chaotic places within the city symbolize transformed dramatically alongside the changing geography of the city. The postwar plan for Dar es Salaam, put together by the British firm Sir Alexander Gibb and Partners, was the first of the three plans in the span of four decades (Gibb and Partners 1949, Marshal Macklin Monaghan 1979, Project Planning Associates 1968). Gibbs' 1949 plans highlighted two outstanding shortcomings in the town's development. The first shortfall was that, despite the planning efforts of first the German and later the British administration, a "labyrinthine triangle where Indian dukas [shops] and dwellings, mingling with the African and Arab huts defied all efforts of municipal administration and sanitation" had survived at the center of the town. The second failure was the "almost entire lack of efficient drainage and sewage system" (Gibb 1949: 14). These concerns reflect the preoccupations of British planning of the period, which were primarily concerned with "health and aesthetics," protecting open spaces, and intervening against sprawl (Armstrong 1986: 45). The plan, Armstrong points out, was not motivated by a desire to solve the glaring housing shortage crisis for the growing African presence in the city but rather to minimize potential outbreak of diseases and populations (Ibid.: 43).[4] As a result, as was true across East Africa, "the government medical service was given almost a stranglehold over urban planning" (Southall 1967: 486) leading to suggestions for "breeze lanes" to improve the city's air and utilizing malaria control maps to justify the depopulation of high density (African) areas of town (Armstrong 1986: 45). The 1949 Master Plan's major acknowledgment of the housing shortage was to propose the construction of "boy's towns" close to low-density (white) areas for Africans who would be working in European neighborhoods. "With proper control we are sure that these 'towns' or 'villages' could be made most attractive and be free from any criticism which might be leveled from the health aspect" (Gibb and Partners 1949: 35). The growing city demanded access to laborers, necessitating their presence in the city. However, their presence was severely circumscribed, both geographically and demographically. Moreover, city planners realized they could utilize the natural contours of the city to create boundaries between neighborhoods. Full of creeks and waterways that served as natural barriers, these "no man's lands" were imagined as extended *cordons sanitaires* (Armstrong 1986: 46). Dar es Salaam's very nature conspired with the British propensity for sprawling towns to lay the groundwork for a host of future problems. However, at the time, planners saw this syncopated cityscape as a fundamental element of a healthy urbanism. Dar became a very spread out city and, as a result, faced increasing problems of site serviceability as it grew. In addition, land set aside as undisturbed sanitary corridors later became contested places for *ad hoc* farming and grazing as urban Africans, unable to live on their wages and overcrowded in their neighborhoods, sought out alternatives. With little success, the colonial government generally tried to prevent these rural encroachments citing concerns of malaria and water pollution.

Twenty years later and after independence, the 1968 plan continued to emphasize beautification and the environment. The concept of "breeze lanes" was resurrected as "landscape corridors," swaths of open land running from the hills to the sea. These peninsulas of open space created buffers across town between neighborhoods or different use zones and proposed "enforcement officers" to keep these areas free from unplanned development. Housing or communities that sprung up would be torn down with no compensation, which had previously been the government's policy (Armstrong 1986: 57). Despite this policy, these sanitary corridors did not stay empty from human use for long.

In prescribing future use on the city, these planners failed to come to terms with how citizens actually used their city. An important example of this was how administrators planned for municipal services. Wilbard Jackson Kombe writes that planners assumed that, if infrastructural services promoted urban growth, the absence of infrastructure would accordingly restrain it (2005). More generally, these initial planners hoped that prescribing ways of use against the grain of current use would be sufficient to dictate future use. This rapidly expanding population of marginal urban residents exploited the city and its environment and confounded the sanitized borders of the colonial city as a way to survive lean economic times. Whereas urban planners imagined a sanitized and segregated future for Dar, a very different reality was extant. J. A. K. Leslie's *Survey of Dar es Salaam* (1963) paints a much livelier and more chaotic version of the city on the cusp of decolonization. This particular excerpt describes the neighborhood of Keko Magurumbasi:

> Even in the morning Magurumbasi is a-humming with life, with enough young men sitting around to make six or seven good football teams. The truth of the saying that houses here are only used for sleeping or sheltering from the rain is shown by the number of people, young men, women, couples presumed to be married, old men and women, and children, who are reclining outside the houses in the sandy soil, playing bao, playing cards, eating, drinking tea, playing with the hobby-wheels which small children make (decorated with balloons, bells, 'wireless aerials', bits of silver paper or what not) or just talking lazily in the warmth of the early morning sun. The 'main street', which is full of Arab shops, is blocked with hawkers selling oranges, vegetables, charcoal, firewood, anything that one can get in the Kariakoo market; and throughout the morning, particularly towards noon, this street is thronged with shoppers. In the compounds there are yet more people, of all ages and of both sexes, clothes being washed and hung on the ubiquitous clothes-line of heavy gauge railway wire (which also goes to make the hobby-wheels' hands)…Much in evidence are the municipal sanitary labourers, many of whom live right here in Magurumbasi, who go round the houses collecting rubbish into baskets and burying it in the ground in little pits all over the place, an effective and sensibly simple way of doing it which obviates the need for motor transport. All these villages suffer from paper litter rather than vegetable waste, so that there is no great danger to health, particularly here where the sandy soil dries out quickly and there is almost no grass or bushes. (Leslie 1963: 208–209)

Leslie's description of the neighborhood is "littered" with references to the abundance of waste and methods of reuse in the everyday, from the toys children made from repurposed objects such as railway wires and bits of paper to the crush of hawkers that Nyerere and the municipal government implicated as the cause of disorderly and polluted streets. Leslie, further, describes how sanitary laborers undertook and enforced order and cleanliness within the community, despite not having garbage trucks. Settlements that sprung up closer to the creeks that extend finger-like across the city from the ocean inwards were some of the most complex places to parse in terms of dirt and sanitation. Inhabitants in the Vingunguti and Hananasif settlements used the river basin for growing vegetables, particularly Mchicha (spinach), which was sold by street vendors. Creeks served as a crucial source of water since they lacked access to piped water while the Pugu Road Industrial area discharged waste into the same creeks. Vingunguti and Hananasif were also affected by being located close to the city dump (Lugalla

1997). Interspersed among all this activity, houses "built of simple and impermanent materials like mud, sticks, poles, mangrove trees, thatched grass and recycled metals" dotted the hillsides of the basin (Ibid.). Issues of sanitation and pollution in these areas were enmeshed in urban economies as much as they were the result of unregulated informal housing. People would migrate to the city hoping to find work at the same factories that were discharging waste into their neighborhood creeks, and then cultivate on small plots by the river to supplement their income.

A 1973 *Daily News* reporter's account of going into the "squatter neighborhood" of Kisutu—a neighborhood in Dar slated for destruction—is, perhaps, one of the more complex descriptions of these informal neighborhoods. The reporter portrays the community as a politically potent symbol both for both those residing in Kisutu and those calling for its destruction (Rweyemamu 1973). The reporter introduces Kisutu as an infamous "kupe's [parasite] paradise" and, nevertheless, mentions that residents playfully call the neighborhood Dar's "Ujamaa village" and "Dodoma."[5] They were either subverting the notion that their community undermined national development goals or suggesting the irony that such neighborhoods were the reality in the face of such lofty political rhetoric:

> I had walked only a few yards when I bumped into two women—wives of key men in the public service. I asked them in all sincerity where they were coming from. They replied with confidence: 'we're coming from Dar's Ujamaa village. Don't you know this village?' They asked as I looked bemused...And lo and behold, I was in Kisutu, a brave new world and a brave new life. It was in a hive of activity. (Rweyemamu 1973)

The reporter is torn about whether Kisutu is a "unique village within a metropolis" or "a conglomeration of old poles, sticks, coconut leaves, oil-drums, cardboards. And all types of scrap metal placed together incongruously to provide for human habitation." Kisutu's materials seemed to contradict its cosmopolitanism. "In short," he writes, "in 'Dodoma' you find the ugliest, messiest and shoddiest compound you could think of right in the heart of a thriving fast-developing modern city" (Rweyemamu 1973). In June 1974, a year after this article, Kisutu was marked for demolition, a move that many citizens endorsed. In a letter to the *Daily News* Lucas Maziku wrote of Kisutu's inhabitants, they "live in terribly dirty huts beyond human habitation which spoil the good view of the city. Hence the fall of Kisutu is exclusively welcome" (Burton 2005: 148). Maziku seems to convey disdain for this community not just based on its dirt, but because these huts mark the neighborhood as provincial and rural rather than cosmopolitan and urban.

As Maziku's dismissal of Kisutu points out, these informal neighborhoods were condemned as sanitation hazards not just due to their tenuous relationship to systems of proper sewage and disposal, but because of the very materials from which these "huts" were constructed. Nevertheless, the state's perspective on acceptable building material was undergoing a transformation in the early 1970s. Gerard Grohs, writing on the housing problem and the National Housing Corporation's slum clearance program attributed traditional Makuti houses (mud and pole houses with palm thatched roofs) with the spread of diseases such as tuberculosis, measles, dysentery, and malaria (1970: 167). Although many diseases certainly originated in crowded, unclean environments, correlating squatter housing with poor public health also allowed officials to demolish neighborhoods as an act of public good. However, at least officially in 1972, Nyerere changed his policy toward informal settlements from one of eradication to upgrading. Furthermore, in a 1977 speech celebrating the 10-year anniversary of *Ujamaa*, he encouraged the acceptance of traditional building materials in house construction, citing a reliance on concrete houses with tin roofs as symptomatic of an unhealthy colonial mindset:

> Although we know that most of our people cannot afford the mortgage or rental costs of the cement house, we persist in promoting its construction... for most people the only effective choice is between an improved and an unimproved traditional house—they cannot afford the cement house... Instead we should concentrate on the development of site-and service projects so that people can build for themselves houses which are appropriate to their income, and which can be gradually improved over time... The present widespread addiction to cement and tin roofs is a kind of mental paralysis. A bati (corrugated iron) roof is nothing compared with one of tiles. But those afflicted with this mental attitude will not agree. Cement is basically earth' but it is 'European soil'. Therefore people refuse to build a house of burnt bricks and tiles; they insist on waiting for a tin roof and 'European soil'. If we want to progress more rapidly in the future we must overcome at least some of these mental blocks! (Nyerere 1977: 29–31)

Realizing they could not stem the tide of informal communities nor afford to build housing at the appropriate scale, officials appeared ready to embrace a "self-help" approach to home building. This was a dramatic reversal of rhetoric on the "health" of informal housing: whereas previously correlated with disease, the mud, pole, and makuti were now the signs of a healthy, decolonized national pride.

With all of these changes at hand, the last master plan in 1979 represented a city (and its contracted foreign planners) beginning to come to terms with its real nature. A large part of this reckoning was recognizing that the exploding informal settlements across the city over the past decade had changed Dar fundamentally. There was no longer any "clearly defined structured growth pattern in evidence in Dar es Salaam" (Marshal Macklin Monaghan 1979: 7). In regards to squatting, the planners wrote that controlling growth of illegal housing would be hard "not only because many of these houses are built very quickly, but also because legal plots will need to be made available and allocated if there is to be any realistic attempt at stopping the growth areas." (Ibid.: 7). The plan proposed graduated levels of service across the city based on people's needs and financial capability. Although this accommodated the reality of poor urban populations more than past plans, it also likely perpetuated the same lack of services in poor neighborhoods that were neglected in the past due to racial segregation (Ibid.: 9).

Beyond housing, the new Master Plan highlighted persistent infrastructural problems that the municipality had failed to address, dating back to the German administration when updates to drainage and sewage updates were put on hold due to the war. The city's decrepit sewage system, despite being slated for improvement in the last plan, had yet to be upgraded, leaving the system constantly vulnerable to "the rapid expansion of residential and industrial areas" and creating "serious potential health hazards for the population" (Marshal Macklin Monaghan 1979: 6). Despite commissioning a drainage scheme from the London Consulting Engineers in 1930, the British had never completed an upgrade (Department of Medical and Sanitary Services 1941). In 1948, officials again sought to fix the ailing system when the colonial secretary warned against more delays arguing that "the built-up areas of the Township have become progressively more cesspit-riddled and sewage-sick" (Department of Medical and Sanitary Services 1948). The community was in danger of contracting waterborne diseases, noted the secretary, "from which the only satisfactory safeguard is the installation of a system of water-borne sewerage and storm-water drainage" (Ibid).

By 1979, parts of the city still relied on the small pipes from decades ago; however, most residential, industrial, and commercial areas had switched to private on-site septic tanks or pit latrines in the absence of municipal developments (Marshal Macklin Monaghan 1979: 7–8). By the 1980s, the dire situation had attracted the World Bank's attention. In a report initiating an improvement project, the Bank noted that only one waste stabilization pond and only one of 17 pumping stations for sewage were in operation, adding that many sewers were completely blocked (World Bank 1982: 8–9). The report noted that the abject state of Dar's sewage maintenance was exacerbated by the 4-year absence of any municipal government from 1974 to 1978, due to a national policy of decentralization.[6] The chronic disrepair of the system led to an estimated 22,000 m^3 of untreated sewage a day being sent out to sea, with peak flows of approximately 56,000 m^3 per day (Ibid).

In concert with persistent sewage disposal issues, the main waste dump for the city in the neighborhood of Tabata reached its maximum capacity by the 1960s, and the 1968 Master Plan suggested the construction of a new site in Kimara. Development on this site progressed only until 1976 due to protests by local residents related to fears of attracting a squatter community (Yhdego 1991: 178).

In reality, only a small fraction of the waste generated by the city made it to the dump in any given week and, over time, the state of waste removal from neighborhoods only worsened. The 1968 Master Plan noted there were 21 lorries for waste removal (Marshal Macklin Monaghan 1968: 158). Nevertheless, in a 1974 *Daily News* article, the regional TANU secretary noted that only 9 of 33 refuse trucks were functioning: "The rest are broken down and could not be repaired" due to "shortage of spare parts or because of the cost of repairing some of them would be almost equivalent to the cost of buying new ones" (*Daily News* March 15, 1974). Due to the dearth of functioning trucks, the amount of waste picked up in the growing city decreased from 175 tons per day to 100 tons between the 1968 and 1979 master plans (Marshal Macklin Monaghan 1968: 168).[7] However, despite the abject situation of garbage and sewage trucks in the city, the regional secretary blamed the proliferation of waste in the city on "people who littered streets freely, hawkers and other people who carried out trading activities in areas other than markets" and "the mushrooming of squatter areas" (Marshal Macklin Monaghan 1968: 168). Thus, although crowded neighborhoods shouldered the blame for the city's state of sanitary disrepair, the most fundamental flaws in sanitation came from structural municipal shortcomings.

The waste footprint of informal settlements was, in actuality, far less than planned residential neighborhoods, which contributed almost double the amount of waste to Tabata per day (Marshal Macklin Monaghan 1968: 157). This likely represented a convergence of many factors including less inorganic waste generation, lack of accessible roads for garbage trucks in squatter areas, and alternative disposal methods such as burning waste and engaging in more conscientious reuse. Unplanned neighborhoods, moreover, posed challenges for waste removal due to their construction and constant transformation. As with water delivery, when neighborhoods grew to be a "mass of twisty lanes with no control over where each house is built" and city trucks could not access them, this encouraged the development of informal industries such as water carriers, kerosene and charcoal sellers and "extra-municipal garbage men" (Leslie 1963: 208–209).

Examining the city in relation to its three master plans offers an interesting composite view of its changing personality and landscape. These crucial documents reveal how calls for preserving public health were often a thin veneer fashioned over desires for a segregated city. Continuing into the independence era, sanitation remained a frequent and blunt instrument of urban control; however, it was control of a different kind. Rather than preserving the borders of a segregated city, sanitation and slum removal projects were a means to control the size of a growing city the government was wont to let expand. Nevertheless, as funds for urban development dried up, Nyerere advocated for a brand of self-help urbanism that began to blur the sanitary lines of the city, particularly as the failure of waste removal and sewage systems pushed the responsibility for maintaining a clean city environment almost solely onto the backs of its residents.

Discipline and Waste: Discursive Urbanization

Calls for a cleaner city in the postcolonial era also intermingled with other campaigns of urban governance and control in provocative ways. During *Ujamaa*, Nyerere employed a rhetoric of discipline in hopes of cajoling a public he often portrayed as lazy and messy. This rhetoric of discipline encouraged self-reliant sanitation and the purging of dirt and "dirty" people from the cities. The rhetoric also emerged in campaigns to control the black market in food and consumer goods and calls for reuse in the face of shortages.

In 1965, for example, the Dar Medical Officer of Health emphasized the health and hygiene burden of food vendors. In the following decades, there were a handful of campaigns to rid the city of traders and hawkers in the name of sanitation and urban order. As Andrew Burton points out in reference to urban purges in the 1960s, the government and press cultivated a correlation "between parasitism and sloth" in an effort to thin out urban populations (2007: 131). It was not just shanty communities but their economic equivalent—itinerant traders—that contaminated official visions of a modern city. An explicit example was the 1973 campaign to rid the city of its itinerant residents called *Operation Kupe*—the Swahili word for tick or parasite. To attack physical signs of poverty was to purge and purify the city of dirty, parasitic elements.[8] Burton also briefly remarks (but it bears further emphasis) that these officials closing down small businesses were often fighting against citizens' ingenious methods of providing resources the government failed to deliver (quintessential forms of self-help). People's "indiscipline" was, thus, in reality, a direct compensation for the undisciplined nature of a failing municipal government. A 1967 roundup and deportation of water sellers captures this ultimate irony as their livelihood was a response to city's failure to construct a viable system of piped water for urban residents (Burton 2007: 142).

One of the most notorious roundups of informal workers was the Human Resources Deployment Act of 1983. Colloquially known as *Nguvu Kazi* (hard work), the act required the registration of all workers along with the issuance of labor-identification cards. The goal was to repatriate those who were unemployed in the city back into the country to work on large farm projects. To encourage the campaign, Nyerere, appealed to the "disciplined" urban public that, "if we don't disturb loiterers, they will disturb us."(*Daily News* September 26, 1983, qtd. in Shaidi 1984). During the campaign, anyone engaged in casual work such as fish and fruit sellers, street hawkers, barbers, and tailors were rounded up and deported from the city if they could not prove formal employment. These campaigns against the city's informal workers sought to purge the city of those perceived as perpetuating disorder and indiscipline, which by these definitions were an increasing margin of the city's population. From 1974 to 1988, real urban incomes had decreased 83 percent, and yet, the numbers moving into cities had unyieldingly increased (Tripp 1997: 3). These marginal urban forms were now clearly mainstream. Interestingly, Nyerere conducted these purges despite publicly bemoaning their ineffectiveness 5 years before initiating the campaign. He had done so in a speech commemorating the tenth anniversary of the Arusha Declaration in 1977:

> It has been announced more times than it is easy to count that every able-bodied person in Tanzania must work, either on the land, in the factories and offices, or in some useful capacity in what is called the 'informal sector' (that is, as a carpenter, blacksmith, full-time trader, etc. etc.) I myself have been leading advocate of the principle that every person must work. Then, on every occasion there is a great drive to 'round up' the unemployed in towns and repatriate them. For a week

> or so the criminals and idle parasites hide in their houses while respectable workers and peasants on legitimate business are harassed, and the people in paid employment otherwise carry on working hard or not as they did previously. Then the whole campaign dies away until it is realized that the problem of criminals in towns, and of people not doing a hard day's work, is still with us—and the process is repeated! The fault in such cases is not the decision itself; the Arusha Declaration says that in a socialist state 'everyone who is physically able to work does so; every worker obtains a just return for the labour he performs'. The fault was in trying to carry out the policy by a temporary 'drive' instead of a well-thought out and planned scheme which has the active support of the people. These hasty campaigns are becoming a disease. (Nyerere 1977: 46–47)

Considering how often terms invoking disease and parasites were used to describe these unemployed populations, it is interesting that Nyerere also calls the government's failing intervention its own disease. Perhaps the zenith of deploying this rhetorical language of urban discipline occurred in 1983, when the Tanzanian government launched a campaign to fight "indiscipline" (the black market) in the economic sector, against those conducting what was known as economic "sabotage." It was also described as "real measures to bring out the brilliant performance of the civil service" (*Daily News* May 8, 1983). By the 1980s, the Tanzanian agriculture sector was in tatters as was its foreign exchange. To procure staple food necessities and common consumer goods such as soap and cloth, residents of Dar often had to wait in line at state co-ops for hours. In some cases, people would run after cars they believed were delivering a new supply of goods in hopes of securing a good spot in line.[9] The black market had developed due to the state's control of pricing and their poor distribution and general scarcity. Virtually everyone used the black market in some way, whether they were buying maize meal or a car. The purpose of the 1983 campaign was to control the amount of goods being diverted to the black market by catching and punishing sellers that were hoarding goods.

At its inception, this campaign was popular and perceived as an attempt to help make goods more affordable for everyone. Nyerere and the press described the campaign as a triumph over chaos, lawlessness, and a polluted, diluted state. Nyerere sought to "carry out a thorough re-examination" of party members and the government "with a view to cleansing themselves by identifying all those who are corrupt and reporting them to the appropriate authorities for appropriate disciplinary action" (*Daily News* May 11, 1983). Moreover, he felt that "cleansing those organs was considered a necessary preliminary step toward waging an all-out war against corruption on a national basis" (*Daily News* May 11, 1983). Over time though, the campaign against these economic "fifth columnists" became problematic for poor people (*Daily News* May 12, 1983). The fight against economic sabotage lost general popularity when the state began prosecuting ordinary people who relied on the black market in some form or another, and left untouched some of the largest operators who gouged prices for huge profits (Tripp 1997: 185).

Ironically, in the aftermath of Nyerere's crackdown on economic saboteurs, an unanticipated problem of disposal arose (*Daily News* June 7, 1983). Although attacking the waste caused by these saboteurs on government resources, it caused a pile up of perishable commodities without the means for distribution. Trying to avoid waste, Prime Minister Sokoine ordered "soap and perishable items still lying in go-downs" to be sold to "prisons, the National Service, schools, armed forces, cooperative and village shops." Containers of "condemned and expired milk" were destroyed by the city council and regional authorities "were tasked with turning food that was no longer fit for human consumption into animal feed" (Ibid). In attacking illegal but efficient means of distribution, the government caused waste to abound rather than dissipate.

In 1984, the government announced yet another campaign for cleanliness. When calling for the campaign, Nyerere described the city as "rotting and stinking." "City roads are gradually deteriorating, and there is no effort by Dar es Salaam leaders to repair them. It appears that the city leaders have failed to improve sanitation despite constant annual allocation of government subvention" (*Daily News* June 14, 1984). Cleanliness was a matter of "habit," Nyerere said, rebuking the idea that the city's dirt had its roots in economic hardship or municipal neglect. "We have a bad habit of taking filth for granted. This is very embarrassing," he said, "the city is rotting" (Ibid).

Dar citizens had long been articulating these same sentiments. Complaining about how seldom the trash was picked up on his street, Juma Ali wrote a letter to the *Daily News* blaming lazy workers: "this is so because the labourers concerned get overtime and hence more money: this just shows the amount of liking they have for work! One would almost think that their motto is 'work only when there is money in sight'" (*Daily News* July 14, 1967). Juma ended his letter with a sentiment many shared about the sanitary state of Dar es Salaam: "On top of all this I must say that during colonial times Dar es Salaam was much cleaner city than what it is today." In a similar letter bemoaning the city's burial under trash during the yearly Saba Saba festival, the writer sarcastically noted that, "the scintillating smell, of decay and rotten goods, is indeed the highlight of our celebrations. Market Street, for example, looks quite picturesque: large drums filled with fly infested rubbish, standing outside the big shops, give them a really majestic bearing" (*Daily News* March 14, 1974). The writer ends his letter remarking that he can no longer be proud of Dar es Salaam, and that it is hardly the "the Dar es Salaam we once knew." Nyerere, the newspapers, and citizens alike wove together narratives of cleanliness and discipline to examine the efficacy of the state, while also trying to rid the city of its burgeoning class of semi-employed hawkers and sellers.

Reuse and Self-Reliance

In *The African Poor*, John Iliffe briefly discusses the flipside of this growing relationship between the urban poor and the pollution of cities (1987). If the urban poor were polluting vectors of disease and wasted rural labor forces, they were also the stewards of objects—developing ingenious methods of repair and reinvention, extending the life of stuff, or creating new objects entirely. They did, in effect, stem the tide of a growing waste stream. This stewardship of waste occurred across colonial Africa. Navigating through the strange new territory of both consumer objects and urban poverty, townsmen—Iliffe writes—created charcoal stoves from car doors, lamps from oil tins, and tambourines from bottles. Beyond reuse at the individual and household level, men and boys, in particular, found employment in recovering waste:

> Boys at Hargeisa in Somaliland have organised themselves into an engineering firm on a rubbish dump. In this way from twenty-five to thirty boys support themselves. They live, rent free, in a disused shed, and grew four sacks of millet on a piece of land lent them for the purpose. Whereas the very poor of Yoruba towns had scoured the bush, the very poor of colonial towns scavenged industrial wastelands. Sanitary workers in Lourenco Marques reworked collected trash and resold bottles, plastic bags, rope, metal, old clothes, and a host of other articles. Ibadan had an Association of Worn Out Tyre Traders. In Abidgan men toured the streets with bathroom scales offering to weigh people for two pence a time. (Iliffe 1987: 175)

Recovering these organizations and networks in African cities can be hard to do in any systematic manner, and Dar es Salaam is no exception. When and if such practices do make it into the records, it tends to be in the criminalization of scavenging. Anthropologist Mark Livengood conducted fieldwork, in the 1990s, in Dar es Salaam looking at the folk recycling cooperative Dar es Salaam Small Industries Cooperative Society (DASICO). Although his study includes little historical information about the coop's origins, he dates the organization back at least to the 1960s (Livengood 2001). These men, known as *mafundi chuma*, forged objects out of used materials such as wire, steel rods, old car doors, empty vegetable oil tins, and oil drums from British Petroleum (BP) and the soap factory. The *mafundi chuma* bought their materials from men called *skrapas* (scrappers) who scavenged across the city, bringing items to DASICO (Livengood 2001: 87).

In another study on scavenging, Michael Yhdego mentions that men and women sorting waste at the dump provided 60 percent of the raw materials for DASICO and similar organizations (Yhdego 1991: 263). By 1987 when Yhdego first conducted his survey, Tabata dump was home to a long-term community of scavengers. The oldest scavenger Yhdego talked to, Mr. Takataka (Mr. Garbage) had been scavenging for 20 years.[10] Mr. Takataka noted a shift over the years from collecting at the dump to scavengers moving into the center of town for more valuable materials (Yhdego 1991: 262). Furthermore, Yhdego reported that the city council was mostly ambivalent to the practice of scavengers: "At first the council fenced off the dumping area, but as the fill grew higher the fence was buried in the waste. Since then the attitude of the city council has apparently been neither in favour of nor against scavenging" (Ibid).

Without being too reductive, this statement can be taken to encapsulate the evolution of the state's approach to waste and disorder in the city. For the first 20 years of independence, the state sought to eradicate and contain "undisciplined" people and landscapes. However, citizens, often out of sheer desperation, continued to exploit their local environments and resources as adequate city services failed to materialize. Government rhetoric then slowly began to redefine the scope and understanding of self-help and self-reliance within urban environments, reluctantly ignoring those who broke the "rules." A brief example is Nyerere's promotion of peasants using compost in 1983, claiming that it could increase yield "without becoming dependent upon an unreliable supply of expensive fertilizers from outside the village" (*Daily News* May 17, 1983). He added, "we have to do this economically on the basis of self-reliance and in a sustainable manner." What had once been considered good practice (using commercial fertilizer), in the face of crushing economic instability and skyrocketing import costs, now fell under the category of unhealthy dependencies just like concrete and tin roofs had come to represent a "mental paralysis." Nyerere nostalgically associated good social conscience with a time when less wastefulness and disorder abounded. He also worried that if people succumbed to laziness, Tanzania's future would be one of continued economic collapse and ruin:

> There was a time, for example, when Agricultural Officers used to walk from village to village on duty, spending the nights in people's houses or in tents. Now we even scorn bicycles! And paper is wasted in our offices; the simplest letters are marked "Secret" and put in two envelopes, circulars are duplicated on one side of the paper only, and so on. Such economies seem petty, and the amounts saved appear so small as to be unimportant in a single office; but they do mount up when 20 Regions and 72 Districts—to say nothing of the Ministries—are added together! Serious attention must be given to every detail of expenditure, and the question asked "How can the job be done more cheaply." (Nyerere 1977: 38)

This chapter observes, writ on the landscape and in public discourse, how the government and citizens negotiated different notions of urban "discipline," sanitation, and waste. The state's perspective shifted from considering sanitation an issue of personal health and virtue to accepting certain elements of the chaotic city. Nevertheless, the state targeted what they saw as a systemic urban laziness. A transformed rhetoric about what constituted a healthy, self-reliant nation emerged. Whereas Nyerere's rhetoric remained generally intolerant of informal or "idle" urban populations, particularly ones contributing to disorder, he also saw an intrinsic discipline in some of the self-reliance that surfaced as a result of municipal neglect. For example, he came to reluctantly accept and ultimately encourage those who blurred sanitary borders of the city's outer edges by cultivating food next to their homes or keeping chickens and livestock.

Reflecting on 10 years of *Ujamaa*, Nyerere emphasized to Tanzanians, "We must increase our *discipline*, our *efficiency*, and our *self-reliance*. In particular we must put more effort into looking always to see what we can do for ourselves out of our own resources—and then doing it" (Nyerere 1977: 55). This seems to be the dual dilemma of waste as Nyerere rhetorically employed it. On the one hand, waste symbolized the agonizing growth of cities and all of the anxieties they embodied for the state: physical waste, disorderly and unproductive spaces, and a self-interested materialist future. On the other hand, waste also symbolized ingenuity and conservation of resources at a time when Tanzania was suffering huge trade imbalances.

The habits and reactions of the average urban dweller to waste are far harder to recover than the state's political rhetoric. In 1968, Michaela von Freyhold conducted a survey that eventually was turned into a book called *The Workers and the Nizers* (1976). The goal of this survey was to examine class formation among new migrants in Dar es Salaam. Von Freyhold and her team surveyed a wide range of residents cutting across the economic and social swath of the city. One question the team asked participants was how should the government improve living conditions in Dar es Salaam. First, two thirds of those surveyed wanted change in the form of economic investments and measures, and more than half of those wanted the disparity between wages and the price of goods addressed, particularly food prices. They were, no doubt, tired of constant reinvention and reuse. Second, residents wanted the creation and expansion of industry and employment. Only after noting significant economic challenges did respondents turn to infrastructural upgrades, including more and improved housing, schools, hospitals, water supplies, improving streets and roads, public transportation, and, lastly, "increased efforts to keep the town clean" (Freyhold 1976: 86). This survey struck me, at first, as contradictory to the amount of public discourse dedicated in to issues of waste and cleanliness. Even if one disregards articles complaining about dirty streets, markets, houses, and roads, a language of dirt and cleanliness pervaded discussions of proper and improper urbanism, creating exclusionary definitions of citizenship in the city. However, despite the attention to waste in public discourse, Freyhold's survey reveals a different and logical set of priorities for people whose economic choices were becoming ever more narrow and desperate. Moreover, due to a legacy of colonial urban neglect, many citizens may have never registered that the failure of basic municipal services fell under the purview of the state. The results of von Freyhold's survey are a word of caution when parsing debates on waste to fully consider first who actually sees the dirt, where and why they see it and for whom it becomes invisible among problems of a greater magnitude. Freyhold's survey suggests that perhaps for many the proliferation of waste was not perceived as a pressing problem. People and communities navigated trash and sanitation woes as best they could, reclaiming waste for new uses when possible, whereas having no money or job posed a far more crushing obstacle.

Notes

1. Andrew Burton (2007) outlines the series of purges during the postcolonial era. In addition, he touches on the metaphors of cleanliness and order at play in these purges of people from the city.

2. *Ujamaa* was the name of Nyerere's development policy he undertook beginning officially in 1967, which he announced in his Arusha Declaration that outlined his philosophy of African Socialism.
3. Lincoln's dissertation (2008) utilizes Douglas' definition to talk about people and neighborhoods as out of place and disposable in African fiction.
4. The first two Master Plans also represent the "only strategic and comprehensive urban planning exercise undertaken by in Tanzania, until the 1970's ushered in a program of foreign aided and executed master planning for many regional towns" (Armstrong 1986: 43).
5. The capital of Tanzania was moved from Dar es Salaam to Dodoma, at the center of the country, following the era of decentralization.
6. Decentralization called for the disbanding of all municipal governments in Tanzania, among other major shifts in national governance.
7. Dar es Salaam was also a port city and the major site for industry in Tanzania; however, these industrial waste streams are hard to track down and are rarely discussed in newspapers or much in the three generations of master plans. However, a World Bank Report from 1982 addressed industrial wastes briefly, mentioning that, "Industrial and trade wastes in Dar es Salaam are substantially uncontrolled and untreated. Of about 700 industries in the area, about 30 should be considered serious sources of pollution. The Msimbazi River, north of the city center, is highly polluted with industrial wastewater. Existing legislation converging the discharge of pollutants to watercourses is not enforced at present."
8. Tanzania is not alone employing these sorts of metaphors for public campaigns. President Mugabe in 2005 deployed a program called Operation Murambatsvinia (Operation Drive Out Trash) in Bulawayo and Harare where police and soldiers destroyed the homes of over 700,000 squatters (Neuwirth 2005: xii).
9. Personal interview with Mohamedi Mikoi, November 2009, Mbagala, Tanzania.
10. Yhdego interviewed Takataka in 1990.

References

Armstrong, A. (1986). "Colonial and Neocolonial Urban Planning: Three Generations of Master Plans for Dar es Salaam." *Utafiti: Journal of the Faculty of Arts and Social Sciences* (University of Dar es Salaam) VIII(1): 43–66.

Burton, A. (2005). *African Underclass: Urbanisation, Crime & Colonial Order in Dar Es Salaam.* London: British Institute in Eastern Africa.

———. (2007). "The Haven of Peace Purged: Tackling the Undesirable and Unproductive Poor in Dar es Salaam, ca.1950s–1980s." *The International Journal of African Historical Studies* 40(1): 119–151.

Department of Medical and Sanitary Services. (1941). "Dar es Salaam Drainage." Memo, March 20, 1941, Box 10 168 File #39/15 "Sewerage Scheme Dar es Salaam" Acc: 450. Tanzanian National Archives.

———. (1948). "Dar es Salaam Sewerage Scheme." Memo, April 22, 1948, Box 10 168 File #39/15 "Sewerage Scheme Dar es Salaam" Acc: 450. Tanzanian National Archives.

Douglas, M. (1966). *Purity and Danger: An Analysis of Concepts of Pollution and Taboo*. New York: Routledge.
Esty, J. D. (1999). "Excremental Postcolonialism." *Contemporary Literature* 40(1): 22–59.
Fanon, F. (2004 [1963]). *The Wretched of the Earth*. New York: Grove Press.
Freyhold, M. v. (1976). *The Workers and the Nizers: A Study in Class Relations*. Dar es Salaam: University of Dar es Salaam Department of Sociology.
Gibb, Sir Alexander and Partners. (1949). *A Plan for Dar Es Salaam: Report*. London.
Grohs, G. (1970). *Urban Challenge in East Africa*. Nairobi: East African Publishing House.
Iliffe, J. (1987). *The African Poor A History*. Cambridge: Cambridge University Press.
Kombe, W. J. (2005). "Land Use Dynamics in Peri-Urban Areas and Their Implications on the Urban Growth and Form: The Case of Dar es Salaam, Tanzania." *Habitat International* 29: 113–135.
LaFontaine, J. S. (1970). *City Politics: A Study of Leopoldville, 1962–63*. Cambridge: Cambridge University Press.
Lerner, D. (1967). "Comparative Analysis of Processes of Modernisation." In Miner, H., ed., *The City in Modern Africa*, pp. 21–38. London: Praeger.
Leslie, J. A. K. (1963). *A Survey of Dar es Salaam*. Oxford: East African Institute of Social Research, Oxford University Press.
Lincoln, S. (2008). "Expensive Shit: Aesthetic Economies of Waste in Postcolonial Africa." PhD diss., Duke University.
Livengood, R. M. (2001). "Mafundi Chuma and Folk Recycling in Dar es Salaam: Case Studies of Material Behavior in Urban Tanzania." PhD diss., University of California, Los Angeles.
Lugalla, J. L. P. (1997). "Economic Reforms and Health Conditions of the Urban Poor in Tanzania." *African Studies Quarterly* 1(2): 19–37.
Marshal Macklin Monaghan. (1979). *Dar es Salaam Master Plan Summary and Supplementary Material*. Toronto: Marshal Macklin Monaghan, LTD. O.
Maude, J. (1938). *City Government: The Johannesburg Experiment*. Oxford: Oxford University Press.
Neuwirth, R. (2005). *Squatter Cities: A Billion Squatters, A New Urban World*. New York: Routledge.
Nyerere, J. (1977). "The Arusha Declaration Ten Years After." Dar es Salaam: Government Printer.
Project Planning Associates. (1968). *National Capital Master Plan*. Dar es Salaam, Toronto: Project Planning Associates Ltd.
Reader, D. H. (1962). *The Black Man's Portion: Xhosa in Town*. London: Oxford University Press.
Shaidi, L. P. (1984). "Tanzania: The Human Resources Deployment Act 1983: A Desperate Measure to Contain a Desperate Situation." *Review of African Political Economy* 31: 82–87.
Southall, A. W. (1966). "The Growth of Urban Society." In Diamond, S. and Burke, F., eds., *The Transformation of East Africa: Studies in Political Anthropology*, pp.463–493. New York: Basic Books.

Southall, A. W. and Gutkind, P. C. W. (1957). *Townsmen in the Making: Kampala and Its Suburbs*. Kampala: East African Institute of Social Research.
Soyinka, W. (1972). *The Interpreters*. London: Andre Deutsch Publishers.
Swanson, M. (1977). "The Sanitation Syndrome: Bubonic Plague and Urban Native Policy in the Cape Colony, 1900–1909." *The Journal of African History* 18(3): 387–410.
Tripp, A. M. (1997). *Changing the Rules: The Politics of Liberalization and the Urban Informal Economy in Tanzania*. Berkeley: University of California Press.
World Bank. (1982). Staff Appraisal Reports for Water Supply and Urban Development Projects. Tanzania Dar es Salaam Sewerage and Sanitation Project, Water Supply and Urban Development Division, Eastern Africa Regional Office, 9 November 29, 1982. Washington, DC: World Bank Archives.
Yhdego, M. (1991). "Scavenging Solid Wastes in Dar es Salaam, Tanzania." *Waste Management and Research* 9(4): 259–265.

Newspaper Articles (Accessed via Microfilm)

Readers' Forum "Dirty Dar Derided," *Daily News*, July 14, 1967.
"Council Plans Clean-Up of the City DSM," *Daily News*, August 20, 1967.
"Hawkers," *Daily News*, August 16, 1967.
"Dar Hit by Shortage of Refuse Trucks," *Daily News*, March 15, 1974.
Rweyemamu, R. "Hive of Activity Where Night is Hell," *Daily News*, February 11, 1973.
"Filthy City," *Daily News*, March 14, 1974.
"Government to Fight Indiscipline," *Daily News*, May 8, 1983.
"War That Must Be Won," *Daily News*, May 11, 1983.
"War Must Be Won," part two *Daily News*, May 12, 1983.
"Nyerere Promoted Compost," *Daily News*, May 17, 1983.
Title unknown (qtd in Shaidi 1984) *Daily News*, September 26, 1983.
"Sokoine Urges Speedy Disposal of Perishables," *Daily News*, June 7, 1983.
"Ministry to Act on Cleanliness," *Daily News*, July 15, 1984.
"Mwalimu Alerts City Fathers Over Filth," *Daily News*, June 14, 1984.

Interviews

Mikoi, Mohammedi. November 2009. Mbagala, Dar es Salaam.

10

"Ambivalent Cosmopolitans"?* Senegalese and Malian Migrants in Johannesburg

Christine Ludl

"Transnationals" or "Cosmopolitans"?

It is shortly after 7 p.m. on a Saturday night. It is getting dark and the living room, the largest room on the ground floor of the house, is lit by the dimmed light of several energy-saving bulbs. A light brown carpet covers the floor, and someone has put a few armchairs and a canapé against the wall to leave a large open space in the middle of the room. A desktop computer, speakers, a DVD and CD player, a TV, and photographs are arranged on a shelf in addition to office equipment. The walls are decorated with text quotes in Arabic in small wooden frames, an Islamic calendar, and several family photographs. A few men chat and watch African music videos. The banging of the iron gate outside and the noise of cars in the courtyard announces the arrival of more visitors. The mostly young or middle-aged men cover the large open space in the center of the room with red, green, black, and gold-patterned shiny blankets and kneel in rows, facing several men in the first row. Four or five women and a few children enter the room. The women have covered their hair and wear dresses made from colorful Dutch wax-prints or single-colored, long, coat-like dresses with a final layer of a light material with laced or embroidered hems. They sit in the last row or in a corner of the room. The largest photograph on the wall shows a man wearing a white *boubou* and fez. It is the portrait of the leader of a branch of a Senegalese Sufi order. The weekly meeting of the *dahira*, one of the numerous local organizations of the order, is about to start. The gathering begins with chants, followed by instructions on a theme relating to religion or morality by one of the leaders who sit in the first row. The meeting ends with a prayer. The men fold up the blankets. Then begins the informal part with greetings and the collection of the weekly contributions to the *dahira* and the women's association. The men have tea and exchange news on their business travels to China or on their latest encounters with the police. The women meet in a separate room where they chat about the children's schooling and exchange *pagnes* or yellow-colored, gold-plated jewelry. Occasionally, the meetings are followed by a dinner brought by the women or prepared by one of the men in the kitchen of the house.

This scene is in Johannesburg, South Africa—a few kilometers east of the city's former exclusively "white" economic and cultural center. After the end of apartheid and the abolition of its restrictive legislation in the early 1990s, white residents and businesses left the city center for the wealthy northern suburbs and South Africans from townships and rural areas moved into the inner city (see Morris 1999, Murray 2011).[1] From the mid-990s on, South Africa also became a major destination for migrants from the rest of the continent. Many of these migrants live in and transit through the inner city.[2]

The *dahira* gathers migrants from all regions of Senegal and provides newcomers with food, housing, and a small starting grant. The weekly assemblies of the *dahira*, its decor and order of events, could take place in almost exactly the same way in Dakar, Milan, Dubai, Bangkok, or New York. Senegalese migrants are a prime example of "transnational migrants"[3] who travel back and forth between their country of origin and one or several destinations across the globe. This holds for the Murid traders, members of the largest Senegalese Sufi order, but also for members of the *Tijaniyya*, the country's second largest brotherhood, as well as for migrants from the Senegal River valley who were historically the first to migrate within North, West, and Central Africa and later to Europe, mainly to France (Daum 1998, Manchuelle 1997, Timera 1996).[4] Several studies have pointed out that these migrants not only travel widely but also recreate their social and cultural organizations wherever they go. The Soninke from the Senegal River valley are known for reproducing their social organizations in French workers residences and Murids, "[i]nside and outside Senegal,...maintain the ritual community as soon as they take up residence in a new locale" (Diouf 2000: 694, Timera 1996).

Ousmane Kane, while acknowledging the critiques raised against the concept, considers transnationalism as the "dominant mode of adaptation" of Senegalese Muslims in the United States. At the same time, he underlines that "the arena in which to exhibit social status is the homeland" and "that it is Senegalese cultural norms (not those of the United States) that determine status in the ethnic sphere of a Senegalese immigrant community" (Kane 2011: 9). Bruno Riccio also insists on the strong orientation of Murid traders in Italy toward their country of origin and, although he recognizes the interactions between locals and the traders and the "hybridity" of the resulting practices, he is skeptical whether transnationalism should be assumed to automatically lead to multiple, hybrid, and cosmopolitan identities (Riccio 2006: 96). Should we conclude, then, that Senegalese migrants are "transnationals" who "move and build encapsulated cultural worlds around them" rather than "cosmopolitans" who "familiarise themselves with other cultures and know how to move easily between cultures"? (Werbner 1999: 19–20).[5]

The concept of cosmopolitanism goes back to the Greek Stoics and Kantian Enlightenment and gained a renewed interest in the social sciences with the emergence of globalization studies and Nussbaum's essay on cosmopolitanism and patriotism (1994, see Nussbaum and Cohen 1996). The concept "proposes a radical decoupling of social action and imagination from national or local anchors" (Skrbis and Woodward 2007: 731) and aims to understand the new forms of sociability and space-time experience that have emerged with increasing global interdependencies (Beck 2002: 30). It is intimately linked to movement, rootlessness, nomadism, and homelessness, and assumes "a broadly defined disposition of 'openness' towards others, people, things and experiences whose origin is non-local" (Skrbis and Woodward 2007: 730, see Kendall et al. 2004: 116). This openness is supposed to lead to cultural cross-pollination, hybridity, and fluidity, but the concept has also become a catch-all phrase devoid of analytical precision (Kendall et al. 2004: 115, 117, Skrbis and Woodward 2007: 731, see Pollock et al. 2000). Typical cosmopolitans are Calhoun's "frequent travellers" (2002), Kanter's "world class" global business elites (1995: 22), or Hannerz's "expatriates" (1990: 243). Contrary to that, Bhabha's "vernacular" (1996), Lamont and Aksartova's "ordinary" (2002), Skrbis's and Woodward's "ambivalent" (2007), Werbner's "working class" (1999), and Landau and Freemantle's "tactical" cosmopolitans (2010, Haupt, 2010) challenge the class and Western bias of the concept. At the same time, these studies try to pin down the concept empirically by developing indicators for a "cosmopolitan disposition" such as mobility, cultural competency, the willingness to engage with others, or the focus on individual identities, shared humanity, and human rights (Haupt 2010: 26–27, Skrbis and Woodward 2007: 732).

"Tactical" cosmopolitanism, together with citizenship and immigration policy approaches, has been one of the major concepts in studies on migration in South Africa.[6] These studies conceptualize cosmopolitanism "not as a philosophy but as a practice and form of experiential culture" (Landau and Freemantle 2010: 375, see Haupt 2010). Landau and Freemantle argue that, in reaction to restrictive immigration policies and "xenophobic resentments," migrants in South African cities must either "become invisible or find ways of justifying and legitimizing their presence" by using a "mixture of rhetorical and organisational tools drawing on a diversity of more established discourses and value systems with strong cosmopolitan content" (2010: 380, 376). As Haupt argues, the migrants consider cultural diversity and engagement with others as normal, enriching, and unproblematic (2010: 98, 101). At the same time, they use a "rhetoric of self-exclusion and transient superiority that distances this group from a South African national project and cultural assimilation," and make "claims to the city while positioning them in an ephemeral, superior and unrooted condition where they can escape localized social and political obligations...allowing them to live outside of belonging while claiming the benefits of it" (Landau and Freemantle 2010: 380–381).

Contrary to the scholarship mentioned earlier, studies on Senegalese and Malian migrations occasionally refer to the term but rarely draw on the concept of cosmopolitanism as an analytical tool or develop it further through empirical research. In his article on the "vernacular cosmopolitanism" of the Senegalese Murid trade diaspora, Mamadou Diouf goes beyond rigid classifications in terms of cosmopolitanism or transnationalism by arguing that the Murids "incorporate their unique temporality and rationality into world time by using their own vocabulary, grammar, and worldview to understand the world and operate within it" (2000: 685). Most importantly, "[t]here is an undeniable *concomitance* between the construction of the point of reference [the holy city Touba, the country and community of origin] and mobility" (Diouf 2000: 698, my emphasis).

This chapter explores representation(s)[7] of mobility and diversity, and related notions of personal ambition and social prestige of Senegalese and Malian migrants in inner-city Johannesburg. It deploys notions of representation(s) and the imagination and shows how these concepts can be pinned down theoretically and empirically. In so doing, I aim to go beyond the dichotomizing question of whether Senegalese migrants can be considered "transnationals" or "cosmopolitans" and reflect on the mechanisms underlying the abovementioned concomitance between mobility and the reference to home. I argue that an approach framed in terms of representation(s) allows for an understanding of how such ambiguities can work.

Although the questions I ask and the theories and methodologies I use depart, in many ways, from concepts of cosmopolitanism, my results directly concern questions of mobility, diversity, and the city. The aim of this chapter, then, is to explore how my approach relates to existing works on cosmopolitanism, migration, and the city in South Africa. Whereas my research confirms that migrants in Johannesburg frequently refer to mobility, home, and a distance from South African society, I will show, on the one hand, that Senegalese and Malian migrants develop complex representation(s) of others, namely, a causal connection between crime and diversity. On the other hand, these representation(s) are not shared by all groups of Senegalese and Malian migrants in Johannesburg: the perception of social diversity and an opposition of cultures also leads to mutual exchange transcending nation, race, and religion. This will also allow me to take a closer look on the often-proclaimed distinctiveness of Johannesburg. Although it is not always clear what this distinctiveness is made of, the city is generally assumed to be an arena which provides new possibilities for its residents and contributes to the emergence of new forms of belonging while remaining strongly fragmented along overlapping socioeconomic, racial, and spatial lines (Murray 2011, Simone 2008).

Understanding Representation(s) and the Imagination

In the social sciences, the notions of representation(s) and the imagination are frequently employed but rarely based on clear theoretical concepts, which translate into concrete empirical research programs. More often than not, they refer to notions like "attitudes," "ideas," or "values" that appear as the smallest—although ill-defined—unit of culture and identity. To employ a more operational methodology and more theoretically precise concept of representation(s) and the imagination, I suggest going back to the German philosopher of culture Ernst Cassirer and to the French anthropologist and psychoanalyst Octave Mannoni. Within a broader concept of representation(s) (Ludl 2008a), both authors provide the key mechanism of how the concept works. In his famous essay entitled "I know very well, but all the same..." Mannoni examines several ways of how reality and imagination can coexist by abandoning and, at the same time, preserving the initial belief (Mannoni 1969). Similarly, Cassirer conceives of representation as relation. At the heart of his definition of representation lies the relation between the particular and the general (2000: 306)—that is to say, of seemingly contradictory elements. For Cassirer, representation and perception is a creative process characterized by both stability and flexibility. The elasticity of representation(s) allows for free movement in all directions while points of reference provide "direction"

(*Richtungscharakter*) (1999: 106, 2002: 232). These "viewpoints" (*Blickpunkte*) are flexible themselves and can change, leading to completely different representation(s) (1999: 24, 2002: 150).

Furthermore, representation(s) do not solely refer to abstract ideas or states of mind but are closely connected to material practices. Cassirer insists on (artistic) creation, symbols, emotions, and "certain fundamental structural elements of our sense experience itself" like lines, design, or architectural and musical forms for the construction and expression of representation(s). These elements are "visible, audible, tangible" (2006: 171). Thus, whereas representation(s) in the sense of ideas or perceptions stay largely implicit, they are expressed in artistic and verbal creations like non-directive interviews, which then become the starting point of analysis (Donegani et al. 2002, Duchesne 1996, 2000, Duchesne and Haegel 2005, Ludl 2008b, Martin and Ebrahim-Vally 2006, Michelat 1975, Rogers 1945).[8]

Therefore, whereas studies on "tactical" cosmopolitanism in South Africa use survey data and semi-structured interviews with a variety of migrant groups, my research relies on non-directive interviews and ethnographic observations and concentrates on migrants from a specific political, social, and cultural arena whose presence in South Africa is—with a few exceptions (Bouillon 1999, Fall 2004, Lekogo 2006, Lliteras 2009, Ludl 2010, Vigouroux 2005, 2008)—severely under-researched. Through focusing on Soninke and Haalpulaar migrants from the Senegal River region (Senegal and Mali) and members of the *Muridiyya* and the *Tijaniyya* orders originating from different regions in Senegal,[9] this theoretical and methodological approach allows me to go beyond common stereotypes about South Africans and migrants to reveal more complex representation(s) of mobility, diversity, and the city.

Representation(s) of Mobility and the Reference to Home

Most of the migrants I met during my fieldwork had lived and worked in other places in Africa, Asia, and, to a lesser extent, Europe before coming to South Africa. Wholesalers travel every month to China or Bangkok to buy clothes, jewelry, or computer supplies, which they sell in South Africa. Furthermore, they are engaged in imaginary travels as they make plans to move to other places. All of them retain close contact with family and friends in their countries of origin and elsewhere, mostly by making frequent but short calls on their mobile phones. Those who have a citizenship status, which allows them to travel, and who can afford it, regularly spend some months of the year in Senegal. With a few exceptions, they plan to return there permanently once they have earned enough money. As one respondent expressed it, "there's no place like home. My objective is to get it all and settle back there."[10]

Representation(s) of mobility and success touch upon a wide and complex variety of aims, aspirations, circumstances, possibilities, and constraints. They depend on shared representation(s) of personal achievements and social prestige and of legitimate ways to accomplish them; they are established with respect to what one imagines is offered by his society of origin compared with other places toward realizing these goals; they are shaped by migrants' relations to their families, the wider community, and to their countries of (temporary) destination. What is more, migration is always—though to different degrees—a social *and* an individual project. As Fariba Adelkhah and Jean-François Bayart expressed it, "travelling is often experienced as a picaresque or epic lifestyle, even if it responds to structural or cyclical economic or political constraints, and is similar to a moral experience of subjectivation, which is one of its main motives" (Adelkhah and Bayart 2007: 9, my translation).[11] To be more precise, representation(s) of mobility, personal achievement, and social prestige of Senegalese and Malian migrants negotiate two basic tensions, which form a fragile balance where the weight of each element is constantly adjusted: first, a tension between the economic and financial aims of migration and acquiring experience and knowledge through travelling; second, a tension between individual aims of freedom from group control and social obligations, hierarchies, and power relations. Thus, "the obsession of survival is at the same time material and social, political, symbolic and even psychological" (Ould Ahmed Salem 2001: 78, my translation).

The remainder of this chapter explores how this quest for money, knowledge, social prestige, and self-realization plays out and transforms in the social, spatial, and political context of Johannesburg's inner-city neighborhoods. Key dynamics in this context include: insecurity, violence and discrimination, high spatial and social density and diversity, and urban renewal (Crush et al. 2008, Murray, 2011, Simone 2008, Palmery et al. 2003, Vigneswaran et al. 2010).

Superiority, Invisibility, and Perceptions of Crime and Diversity

As the description of the weekly gathering of the *dahira* shows, the migrants maintain and recreate their cultural and religious references in South Africa. In Amadou's account, the importance of these references becomes even clearer:

> The Senegalese are known as hard workers, they pray, they are always correct...Well, that's the luck we had and it's because of our education in Senegal. Education in Senegal is very thorough. We have a very, very thorough education in Senegal. Family, decency...discipline, work, prayer...With your will, you can succeed. This is what makes our strength. Even if it's a small country, we say: small country, great name. (Laughs). There are also intellectuals, people who have shown what they can do, scientists, historians; in Senegal, that's where the brains are.[12]

This strong positive reference to the home country contributes to a feeling of superiority. The migrants think that South Africans are "not educated," "not willing to work" and that they "don't like to travel which is a way of education."[13] Some Senegalese who employ South Africans in their shops consider them as "mentally ill people who only think of partying, of girls and of alcohol," "who want a comfortable life," who are not "disciplined" and "don't know how to save money."[14] However, the migrants see themselves as also challenged by this "depraved" society. In their narratives, it is precisely their education in Senegal and the strength they take from it that helps them to resist temptation and to distinguish the good from the bad. Amadou put it in these words:

> Everything is within reach. Alcohol is, how should I say, is like for free, women are exposed, there is everything here. So, if you have some money and you are not aware of where you are coming from, if you don't know what you are doing, you can easily drift off. You can go astray. It's very easy here in South Africa. You can go astray if you don't have a strong consciousness...But if you know what you want, if you know where you are coming from, if you know where you are going to, you can succeed. There are people who benefited from the things here, people who made it.[15]

The Senegalese and Malians perceive the migrant communities in South Africa as a cornerstone in this task. Moreover, this holds for situations where support turns into social control. Mamadou mentions that "here, you cannot go out in a bar and have a drink,"[16] referring to one's reputation which depends on how fellow migrants judge one's behavior. With a more positive tone, Malik explains why he would like to go to Europe: "You can't make a mess of it because I have lots of brothers there. If I go there and if I'm going to do something stupid, there will be an elder brother who will tell me 'ah, little brother, you need to stop this, this is not good, you need to work and you will get your money'."[17]

The feeling of superiority, based on religious and moral "values" transmitted by the home country, also plays a role when it comes to the most burning issue for the migrants in South Africa, namely, insecurity and discrimination. The importance of the subject in interviews and conversations stems from frequent accounts of violent attacks in the South African Press[18] and from concrete personal experiences like being robbed for money or a cell phone or even attacked, sometimes quite severely. More precisely, it is the combination of risk and the feeling of not being able to get assistance that makes South Africa a "dangerous place."[19] As Mamadou states, "here, if you are in trouble, you are alone... We are afraid. There is no trust. If you are attacked, no one will help you."[20] Therefore, migrants are in a "constant state of preparedness" and "hyperawareness" (Simone 2008: 85, 76).

The migrants hold several explanations why there is crime and insecurity in South Africa that refer to the ways they relate to South African society. They mention, for example, colonial history and religious faith to explain the high crime levels and the reticence to help others without an immediate compensation. Most significantly, the Malians perceive a causal connection between the diversity of South African society and the existence of crime and racism, which reconnects directly with the question of a "cosmopolitan disposition." Malik states:

> This is why there is so much crime here. Because this is a very racist country. It's a country of mixed races! Whites, Blacks, persons of mixed race, Indians, everyone is mixed here... The Blacks stay apart, the Whites stay apart, the Indians stay apart. This is why there is too much crime. The Blacks don't like the Indians, they don't like the Whites either, the Whites don't like the Blacks, the Indians don't like the Whites, really, this is the big problem here.[21]

In this line of argument, he draws a parallel between South Africa and the United States by linking the diversity of American society to his perception that in the United States, "the Blacks are such criminals" and that "you will quickly become a criminal or a down-and-out" there.[22]

The migrants try to control the risk of crime by controlling social relations and space. They limit their social network to trustworthy persons, avoid moving around, and follow a strategy of invisibility. For some, this means not to wear *boubous* or colorful dress in public or to obtain a South African driver's license to avoid problems with the police. Neither the Malian mosque nor the house where the *dahira* meets is recognizable as such from the outside.

Thus, South Africa is an ambivalent destination for the migrants on their journey for money, experience, prestige, and self-realization. In an environment that the migrants perceive as unsafe and depraved, they lend particular importance to networks of people deemed trustworthy. As a consequence, power relations and social control remain tight and limit the potential of freedom from the group, which is an important part of migration projects. In addition, crime and insecurity cast a shadow on the relatively good economic possibilities in South Africa, and if the migrants consider Johannesburg as the only prestigious city on the African continent which "one can present well everywhere,"[23] it remains a far less glamorous and economically attractive destination than Europe, especially for young migrants who feel the pressure not only to migrate and to earn money, but also to go to prestigious places. As Malik says, "my brother is in Paris . . . all my older brothers are there and I am the only one here in Africa. What can I do? I didn't have the chance to leave."[24] And one of his friends concludes: "We came, but we didn't get anything."[25] As a consequence, the majority of the Malians planned to leave for Europe.

Should the Senegalese and Malians in Johannesburg be considered "transnationals" who recreate their social and cultural references wherever they go and who are rarely in contact with the local population? As I have shown, all of them have widely travelled and acquired the necessary competencies to live and work in different cultural and social contexts in Africa, Asia, and Europe and believe that acquiring knowledge and experience is an integral part of migration. At the same time, they remain strongly rooted in their home countries, place themselves in a morally superior position, and establish a causal connection between crime and racism and the diversity of South African society.

The case of Malian migrants in Johannesburg also seems to confirm Simone's account of the inner city's "complex geography that residents must navigate according to a finely tuned series of movements and assumptions. There are places where they know they must no go or be seen—but this knowledge often depends on highly variable notions about which places are safe and which are not" (2008: 82). More precisely, the coupling of insecurity and strong networks has a limiting effect on spatial mobility, the creation of new social forms, and freedom from the group.

Transcending Difference

Despite mutual resentments and social enclosure, the inner city neighborhoods bring together a socially and culturally diverse population and can provide spaces of interaction. Examples include, workplaces, marriages between migrants and South Africans, and the *dahiras*. In the following, I will examine some of these spaces of interaction.

Migrants and locals meet and interact most frequently in the workplace. Some Murids hold stalls at crafts markets that bring together Africans of different nationalities, well-off South Africans shopping for African curios, and international tourists in search of souvenirs (Wa Kabwe-Segatti 2009). At food and neighborhood markets like the Yeoville Municipal Market, migrants have their stalls next to South Africans. Together, they negotiate better relations with the municipality and serve a clientele coming from all parts of Africa (Palomares and Quiminal 2012). Those who run shops or internet cafés often have equally diverse costumers. My research shows that despite the numerous stereotypes between migrants and South Africans, mutual assistance, exchange, and friendship does exist. For example, Mamadou, a young Senegalese man who runs several internet cafés in the Central Business District (CBD), complained that there was no trust between people and that South Africans were closed and unpleasant. Nevertheless, he also had some South African friends whom he considered to be "different" and "nice" and whom trusted enough to lend money.[26] Furthermore, one of the Senegalese migrants who has a stall at the market in Yeoville insisted on being alone, on having no family and no friends in South Africa, and on not being able to get help from anyone. However, during my visits at the market, I noticed that he gave advice on housing issues with people who passed by, borrowed small sums of money from colleagues, and asked the vendor next door to watch his stall while he was attending to business or renewing his permit at the Department of Home Affairs. Moreover, he mentioned that he would be able to borrow up to ZAR 2000 (US $220) from the same person, "because she's my neighbor."[27] In this case, a particular definition of friendship explains the apparent contradiction between the perception of solitude and lack of assistance and the daily forms of mutual assistance practiced in his immediate social environment. In Seydou's understanding, the term "friends" refers exclusively to people he would have known in Senegal before coming to South Africa—and there are none. Seydou was, indeed, a loner. He had not married and had almost completely dropped out of migrant networks, did not earn enough money to sustain his family in Senegal, and, after nearly 20 years in Europe and South Africa, struggled to save money for a visit or a house in Senegal. At the same time, insisting on hard work, loneliness, and insecurity is also part of a narrative of success where enduring suffering and overcoming hardship contributes to the social prestige of migrants.

These examples reveal the common phenomenon that, despite widespread stereotypes and mistrust, interactions and assistance between different groups exist and that there is a need to dig beneath migrants' narratives to examine their underlying representation(s). In the following, I will show more in detail the ways in which these interactions transform migrants' representation(s). Apart from workplaces, marriages between male migrants and South African women are important spaces of social interaction. Whereas none of the Malians were married in South Africa and the percentage was low among members of the *Tijaniyya* who were often married in Senegal or had brought their families to South Africa, according to an internal census of the Murid *dahiras*, 75 percent of their members are engaged in real (or fictitious) marriages with South African women.[28] On the one hand, the Murids consider relations with South African women to be difficult because "the two cultures oppose each other" and because there are "problems of communication." "To be honest, the cultures are different... They are opposed to each other just like the climate is the opposite."[29] This refers mainly to language and communication, to "traditions," "beliefs," to "ways of doing things," to "ways of conceiving of life," to "ways of dressing," or to food habits. Oumar has been living in South Africa for 12 years and has "two families": one in Senegal and one in South Africa. For him, to "unite the two families" so that they can "adopt each other" is an "impossible mission." At the same time, he considers that "this is work... It's a long-term process... for the cultures to adopt each other. Well, it is work. It's not easy... With the future generations... there will be a real exchange of ideas, not between the women but between the children."[30] Oumar applies here the Murid's work ethic of economic achievements through discipline, endurance, and hard work, which he had outlined at the beginning of the interview, to the question of cultural differences on a personal level. What is more, Murids use a related narrative of a long-term process of individual and collective efforts to characterize South African society as a whole. They consider South Africa as a country "which just had opened," where people "didn't even know what an adventurer was," which led to "differences" and a "lack of understanding." However, just like with marriages between migrants and South Africans, "it takes time for things to get better, to adapt to the people... We in Africa know very well what's a country like that just had opened. It won't be easy but as we mix more and more, things will get better and better."[31] Therefore, the migrants use a representation of economic and personal achievements, accomplished through hard work and the endurance of hardship in a long-term process, on two levels: their migration experience and the overcoming of cultural differences on a personal and societal level.

Finally, the *dahiras* are an important site of social exchange, as they gather not only Senegalese but also migrants coming from other African countries and South Africans of Indian origin. One migrant describes this exchange as being "ready to connect" in order to "accept" and to "adopt" each other. We "connect by what we have in common," we "communicate," we "discover," we "go towards the positive things." "This has neither to do with race, nor religion, nor nationality."[32] In the line of this argument, Amadou thinks that "you need to judge people according to their mind...It's not the color of your skin...but it's the mind...It's not skin color,...it's not the way you dress, clothes don't make the man...It's according to one's behavior that one will be judged, whether this person is really human".[33] Therefore, contrary to the Malians, the members of the Senegalese Sufi orders engage more frequently with locals. They "circulate across and become familiar with a broad range of spatial, residential, economic, and transactional positions" (Simone 2008: 69). They develop a universal notion of personhood and consider cultural diversity as surmountable.

The differences between the two groups stem mainly from three interrelated factors: the size and diversity of their networks, their socio-economic situation, and the places in the city where they spend most of their time. Whereas the Malians rely on two small family networks coming from a similar socio-cultural background and the same region in Mali, the *dahiras* of the *Tijaniyya* and the *Muridiyya* gather diverse communities with different socio-economic backgrounds hailing from all over Senegal and other African countries. What is more, contrary to the Senegalese, the Malians have arrived only recently in South Africa and are mostly young unmarried men who are pressed to succeed. They are economically less stable than the Senegalese who have migrated since the 1990s and who often run their own businesses, which has allowed them to leave neighborhoods considered unsafe, such as Yeoville or Hillbrow.

Rooted in the "Search for Something"

Like other migrant groups, Senegalese and Malian migrants in Johannesburg are highly mobile. Nevertheless, they are neither rootless nor homeless. They remain firmly anchored in their countries of origin and regularly return home if their administrative and financial status allows for it. They retain wives and children at home, stay in close contact with family and friends, and invest there in real estate or in businesses. In the case of the Murids, the majority plan to return to the holy city of Touba, the source of the education, values, and national pride from which they draw comfort and strength when they travel abroad. Some of them are also rooted in South Africa where they are married and have children and where some of them plan to stay. Furthermore, contrasting with Landau and Freemantle's study (2010), Senegalese and Malians migrants in South Africa and elsewhere rarely avoid social obligations. They regularly send money back home and support newcomers with food, housing, and starting grants. Even if questions of power relations and individual freedoms come into play, Senegalese and Malian networks in Johannesburg remain strong, and internal conflict and competition remain low. This is remarkable in a city where, more often than not, ethnic and national affiliations tend to disappear (see Simone 2008: 77–78).

I suggest that this concomitance of mobility and a reference to home can be understood as "rootedness in search itself." As one migrant stated, "we move from country to country, in search for something."[34] This "search for something" characterizes the great majority of migration projects and becomes a point of reference in itself. What they search for is an ideal, an imagination of the future,[35] "a good life" (*la belle vie*).[36] This "good life" is difficult to define and almost never attained. For one, it includes the abovementioned balance between economic and social objectives of migration, between commitment to and freedom from the group. It also refers to a state where living together with one's family and being able to earn enough money is possible. For many, it is ultimately the goal of achieving economic success, social prestige, and the ability to retire and rest as a respected elder. If some of the successful migrants attain this state, this does not erase the ambiguities and "sufferings" of migration, such as solitude and being separated from their families in exchange for a long-term process of hard work. Nevertheless, in the course of their migration projects, most migrants develop life projects (*projet d'existence*) (Ricœur 2004: 19), that is to say a coherent construction of their experience where ambiguities and disturbing elements are not erased but accommodated. As in Octave Mannoni's "I know very well, but all the same…" or Cassirer's "elastic" representation(s), they are included in the narrative by conferring a particular meaning to them.

Ambivalent Cosmopolitan(ism)s

Senegalese and Malians migrants in Johannesburg do not make claims to the city. Rather, they become invisible, the second option mentioned by Landau and Freemantle (2010: 380).[37] In these spaces of invisibility, situations and the representation(s) to which they give rise vary considerably. The migrants develop complex representation(s) of diversity which go beyond common stereotypes and which lead to further "concomitances": a concomitance between positive and negative representation(s) of diversity and a concomitance between an openness toward others and a rootedness in cultural references of the home country—for example, when they apply the Murid work ethic to cultural differences.

Whereas in the case of the Malians—despite the commitment to universal human rights—strong but small and homogenous networks lead to a causal connection made between crime, racism and social diversity, in the case of the two brotherhoods, despite the presence of common stereotypes and a discourse meant to reassure the migrants of their own cultural references amid a depraved environment, tight but large and diverse networks foster cultural exchange and the emergence of a universal notion of personhood. This notion of personhood is grounded in a person's "interior," in his or her "mind" and behavior, and transcends "nation, race, and religion." In the first case, this can be seen as the absence of an "ability to compartmentalize a diverse world into recognizable, manageable and consequently more easily accommodated portions," an important although often neglected aspect of cosmopolitanism in the literature (Calcutt et al. 2009: 172). In the second case, the development of a universal notion of personhood and the related representation(s) of social and cultural differences as surmountable can be seen as an effective way of "dealing with otherness and cultural difference" (Ibid.: 174). Therefore, Senegalese and Malian migrants in Johannesburg resemble Skribs and Woodward's "ambivalent cosmopolitans" where cosmopolitanism is "a tool for the negotiation of life chances in an increasingly interconnected and open world" and an ideal "that conflicts with an array of other social and personal imperatives, and thus does not always find full flowering" (Skrbis and Woodward 2007: 746, 735).

If this ideal does not always come to full flowering due to conflicting social and personal imperatives, this chapter shows that the migrants accommodate and transform these imperatives through the creative construction of life projects and, thereby, contribute to the transformation of the city itself.

Notes

*The title refers to Skrbis and Woodward (2007: 746). This chapter builds on fieldwork conducted within the framework of a larger project on "Transit migration in Africa" (MITRANS) funded by the French National Agency of Research (ANR). Earlier versions have been presented at the African Center for Migration and Society (ACMS) (University of the Witwatersrand, Johannesburg), at the Konstanzer Meisterklasse 2010 (University of Konstanz), at the Art of Citizenship Conference (Columbia University, New York City), and at the Centre Marc Bloch (Berlin). I wish to thank all of those who have contributed with their comments to the final version of the chapter.

1. Among other legal instruments, which perfected the country's social and spatial segregation, the Group Areas Act, Act No 41 of 1950, assigned specific residential areas to specific groups. The apartheid regime distinguished between "Africans," "Asians/Indians," "Coloureds," and "Whites."
2. In 2007, internal migrants constituted 37.4 percent of the population of Gauteng and foreign-born persons represented 5.6 percent (Landau and Gindrey 2008: 11).
3. One of the first definitions of transnationalism goes back to Glick-Schiller et al. (1992). The approach focused on the formation of "transnational social spaces" and questioned binary conceptions of sending and host countries (Faist 2000, Portes et al. 1999, Pries 1996, Vertovec 1999). Doubts have been raised against the novelty of the phenomenon and African migrations are a prime example to support this argument (Riccio 2006: 98). Furthermore, the systematization of types of migrants and their networks has attracted critiques regarding the appropriateness of the established categories (Pries 2002: 268).
4. The Senegal River valley spreads over Northern Senegal, Southern Mauritania and Western Mali. Migrants from this region are less frequently organized in brotherhoods as in this area Islam developed within the families of religious leaders (*marabouts*) who were allies of—but subordinated to—local political leaders (Chastanet 1999: 175). Contrary to that, within the *Muridiyya*, religion, migration, and economic success are intimately linked (Buggenhagen 2004: 30, Diouf 2000: 691).
5. Werbner refers here to Hannerz's distinction between "transnational cultures, structures of meaning carried by social networks which are not wholly based in one single territory" (1992: 249) and "cosmopolitans" willing "to engage with the Other" (1992: 252).
6. See Neocosmos (2006), Peberdy (2009), Segatti (2011), Klaaren (2001), and Posel (1991). Against the backdrop of the May 2008 collective violence that targeted mainly foreign nationals in townships and informal settlements across the country and left 62 persons dead, 670 injured, and more than 100,000 displaced (Polzer and Igglesdon 2009), Landau (2011) provides a historically embedded analysis of mobility, diversity, and statecraft in post-apartheid South Africa.
7. The spelling "representation(s)" reflects the notion's twofold meaning of "ideas" (*Vorstellungen*) and "presentation" (*Darstellung*).
8. Non-directive interviews usually start with a verbal, visual or auditory prompt—the only question the interviewer asks—and then rely on the interviewee's free exploration of the proposed theme. They foster the expression of contradictions but also allow for an understanding of how individuals deal

with these ambiguities and of how representation(s) are organized on different scales (Haegel and Lavabre 2010).

9. In total, I conducted 23 non-directive interviews, mostly in French, some in English, lasting between 60 and 150 minutes and numerous conversations between November 2008 and May 2010 in Yeoville, Ellis Park, the Central Business District, Troyeville, Bezuidenhout Valley, Rosebank, and at the Chameleon Village Market near Hartbeespoort Dam. All interviews were taped and transcribed. Translations from French to English are mine. I have replaced the names of my respondents with pseudonyms.
10. Personal nterview, Amadou, Chameleon Village Market, May 23, 2010.
11. Adelkhah and Bayart refer here to the Foucauldian notion of subjectivation, defined as "the production of modes of existence or lifestyles" (Deleuze 1990: 156, referring to Foucault, cited by Bayart 1996: 157, my translation).
12. Personal interview, Amadou, Chameleon Village Market, May 23, 2010.
13. Personal interview, Cissé, Yeoville, March 25, 2009.
14. Personal interview, Yero, Troyeville, October 10, 2009.
15. Personal interview, Amadou, Chameleon Village Market, May 23, 2010.
16. Personal interview, Central Business District, May 07, 2010.
17. Personal interview, Ellis Park, August 12, 2009.
18. Personal interview, Aminata, Troyeville, October 10, 2009.
19. Personal interview, Yeoville, April 06, 2009.
20. Personal interview, Central Business District, May 07, 2010.
21. Personal interview, Ellis Park, August 12, 2009.
22. Ibid.
23. Ibid.
24. Ibid.
25. Personal interview, Yeoville, April 06, 2009.
26. Personal interview, Central Business District, May 07, 2010.
27. Personal interview, Seydou, Yeoville, April 03, 2009.
28. Personal interview, Moustapha, Rosebank, November 12, 2008. When they arrive, most Senegalese apply for refugee status—for which they are not eligible—but which allows them to circulate in the country for 3 months (renewable). Although some manage to obtain successive permits with durations between 3 and 18 months, marriages with South African women are one of the few possibilities to obtain a stable administrative status in South Africa.
29. Personal interview, Oumar, Rosebank, August 04, 2009.
30. Ibid.
31. Personal interview, Aziz, Rosebank, August 04, 2009.
32. Ibid.
33. Personal interview, Amadou, Chameleon Village Market, May 23, 2010.
34. Personal interview, Oumar, Rosebank, August 04, 2009.
35. I understand the imagination as a subcategory of representation(s), referring to what may be, to what is possible or desirable. See Turner (1977: 71), Schiffauer (2006), Geertz (1993: 89, 93–94), or Jewsiewicki (1999: 73).
36. Personal interviews, Aziz, Rosebank, August 04, 2010, Moussa, Yeoville, March 26, 2009. The expression *avoir la belle vie* / "to have a good life" is

ambiguous as it also can refer to laziness. Therefore, in the interviews the expression often appears in ambiguous phrases like "not to have a good life but to have a good life" / *pas pour avoir la belle vie mais pour avoir la belle vie.*
37. Vidal has observed the same strategy of invisiblity among Mosambican migrants in Johannesburg (2008, 2010).

References

Adelkhah, F. and Bayart, J.-F. (2007). "Introduction. Pour une anthropologie politique du voyage." In Adelkhah, F. and Bayart, J.-F., eds, *Voyages du développement: Emigration, commerce, exil*, pp. 5–29. Paris: Karthala.

Bayart, J.-F. (1996). *L'illusion identitaire.* Paris: Fayard.

Beck, U. (2002). "The Cosmopolitan Society and Its Enemies." *Theory, Culture & Society* 19(1–2): 17–44.

Bhabha, H. (1996). "Unsatisfied: Notes on Vernacular Cosmopolitanism." In Garcia-Morena, L. and Pfeiffer, P. C., eds, *Text and Nation: Cross-Disciplinary Essays on Cultural and National Identities*, pp. 191–207. London: Camden House.

Bouillon, A. (1999). *L'immigration africaine en Afrique du Sud. Les migrants francophones des années 90.* Paris: Karthala.

Buggenhagen, B. A. (2004). "Domestic Object(ion)s: The Senegalese Murid Trade Diaspora and the Politics of Marriage Payments, Love, and State Privatization." In Weiss, B., ed., *Producing African Futures: Ritual and Reproduction in a Neoliberal Age*, pp. 21–53. Leiden: Brill Academic Press.

Calcutt, L., Woodward, I., and Skrbis, Z. (2009). "Conceptualizing Otherness." *Journal of Sociology* 45(2): 169–186.

Calhoun, C. (2002). "The Class Consciousness of Frequent Travelers: Toward a Critique of Actually Existing Cosmopolitanism." *South Atlantic Quarterly* 101(4): 869–897.

Cassirer, E. (1999). *Ziele und Wege der Wirklichkeitserkenntnis.* Nachgelassene Manuskripte und Texte (ECN), vol. 2, ed. by Krois, J. M. and Köhnke, K. C. Hamburg: Meiner.

———. (2000). *Substanz- und Funktionsbegriff. Untersuchungen über die Grundfragen der Erkenntniskritik.* Gesammelte Werke, Hamburger Ausgabe (ECW), vol. 6, ed. by B. Recki. Hamburg: Meiner [1910].

———. (2002). *Philosophie der symbolischen Formen, Teil 3. Phänomenologie der Erkenntnis.* Gesammelte Werke, Hamburger Ausgabe (ECW), vol. 13, ed. by Clemens, J. and Recki, B. Hamburg: Meiner [1929].

———. (2006). *An Essay on Man. An Introduction to a Philosophy of Human Culture.* Gesammelte Werke, Hamburger Ausgabe (ECW), vol. 23, ed. by Recki, B. Hamburg: Meiner [1944].

Chastanet, M. (1999). "Les migrations soninkées dans la longue durée: stratégies et identités." *Cahiers d'Etudes Africaines* 39(153): 169–177.

Crush, J., Mc Donald, D., Williams, V., Lefko-Everett, K., Dorey, D., Taylor, D., and la Sablonnière, R. (2008). *The Perfect Storm: The Realities of Xenophobia in Contemporary South African Discourses on Immigration: Changes and Continuity in the Transition Period*. Migration Policy Series, 50. Cape Town: Southern African Migration Project.

Daum, C. (1998). *Les associations de Maliens en France. Migration, développement et citoyenneté*. Paris: Karthala.

Deleuze, G. (1990). *Pourparlers, 1972–1990*. Paris: Minuit.

Diouf, M. (2000). "The Senegalese Murid Trade Diaspora and the Making of a Vernacular Cosmopolitanism." *Public Culture* 12(3): 679–702.

Donegani, J.-M., Duchesne, S., and Haegel, F. (2002). "Sur l'interprétation des entretiens de recherche." In Donegani, J.-M., Duchesne, S., and Haegel, F., eds, *Aux Frontières des attitudes entre le politique et le religieux. Textes en hommage à Guy Michelat*, pp. 273–295. Paris: L'Harmattan.

Duchesne, S. (1996). "Entretien non préstructuré, stratégie de recherche et étude des représentations. Ou: Peut-on déjà faire l'économie de l'entretien 'non-directif' en sociologie?" *Politix* 9(35): 189–206.

———. (2000). "Pratique de l'entretien dit non-directif." In Bachir, M., ed., *Les méthodes au concret. Démarches, formes de l'expérience et terrains d'investigation en science politique*, pp. 9–30. Paris: PUF.

Duchesne, S. and Haegel, F. (2005). *L'enquête et ses méthodes. L'entretien collectif*. Paris: Armand Colin.

Faist, T. (2000). *Transstaatliche Räume: Politik, Wirtschaft und Kultur in und zwischen Deutschland und der Türkei*. Bielefeld: Transcript.

Fall, P. D. (2004). "Les Sénégalais au Kwazulu-Natal (Afrique du Sud) ou les 'naufragés' de la migration internationale." Conference paper, *Congrès international d'études africaines*, Barcelona, Spain, 12–15 January 2004, available: http://www.matrix.msu.edu/~ucad/papadembafall/maoumy/Texte/barcelone_version provisoire.pdf. Accessed April 27, 2013.

Geertz, C. (1993). "Religion as a Cultural System." In Geertz, C., ed., *The Interpretation of Cultures*. Hammersmith, London: Fontana Press.

Glick-Schiller, N., Basch, L., and Blanc-Szanton, C. (1992). "Transnationalism: A New Analytic Framework for Understanding Migration." In Glick-Schiller, N., Basch, L., and Blanc-Szanton, C., eds, *Towards a Transnational Perspective on Migration: Race, Class, Ethnicity, and Nationalism Reconsidered*, pp. 1–24. Annals of the New York Academy of Sciences. New York: Blackwell Publishing Ltd.

Haegel, F. and Lavabre, M.-C. (2010). *Destins ordinaires. Identité singulière et mémoire partagée*. Paris: Presses de Sciences Po.

Hannerz, U. (1990). "Cosmopolitans and Locals in World Culture." In Featherstone, M., ed., *Global Culture: Nationalism, Globalization and Modernity*, pp. 237–251. London: Sage.

———. (1992). *Cultural Complexity: Studies in the Social Organization of Meaning*. New York: Columbia University Press.

Haupt, I. (2010). "'You Can Only Claim Your Yard and Not a Country': Exploring Context, Discourse and Practices of Cosmopolitanism Amongst African Migrants in Johannesburg: Emerging/Diverging Metropolis." PhD diss., Forced Migration Studies Programme, Graduate School for the Humanities and Social Sciences, University of the Witwatersrand.

Jewsiewicki, B. (1999). "Congolese Memories of Lumumba: Between Cultural Hero and Humanity's Redeemer." In *A Congo Chronicle. Patrice Lumumba in Urban Art*, pp. 73–91. New York: The Museum of African Art.

Kane, O. O. (2011). *The Homeland Is the Arena: Religion, Transnationalism, and the Integration of Senegalese Immigrants in America*. New York: Oxford University Press.

Kanter, R. M. (1995). *World Class: Thriving Locally in the Global Economy*. New York: Simon and Schuster.

Kendall, G., Skrbis, Z., and Woodward, I. (2004). "Locating Cosmopolitanism: Between Humanist Ideal and Grounded Social Category." *Theory, Culture & Society* 21(6): 115–136.

Klaaren, J. (2001). "Contested Citizenship in South Africa." In Andrews, P. and Ellmann, S., eds, *The Post-Apartheid Constitutions: Perspectives on South Africa's Basic Law*, pp. 304–325. Athens, OH: Ohio University Press.

Lamont, M. and Aksartova, S. (2002). "Ordinary Cosmopolitanisms: Strategies for Bridging Racial Boundaries Among Working-Class Men." *Theory Culture & Society* 19(4): 1–25.

Landau, L. B., ed. (2011). *Exorcising the Demons Within: Xenophobia, Violence and Statecraft in Contemporary South Africa*. Johannesburg: Wits University Press.

Landau, L. B. and Freemantle, I. (2010). "Tactical Cosmopolitanism and Idioms of Belonging: Insertion and Self-Exclusion in Johannesburg." *Journal of Ethnic and Migration Studies* 36(3): 375–390.

Landau, L. B. and Gindrey, V. (2008). *Migration and Population Trends in Gauteng Province 1996–2055*. Migration Studies Working Paper Series 42. Johannesburg: Forced Migration Studies Programme, University of the Witwatersrand.

Lekogo, R. (2006). "Francophone Africans in Cape Town: A Failed Migration?" In Cross, C., Gelderblom, D., Roux, N., and Mafukidze, J., eds, *Views on Migration in Sub-saharan in Africa: Proceedings of an African Migration Alliance Workshop*, pp. 207–219. Cape Town, South Africa: HSRC Press.

Lliteras, S. M. (2009). "A Path to Integration: Senegalese Tijanis in Cape Town." *African Studies* 68(2): 215–233.

Ludl, C. (2008a). "La (les) Représentation(s) de la migration, entre pouvoir et réussite. La mobilité des migrant(e)s originaires de la Vallée du fleuve Sénégal entre leurs pays d'origine et la France." PhD diss., Institut d'Etudes Politiques de Paris/ Otto-Suhr-Institut für Politikwissenschaft der Freien Universität Berlin, microfiche, Lille: A.N.R.T. Université de Lille III, Lille-Thèses ISSN 0294–1767.

———. (2008b). "'To Skip a Step': New Representation(s) of Migration, Success and Politics in Senegalese Rap and Theatre." *Stichproben. Wiener Zeitschrift für kritische Afrikastudien* 14: 97–122.

———. (2010). "Repli sur soi et ouverture vers l'autre dans l'Afrique du Sud contemporaine. Représentation(s) de la mobilité et insertion des migrants sénégalais et maliens à Johannesburg." *Transcontinentales* 8/9 available: http:// transcontinentales.revues.org/790. Accessed December 20, 2010.

Manchuelle, F. (1997). *Willing Migrants: Soninke Labor Diasporas, 1848–1960*. Athens, OH: Ohio University Press.

Mannoni, O. (1969). "'Je sais bien, mais quand même.'" In Mannoni, O., ed., *Clefs pour l'imaginaire ou L'autre scène*, pp. 7–33. Paris: Seuil.

Martin, D.-C. and Ebrahim-Vally, R. (2006). *Viewing the "New" South Africa. Representations of South Africa in Television Commercials: An Experiment in Non-directive Methods*. Questions de Recherche/Research in Question 19. Paris: Centre d'études et de recherches internationales, Sciences Po.

Michelat, G. (1975). "Sur l'utilisation de l'entretien non directif en sociologie." *Revue française de sociologie* 16(2): 229–247.

Morris, A. (1999). *Bleakness and Light: Inner City Transition in Hillbrow, Johannesburg*. Johannesburg: Witwatersrand University Press.

Murray, M. J. (2011). *City of Extremes: The Spatial Politics of Johannesburg*. Durham, NC: Duke University Press.

Neocosmos, M. (2006). *From 'Foreign Natives' to 'Native Foreigners'—Explaining Xenophobia in Post-Apartheid South Africa: Citizenship and Nationalism, Identity and Politics*. Dakar: Codesria.

Nussbaum, M. C. (1994). "Patriotism and Cosmopolitanism." *Boston Review* 19(5): 3–34.

Nussbaum, M. C. and Cohen, J., eds. (1996). *For Love of the Country: Debating the Limits of Patriotism*. Boston, MA: Beacon Press.

Ould Ahmed Salem, Z. (2001). "'Tcheb-tchib' et compagnie. Lexique de la survie et figures de la réussite en Mauritanie." *Politique africaine* 82: 78–100.

Palmery, I., Rauch, J., and Simpson, G. (2003). "Violent Crime in Johannesburg." In Tomlinson, R., Beauregard, R. A., Bremner, L., and Mangcu, X., eds, *Emerging Johannesburg: Perspectives on the Postapartheid City*, pp. 101–122. New York: Routledge.

Palomares, E. and Quiminal, C. (2012). "Migration in South Africa. Tensions and Post-Apartheid Interethnic Compromises in a Central District of Johannesburg." In Streiff-Fénart, J. and Segatti, A., eds, *The Challenge of the Threshold: Border Closures and Migration Movements in Africa*, pp. 121–139. Lanham, MD: Lexington Books.

Peberdy, S. (2009). *Selecting Immigrants: National Identity and South Africa's Immigration Policies, 1910–2008*. Johannesburg: Wits University Press.

Pollock, S., Bhabha, H. K., Breckenridge, C. A., and Chakrabarty, D. (2000). "Cosmopolitanisms." *Public Culture* 12(3): 577–589.

Polzer, T. and Igglesdon, V. (2009). *Humanitarian Assistance to Internally Displaced Persons in South Africa: Lessons Learned Following Attacks on Foreign Nationals in May 2008*. Johannesburg: Forced Migration Studies Programme, University of the Witwatersrand.

Portes, A., Guarnizo, L. E., and Landolt, P. (1999). "The Study of Transnationalism: Pitfalls and Promise of an Emergent Research Field." *Ethnic and Racial Studies* 22(2): 217–237.

Posel, D. (1991). *The Making of Apartheid 1948–1961: Conflict and Compromise*. Oxford, New York: Clarendon Press, Oxford University Press.

Pries, L. (1996). "Transnationale soziale Räume. Theoretisch-empirischee Skizze am Beispiel der Arbeiterwanderungen Mexico-USA." *Zeitschrift für Soziologie* 25(6): 456–472.

———. (2002) "Transnationalisierung der sozialen Welt?," *Berliner Journal für Soziologie* 12(2): 263–272.

Riccio, B. (2006). "'Transmigrants' mais pas 'nomades': Transnationalisme mouride en Italie." *Cahiers d'Etudes Africaines*, XLVI(1), 181: 95–114.

Ricœur, P. (2004). "Cultures, du deuil à la traduction." *Le Monde*, May 25, 2004: 1, 19.

Rogers, C. (1945). "The Non-Directive Method as a Technique for Social Research." *American Journal of Sociology* 50(4): 279–283.

Schiffauer, W. (2006). "Transnationale Solidaritätsgruppen, Imaginäre Räume, Irreale Konditionalsätze." In Berking, H., ed., *Die Macht des Lokalen in einer Welt ohne Grenzen*, pp. 165–180. Frankfurt and New York: Campus Verlag.

Segatti, A. (2011). "Reforming South African Immigration Policy in the Postapartheid Period (1990–2010)." In Segatti, A. and Landau, L. B., eds, *Contemporary Migration to South Africa: A Regional Development Issue*, pp. 31–66. Washington, DC and Paris: World Bank Publications, Agence Française de Développement.

Simone, A. (2008). "People as Infrastructure: Intersecting Fragments in Johannesburg." In Mbembe, A. and Nuttall, S., eds, *Johannesburg: The Elusive Metropolis*, pp. 68–90. Johannesburg: Wits University Press.

Skrbis, Z. and Woodward, I. (2007). "The Ambivalence of Ordinary Cosmopolitanism: Investigating the Limits of Cosmopolitan Openness." *The Sociological Review* 55(4): 730–747.

Timera, M. (1996). *Les Soninké en France. D'une histoire à l'autre.* Paris: Karthala.

Turner, V. (1977). "Process, System, and Symbol: A New Anthropological Synthesis." *Dædalus* 106(3): 61–80.

Vertovec, S. (1999). "Conceiving and Researching Transnationalism." *Ethnic and Racial Studies* 22(2): 447–462.

Vidal, D. (2008). "Vivre sur Fond de Frontières: Les migrants du Mozambique à Johannesburg." *Culture et Conflits* 72: 101–117.

———. (2010). "Living in, out of, and Between Two Cities: Migrants from Maputo in Johannesburg." *Urban Forum* 21(1): 55–68.

Vigneswaran, D., Araia, T., Hoag, C., and Tshabalala, X. (2010). "Criminality or Monopoly? Informal Immigration Enforcement in South Africa." *Journal of Southern African Studies* 36(2): 465–481.

Vigouroux, C. B. (2005). "'There Are No Whites in Africa': Territoriality, Language, and Identity Among Francophone Africans in Cape Town." *Language & Communication* 25(3): 237–255.

———. (2008). "'The Smuggling of La Francophonie': Francophone Africans in Anglophone Cape Town (South Africa)." *Language in Society* 37(3): 415–434.

Wa Kabwe-Segatti, A. (2009). "'We Offer the Whole of Africa Here!' African Curio Traders and the Marketing of a Global African Image in Post-Apartheid South African Cities." *Cahiers d'Etudes Africaines* 1–2(193–194): 285–308.

Werbner, P. (1999). "Global Pathways: Working Class Cosmopolitans and the Creation of Transnational Ethnic Worlds." *Social Anthropology* 7(01): 17–35.

11

Walls and White Elephants: Oil, Infrastructure, and the Materiality of Citizenship in Urban Equatorial Guinea*

Hannah Appel

Hurricane Ike struck Houston and much of eastern Texas in September 2008. At the time, I was living in Malabo, the capital of Equatorial Guinea, doing fieldwork in the burgeoning oil and gas industry. Many of my informants were Texans, living as expatriate oil industry managers in the tiny Central African country. Days after Hurricane Ike hit, I stood in a security checkpoint building with a few other American women—wives of male expatriate management—going through the rituals of security clearance for admission to a private oil compound. As we waited, the women began to talk about home. They had family and friends in Texas, who, in the wake of the hurricane, had been living without electricity or running water for several days. One woman worried out loud about her 24-year-old daughter in Houston who had told her that there was no more gasoline, ice was sold out at local stores as were ice chests. "*How will she eat?*" she asked. However, in the next breath, she noted the incongruity, the strangeness, that here in Equatorial Guinea people live without electricity and running water every day. "Study a city and neglect its sewers and power supplies," Susan Leigh Star wrote, "and you miss essential aspects of distributional justice and planning power" (1999: 379).

The transnational oil industry in Equatorial Guinea is based in and around the capital city, not only in walled residential and business compounds, but also on the rigs that sparkle and blaze at night off Malabo's shores. Since 2000, this long-impoverished micro-state of 600,000 people has received over $50 billion in capital deployment from American-based oil and gas companies alone.[1] Among the most important new oil producers in Africa, Equatorial Guinea is at the center of the petroleum industry's "new Persian Gulf," from which upwards of 17 percent of US net crude oil and oil products now come (USEIA 2010). Perhaps not surprisingly, everyday life in the capital city and around the small country reflects neither this spectacular inflow of wealth nor the statistical fantasies it produces—that Equatorial Guinea, for example, has the highest per capita wealth in Africa, on par with that of Denmark or Taiwan (CIA 2010). Instead, Equatoguineans live with sporadic electricity, endemic typhoid and malaria, and without potable running water. In affluent areas, the lack of public infrastructure gives way to private provision, and those who can afford it buy generators for electricity or put tanks on their roofs for water. However, even my next-door neighbor—the Ministry of Finance and Budgets—was routinely dark for days and even weeks at a time. Education and healthcare systems were similarly erratic, as were food staples in Malabo's import-reliant markets. With no industrialized agriculture, when the border with Cameroon closed (which it often did), fresh vegetables rapidly disappeared and prices skyrocketed on the dwindling piles that remained.

Meanwhile, on the border of that same city, next to the airport, the gates and walls of private oil industry compounds open onto manicured lawns, landscaped hedges and flowers, paved roads with speed limits and fire hydrants, stately suburban homes with SUVs in garages, and sprawling office and industrial complexes. The largest complex alone generated enough electricity to power the entire country's electricity needs 24 hours per day, every day. Food to feed expatriate employees was shipped from Europe and the United States. The luxurious homes in which expatriate management lived were serviced by their own sewage and septic systems, and appointed with flat screen televisions, wireless internet, and landline phone service with Houston area codes. Moreover, the compounds included pools, gyms, basketball and tennis courts, restaurants, bars, and at one, a movie theater, and small golf course. Malaria, endemic to the Equatorial Guinea just on the other side of the wall, had been all but eradicated on the compounds. Management-level expatriate oil workers and their wives living in these lavish "suburbs of Houston" received a 75 percent salary increase for working in a "hardship" post.

Enclaving, Urban Infrastructure, and Citizenship

Enclaving, or the unequal distribution of urban infrastructure, is nothing new and certainly not unique to tiny Malabo or the oil industry. Critical urbanists increasingly encourage our attention to the sociotechnics of the built environment, highlighting the infrastructural (dis) connections constructed along the fault lines of class, race, the aesthetics of security, neoliberalism, and planning power (Caldeira 2000, Davis 2006, Gandy 2006, Graham and Marvin 2001, Low 2003, Soja 2000). These disconnections are present everywhere in Equatorial Guinea's oil enclaves, and yet, there are productive ethnographic peculiarities to consider as well: All compound residents are foreign, and work for a single company or group of companies. In other words, only expatriate employees are allowed (in fact, often required) to live on the compounds, and Equatoguineans, regardless of their class position, governmental authority, or employment with the company, are prohibited from living therein. Compound residents live and work within the enclave, where housing is zoned by "skill level"—barrack-like conditions for mostly Indian and Pakistani workers, shared dormitory accommodations for midlevel (mostly Filipino) workers, and luxury homes for (mostly white, North American, and Western European) managers. With companies acting as both landlord and employer, compounds create an elevated level of employee/inhabitant control, all of which make Equatorial Guinea's enclaves arguably closer to a company town model (Crawford 1995, Ferguson 1999, 2006, Porteus 1970, 1974, Vitalis 2007) than they are to the forms of privatized urbanism increasingly typical in Africa and around the world. To put it in Mann's (1984) formulation, companies, not the state, exercise infrastructural power in these sites. Beyond renting the land, the Equatoguinean government does not participate in the building, maintenance, or regulation of these spaces.

For Equatoguinean citizens, enclave construction not only entails dispossession, but also dramatizes the lack of access to potable water, reliable electricity, and other forms of domestic comfort beyond compound walls. The enclaves' private luxury, in other words, stands as a securitized monument to escalating petro-inequality and the failure of the state to invest its newfound wealth in public services, situating the enclaves within what Ong has called graduated sovereignty, spaces within the nation-state "that are subjected to different kinds of governmentality and that vary in terms of the mix of disciplinary and civilizing regimes" (1999: 7). As this chapter will go on to detail, the infrastructural power of companies does not stop at the apparent border of enclave walls (despite companies' work-intensive attempts to make it seem so), but extends far into the capital city and beyond.

In a situation where transnational companies wield inordinate infrastructural power, and the state is simultaneously called upon to invest its newfound wealth in public services, where does the locus of responsibility sit for the distributional properties of infrastructure? What alloys of private and public, state and corporation, determine to whom water or electricity flows, to whom roads might reach, let alone the "soft" infrastructures of health or education systems? In Equatorial Guinea, the distributive potentials of infrastructure became a zone of contestation. The infrastructural entitlements often associated with substantive citizenship—water, electricity, roads, schools, and healthcare—became an unequally and uneasily shared project between the state apparatus and transnational companies. Here, infrastructure became a stage on which companies and the state alike talked about, performed, and renounced the responsibilities attached to the provision of citizenship's materialities. Sovereignty itself was at issue. Oil companies were "happy to invoke [Equatorial Guinea's] sovereignty when pressures are placed on them to improve their human rights or social responsibility records; and yet only too happy to operate in an environment in which they could get away with just about anything" (Kashi and Watts 2008: 46). State actors on the other hand, willfully signed contracts with oil companies that compromised their authority, thus taking the opportunity "to support unfettered capitalism while denouncing it: to bemoan their loss of power and sovereignty while contributing to that very loss" (Palan 2006: 190). The enclave in particular, I will suggest, is a framing device, a site of intentional but asymptotic disentanglement, on behalf of which oil companies do a tremendous amount of work, intended to structure risk, liability, and responsibility in such a way that the industry can *seem to* remove itself from the legal, environmental, political, and economic situations in which it is, in fact, urgently implicated.

I start the chapter by thinking through the enclaves both in their capacity as residential oases of comfort and privilege, and as ring-fenced corporate spaces in which the industry can work toward a separation from the "corruption" that surrounds them. In the second half of the chapter, I turn to Malabo II, and the ways in which new infrastructural developments "outside the walls" are both entangled with the oil industry in surprising ways, and become central to the negotiation of governmental responsibility for the outcomes of becoming an oil exporter.

Enclaves I: *Una Limpieza Terrible*

After attending college in Texas, Mauricio returned home to Equatorial Guinea where he worked for the Major Corporation. Intimate both with life inside the enclave (as an employee) and outside as a Malabo resident, Mauricio explained that expatriate residents "don't live in Malabo. They live in Houston." Indeed *suburbs of Houston* was the emic label residents often used, with a touch of guilt and a touch of humor, to describe compound life. As one American wife put it, "I love the fantastic houses and facilities. More than anything, I love the quiet. I feel protected. You feel like you're in the United States—our own suburb of Houston—and that's what the enclaves are for, so that the expatriates can feel like they're at home." Although there was much on the compound to indicate that expatriate residents were not at home—Equatoguinean service personnel, the occasional goat munching well-maintained grass, a greatly diminished but still-present threat of malaria—there was also a great deal to indicate that they were.[2] Facilities invariably displayed adjacent clocks, one set to Houston time and the other to Malabo time. English was the lingua franca of the compounds. Companies facilitated the delivery of an overseas shipping container to each compound household, bringing the family piano to one home, extensive printmaking equipment to another. Each home was filled with the much-loved trinkets, artwork, and indispensable kitchen supplies that had followed expatriate management through many overseas postings. These personal effects supplemented high-end standardized furniture and state-of-the art KitchenAid, Cuisinart, and Sub-zero appliances, powered by 120-volt currency to accommodate American voltage settings. Satellites facilitated landline phones with Houston area codes, allowing local calls to and from the United States, wireless internet, and expansive cable offerings. Although not all expatriate managers were American, all had worked for American oil and gas companies long enough to have lived in Houston for years, and had come (often grudgingly) to accept a Houston-centric domestic and corporate culture.

The making of an American suburban experience was also evident in the spatial layout of the enclaves. The management homes in the Endurance compound, for example, were set atop a gently sloping hillside overlooking a manmade lake. All the houses were painted either neutral gray or dusky sand. Because residents were forbidden to paint their homes, display flags or lawn ornaments of any kind, or tend to their own gardens, there was an anonymity to the built environment, to the extent that residents often joked about walking into the wrong house. Meticulous landscaping assured that no flower, palm, or blade of grass was overgrown, though a handful of towering old-growth ceiba trees had been thoughtfully spared. The various compound areas—houses, the pool, the restaurant and recreation center, the office complex, the liquid natural gas plant—were connected by smooth, wide paved roads on which speed limits were strictly enforced. Security checkpoints and card-activated gates punctuated the unhurried circulation of golf carts and company-issued SUVs. Because Malabo proper was claustrophobically small, essentially without greenery, and crosscut with narrow roads newly congested and dusty with oil-fueled construction projects, my Equatoguinean friends and informants who had spent any time on the compounds were often struck by the pastoral atmosphere of the enclaves, nevertheless redolent with containment and control. In one particularly evocative description, an older Equatoguinean man described the scene behind the walls as *una limpieza terrible*. Literally, "a terrible cleanliness," but perhaps more accurately a fearsome cleanliness, where fearsome can mean both terrifying and awesome.

Comings and goings from the compounds were strictly monitored. Non-residents and non-employees needed an invitation to enter, and even with an invitation had to stop at a guard house to leave their passport and a local contact number, in exchange for a badge to be visibly displayed at all times when inside the compound. Non-resident personnel spending the night on the compound was permitted only in exceptional circumstances (family visiting from afar), and curfews—the time by which residents had to be back on the compound if they chose to leave—were observed, if not strictly enforced. The compounds were also occasionally "locked down" in response to perceived geopolitical unrest, whether local or in Nigeria, Cameroon, or along various borders. Because public transportation could not circulate within the compound, local workers were picked up on company buses in the morning and dropped off again in the evening. Compound residents frequently explained their lives to me in metaphors of fishbowls and golden cages, indicating infrastructural luxury within which they felt constantly monitored and contained. This level of controlled circulation and claustrophobic monitoring, in addition to the prohibition against Equatoguinean residents, contributed to the "lived" sense that the enclaves were somehow hermetic—completely detached from and indeed fortified against the world outside their walls (Caldeira 2000).

To be dropped outside the Endurance compound by taxi, one needed only ask the driver for "la planta." A cognate with the English word "plant," asking to go to "la planta" was in part to ask to be taken to the factory. However, for Equatoguineans, "la planta" is also an abbreviated reference to "la plantación" or the plantation, and the picturesque isthmus on which the massive Endurance compound now sits was a large cocoa plantation during the colonial era. The isthmus itself is known as Punta Europa—Point Europe. Along with many of Equatorial Guinea's largest plantations, it fell into disuse in the 1970s, and President Obiang eventually claimed it as his own. Through the 1980s and 1990s, small informal settlements emerged among the cacao trees, by that point overgrown with ferns, vines, and other secondary growth. The first contract for oil-related infrastructure development on Punta Europa in the late 1990s was between Endurance's predecessor company and Obiang, to whom they paid rent as a private property owner. During the second phase of Endurance's major expansion, Obiang made a large and public display that the state was "expropriating him too," as he officially sold his property to the government. The President's brazen display of solidarity-in-dispossession came as the dispossession of many communities in the greater Malabo area, including those who inhabited Punta Europa, began to rapidly accelerate. On their sundown walks through the compound, expatriate employees would collect shards of pottery that dotted the ground, remnants of a recent past of habitation rendered historically distant in their minds by the ceramic material and the romance of archaeological discovery.

Despite these contemporary histories of ownership and habitation, much of the work of disentanglement is predicated on an idea of the enclave's physical isolation, remote not only from surrounding unpredictability, but also from local histories of use, ownership, and dispossession. The company town has to be a frontier, a "zone of unmapping" wherein "frontiers aren't just discovered at the edge; they are projects in making geographical and temporal experience" (Tsing 2005: 29). Wendy reminisced about this frontier project to me from her spacious patio overlooking the ocean inlet that separates the Endurance compound from Malabo. The city was low and visible through the heated haze just across the water, as if a mirage. She and her husband had been coming in and out of Equatorial Guinea since 1999, by far the longest of any of the expatriate families I came to know. Her husband had come to Equatorial Guinea in 1998, and she accompanied him a year later to determine if the place was a viable living and working option for them, after other lengthy expatriate stints (as Brits) in Ecuador, Indonesia, Texas, and Los Angeles.

> The project was here. It was actually on this spot. There were very little lights around here. Nothing existed. This was jungle, total jungle. So we just saw the whole thing develop. [My husband] went on a 'reci,' you know, he actually did a reconnaissance mission. He actually walked through the jungle to see whether it would be suitable to start building houses, and where they would build the plant. That's how they mapped it out.

In Wendy's narrative of adventure and discovery, "nothing existed" on Punta Europa when her husband arrived in 1998. "It was jungle, total jungle." Then, using a term common both in the military and survey or civil engineering, Wendy remembered that her husband had "actually" walked through the jungle on reconnaissance, mapping a place where nothing existed into the potential for houses and a methanol plant. The work of disentanglement starts in origin stories like Wendy's.

With the land cleared of inhabitants and their histories (save for the romantic pottery shards decorating the mantle), the work of building an enclaved world can begin. It is through exceptional infrastructure—potable hot and cold water, constant electricity, and sewage and waste systems—in a country that had none of these things, that disentanglement is built. Paul is a white Zimbabwean who managed the building of the Smith Corporation compound, the only major compound on Equatorial Guinea's mainland, located just outside the city of Bata. Like many expatriates I came across in the industry, Paul's professional background was military and paramilitary, but he had been "cooling his heels" for a while, working in various tourism and game park development projects throughout Africa. He jumped at the chance to manage the building and maintenance of the Smith compound, but attested to the strenuous work required to assure that the exceptional infrastructure worked.

> Opening a facility like this takes twelve months. We had teething problems: generators black out, the incinerator wouldn't work. Potable water wasn't really potable. We had to modify filtration systems, massive problems with AC. The camp was designed by an American company in Houston and this isn't Houston, this is Africa. It has its own relative humidity, its own dew point.

Paul narrated to me a long year in which a Danish construction company, Spanish, Portuguese, Icelandic, and Greenlandic journeymen, along with 800 temporarily employed local Bata residents, built the camp according to a Houston-based design. "Africa" interfered every step of the way, with Harmattan dust clogging the air conditioning and filtration systems. However, once the international crew was able to reconcile the Houston-based design with local dew points and humidity levels, the camp became, according to Paul, "completely self-contained." Having folded local weather patterns and other climatic considerations into the materiality of the infrastructure, the provision of electricity, water, sewage, garbage disposal, and even food was organized and systematized to serve those within the walls.

> Electricity, water, sewage, [we] handle our own garbage, incinerate it all here. The bulk of our food comes from Houston. We ship it all in because it's cheaper and the quality is good and it eliminated the need to

> deal with a highly inefficient local economy. We spend $150 million dollars a year [in the local economy] but in a manner that doesn't negatively impact efficiency offshore. [Our] social development program [is] one hundred percent local content.

Despite Paul's insistence on self-containment, provisioning the compound of course relies not only on infrastructure outside the compound walls—roads, sea ports, and airports—but also on the locals who manage those resources, as well as those who come into the compound on a daily basis as employees (Caldeira 2000). Nevertheless, in Paul's mind, these ties do not detract from the compound's self-sufficiency. Instead, the effect of these substantial investments is to "eliminate the need to deal with a highly inefficient local economy." Facilitated by this idea of separation, the only relationship Paul sees with the outside world is the $150 million per year spent "in the local economy" on social development programs. Note the incongruity here of imagining that there is something called an "economy" in Equatorial Guinea separate from the industry which literally constitutes it (Mitchell 2002). Corporate social responsibility becomes the detached way in which oil companies intervene, from the other side of the wall, redoubling the effect that they are somehow separate, but willing to "help" those on the "outside" (Shever 2010, Zalik 2004).

From meticulous landscaping to the monitoring of human movement, from reconnaissance missions in uninhabited jungle to construction projects that struggled to wall Houston-designed infrastructure away from its absence on the other side, the effect of this work of separation was to make the enclave into a framing device, a site of intentional disentanglement. Although ostensibly meant to solidify a line that already existed—between company and state, between Western standards and "Africa"—the separation is, in fact, partial, strategic, and performative, with many people doing a tremendous amount of work to maintain its boundaries. However, the "effect" of this work of separation is eerily successful: it allows companies—as individual employees living in Equatorial Guinea *and* as juridically dispersed institutions with shareholders and Houston central offices—to inhabit a space of uneven disentanglement, to bemoan what goes on outside their gates, as if they have nothing to do with it, when, in fact, their industry constitutes 98 percent of Equatorial Guinea's national economy. Insofar as the enclaves enclose not only residential life but also daily office life, they are a spatial representation of the extent to which the industry claims to ring-fence corporate practices away from an external business environment widely regarded by the industry as unpredictable, personalistic, and corrupt. It is to this enclaved corporate culture that I now turn.

Enclaves II: Zonal Capitalism

In my 14 months of fieldwork in Equatorial Guinea, the Ministry of Mines, Industry and Energy (MMIE) remained jarringly empty. Located in a Lebanese-built apartment building on the airport road, the Ministry was floor after floor of empty hallways, plastic-covered furniture apparently unused, and outdated concession maps. Seated at desks that were completely bare save for computers (no papers, files, or calendars), secretaries chatted happily to one another, windows open to let in the breeze necessitated by electricity outages. The functionaries were often impossible to find in their offices. This was a radical contrast to the office environments I found on the oil compounds: large buildings with open floor plans crowded with cubicles and swivel office chairs; graphs, charts, and posters touting company slogans and achievements covered the walls; enormous white board calendars and schedules were animated by uncannily legible handwriting and meaningfully placed magnets; stacks of paper, books, labeled binders, file cabinets, computers, printers, and fax machines crowded office desks and shelving; the thrum of phones and photocopying; and the hustle and bustle to and fro between personalized work spaces with photos of families, inspirational quotes, and sports team memorabilia, was constant.

The infrastructure necessary for constant electricity, wireless internet, running water, and Houston area codes was not, of course, only for the domestic comfort of expatriate employees, but also facilitated the movement of oil and gas to market. Moreover, the industry points to the ostensible infrastructural "ring fence" within which corporate operations take place as spatial and procedural proof that they are separate from the "corruption" outside their walls (Barry 2006, Ferguson 2006, Reno 2001). Considered in their commercial capacity, these enclaves, in fact, functioned as Ong's "noncontiguous zones" (2006) or Winters' "zonal capitalism" (1996). Separate business practices ranged from the independent telecommunications systems, to private ports, to differential laws, regulations, and taxation regimes.[3] The means of production too were freed from state involvement: companies were permitted the duty-free importation of all equipment, materials, machinery, supplies, and components (Cameron and Palan 2004, MacLachlan and Aguilar 1998, Sklair 1993).

Justifications for these separate business practices stretched beyond arguments for efficiency and profit maximization. Corporate processes "within" the enclave cloaked themselves in discursive and procedural regimes of the global, the standard, the compliant, the objective, to be differentiated from the arbitrary, the personalistic, the incomprehensibly local beyond their walls. As Barry (2006: 250) puts it, "the formation of technological zones has become critical to the constitution of a distinction between global/Western political and economic forms, and their non-Western others." Reno (2001: 4) has gone so far as to say that "the private enclave exploitation of resources is a salutary imposition of market discipline and standards of efficiency on corrupt economies." Although I disagree with Reno's assertion for the extent to which it succumbs to the ostensible separation between the enclave and its outside, his is a prescient summary of the performativity of the enclave, the *desire* and work toward creating a line between compliant and corrupt, American and African. And yet, considered ethnographically, zonal capitalism in Equatorial Guinea was made through deep entanglements with that from which it claimed to be separate. The Smith Corporation's country manager described the exceptional status his company enjoyed as follows:

> There's so much revenue generated. Corruption and inefficiency exist in spades in West Africa. The fact that we generate so much revenue, we have direct contacts in [the Ministry of Mines, Industry and Energy] and tremendous influence. If there are difficulties—[given our] $700,000 per day [rig] rental—negative impact by customs, immigration, [we are] able to make a few phone calls and it gets cleared away.

He continued by explaining that they use their global, compliant standards to call their highly placed connections at the Ministry of Mines and ask them to please grant the favor of calling the lowly customs official holding their needed technology at the port, and telling him to snap out of it. This is how they differentiate themselves from the "corruption that exists in spades in West Africa." Thus, although Barry (2006) is right that the formation of technological zones is critical to the making of distinctions between us and them, compliant and corrupt, the work of making those distinctions cannot be characterized by separation alone, but must also include the Spanish word that locals used most often to explain the relationship between the oil industry and local power structures: *compinchados*—accomplices.[4] As one Equatoguinean lawyer put it:

> Obiang gives the companies free reign, and in turn they protect his regime. They operate on the margins of local law but it doesn't affect them. This theme of having their own telecommunications system, it

> guarantees that the government cannot interfere. This is on the margins of current legality and of the country's interests. They are commercial relations in which the industry closes its eyes to what is obviously illegal according to international law in order to do business with the regime. [...] The government has tacitly renounced control of the activities of these companies. As they renounce control, company activities damage the interests of the population.

The deep complicities between oil companies and those in power here stretch from the state's granting of corporate sovereignty within the enclaves to companies' willful blind eye to blatant illegalities. However, the "effect" to which Barry and Ferguson point—a border between the industry and the economy and society thought to be "outside" it—is pervasive. Despite the sticky entanglements through which hydrocarbons get to market, the infrastructural separation allows a consequential inhabitance of a partition. Looking out at Equatorial Guinea from the enclave, expatriates told me about how locals should really learn to stop burning their small piles of garbage, even as gas flares blazed constantly around us; or they paused in security buildings, struck by questions of responsibility and framing that Hurricane Ike made momentarily visible.

Responsibility Outside the Walls

In 2004, an American congressional subcommittee tasked with investigating money laundering and foreign corruption released a report accusing Riggs Bank (a Washington DC firm) and President Obiang of theft of public oil revenue and money laundering on a grand scale. The report also implicated American oil companies, revealing large payments into the offshore accounts of highly placed Equatoguineans (Coleman and Levin 2004). The marketization of oil requires entanglements from the mundane to the cinematic.

In response to what became known as the Riggs report, the Equatoguinean state released a report of its own, entitled "Statement of the People & Government of Equatorial Guinea in Response to the report on Riggs Bank" (República de Guinea Ecuatorial 2005). After a scant 19 pages of explanation, 66 pages of the statement went on to offer charts and photographs documenting infrastructure investment as the "real" site of the missing billions.

Part of the performance of private enclaves is, of course, the abdication of responsibility for infrastructure provision outside the walls, even as their construction demanded complicity in dispossession and illicit payments to Equatoguinean dignitaries. However, there are other, unexpected overflows that directly implicate the oil industry in Malabo's wider infrastructural development, or lack thereof. Further, through an ethnographic consideration of Malabo II, I explore the ways that infrastructure became a terrain in which the state negotiated responsibility for the outcomes of oil extraction, with ensuing and unexpected entanglements of oil and gas companies in Malabo's infrastructure provision.

The Equatoguinean government's response to the Riggs Bank report offered innumerable and costly infrastructure projects as a defense against charges of theft and money laundering; the money had not been stolen or invested for personal gain, rather it had been spent in the building and maintenance of public infrastructure. Despite the dubiousness of many of the report's claims, the long term lack of certain kinds of infrastructure in Malabo is arguably eclipsed today by the breakneck speed at which "other" kinds of infrastructure are being built. Highways, high-rises, governmental palaces, airports, sea ports, national stadiums, and national oil company headquarters appear in vast swaths of new construction. Equatoguinean friends and I often joked that the National motto—Unity, Peace, and Justice—should be changed to Unity, Concrete, and Glass.[5]

Construction booms in newly resource-rich states are a well-documented phenomenon. Often pejoratively labeled "white elephants" for their unique combination of grandiosity and impracticality, critics deride prestige projects as irresponsible in the face of populations who watch aging infrastructure crumble around them as oil wealth builds airports from which they will never leave (Apter 2005, Coronil 1997, Watts 2008, Vitalis 2007). Following the Riggs Bank retort, however, I would like to suggest here that white elephants are in fact central to the negotiation of governmental responsibility, negotiations in which the projects' grandiosity and impracticality are not necessarily liabilities.

After education abroad, and extensive travel in Europe and the United States, Alberto came home to Equatorial Guinea to work as a human resources manager with the Smith Corporation. Noting that the company had been in neighboring Gabon for 18 years, Alberto commented that Equatorial Guinea had not learned from places that had made the same mistakes before:

> I don't believe that the state has learned. For example, the coastal promenade, (*paseo marítimo*)...is being extended. It has cost a fortune, but the value that it brings the population is infinitesimal compared to the value that could be produced by investment in the University to train

> technicians. This same concrete jungle went up in Gabon, in Nigeria, and it's the same thing we're doing here. There's concrete everywhere. The tendency is unstoppable: concrete, skyscraper, concrete, skyscraper. The only concrete that is good in my opinion is roads. All the rest—airports in the interior, promenades—it's all a waste. When you start investigating the wasteful use of resources, go to Gabon and look at the train. It's awfully wasteful, but mine isn't a common opinion. People like visible infrastructure. It's because we're a colonized people. We want to portray ourselves as having achieved what they have in other parts of the world. If we look like New York we feel very happy. I'm not happy. I'd rather have the university well-funded and the schools and the scholarships and the hospitals and then small houses. No more concrete.

Although Alberto's comparative frame—to Gabon and Nigeria—was unavailable at earlier times and places of oil development, the substance of his critique is as old as the infrastructure development patterns he points to. Despite his insistence that his is not a common opinion, Alberto comes from a long line of critics who characterize these empty construction booms as mimetic, hollow versions of the trappings of "modernity," sedimenting the given place in a mess of semi-finished palaces destined more to crumble than to improve the quality of life of the majority (Coronil 1997, Vitalis 2007, Watts 2001). Alternatively, we might read these construction booms through Ferguson's (2006: 161) argument about the politics of membership, by which the appearance of architecturally modern buildings would not merely be empty gesture or mimicry, but the pressing of a claim "to the political and social rights of full membership" in a global club visually defined by the shared infrastructure of skyscrapers and superhighways.

Although an instantaneous modernity (albeit it one modeled more after Abu Dhabi than New York,) as well as assertions of global membership were both at work in Equatorial Guinea's infrastructure boom, the Riggs report and beyond suggest that the rapid construction of conspicuous infrastructure also plays a central role in high-profile international wrangling over what should be done with oil money in impoverished places. Pressure on oil-exporting state apparatuses to combat "corruption" and foment "social investment" of oil monies has intensified over time as the social, environmental, and political ravages of becoming an oil exporter grow clearer. New infrastructure in Malabo then becomes a site of visible investment (Apter 2005), a site to which the government—accused of squandering or outright stealing oil money—can gesture to show where the money has gone. Just as the enclave offers transnational oil companies a stage on which to negotiate responsibility through the performance of removal and superiority, oil-funded public infrastructure development offers the Equatoguinean state a similar stage on which to negotiate their role in infrastructural violence. Stefán, a resident of the impoverished Campo Yaounde settlement, explained, "What matters to the state is the outcome. There will be a time when people will ask questions and they need to be able to point to a stadium, a road."

As built responsibility, the conspicuousness of white elephant projects and the haste with which they go up—often cited as evidence of their hollowness—are, in fact, integral to their function. Compared to water and electricity systems, for instance, prestigious buildings go up quickly. Past the expertise required for their construction, no other expertise is required to make them "work." Once constructed, the work they do is to be seen (Apter 2005). That many of Equatorial Guinea's new prestigious buildings were, in fact, without pipes to facilitate running water, sewage systems, or electrical wiring was neither visible from the outside nor central to the immediate work required of them by the Equatoguinean state. Oil and gas companies are also involved in these white elephants in unexpected ways as the case of Malabo II (*Malabo Dos*) highlights well.

Malabo II

When I first arrived in Equatorial Guinea in summer 2006, Malabo II was a swath of second-growth jungle and overgrown cacao plantations, with one new red-dirt road through the middle. Moreover, a series of billboards around town on which the president's face was superimposed over a photo-collage of idyllic, deterritorialized residential and financial districts. He gazed meaningfully out into the distance/future, and the caption read, *Este hombre tiene un sueño,* this man has a dream. When I returned in fall 2007, Malabo II was hectares of cleared land, dotted with bulldozers. When I left in fall 2008, it was a series of paved roads with a handful of large buildings, none of which were occupied, although cars had begun to circulate on the new roads. GE Petrol (the national oil company) had erected a 20-story headquarters; China Dalian was building 100+ unit apartment buildings; and many other architectural growths were in various stages of completion. During my 14 months in Equatorial Guinea, watching Malabo II spring up was like watching time-lapse photography of a plant growing from seed to flower—it is a process with which you are familiar, but one that looks altogether strange in fast-forward.

Despite, or perhaps because of, the spectacular rate of construction, Malabo II was without water, sewage, or electricity systems. It was a series of empty, glass-skinned buildings sitting in the middle of recently-felled jungle. As such, Malabo II not only constituted a framing project for governmental responsibility for the investment of oil monies, but also offered a medium through which to rethink the materialities and histories entailed in infrastructural violence—what assemblage of who, what, and how might be responsible for the persistent absence of water, electricity, and sewage systems?

Considered processually, on the one hand, these buildings require one contract with one construction company, and a matter of months to construct. On the other hand, city-wide water or electricity grids (let alone national systems) require a much wider range of expertise—from the bacteriological to the distributive, engineering to chemistry—and, therefore, a wider range of contracts, a longer time frame, and far more logistical coordination. A Spanish city planner working for a firm with multiple contracts in Malabo and Malabo II explained to me some of the intricacies of these processes. There was a company with a contract to build a water system for Malabo, he explained, but "right now they're only placing the tubes at the initial point of capture, the river."

> Then there's the work of treatment, of purification, to take out the sand. There are mechanical, chemical, and bacteriological filtration processes. Then there has to be a storage system, with capacity for two days of treated water. [...] Here, one company is doing the tubes, but I don't know where they're capturing water or treating it. The water that comes to the city comes directly from the river without treatment.

To understand the complexities of contracting water or electricity systems is to think through Equatorial Guinea's history, in which "public service" infrastructure has long been a patchwork of private or enclaved development, set up either to facilitate the extraction, production, and export of commodities—enslaved people, palm oil, cacao, or petroleum—or to provision the colonial and postcolonial elite. Pieced together with private contracts and private interests, throughout the colonial and postcolonial periods, infrastructure has been a profitable locus of what Bayart (1993: 70) calls "the symbiosis between the worlds of administration and business," or Mbembé (2001: 78), "the privatization of sovereignty." Since independence, remuneration for governmental work in Equatorial Guinea—from police to ministers—has come not in the form of salary, but in the opportunity provided by the position to accumulate connections and wealth. In the same time period, contracts with foreign firms or development organizations have more reliably produced kickbacks than the more elusive final product they promise, especially when it comes to systemic projects such as water and electricity, which entail expansive and overlaid networks of pipes and wires, and require diverse and protracted forms of expertise and maintenance. Because projects like this take so long, and rely on external expertise that, in turn, relies on fickle and ever-changing international relationships, precisely the kinds of infrastructure needed to alleviate the violence at issue here are also the kinds most vulnerable to false starts, incompletions, and incompatibilities. As the Spanish city planner cited earlier continued,

> Instead of having a single contract for someone to install a water system, they have the Chinese, the Arabs over here, mixed companies. At this moment it's chaos. One company comes in to lay asphalt, and then [another] comes to break it and put in water tubes. Sometimes, electricity tubes cross water tubes and they're different companies so no company wants to repair anything. In the end there's no solution and there's chaos. It's a delicate problem because there are no international standards. Electrical installations by Chinese companies are very different that those done by the Egyptians or the Americans. Chinese measure in millimeters, Americans in inches. But you can't mix technology or measuring systems if you want water to run. Over time the Russians have been here, the Chinese, the French, the Spanish, now the Egyptians too. Because of political relationships between nations, favored contractors change over time. One company lays one cable. Later another company lays another cable. They cross... Another company comes in to fix it and another one collapses. It's a repeating cycle.

This account of crossed cables and incompatible measuring systems offers a material history of the fickle involvement of global superpowers in Equatorial Guinea—the Spanish as the former colonial power; the French as the regional colonial power; and the Chinese and the Russians, who invested heavily in the post-independence, Cold War era. Today, the Chinese are back along with Arab Contractors—Egypt's largest parastatal construction firm. The planner's rhetorical archaeology of infrastructure technologies indexes changing colonial and postcolonial relationships in which infrastructure is first a vehicle for, and later the ruins of, fickle geopolitical solidarities. This is a long history of entanglement in which American oil companies, despite their best efforts at framing their involvement otherwise, are only the most recent participants.

As oil companies work so furiously to enclave their exceptional infrastructure, and abdicate responsibility for its absence outside the walls, there are overflows. Contracts signed with the Republic of Equatorial Guinea in fact *require* oil and gas companies to "construct a prestigious building" in Malabo II, "using modern and permanent materials." Article 6.22 of a sample contract between Equatorial Guinea and an oil company, entitled *Premises*, reads in part: "Upon the first Commercial Discovery, the Contractor shall [...] construct a prestigious building for its offices in Equatorial Guinea using modern and permanent materials and of an appropriate size and design as shall be approved by the Ministry" (MMIE 2008: 26). *Congosa* (gossip) around Malabo among both expatriates and Equatoguineans was that the requirements of Article 6.22 were more specific than those in the document to which I have had access. Multiple informants told me, for example, that "appropriate size and design as shall be approved by the Ministry" required that each "prestigious building" be at least six stories high. This was plainly ludicrous for most transnational companies with small E. G. subsidiaries and rotating subcontractors, often with ten or fewer in-country employees, but no matter, one of my expatriate management informants explained:

> Companies are required by law to have a presence in Malabo II, even if they don't need it, and even if they certainly don't need six floors. If they don't build it themselves, someone, the Chinese, will build it for them, and they will have to pay for it.

This privatized development plan extends not only to the building of superfluous company headquarters, but also to the financing, renting, and eventual ownership of the buildings. Once construction costs have been recovered by the company, the state then owns the building and the company inhabiting it will pay rent to the state.

> All installations, facilities, goods, equipment, materials, or land acquired by the Contractor for Petroleum Operations shall become property of the State from the point at which their costs are fully recovered by the Contractor. [...] Upon termination, rescission, or cancellation of this Contract, for any reason whatsoever, in relation to all or part of the contract area, the ownership of said installations, facilities, goods, equipment, materials, or land,...and any other items acquired and used for Petroleum Operations shall become the sole property of the State and shall be conveyed directly to it. (MMIE: 43)

Without any other large productive sectors (agriculture, manufacturing, tourism, etc.) the government has subsidized and subcontracted the transnational oil industry to build them a new city. Where the enclave involved costly investments and actions toward cutting certain ties—not only to systems of food, water, and electricity provision outside the walls, but also to the daily practices of Equatoguinean governance and commerce—these investments have also necessitated the internalization of other ties, including the development of Malabo II. All disentanglement, Callon (1997) reminds us, provides the opportunity for new entanglement. From the abdication of responsibility for wider infrastructure provision that is so clear in the enclave, in Malabo II oil companies (or the construction companies they subcontract) effectively become reluctant architects and city planners, entangled not only in the proliferating presence of six-story buildings of modern and permanent material, but also in the renewed absence of water, electricity, and sewage systems to serve the new city. More broadly still, contractually enforced participation in the Malabo II project entangles American oil companies in much longer histories and archaeologies of infrastructure that foreign experts—engineers, capitalists, development practitioners—have left behind. Article 6.22 and Malabo II incontrovertibly belie the oil industry's work of separation from and abnegation of responsibility for infrastructural violence in Equatorial Guinea today.

Conclusion

> *When I lived in Equatorial Guinea I didn't complain about the running water. This is a shared reality that we all bear. But I had to complain that my country wasn't habitable by all. Electricity? We all share a difficult situation. But that not everyone is allowed to share even that situation? Unbearable.*

Donato Ndongo, the Equatoguinean writer-in-exile who spoke these words in 2009 offers two orienting admonitions by way of conclusion. First, he reminds us of the dangers of the narrowly biopolitical humanitarian concern that attention to infrastructure can summon. Sporadic water and electricity are bearable, he says, more so when they are a shared life condition. However, that many Equatoguineans (including the speaker) live in exile—unable even to share in the bearability of unreliable infrastructure—is, to him, unbearable. Second, his insistence that the lack of basic public infrastructure is, in fact, bearable, is a useful reminder. It is useful in particular to those of us who live with the normative assumptions that potable water and usable electricity should flow constantly, and that their absence represents an intervenable humanitarian situation. Taking liberties with Stoler on ruins, I think it could be equally said of infrastructure that "melancholy, compassion, and pity nourish imperial sensibilities of destruction." Infrastructures "hold histories but are less than the sum of the sensibilities of people who live in them. Instead we might turn to [infrastructure] as epicenters of renewed claims, [...] as sites that animate new possibilities, bids for entitlement, and unexpected political projects" (2008: 197–198).

In newly petroleum-rich Equatorial Guinea, infrastructure indeed became a site of unexpected political projects, as companies and the state alike used it as a newly visible stage on which to strategically assert or deny their sovereignty. All the while, however, both companies and the state were mutually entangled in the provision of services, or their absence, in the lives of Equatoguinean citizens. For companies, infrastructure becomes central in its capacity as architectural, liability, and performative wall between the production of profit and the place in which it happens to be occurring. For the Equatoguinean state, its centrality derives from its position at the heart of debate and evidence of the "responsible" investment of oil money.

Peter Benson draws on Levinas, Deleuze, and Guattari to consider "faciality," the practice by which people see each other "as typified objects and, on that basis, [circumscribe] suffering as an event that belongs to or was even caused by the sufferer. The other's suffering dangerously and easily becomes an event in which the self is not complicit [...] "Faciality...allows [people] to maintain distance between each other despite realities of having conjoined lives" (2008 595, 605). But, how does this "isolation and partitioning of responsibility" occur? What can so convincingly isolate and partition conjoined lives? In the oil and gas industry in Equatorial Guinea, I have suggested, this effect is made in part through infrastructure, which, through concrete and glass and food and water, produces the effect of separation in people whose lives are deeply conjoined. Today, this effect gleams in the glass of Malabo II, sparkles off the swimming pool in the Endurance compound, but tomorrow it will be ruins, or maybe a hotel. *The rot remains with us. The men are gone* (Walcott 1986: 5).

Notes

*A version of this essay originally appeared in *Ethnography* (2012, 13:4). It has been revised here to reflect the themes of the volume. Thanks to Sage Publications for permission to use the article here and to the editors of this volume for including the article here.

1. I use "capital deployment" here to specify that both Foreign Direct Investment (FDI) and capital investment calculations are not sufficient to measure the

quantity and diversity of hydrocarbon-related investment in Equatorial Guinea. In FDI alone (a narrow calculation based on balance of payment statistics and business registers, see UNCTAD 2009; Zhan 2006) Equatorial Guinea had received 13.676 billion by 2009. Assuming a stasis in FDI numbers (which is cautious given major pending projects including a second natural gas train) FDI will top 17 billion by FY 2011 (UNCTAD 2009; Kraus 2010 and personal communication). Capital deployment then widens this statistic out to include both capital investment (in the purchase of equipment and buildings) and operating costs, in which rig rental alone requires upwards of $1 million *per day* for each rig. Finally, it is my intention that this estimated figure include the millions of dollars paid into offshore accounts of powerful Equatoguineans (see Coleman and Levin 2004).

2. I focus here on the experiences of expatriate management who lived for three-year stretches in the compound's most luxurious homes. Other expatriate workers—mostly Filipino—rotated in and out of the compound's less luxurious residential facilities, and did not have the opportunity to cultivate "homes" in the same way.
3. Which ports oil companies used for the import and handling of which materials was a complicated and ever-changing question. From the late 1990s through at least 2005, the major US companies brought all their imported assets—from the technical to the domestic—through the Malabo and Bata ports. When that proved to be too cumbersome, as port officials would hold their goods at sea and demand extortionate sums of money, the Endurance corporation built their own port, through which they were permitted to import some, although not all, of their inputs. The relevant regulations and enforcement are constantly in flux and subject to negotiation. Suffice it to say that the oil industry, its proliferating subcontractors, and attendant construction industry greatly increase traffic at local ports, even as they begin to build the private infrastructure that allows them to bypass national infrastructure.
4. The term *compinchados* has rich inferential meanings beyond "accomplices." Although the term suggests a superficially equal relationship, it is derived from *pinche*, or helper, and thus implies inequality between the parties. This is certainly the case in Equatorial Guinea where it was widely agreed upon that the government was merely the oil companies' *pinche*.
5. *Unidad, Paz, y Justicia* becomes *Unidad, Hormigón, y Cristál*.

References

Apter, A. (2005). *The Pan-African Nation: Oil and the Spectacle of Culture in Nigeria*. Chicago: University of Chicago Press.

Barry, A. (2006). "Technological Zones." *European Journal of Social Theory* 9(2): 239–253.

Bayart, J.-F. (1993). *The State in Africa: The Politics of the Belly*. London and New York: Longman.

Benson, P. (2008). "El Campo: Faciality and Structural Violence in Farm Labor Camps." *Cultural Anthropology* 23(4): 589–629.

Caldeira, T. P. R. (2000). *City of Walls: Crime, Segregation, and Citizenship in Saõ Paolo*. Berkeley: University of California Press.
Callon, M. (1997). "Actor-Network Theory: The Market Test." Keynote Speech. Vol. 2010: Lancaster University Department of Sociology.
Cameron, A. and Palan, R. (2004). *The Imagined Economies of Globalization*. London: SAGE Publications.
CIA. (2010). GDP Per Capita based on Purchasing Power Parity. World Factbook. https://www.cia.gov/library/publications/the-world-factbook/rankorder/2004rank.html.
Coleman, N. and Levin, C. (2004). "Money Laundering and Foreign Corruption: Enforcement and Effectiveness of the Patriot Act." Case Study Involving Riggs Bank. Recovered from http://hsgac.senate.gov/public/_files/ACF5F8.pdf (June 23, 2011).
Coronil, F. (1997). *The Magical State: Nature, Money, and Modernity in Venezuela*. Chicago: University of Chicago Press.
Crawford, M. (1995). *Building the Workingman's Paradise: The Design of American Company Towns*. London: New Left Books.
Davis, M. (2006). *City of Quartz: Excavating the Future in Los Angeles*. London: Verso.
Ferguson, J. (1999). *Expectations of Modernity: Myths and Meanings of Urban Life on the Zambian Copperbelt*. Berkeley: University of California Press.
———. (2006). *Global Shadows: Africa in the Neoliberal World Order*. Durham NC: Duke University Press.
Gandy, M. (2006). "Planning, Anti-planning and the Infrastructure Crisis Facing Metropolitan Lagos." *Urban Studies* 43(2): 371–396.
Graham, S. and Marvin, S. (2001). *Splintering Urbanism: Networked Infrastructures, Technological Mobilities and the Urban Condition*. London: Routledge.
Kashi, E. and Watts, M. (2008). *Curse of the Black Gold: 50 Years of Oil in the Niger Delta*. Brooklyn, NY: PowerHouse Books.
Kraus, J. R. (2010). "The Business of State-building: The Impact of Corporate Social Responsibility on State Development in Equatorial Guinea." PhD diss., University of Florida Gainsville.
Low, S. (2003). *Behind the Gates: The New American Dream*. New York and London: Routledge.
MacLachlan, I. and Aguilar, A. G. (1998). "Maquiladora Myths: Locational and Structural Change in Mexico's Export Manufacturing Industry." *Professional Geographer* 50(3): 315–331.
Mann, M. (1984). "The Autonomous Power of The State: Its Origins, Mechanisms, and Results." *European Archive of Sociology* 25(2): 185–213.
Mbembé, A. (2001). *On the Postcolony*. Berkeley: University of California Press.
Mitchell, T. (2002). *Rule of Experts : Egypt, Techno-politics, Modernity*. Berkeley: University of California Press.
MMIE (2008). Production Sharing Contract (Sample).
Ndongo, D. (2009). "Between Three Continents: Rethinking Equatorial Guinea on the Fortieth Anniversary of its Independence from Spain." Conference Presentation, Hofstra University, April 4, 2009.

Ong, A. (1999). *Flexible Citizenship: The Cultural Logics of Transnationality.* Durham, NC: Duke University Press.

———. (2006). *Neoliberalism as Exception : Mutations in Citizenship and Sovereignty.* Durham, NC: Duke University Press.

Palan, R. (2006). *The Offshore World: Sovereign Markets, Virtual Places, and Nomad Millionaires.* Ithaca, NY: Cornell University Press.

Porteus, J. D. (1970). "The Nature of the Company Town." *Transactions of British Geographers* 51: 127–142.

———. (1974). "Social Class in Atacama Company Towns." *Annals of the Association of American Geographers* 64(3): 409–417.

Reno, W. (2001). *Foreign Firms, Natural Resources and Violent Political Economies.* University of Leipzig papers on Africa. Politics and Economics Series (46). Leipzig : Institut für Afrikanistik, Universität Leipzig.

República de Guinea Ecuatorial (2005). "Statement of the People and Government of Equatorial Guinea in Response to the Report on Riggs Bank of the Permanent Subcommittee on Governmental Affairs of the Senate of the United States of America."

Shever, E. (2010). "Engendering the Company: Corporate Personhood and the 'Face' of an Oil Company in Metropolitan Buenos Aires." *PoLAR* 33(1): 26–46.

Sklair, L. (1993). *Assembling for Development: the Maquila Industry in Mexico and the United State.* San Diego, CA: University of Californial Center for US-Mexican Studies.

Soja, E. W. (2000). *Postmetropolis: Critical Studies of Cities and Regions.* Malden, MA: Wiley-Blackwell.

Star, S. L. (1999). "The Ethnography of Infrastructure." *The American Behavioral Scientist* 43(3): 377–391.

Stoler, A. L. (2008). "Imperial Debris: Reflections on Ruins and Ruination." *Cultural Anthropology* 23(2):191–219.

Tsing, A. L. (2005). *Friction: An Ethnography of Global Connection.* Princeton, NJ: Princeton University Press.

UNCTAD. (2010). *World Investment Report.* Country Fact Sheet: Equatorial Guinea.

USEIA. (2010). US Net Imports by Country. http://www.eia.gov/dnav/pet/PET_MOVE_NETI_A_EP00_IMN_MBBLPD_A.htm. Accessed June 20, 2011.

Vitalis, R. (2007). *America's Kingdom: Mythmaking on the Saudi Oil Frontier.* Stanford: Stanford University Press.

Walcott, D. (1986). *Collected Poems, 1948–1984.* New York: Farrar, Straus & Giroux.

Watts, M. (2001). "Petro-Violence: Community, Extraction, and Political Ecology of a Mythic Commodity." In Peluso, N. and Watts, M. eds, *Violent Environments*, pp. 189–212. Ithaca, NY: Cornell University Press.

———. (2008). "Oil as Money: The Devil's Excrement and the Spectacle of Black Gold." In Barnes, T. J., Peck, J., Sheppard, E., and Tickell, A., eds, *Reading Economic Geography*, pp. 205–219. Oxford: Blackwell.

Winters, J. A. (1996). *Power in Motion: Capital Mobility and the Indonesian State.* Ithaca, NY: Cornell University Press.

Zalik, A. (2004). "The peace of the graveyard: The voluntary principles on security and human rights in the Niger Delta." In: van der Pijl, K. and Wigan, D., eds. *Global Regulation: Managing Crises After the Imperial Turn*, pp. 111–127. London: Palgrave.

Zhan, J. (2006). *FDI Statistics: A Critical Review and Policy Implications.* Geneva: World Association of Investment Promotion Agencies.

12

Nigerian Modernity and the City: Lagos 1960–1980

Giles Omezi

Introduction

As you drive onto the Third Mainland Bridge from the Apapa Oworonsoki Expressway heading south to the main city of Lagos, the adjoining slip road is terminated by a stop line where the two roads meet. Traffic permitting, you are forced to stop. Off peak, the traffic is fast, a mix of vehicles within a road corridor defined by continuous concrete upstands which endow this momentary scene with a horizontal emphasis further reinforced to the west by a cityscape of rusty rooftops occasionally punctuated by radio masts and the odd 6-storey building. To the east of the expressway, a settlement emerges from the dark green vegetation of the marshes on the western banks of the Lagos Lagoon. On the horizon, the vertical outlines of the tall buildings on Lagos Island are shrouded in the smog of the city, a partial "manhattanized" strip on its southern shore.

The concrete of the third mainland bridge and the rust roofed buildings have been weathered by city's sweltering equatorial climate. As the speed picks up, the expanse of the Lagoon is revealed to the east of the bridge, as the dense horizontal city districts of Abule Okuta and Akoka to the west push hard against the bridge as it soon detaches fully from land and floats over the Lagoon heading toward Lagos Island.

At the Yaba interchange, approximately two thirds of the way on this 12-kilometre long bridge, the waterside settlement of Makoko and the timber sawmills on the shoreline of Ebutte Metta to the west sit in stark contrast to this piece of modern civil engineering. The otherwise horizontal western horizon is dominated by the floodlight masts of the National Stadium in Surulere and the staid bulk of the National Theatre in Iganmu. Viewed together, the "partial Manhattan" of Lagos Island

and the dominating hulks of these two civic buildings poised at two ends of the city, and the fast expressway of Third Mainland Bridge, the essence of the modernity of Lagos is revealed. The city districts bound by the expressway network appear as infill produced as a horizontal rusty roof-scape that somehow underscores the contradictions of modern and traditional, or perhaps, it could be argued, articulates the notion of duality that informs and maybe defines ideas of a Nigerian modernity.

This six-lane expressway built as part of the Road Building Programme of the Third National Development Plan (1975–80), inscribes onto the urban fabric of the city a fragment of an "imagined modernity." The network of expressways that shape the city seen as a consequence and direct product of a concerted modernization and development effort enshrined in the series of National Development Plans spanning three decades from 1960 to 1980.

Nationalism, Modernity, and the Politics of Space

Within the context of the postindependence Nigerian State, aspirations to modernize and strands of nationalism appear to converge, with modernization viewed as a means of equalizing the colonized with the colonizer. We must, however, seek to understand both terms as universal concepts and their meaning within the Nigerian context. Further questions more relevant to this chapter are: How might we understand an evolving Nigerian Modernity and its possible spatial expression in the city? How have the formal processes of the "Nigerian Project" of modern state formation been formulated and actualized? How has the city of Lagos been shaped by these somewhat abstract notions and forces so as to shape and impact its urban structure and space?

Firstly, it will be prudent to state that the objective of this inquiry is neither a study of the successes or failures of the Nigerian state, nor is it a critique of the international events that form the short case studies. It must be stressed that the focus is one of reconstituting a historical narrative of urbanization of Lagos through the prism of formal state planning and related notions of a Nigerian Modernity that were subsequently acted out in this process. Secondly, a brief examination of the terms—modernization and modernity and how these are bound up in the development of the two strands of nationalism—the first strand centered around the agitation for self determination prior to independence and the latter strand, post the civil war, centered on a project of national integration. We can locate these strands temporally, the former occurring in the decades preceding independence and the latter emerging in the immediate decade after the civil war of 1967–1970, respectively.

The preindependence constitutional development of Nigeria has been acknowledged as a major catalyst in the shaping of nationalist politics leading to independence (Dudley 1982). The fragmented approach to British imperial expansion in the area named Nigeria effectively fused together distinct subjugated territories with their varied precolonial histories. In 1946, the so-called Richards constitution established autonomous regional administrative units shaped broadly around the three dominant ethnic groups: Ibo, Hausa, and Yoruba. Geographically, these groups were conveniently delineated by the meeting of the River Niger with its tributary, the River Benue, consequently placing the three groups in distinct land territories. From the much-criticized 1946 constitution emerged the revised Macpherson Constitution of 1951, which further reinforced the regional character of Nigeria by assigning partially devolved powers to these ethnic-based regions. Viewed as unworkable in its partial devolution of power, the more or less unitary state still retained control over budget disbursements, in contrast to the generally held preference for stronger regional autonomy by the Nigerian political leaders of the time. In 1954, the Lyttleton Constitution was adopted, effectively establishing federalism as the binding structure of Nigeria. The emergence of "true" political activity is attributed to the structure of this revised constitution which now permitted the election of Nigerians into Federal and Regional Assemblies and the freedom of each region to achieve self government at its own pace.

The political leadership of the regions congealed into political parties with a strong ethnic bias, their identities typically referencing precolonial states and empires. In the case of the northern (NPC) and western (AG) parties, ethnic national basis was established around geographic and cultural (northern—Hausa Fulani) and linguistic and cultural (Western—Yoruba) lines (Coleman 1958). The third party, the NCNC, historically the oldest and forged out of metropolitan nationalist tendencies whose support was drawn from an eclectic base, spanned cultural ethnic associations, labor unions, and was ideologically placed as a left-leaning party. Eventually, as its purist nationalist stance gradually weakened relative to the ascendancy of more ethnic bias, it became the party of the eastern ethnic group (Igbo) (Dudley 1982). These cleavages were, thus, amplified by the power of the autonomy of regional units and their access to and control of resources at both tiers of government. Effectively, the preindependence federation of Nigeria comprised three "Nations." Each viewed socioeconomic development as a means to improving the welfare of its various ethnic constituencies, and in the process, sought to consolidate power through loyalties that increased their access to resources required to maintain the attendant patronage networks.

The political landscape for postindependence Nigeria thus set, the modernization of the country was fashioned through the prism of the state-led economic planning that effectively fused the aspirations of three regional plans encapsulated by a Federal Plan to form the First National Development of 1962–1968. The development aspirations of the newly independent state through its semi-autonomous political units essentially sought to modernize society in their respective territories. Strategies varied, but the common strand and, therefore, national position was the recognition that modernization would imply "the enlargement of the directly productive capacity of the economy" and also that "the level of living of the people is to rise" (Federal Ministry of Economic Development 1962: 21). These aspirations were to be achieved with an economic growth target of 4 percent per annum compounded over the period of the plan. Consequently, with the entrenching of regional blocs in the country, the city of Lagos was reconfigured from the administrative entity of the old Lagos Colony and mostly absorbed into the Western Region, leaving a small enclave that housed the Federal Government and strategic economic assets: the airport, port, and railway terminus. The Federal Government set out to address the urban issues in Lagos, commissioning a Metropolitan Area study, which was published in 1964. The study developed national objectives for Lagos articulated in the First National Plan. The Federal government placed a priority on the development ports component of the transport sector seeking to also integrate this nationally with the wider road network. Decongestion of port traffic at the complex in Apapa and the evacuation of goods to and from the Nigerian hinterland by road had a direct impact on the scope of a sketchily described Federal Road program. Nonetheless, the plan hinted at the beginnings of an additional layering to the Lagos road network, conceiving the idea for the Second Mainland Bridge, and the Apapa—Ijora—Western Avenue Causeway system. The detail for these roads were located in the 1964 Metropolitan Area study where a demand forecast-driven study of the Lagos road transport and mass transport was established, and projections that shaped a network of roads and bridges up to 1970 were made to suit the numbers. The purpose of the 1964 study was to plan for the expansion of the city, noted as growing at a rate of 14 percent from 1952 to 1962 census figures. Acknowledging that the areas of Metropolitan Lagos outside of the Federal Territory would experience the bulk of population growth, the study set the scene for the next decade based on the current growth rate stating that "it would be unwise to plan for anything less than the continuation of the average growth rate of the past ten years" and that "it is not extravagant to expect that the figure of one million inhabitants will be reached by the end of the present Development Programme in 1968" (Koenigsberger et al. 1964: 6).

The genesis of the ubiquitous network of expressways of Lagos can therefore be traced back to the modernizing aspirations of the First National Plan and its appendage, the 1964 Metropolitan Study. The latter projected an urban infrastructure that appears to be sourced from a project of modernization underpinned by aspirations for industrialization. The road network was also viewed as a key solution to the already emerging traffic congestion in Lagos, as emphasized in the First Plan, that: "The Lagos transport problem is made even more acute by the fact that the island is at present linked to the mainland by only one bridge and one ferry service. The delays due to traffic hold-ups can, and do, contribute to increasing costs of badly needed development goods" (Federal Ministry of Economic Development 1962: 95). Plans for interventions to resolve this traffic issue revolved around proposals for two north south highway systems, which included requisite cloverleaf interchanges and bridges. In addition, a monorail system was proposed to convey up to 15,000 people per hour in one direction between the built up districts of Yaba and Ebute Metta on the mainland of the city with employment centers on the island of Lagos.

The welfarist Western Regions component of the First National Development Plan placed a strong emphasis on industrialization, devising direct spatial interventions in support of this policy in the guise of industrial estates, two of which were already in existence in the Western Region parts of the Lagos metropolitan area. In total, approximately 570 acres of land was to be developed as industrial estates, 262 acres in existence in the districts of Ikeja and Mushin. Both sites conveniently straddled the key urban rail and road routes providing direct access to the Federal owned Apapa Port complex. The terms of reference for Otto Koenigsberger's team of planners recognized the need to fuse Lagos into a single entity, even if only for the purpose of the study, stating that: "The island on which Lagos stands is Federal Territory, but the surrounding area comes within the jurisdiction of the Western Region. It is expected that any plan for the expansion of the city will have to include the administrative areas of both the Federal and Western Governments" (Koenigsberger et al. 1964: v). This sensible position was set against the acrimonious backdrop of the two territories being governed by rival parties: The Northern People's Congress

(NPC)-led Federal Government oversaw the Federal Territory of Lagos with the Western Region led by the opposition Action Group (AG). Effectively, the parties represented two separate sub-national interests that emerged out of the preindependence ethnic nationalism that had shaped the political geography of Nigeria. The Lagos Colony fused into the Western Region by the Macpherson Constitution of 1951 effectively created a "fragmented political and administrative authority between two antagonistic governments" (Olowu 1990: 43)—the NPC controlling the Federal Territory and the AG controlling the Colony Provinces. This fragmentation implied a skewing of urban investment to the Federal-controlled Territory with a gap opening up between the peripheral metropolitan area and the center.

Nationalism, as construed in the period immediately proceeding and after independence, was fraught with the ambiguity of two tiers of nationalism congruent with the regional territories and the national territory. The powerful party heads recognized the strength and potency of the regions and opted to rule the regions rather than participate directly at the center. Bound up with these cleavages was the fragile notion of a unified Nigerian State whose somewhat ambiguous projection onto the world stage was notably cool and at best aligned with global Western interests. The unity of Nigeria sat as a priority with economic development fusing an "imagined nationalism" (Anderson 1983) with an aspiration to modernity. In other words, the modernization of Nigeria and the subsequent benefits to its disparate components, at least on paper, might eventually reduce the ethnic cleavages that formed an existential threat to the state. The political crisis of 1965 led to a series of violent coups by the army in 1966 that reconfigured the political landscape and power formations of Nigeria. The overthrow of the old political order was legitimized as a "Revolution" (Ayida 1973) and the initial military government sought to reconfigure the state from a Federal to a unitary one. The outbreak of civil war in 1967 fractured the federation, with the eastern region seceding to form Biafra. The response of the military government among others was the creation of 12 states, thereby fracturing the regions by military decree, of which a core principle was that "no one state should be in a position to dominate or control the Central Government" (Ayida 1973: 6). Following the end of the civil war in 1970, with the subsidence of the existential threat to Nigeria, came the transformation of an ambivalent notion of nationalism underpinned by strong ethnic sub-nationalisms, to one where the unified state appeared to be reconfigured as the sole national entity and a project to enshrine unity commenced. The military government sought to reconstitute the space of the state, by fragmenting the regions and institutionally redefining and erasing territorial clarity of the attendant sub-nations. Moreover, by evolving a national rhetoric of "national integration" and "unity" intended as benefit of the project of industrialized modernization, the military government, at least superficially, consolidated the primacy of the nation state over the precolonial regional ethnic groupings.

Created in 1967, with its capital located to the north of the city in Ikeja within the area administered by the defunct Western Region, Lagos State also played host to the Federal Capital now shorn of a distinct territorial identity. The project of modernization continued by the military state at the close of the civil war was buoyed by a confidence emerging from the resilience demonstrated by the wartime economy. Growth figures of 6.6 percent and manufacturing output up by 25 percent per annum exceeded the 4 percent forecasts of the 1962–1968 Plan. The wartime Finance Commissioner Obafemi Awolowo admitted that "the exigencies of the war did well to shock us out of our traditional complacencies, and compel us to make a clean break with the injudicious and injurious policies of the past" (Zwingina 1992: 73). This infused the Federal Government with a measure of confidence in the shaping of the Second National Development Plan 1970–74. This plan effectively being "a Federal Government Plan and could justifiably be described as an exercise in planning from above" (Dudley 1982: 232), thus making it very much a national venture. What was emerging in parallel was a more confident and internationalist stance by the Nigerian state. The civil war forced an internationalizing of Nigeria's outlook, fought globally as a sophisticated propaganda battle, the consequence of which was the blurring of the traditional Western-leaning allegiances of the Nigerian state to accommodate a supportive Eastern Bloc. A consciousness had developed, that on one hand inspired a more strident international attitude to African matters and, therefore, the binding of a sense of national interest with integration at the regional, continental and global scales (Akiba 1998). This sat in contrast to the "gradualist and conservative" (Apter 2005) attitude of the 1960–1966 period. Nigeria's awakening on the global scale is reflected within the Second Plan with a section that clearly stressed trade integration with West Africa, with the goal of opening up markets as destinations for Nigerian manufactured products that would pour out of the newly planned industrial complex the state was crafting. An intention underscored by a comment in the plan that stated: "But it is absolutely essential for the country's external policy to be seen, henceforth, as an integral aspect of national policy; it is to serve, at all times, the nation's primary interest, particularly in the economic field" (Federal Ministry of Economic Development 1970: 78).

This emerging Pan Regional and Pan African outlook, no doubt, influenced Nigeria's offer to host the second edition of the quadrennial All Africa Games in Lagos. Scheduled to be held in Mali in 1966, a military coup forced a postponement and rescheduling of the event for 1971 in Lagos. Similarly, following the first World Festival of Black and African Arts and Culture held in Dakar, Senegal in 1966, Nigeria agreed to host the next edition in Lagos. A Nigerian modernity was emerging that acknowledged difference as expressed tangibly in its inherent ethnic complexity and consequently sought to incorporate a Pan Black and Pan African dimension into its national identity. Fuelled literally by oil, as Andrew Apter observed in his 2005 book *Pan Africa Nation*: "Oil thus underwrote the veracity of a range of discourses, from the technical and scientific to the national and even racial, as the redeemable and redemptive wealth of the black and African world" (225). The increase in revenue receipts from oil production as a consequence of the 1973 Arab Oil embargo and Nigeria's entry to the producer's cartel OPEC in 1971 lent real substance to the modernizing rhetoric as it provided the means to actualize the projects in the Second Plan.

The Modernist Overlay: Lagos 1970–80

> Running north and south, and east and west, and forming the two great axes of the city, there would be great arterial roads for fast one way traffic built on immense reinforced concrete bridges 120 to 180 yards in width and approached every half mile or so by subsidiary roads from ground level. These arterial roads could therefore be joined at any given point so that even at the highest speeds the town can be traversed and the suburbs reached without having to negotiate any cross roads.
>
> —Le Corbusier (1987 [1929]: 168).

Hilde Heynen offers an instructive conceptualization of the relationship between concepts of modernization and modernity. She views the former, the term "modernization," as describing "the process of societal development, the main features of which are technological advances and industrialization, urbanization and population explosions, the rise of bureaucracy and increasingly powerful national states, an enormous expansion of mass communication systems, an expanding (capitalist) market world market etc" and the latter, "modernity," as that which "stands for the attitude to life that is associated with a continuous process of evolution and transformation with and orientation towards a future that will be different from the past and from the present" (Heynen 2003: 22). Within the Nigerian context, a clear modernizing project was underway: one led by the state and in its totality an aspired end state of a modernity that included the reconfiguration of the modes of production at both the economic and cultural scales. The nation "imagined" not by its people but by the state, which in constituting the material skein of socio-economic development both nationally and at the scale of the urban, produces a social space inscribed and reinforced by an iconography of modernity which more or less fused concepts of modernization into the consciousness of the people. Flows of production were articulated, therefore, in an infrastructure overlay that recalled the modernist city vision of the early twentieth century and were literally constituted as a metaphor to an aspired modernity buttressed further by the inclusion of sites cultural production within this framework.

The road network at the national scale as proposed by the state, was founded on an overt requirement to link sites of production, raw material sources, markets, and extraction nodes. These national assets were brought under the direct control of the Federal state that had embarked on a takeover and reclassification of the colonial era roads, leading to a fourfold increase in mileage from 5,603 miles in 1967 to over 20,000 miles in 1974 (Okunnu 2010). The road—viewed as central to the distribution of the material in the industrialization project—benefitted from substantial investment in the road programs of the First, Second, and Third National Development Plans with figures of 64, 88, and 86 percent (Olayemi 1981: 99–121) of total public expenditure on land transportation and capital expenditure components of 25, 24, and 22 percent, respectively. The reconstituted state, *vis-a-vis* the spatial consequences of the departure from the regional structure to the 12 states, is directly envisioned as the driver of the structure of the Federal Road Programme. As an iconograph of Nigeria's modernity, the image of the modern road network, particularly the expressway, begins to crystallize in the mind of the state and its citizens as the tangible benchmark of progress. The former Federal Works and Housing Commissioner Femi Okunnu stated in an interview in 2011 that "with the new 12 state structure, it was necessary to have direct links between not just the federal capital and the state capitals but between the various state capitals..."[1] The ensuing road network sought to intensify the connectivity within the state and shifted communication at the national scale away from the north–south-dominated rail and road system that complemented the extractive economy of the colonial state. The new network appeared to inscribe a national focus and gave spatial expression to the "National Integration" aspirations that accompanied this modernization project.

The impact of this attitude to mobility infrastructure in Lagos can be seen in the initial attempts to resolve the traffic congestion issue and urban expansion in the city in the First National Plan, as clearly articulated in the 1964 Metropolitan Area Study. The 1964 Study proposed two major north–south expressways: The Axial Motorway, which:

> will be the artery of transport for Metropolitan Lagos. It will bring Agege to the north, as well as huge areas to the east of Victoria Island, to within 30 minutes drive to downtown Lagos. Developments will take place alongside, and to the north and east of its extremities. Lagos will thus be not a circular but and L—shaped metropolis with Lagos Island in the centre at the bend on the south—west corner.' and 'The Western Avenue, extended straight southward to join the Second Mainland Bridge, will become an important arterial throughway from Lagos and Apapa northward. It should be widened, and made into a limited access road, joining the Axial Motorway at the interchange at Yaba Roundabout. (Koenigsberger et al. 1964: 83)

The functionalist expressway section extruded along the described alignments providing in the mind of the planners, a purist vision for vehicle movement through the city:

> This road is a super expressway, and should be flanked on both sides by parallel access or service roads, bicycle tracks and pedestrian walks. Where crossings is necessary, the motorway can be elevated or on the street level with service roads crossing over it. Where it is on the same level as access roads it should be fenced off: for a motorway is designed for a speed of 50 to 60 m.p.h or even higher. (Koenigsberger et al. 1964: 82)

The 60-mph design speed eventually formed the benchmark design speed for Federal Highway Design Standards based on US standards and formally adopted in 1973 (Okunnu 2010). The 1964 Metropolitan Area Study was not formally adopted by the Federal Government, which also had to contend with a similar study by the Lagos Executive Development Board on behalf of the Western Region. However, as noted by Fapohunda, elements of both studies were implemented as major infrastructure projects over the next decade, despite formal adoption of recommendations not having taken place (Fapohunda 1978).

Major elements of the expressway system for Lagos were carried over to the Second National Development Plan, as the 1967 war interrupted the late phase. This interruption, coupled with an over reliance on foreign aid to fund the First Plan that only partially materialized, forced a reprioritization of the programs in the First Plan by the government. The works contract for the Second Mainland Bridge was awarded to the German firm of Julius Berger AG on August 24, 1965; it completed the bridge in 1968 ahead of schedule by 3 months and was named "Eko Bridge" by the then Federal Commissioner of Works Femi Okunnu. The war had forced an embargo on foreign loans from most Western countries directly impacting the ability of the state to deliver on the capital expenditure programs in the 1962–1968 plan. West Germany's willingness to provide soft loans for the construction of the Western Avenue and Ijora causeway system encouraged the appointment of Julius Berger AG to build this road corridor which provided increased traffic capacity and also linked the potential sites for the proposed National Stadium at Surulere and the National Theatre at Iganmu with the airport to the north and the capital located on Lagos Island. The nationalism that infused the post-war Nigerian state gathered momentum through a rationalized military–civilian government. Still in wartime mode, this government could effectively manage and direct the affairs of state through its vertically integrated command and control structure.

All Africa Games 1973

The National Stadium project was earmarked for construction during the 1962–1968 plan and was located within the Federal Territory on a 78-acre site set aside on the city fringes. The initial aspiration was to develop the stadium—and sports, in general—as part of a wiser social program in the plan. However, the opportunity to host the 1973 All Africa Games pushed the project high up the development agenda of the state. Designs for the stadium were completed in 1962 by the British architectural partnership of Mence, Moore & Mort (W.A) in collaboration with their London Office and the engineering firm Ove, Arup and Partners. The complex allowed for a 60,000 spectator main stadium bowl to accommodate athletics and field sports including football, an indoor multi use sports hall, and swimming complex. Work commenced in 1970 by the Italian construction firm Cappa and D'Alberto and was completed in 1972 in time for the All Africa Games. Rendered in a Brutalist style of Modernist architecture with its board-shuttered concrete finishes and strong formal expressions, the intention for Nigeria's image seem clear. With the revenue receipts from oil exceeding expectations by 206 percent in 1973 (Apter 2005), a modern

African state was projecting a new modernity conceived by the state that sought to meld the divisions of the 1967–1970 civil war and incorporate a Pan African idea into both international and national perceptions. New student halls of residence were built at the University of Lagos to provide accommodation for the athletes. Held from January 7 to January 18, 1973, the Games offered a platform for Nigeria to flex its sporting muscle. Nigeria entered the top five of the medals table, which was, paradoxically, a regression on its performance in the 1965 edition held in Brazzaville, Congo. The event laid the foundation for a nationwide sports infrastructure that led to the country's dominance of next seven editions of the games where it consistently topped the medal tables.

Entry to the stadium was off the Western Avenue—a newly completed expressway system with a complex set of elevated bridges and interchanges sweeping traffic from the sites of extraction and production at Apapa and Iganmu, respectively. The expressway intersected with the Alhaji Masha Street from Surulere, the road rose to avoid the bottleneck as a sweeping concrete bridge, simultaneously permitting traffic from Alhaji Masha to flow north and south and mark an entry arch to the Stadium. More importantly, it obeyed the simple diktat in the 1964 Study: rising to avoid the junction and returning to grade north of the Stadium. The carrying over of the stadium project from the 1962–1968 plan was attributed to a reprioritizing of the project due to the inability of the state to generate finance directly or indirectly via contractor finance. Its implementation was, therefore, a direct beneficiary of the fiscal confidence of the resilient wartime economy and rising oil revenues. It marked the beginning of the transformation of the Nigerian political economy from a neo-colonial to neo-welfarist (Zwingina 1992) mode, the latter consolidating the essence of post-civil war Nigerian nationalism.

The early phase of the project consisted of temporary grandstand, field, and running tracks utilized for sporting at the 1960 Independence Celebrations, whereas the latter phases constituted the permanent complex to be utilized for the Games. In his handover speech at the opening of the Stadium in December 1972, the Federal Commissioner for Works, Femi Okunnu, underscored the essence of the project and its impact on Lagos. He stressed that:

> The construction of the National Stadium has brought with it, vast improvements to roads in the vicinity to enhance smooth flow of traffic, and structural improvements to some public buildings including some schools and the University of Lagos. Not only will the All-Africa Games

> thus be leaving some permanent marks in the city, but in its own right the National Stadium is an important landmark on the changing face of Lagos. (Okunnu 2003: 278)

In acknowledging this relationship between state intentions for modernity and urban space, Okunnu confirms the potency of the top–down project of national reconfiguration and integration which inadvertently found a clear expression in Lagos. This signals a new power and space relationship emerging in the city. The lozenge-shaped plan of the main bowl was designed to be accessed by 12 concrete ramps, ten of which terminated with circular discs radiating out into the parking areas. The grandstand on the west was shaded by a canopy and four tall lighting masts for floodlights punctuating the Lagos skyline—clearly marking out the location of the National Stadium in the city.

As a site of emerging industrial production, resource extraction, and the evacuation of input goods to the hinterland, the city was beginning to be layered with a skein of cultural production infrastructure as part of the national modernization project. The trend was further entrenched by the next major event, FESTAC. Initially scheduled for 1975 and postponed indefinitely by General Gowon, FESTAC was eventually held in 1977.

FESTAC 77

The Second Festival of Black and African Arts and Culture held in Lagos involved a concerted effort and opportunity to incorporate architecture and urban infrastructure into a state-directed project of cultural production. Postponed twice—first, in 1970 due to the civil war and, then, in 1974 due to the incomplete facilities—the Federal Government conceived a series of new buildings for completion by the opening date of the Festival. These included: a new airport, two new hotels, a 15,000-unit housing estate, a national parade ground, and the jewel, the National Theatre, all connected by the rapidly expanding expressway system. The city of Lagos, thus, benefitted from a fusion of modernist architecture and city planning that, at once, recalled aspects of Le Corbusier's City of Tomorrow and forcefully projected a national consciousness that subsumed a notion of global "blackness," thereby, underpinning Nigeria's modernity aspirations through culture.

The architectural language was incidental, a product of the preindependence influx of British Modernist architects that was broadened to include Eastern Bloc architects as well. A late modernist style prevailed that somehow lost the sensitively scaled and responsive thrust of the early works of Maxwell Fry and Jane Drew or John Godwin and Gillian Hopwood from a decade earlier, resorting instead to muscular expressive forms. The inclusion in the circuits of architectural production for these sites brought an array of unlikely international firms, ranging from the Greek planner Constantine Doxiadis whose practice designed the Festac Town, the British architect Robin Atkinson now in charge of the Fry–Drew practice in charge of designing the Parade Ground at Onikan, and the Bulgarian Consulting and Contracting Group Technoexportstroy in charge of the National Theatre at Iganmu. The spread of international participation, particularly the turn to Eastern Bloc countries may be viewed through the prism of Nigerian post-civil war foreign policy that marked a shift from traditional Western partners to a wider gamut of imported technical expertise. The perceived lukewarm support for the Federal war effort by Great Britain, whose initial arms embargo was supplemented by a willing Soviet and Czech response, pushed the state to seek stronger ties with this bloc. The communist countries benefited through the awards of contracts for lucrative capital projects, including the extensive steel complex at Ajaokuta for which Soviet expertise was sought.

These capital projects, embedded in the Second and Third National Development Plans, were viewed as central components of a conscious cultural program. The Third Plan's policy objectives stated the intention clearly: "The major policy measures in this sector will be to make information services more efficient in the task of promoting the nation's basic ideals of unity and the projection of the nation's image abroad" (Federal Ministry of Economic Development 1975: 275). Going further to set out the projects and programs, the report commits to: "Programmes connected with the Second World Black and African Festival of Arts and Culture and which will be completed in the first year of the Third Plan include the Theatre Complex, the redecoration of Tafawa Balewa Square in Lagos and the Race Course in Kaduna" (Ibid.: 277). The inclusion of these projects, not as a separate section on culture, was clearly instrumental to the Nigerian state's intentions and its view of culture as a component under the purview of the Information Ministry. Culture was key to the propaganda of the state's modernization project as it sought to not only unify the country, but also project globally its view of Nigeria.

Two projects are worth considering in some detail: the National Theatre and FESTAC Town. The former was conceived as one of the stages to host major events during FESTAC, whereas the latter provided accommodation for the foreign participants. The sites for the projects were dispersed across the Lagos: FESTAC town to the west along the corridor leading to the old town of Badagry, and the National Theatre on marshlands north of the Apapa Port Complex and Tafawa Balewa Square, occupying the site of the former colonial Race Course in central Lagos.

FESTAC Town emerged from a convergence of an emerging National Housing Programme and the festival, with the former seeking an additional 10,000 to 15,000 housing units in Lagos. The Federal Government established the Federal Housing Authority directly under the Cabinet office to oversee the project, despite reservations from the Federal Works and Housing Commissioner Femi Okunnu. He argued against it, stating that: "the Cabinet Office [was] saddled with executive functions, [and] should be left to play its traditional role, coordinating the activities of the various ministries and streamlining government policies" (Okunnu 2010: 300). The housing authority established by decree in 1974 was the agency through which the government sought to intervene directly in the provision of housing, earmarking a sum of NGN 1.5 billion for the program tying the welfarist tendencies of the state to the broader modernizing project. The Doxiadis Associates plan was based on a loose grid of numbered avenues and roads located north of the newly constructed Lagos–Badagry Expressway (DA Review). Intended as a project for "24,000 dwelling units for a population of 120,000 distributed in seven communities over an area of 1,770 ha," approximately 40 percent of the original area of the masterplan was built, generating 5,000 housing units for low- and middle-income earners. Transferred much later after FESTAC to the now established Federal Housing Authority, the estate established itself as a sought-after destination and district along the western corridor of Lagos. The co-opting of Constatine Doxiadis to plan the estate underscored the state's intentions, bringing in the cutting edge of knowledge and ideas to produce the space of the new nation. Having worked on a regional plan for Lagos and the site for the new capital Abuja, Doxiadis had prior experience over the previous decade or two working on Pakistan's new capital Islamabad, Khartoum in Sudan, Baghdad in Iraq, and the new port town of Tema in nearby Ghana. Doxiadis represented a new tradition of urban planning in new nation states, and was therefore relied on to craft a vision appropriate for the new Nigeria.

Streets ordered by a rational system of numbers enabled the occupants and visitors to orient themselves in the estate. "If you lived at 5112, you knew you were on 5th Avenue. 721 is 7th Avenue" (Apter 2005: 49). An ordering of space and, thus, society was evident in the intentions of the state and the model on which the housing problem would be addressed. The development was envisaged as a self-sustaining community as opposed to a dormitory town, with light industry, community, and social uses incorporated in that vision.

Further along the Lagos Badagry expressway to the east, the expressway terminates at the spaghetti intersection that forms a triangle within which the National Theatre nestles. The Eko Bridge system running north south along the eastern edge, the Apapa Road on the western edge, and Ijora Causeway to the south are all elevated road sections which set up a distinct relationship between the city motorist and the building. Symbolically, the convergence of the prime site of cultural production and the mobility system linked to sites of strategic production and extraction in the city reinforced the intentions of the state as it sought to weave layers of complexity into its overarching modernization project. The complex consisted of a circular-plan building topped with a saddle-shaped roof under which were laid out a 5,000-seat auditorium, 1,600-seat conference hall, two exhibition halls able to seat 800, and two cinemas of the same capacity. Surrounded by lush green lawns and trees, the theater appeared to settle on the ground. Supported by a generous podium that housed the wedge-shaped halls, offices, and ancillary spaces, ramps led from the grounds to the main concourse running right round the building. The concrete spokes rising from the podium were held together by similarly scaled transoms, an infill of a dark skin of glazed curtain walling and fenestration set back from and sliding past the structure. Incorporated into the façade is the Nigerian national coat of arms, an arrangement that echoed the caps of the military generals who ran the state. At a cost of 144 million Naira (Apter 2005), the architecture of the Theatre incorporated contemporary Nigerian art: friezes and sculptures were woven into the building's fabric—in effect, stamping the identity of country's traditions onto a building styled as a late modernist building. The National Theatre is, however, a simulacrum of the National Palace of Sports and Culture in Varna, Bulgaria designed by the architect Stefan Kolchev. A delegation of the Nigerian government on a visit to the site in 1968 asked that the Bulgarian Palace of Sports and Culture be replicated as the National Theatre in Lagos with a different use program that emphasized high culture, not sports. The Nigerian version was scaled up five times from the original.

Conclusion

The fast expressway system now encircling Lagos in the late 1970s established itself as a metaphor for the dynamic progress the state had made since independence and particularly after the civil war. Obliquely, the integration of sites of strategic import within Lagos with the expressways echoes, perhaps, an urgent response to the crisis of disintegration recently overcome with the conclusion of the war. The expressways rise above the city in elevated bridge sections that either avoid contact with the marsh terrain or the congested city, a curious configuration that stresses the efficiency of movement as a purely functional exercise or, perhaps, a conscious detaching from the city and, therefore, citizens that lays the foundations for the two-speed city of today. The insertion of symbolic civic interventions placed in proximity to the expressways can be read as a means of reinforcing in the minds of the citizens the primacy of the state and nation above the ethnic cleavages of old and colonial past.

Modernity as a process in the case of the development of Lagos, borrowing from Hilde Heynen, is of the programmatic—that is, "a project of progress and emancipation" (Heynen 2003). The genealogy of the modernizing process post-independence in Nigeria was increasingly appropriated by the strengthened state as a nationalist ideal transformed from an initial struggle for emancipation from colonial rule to one that sought emancipation from underdevelopment and the threat of fragmentation. The imprint of this project reconfigured the city at the macro scale, illustrating, perhaps, the limitations of the top–down approach that the military deployed. The silencing of the citizen's voice in this race for development, the chasms opened up by the state's deficiencies in delivering the plans, joined with the sudden availability of capital surpluses (generated not by industrial production but by extraction) to implement this national project, appear as a contradiction that remains unresolved. It highlights the lack of a concerted "subjective" aspect of modernity that mediates between the modernization process and the collective and individual processes that it sought to transform. The subsuming of the elements of society that may have constituted this mediation into the production of culture could be argued to have diverted these otherwise critical energies.

The series of interventions in Lagos inadvertently imbibed the military regime with the confidence to directly link the national modernizing project with urban space in its move to create from scratch a new capital that would foster national unity. The new Federal Capital, sited in Abuja, is structured around rapid movement and symbolism of unity and democratic institutions in a clear vision for the national project: a new city built on a virgin site directed by the state and delinked from primordial claims of divisive ethnic groups and memories of colonial subjugation. Is it possible, therefore, to read a Nigerian Modernity in the urban space of Lagos, given that its development resulted from two differing nationalist positions? Taken as a whole, it could be argued that the city, in its partial production prior to the move to Abuja, represents the initial concrete attempts to forge, literally, a modernity cast around nationalism of difference.

Notes

1. Personal interview (January 14, 2011). Waterstones, Picadilly, London.

References

Akiba, O. (1998). *Nigerian Foreign Policy Towards Africa*. New York: Peter Lang Publishing.

Anderson, B. (1983). *Imagined Communities*. London: Verso Editions.

Apter, A. (2005). *The Pan African Nation: Oil and the Spectacle of Culture in Nigeria*. Chicago, IL: University of Chicago Press.

Ayida, A. A. (1973). *The Nigerian Revolution, 1966–1976*. Ibadan: Ibadan University Press.

Coleman, J. (1958). *Nigeria: Background to Nationalism*. Berkeley: University of California Press.

DA Review. (October 1974 and April 1977). *Funnelme*. March 05, 2011. http://funnelme.wordpress.com/2011/03/05/doxiadis-%E2%86%92-lagos-festac-1977/. Accessed May 02, 2011.

Dudley, B. (1982). *An Introduction to Nigerian Government and Politics*. Bloomington, IN: Indiana University Press.

Fapohunda, O.J. (1978). *Lagos: Urban Development and Employment*. Geneva: International Labour Office.

Federal Ministry of Economic Development. (1962). *National Development Plan 1962–68*. Lagos: Federal Ministry of Economic Development.

———. (1970). *Second National Development Plan 1970–74*. Lagos: Federal Ministry of Information Printing Division.

———. (1975). *Third National Development Plan 1975–1980*. Government Report. Lagos: The Central Planning Office, Federal Ministry of Economic Development.

FESTAC 77. (1977). FESTAC 77: Souvenir Book of the Second World Black and African Festival of Arts and Culture. African Journal ltd and the International Festival Committee.

Heynen, H. (2003). "Team 10—Between Modernity and the Everyday—Conference Papers—June 5–6, 2003 TU Delft." *Team 10 Online*. 2003. http://www.team10online.org/research/papers/delft2/heynen.pdf. Accessed April 20, 2011.

Koenigsberger, O., Abrams, C., Kobe, S., Shapiro, M., and Wheeler, M. (1964). *Metropolitan Lagos*. New York: United Nations Technical Assitsance Programme.

Le Corbusier. (1987[1929]). *The City of Tomorrow and Its Planning*. New York: Dover Publications Inc.

Okunnu, F. (2003). *Engaging with History*. Benin City: Sankore Publishers Ltd.

———. (2010). *In the Service of the Nation*. Benin City: Sankore Publishers.

Olayemi, O. A. (1981). "Land Transportation: Its Problem and Effects on Nigeria's EconomicDevelopment." In Onakomaiya, S. O. and Ekanem, N. F., eds, *Transportation in Nigerian National Development*, pp. 99–121. Ibadan: Nigerian Institute of Social and Economic Research.

Olowu, D. (1990). *Lagos State: Goverenance, Society and Economy*. Lagos: Malthouse Press Limited.

Zwingina, J.S. (1992). *Capitalist Development in an African Economy*. Ibadan: University Press PLC.

Contributors

Hannah Appel is an assistant professor of Anthropology at the University of California, Los Angeles. She was previously a postdoctoral research fellow at the University of California, Berkeley, and with the Committee on Global Thought at Columbia University. Her research focuses on the daily life of global capitalism, the private sector in Africa, and the economic imagination.

Rémy Bazenguissa-Ganga is a sociologist, and the Directeur d'Études at the École des Hautes Études en Sciences Sociales (EHESS), Paris, France. Before joining the École, he was a professor at the Université of Lille 1 in the Institute of Sociology and Anthropology. He is the author of *Congo-Paris: Transnational Traders on the Margins of the Law* (with Janet MacGaffey, Indiana University Press, 2000) and *Les Voies du Politique au Congo* (Karthala, 1997).

Emily Brownell is an assistant professor of African History at the University of Northern Colorado. She is currently working on her first book, *Going to Ground: An Environmental History of Urban Crisis in Dar es Salaam, Tanzania*. In addition to her interest in the environmental history of African cities, she has written on the history of international waste trading.

Mamadou Diouf is the Leitner Family Professor of African Studies and the Director of Columbia University's Institute for African Studies. He holds a PhD from the University of Paris-Sorbonne. Before joining the faculty at Columbia University, he was the Charles D. Moody Jr. Collegiate Professor of History and African American Studies at the University of Michigan, from 2000 to 2007. Before that, he was Head of the Research, Information, and Documentation Department of the Council for the Development of Social Science Research in Africa (CODESRIA) and faculty member of the History Department of Cheikh Anta Diop University in Dakar, Senegal. His research interests include urban, political, social, and intellectual history in colonial and postcolonial Africa. His publications include: *Les Arts de la Citoyenneté au Sénégal : Espaces Contestés et Civilités Urbaines* (edited with Mamadou Diouf) (with R. Fredericks, 2013). *Tolerance, Democracy, and Sufis in Senegal* (ed. Columbia University Press, 2013), *New Perspectives on Islam in Senegal: Conversion, Migration, Wealth, and Power* (with Mara A. Leichtman, Palgrave, 2009), *La Construction de l'Etat au Sénégal* (with M. C. Diop & D. Cruise O'Brien, Karthala, 2002), and *Histoire du Sénégal: Le Modèle Islamo-Wolof et ses Périphéries* (Maisonneuve & Larose, 2001).

Rosalind Fredericks is an assistant professor at the Gallatin School of Individualized Study at New York University. Fredericks received her PhD in Geography at the University of California, Berkeley. After her PhD, she was a Postdoctoral Research Scholar with the Committee on Global Thought at Columbia University, where she taught in the Institute of African Studies. Her research interests include urban development and politics in postcolonial Africa, with a particular focus on youth social movements and labor politics in contemporary Dakar, Senegal. She is currently completing a book manuscript on the cultural politics of garbage infrastructures in Dakar. Her other publications include *Les Arts de la Citoyenneté au Sénégal*: *Espaces Contestés et Civilités Urbaines* (edited with M. Diouf) (Karthala, 2013).

Peter Geschiere is a professor of African Anthropology at the University of Amsterdam and co-editor of Ethnography (SAGE). Since 1971, he has undertaken historical–anthropological fieldwork in various parts of Cameroon and elsewhere in West Africa. His publications include *The Modernity of Witchcraft: Politics and the Occult in Post-colonial Africa* (University Of Virginia Press, 1997), *Perils of Belonging: Autochthony, Citizenship and Exclusion in Africa and Europe* (University of Chicago Press, 2009), and *Witchcraft, Intimacy and Trust: Africa in Comparison* (University of Chicago Press, 2013).

Christine Ludl earned a PhD in Political Science from the Freie Universität Berlin and Sciences Po Paris. She held postdoctoral positions at the African Centre for Migration and Society at the University of the Witwatersrand (jointly with the French Institute of South Africa) in Johannesburg and the Bayreuth International Graduate School of African Studies, Germany. She is currently an associate Senior Fellow at the Bayreuth International Graduate School of African Studies and an associate researcher at the Centre Marc Bloch in Berlin. Her research focuses on the transformation of representation(s) in contexts of migration, diversity, and urban change.

Ruth Marshall is an associate professor in the Department of Political Science and the Department for the Study of Religion at the University of Toronto. She is the author of *Political Spiritualities: The Pentecostal Revolution in Nigeria* (University of Chicago Press, 2009) and numerous scholarly articles on the study of the political implications of Pentecostalism, postcolonial politics, and war in West Africa, particularly on questions of religious and political subject formation in the context of anarchic postcolonial states. Her current work examines the ethicopolitical force of religious language in the postcolonial world, critically reflecting on the problematic treatment of radical religious "otherness" by contemporary political theory.

Juan Obarrio is an assistant professor of Anthropology at Johns Hopkins University. He holds a PhD from Columbia University. He has published essays on law, custom, local politics, and magicality. He is the author of *The Spirit of the Laws in Mozambique* (University of Chicago Press, 2014).

Giles Omezi is the Director of London-based Laterite—an Architecture and Urban Design practice whose current work is focused on urban projects in Africa. He has developed interests in contemporary African architecture and urbanism, has lectured and tutored at various universities, and is currently completing doctoral research on post-independence urbanization of Lagos, Nigeria, at the University College London.

Adedamola Osinulu is an assistant professor of Afro-American and African Studies at the University of Michigan and a postdoctoral scholar with the Michigan Society of Fellows. He holds a PhD in Culture and Performance from the University of California, Los Angeles Department of World Arts and Cultures. He also received a degree in Architecture from the University of Houston.

Jinny Prais is Assistant Director of the Institute of African Studies at Columbia University. Her teaching and research expertise include twentieth-century West Africa and the African diaspora, with emphasis on urban cultures, colonial identity formation, and gender.

AbdouMaliq Simone is an urbanist, with particular interest in emerging forms of social and economic intersection across diverse trajectories of change for cities in the Global South. Simone is presently a Research Professor at the University of South Australia and Visiting

Professor of Urban Studies at the African Centre for Cities, University of Cape Town. Key publications include: *In Whose Image: Political Islam and Urban Practices in Sudan* (University of Chicago Press, 1994); *For the City Yet to Come: Urban Change in Four African Cities* (Duke University Press, 2004); and *City Life from Jakarta to Dakar: Movements at the Crossroads* (Routledge, 2009).

Index